Working in American Theatre

A brief history, career guide
and resource book for
over 1,000 theatres

Jim Voltz

methuen | drama

Methuen Drama

1 3 5 7 9 10 8 6 4 2

Methuen Drama is in imprint of Bloomsbury Publishing Plc

Methuen Drama
Bloomsbury Publishing Plc
36 Soho Square
London W1D 3QY
www.methuendrama.com

First edition published in 2007 by Back Stage Books,
an imprint of Watson-Guptill Publications, a division of
VNU Business Media, Inc.

Jim Volz has asserted his rights under the Copyright, Designs and
Patents Act, 1988, to be identified as the author of this work

A CIP catalogue record for this book is available from
the British Library

ISBN: 978 1 408 13473 3

Available in the USA from Bloomsbury Academic & Professional,
175 Fifth Avenue/3rd Floor, New York, NY 10010.
www.BloomsburyAcademicUSA.com

Typeset by Country Setting, Kingsdown, Kent CT14 8ES
Printed and bound in Great Britain by Martins The Printers,
Berwick-upon-Tweed

Contents

This book is dedicated to five brilliant men of the theatre and men of the world – educator/world traveler Abe J. Bassett; Renaissance man and scholar, the late Eugene B. Cantelupe; brilliant novelist and kind friend John Jakes; the jubilantly irascible Irishman John Kelly; and the finest gentleman I ever knew – the late, great Philip A. Sellers.

Acknowledgements

Sincere thanks go to my Methuen Drama Publisher Jenny Ridout and Managing Editor Inderjeet Tillier as well as my myriad consulting friends and longtime colleagues who do so much for the American theatre through the National Theatre Conference, Shakespeare Theatre Association of America, American Theatre Critics of America, League of Resident Theatres, Association of Theatre in Higher Education, Theatre Communications Group, Institute of Outdoor Drama, National Association of Schools of Theatre, and *Back Stage*. Special recognition goes to Mark Glubke and Michele LaRue for their early work on my books and to Milton Gordon, Joseph Arnold, James R. Taulli, Bruce Goodrich and my many associates at California State University, Fullerton, who were invaluable in providing professional advice and/or support.

In addition, I need to acknowledge my team of researchers, including Brian Rickel, Nicholas Volz, Joseph Hill, Lissa Supler, Jenny Spear, Caitlin Volz, Jeni Galli-Perdue, Andrea Ramirez-Martinez, Kirsten Kuiken, Ruby Hanger, Ben Lambert, Jocelyn Pronovost, Sean Scofield, Megan Pickerel, Jonathan Castanien, and Brooke Flint. Heartfelt thanks to Cindy Melby Phaneuf and Abe J. Bassett, who reviewed an earlier manuscript and offered important editorial, artistic, and historical guidance. Also, many thanks to Ben Cameron, Dana Gioia, Gilbert Cates, Paul Baker, Arthur Bartow, Robert Schenkkan, Gerald Freedman, Vera Mowry Roberts, Scott L. Steele, Sanford Robbins, Sid Berger, Kate Pogue, Roche Schulfer, John Jakes, Paul Nicholson, Dan McCleary, Richard Garner, Lesley Schisgall Currier, Fred C. Adams, R. Scott Phillips, Stephen Rothman, Richard Rose, James O'Connor, Kate Ingram, Tad Ingram, Andrew Barnicle, Rick Stein, Dick Devin, Steven Woolf, Ed Stern, Alan Rust, Gil Lazier, David W. Weiss, Scott J. Parker, Tom Markus, Ted Herstand, Kent Thompson, Emma Walton, Kevin Maifeld, Cindy Gold, Sidonie Garrett,

Michael Detroit, Peter Brosius, Risa Brainin, Emily Petkewich, David Heath, Mark Hofflund, Michelle Kozlak, Ben Donenberg, Iris Dorbian, Jan and Griff Duncan, Julia and Geoff Elliott, Richard G. Fallon, Joel G. Fink, Bernard Havard, Susie Medak, Howard J. Millman, Charles Morey, Jonathan Moscone, Robert Moss, Jim O'Quinn, John Quinlivan, Murray Ross, Craig Belknap, Ralph Cohen, Kathleen Conlin, Lynn Landis, Timothy Near, and Victoria Nolan, who shared their wisdom and thoughts for the text.

Grateful thanks to Mark R. Sumner, Sallie Mitchell, Edwin Duerr, and Allen Zeltzer, for their theatre history collections that provided vital background for the 'Brief History of American Theatre' and for their library contributions that have opened up the worlds of Eva Le Gallienne, Margo Jones, Nina Vance, and countless other American theatre pioneers to new generations of theatre students who appreciate theatre history.

Special thanks to those who helped with regional theatre and city information, including Chicago's Valerie Black-Mallon, Seattle's Stephanie Shine, San Francisco's Toby Leavitt, Atlanta's Marc Gowan, San Francisco's Dale Albright, and LORT's Adam Knight and Stephanie Drotar. Thanks to Gordon Goodrich, Dan Evers, Nikki Allen, Samantha Smith, Heather Biehl, Mary Waldron, Jenifer Olivares, Adrianna Maynes, Charlotte Williams, Richard Vieyra, Chantel Adedeji, and Renee Watkins for their Orange County assistance.

Most grateful thanks to London author Hilary Lissenden for her editorial assistance on both *How to Run a Theatre* and *Working in American Theatre*.

Most importantly, I would like to thank actress and award-winning educator, Evelyn Carol Case, who has helped me with book ideas, editing, research and resources during the many years that this book has been in the making.

Preface

> *Small opportunities are often the beginning of great enterprises*
>
> Demosthenes

Over the past few years, I've received an outpouring of sage advice, pithy sayings, and fascinating words of wisdom from theatre leaders throughout the world. Artistic directors, producers, managing directors, casting directors, playwrights, freelance directors, and others have been amazingly generous in sharing their vision of theatre and offering 'tips of the trade' to help you.

There's great joy in assisting the next generation of American theatre artists. Whether you live in San Francisco or Shanghai, New York or New Zealand, Las Vegas or London, this book offers you an overview of the American theatre and many of the career-planning resources you need to create, build, and nurture a life in the theatre. From past experience, it's clear that the information contained in this book has the power to:

➤ Assist you in identifying and defining your options for working in America's theatres.

➤ Help you clarify your job-search, career-planning, and life-planning expertise.

➤ Educate entry-level employees in the rich history, astounding artistry, risk-taking legacy, and self-sacrificing contributions of so many American theatre leaders and institutions.

➤ Contribute to your future earning power through savvy career strategies.

➤ Change your life with ethical, straightforward outreach, and networking that helps put you in control of your destiny and allows you to anticipate and plan for your future in the theatre.

This guide to working in American theatre offers immediate strategies for breaking into the business, coupled with advice on how you can develop long-range career-planning skills that may serve you in every area of your life. It also offers an overview of many of the largest and most successful professional theatres in America, and contact information regarding many of the most successful service organizations, useful nonprofit theatre support groups, and dedicated unions and collective bargaining organizations.

As a longtime producer, theatre professor, and consultant to many of the world's theatres, arts centers, cultural parks, and universities, I've been privileged to coach, lead, direct, or assist actors, directors, designers, choreographers, dancers, singers, craftspeople, board members, artistic directors, producers, and presidents of nonprofit operations while teaching in BA, BFA, MA, and MFA programs in a number of America's universities.

This book has been in the making for decades and began with a series of 'Business of Acting,' 'Assertive Personal Marketing,' and 'Working in American Theatre' seminars and workshops I used to conduct for regional and national theatre organizations, undergraduate theatre classes, graduate acting classes, and professional conservatory training programs.

There are already dozens of timely books on the market dealing with the evolving basics of the job search: résumés, interviews, cover letters, auditions, photographs, etc. This book identifies many of these resources for you, fills in the blanks, and details resources that have never been captured before in one book on American theatre.

My sincere thanks to the many theatre leaders who contributed to this book, and my absolute apology to all the brilliant artists and theatre leaders whose names aren't included in this attempt to meld a bit of history with the realities of the job search. Here's hoping this book ends up being worth at least 100 times what you paid for it. If you haven't already, consider adding a copy of *How to Run a Theatre*, 2nd Edition (Methuen Drama, London, 2011) to your library. Together, these two volumes offer a unique insight into the sometimes harsh, oftentimes fabulous, oh-too-often surreal realities of the theatre. Do write me (jvolz@fullerton.edu) and let me know what you'd like included in the next edition or a future book on the theatre.

Part 1
Everything you need to know about working in American theatre . . . from the professionals!

Life lessons from America's artists and professionals

> *The fool wonders, the wise man asks*
> Benjamin Disraeli

Whether you are wailing on stage or welding in the scene shop, there's the potential for a great life in the theatre. Career choices in theatre range from acting, directing, playwriting, and designing to costuming, set building, marketing, stage managing, fundraising, and a whole host of other challenging, potentially career-satisfying positions that offer employees the opportunity to create theatre.

Fortunately, for those just heading into a high school, college, or theatre training program, I've asked many of the nation's theatre professionals to help guide you in your decision-making. Happily, they don't all think alike – many have found their own creative avenues to successful careers – and all have been stunningly candid, unpredictably blunt, graciously helpful, or all of the above! The great news is, it is your life and you can read through all this grand advice, listen to the debates of theatre professionals who also had to make key life choices, and decide for yourself what's best for you!

Nobody's sweetheart is ugly

Good news! If you are already in college or preparing for a career in the theatre in other training programs, or already working in professional, community, university, or myriad other theatres, there are still plenty of extraordinary tips for managing your career and strategically planning for your life in the theatre. An old Dutch proverb declares that 'nobody's sweetheart is ugly,' and regional theatre is the 'sweetheart' and artistic home of many quoted in this text. Keep this in mind as you weigh the advice. No doubt many Broadway producers would regale you with the joys of life in New York and the thrills of Times Square. My contributors strive mightily to strike a balance in their advice about working in regional theatre and commercial theatre – but it's up to you to make your own choices.

As you might suspect, when you are fresh out of school, it sometimes seems impossible to break into the larger, more financially stable theatres or work your way past the volunteer or low-paying intern stages of any theatre. For most of my career in the theatre of over thirty years, it has driven me crazy when not-very-well-informed Broadway agents or film or television casting directors advise students and young actors, directors, designers, and craftspeople to go 'Cut your teeth and get experience in the regional theatres and come back when you've grown up.' Ha! Generally, this is ridiculous advice as it's often harder to get a job in a League of Resident Theatres (LORT) venue than in any other theatre in America. Perhaps community theatres, membership companies (where you pay to support the company), or smaller, generally volunteer-based companies allow you to 'cut your teeth' with less-than-brilliant skills, but be ready for a highly competitive regional theatre marketplace rivaling Broadway's employment challenges where polished skills and soaring potential are expected to mesh with unrelenting dedication, fervent loyalty, and long hours.

So where do you start and what do the leaders of American theatres have to say about working in their venues? It's great to have a career mentor and ongoing advisor, and I hope you will seek out many along the way. In the meantime, how wonderful to have so many theatre professionals share their lifelong lessons and career advice with you in this book. I am so indebted and grateful to the many industry leaders and artists who 'answered the call' to share their 'best practices' with you.

This is the moment!

Before you plunge in, let me remind you that there are so many ways you can prepare *now* for your life in the theatre. Seek counsel from your high school teachers, from your university professors, and from professionals with theatre experience in your home community. Nurture relationships and gather written recommendations that will help you in the future. Research the websites of schools and/or training programs that interest you and sit in on classes, workshops, and seminars to determine if the work is right for you. Attend performances, read theatre reviews, peruse trade papers, go to the library or bookstore and devour Theater Communications Group's *American Theater* magazine, Todd London's *The Artistic Home,* Robert Cohen's *Acting Professionally,* Tom Markus's *An Actor Behaves,* Sherry Eaker's *The Back Stage Handbook for Performing Artists,* William Ball's *A Sense of Direction,* and the myriad other books on the market.

Conduct an informational interview with someone who has the life and career you think you want and ask how he or she achieved success. Most people enjoy sharing their life stories – especially if they think they may be of help to you. An informational interview is a fact-finding session that you create by calling someone who has been successful at your dream job or a related job in the profession. You call them up, make it clear that you aren't applying for a job – that you would just appreciate fifteen minutes of their time. Ask them to share their thoughts about how to break into their business, how they have enjoyed their career climb, and what advice they might have for you in regard to the profession.

Mentors and mottos

Ben Cameron, past executive director of the national organization for the American theatre, Theater Communications Group (TCG), is one of the most articulate, engaging, embracing, and respected professionals in the field. He worked on the American theatre's front lines for a number of years, was lured into the philanthropic and service communities, then returned to head TCG and devote time to 'strengthen, nurture, and promote the professional not-for-profit theatre.' He discusses the mentoring process and offers advice about training and a life in the theatre:

> *I was blessed by being mentored by a number of people, of whom two rise to the top: the late Tom Haas, who was perhaps the most important figure for me, steering me toward graduate school, nurturing me as a director, teaching me how to read text in an uncluttered but heartfelt way; and the late Peter Zeisler, who during my NEA days taught me to see a field, not a string of separate theatres, while teaching me to value the concepts of*

service and leadership. Conservatory training is, for many in our field, indispensable: it provides a basic framework for thinking and instills a basic vocabulary and approach for work – a vocabulary that (like Picasso breaking out of the realistic tradition in which he had been trained but which was pivotal to his development) we will be increasingly shattering as we solve the problems and challenges that lie ahead for us, artistic and managerial alike. That said, mentor relationships are critical. I heard Lloyd Richards once say, when asked whether someone should enroll in a grad program, that the more important thing was to find the person with whom you needed to study and attach yourself to them – a counsel that embraced, but did not mandate, formal grad programs. My motto: life is too short to be serious and too serious to be frivolous.

Paul Nicholson, executive director of the Oregon Shakespeare Festival, offers these seven thoughtful bits of advice:

1) Remember that we work for a theatre that does not exist.

2) Before anything can be accomplished, some poor fool has to put something down on paper.

3) If you keep doing what you're doing, you'll keep getting what you're getting.

4) Winston Churchill's definition of planning: 'Ponder deeply, then act.'

5) You cannot afford not to make the time for strategic planning.

6) There is nothing like the threat of being hanged in a fortnight to concentrate your mind.

7) The goal of every theatre artistic director, managing director or general manager should be to enable the people they work with to make a life in the theatre; just making a living is not enough.

Advice to the players: get out of that suitcase!

Former National Endowment for the Arts chair Dana Gioia helped inspire and revitalize America's arts community. A working artist himself, Mr. Gioia directs those interested in regional theatre 'to keep working – no matter what the obstacles.

I have only impractical advice, but for artists impractical idealism is ironically the most pragmatic: to read as much as possible, to act as much as possible, and to put your art at the center of your life.'

Former *Stage Directions* magazine editor-in-chief Iris Dorbian encourages aspiring theatre professionals to 'be curious and open-minded. Learn something else besides theatre – read newspapers, cultivate your brain, and get out there! Do some investigation of the theatres where you'd like to work and then find out if they offer internships in your desired area.'

Jan and Griff Duncan, producer and artistic director of one of America's premier musical theatres, California's Fullerton Civic Light Opera, explain the upside and downside of a career in the theatre:

Theatre requires endless devotion/perseverance and a personal constitution that can accept rejection and a willingness to try again after failure. As a performer, it is 'life out of a suitcase' and the constant judging of your ability (auditions). Theatre is fickle and there will be failures. Each new production offers hope of success and it is enormously rewarding when that happens.

Sweep the floors and stay out of debt!

Near the breathtaking Zion National Park is Cedar City, Utah – home to a glorious complex of professional theatres and the Tony Award–winning Utah Shakespeare Festival. Fred C. Adams, one of America's wisest, most active, and most experienced theatre producers, offers sound advice for all theatre job seekers:

I beg young promising theatrical entrepreneurs to refrain from debt. Borrowing money has proven to be the kiss of death to young and promising theatre groups. Build first an audience, and that is done with credible high-quality work, then when the demand is great talk about building a theatre. Sweep floors, usher, volunteer in the box office, learn everything you can from the ground up. My university courses were wonderful ways of learning what makes a script great, how you market, how to measure the taste of your audience – these were all great topics. But no class can teach you how to approach a foundation for funding, what to look for in potential actors, how to maintain the theatre's restrooms. So learn what you can in school, then go out and immerse yourself in the actual day-to-day operation of a regional theatre.

I would tell any young dreamer to remember the advice my father gave me: 'Hell is going to work eight hours a day at a job you do not love.' Stay the course, pay your dues, and remember that the American theatre is a very small family, so make no enemies, do not spread tales, and be honorable to your peers and even more to the people you hire.

Pseudolus, Pericles, or the cover of *People* magazine?

Perhaps the best placed LORT theatre in America is California's Laguna Playhouse, a brisk walk from the Pacific Ocean and surrounded by glorious cliffs, leaping dolphins, and international intrigue. Longtime Laguna Playhouse artistic director Andrew Barnicle offers sane, sound, practical advice:

Recognize what the ultimate goal is and be honest with yourself. If you dream of being on the cover of TV Guide, by all means move to LA without regret. If visions of accepting a Tony put you to sleep at night, by all means move to New York. If playing Hamlet maybe in a storefront in South Dakota – even if you're too young – gets you hot, then by all means move to South Dakota; just don't expect many people to notice. For non-actors (development directors, managers, designers), recognize that you will be overworked and not remunerated at the level of the regular commercial sector. You must love making a contribution to an art form you truly believe in, or that one-bedroom apartment and the ten-year-old Hyundai will get boring very quickly.

New York University's Tisch School of the Arts is one of the premier training grounds for theatre students in many disciplines. Arthur Bartow, former artistic director of the undergraduate Department of Drama, offers this canny advice:

See the work of as many regional theatres as you can and study their histories. Look at their current repertoires. Determine those artists who you admire and how you can fit into the structure of their theatres. Develop the skills necessary to do the work of those theatres. Once you are ready, start a communication with their casting directors and their artistic directors. Keep at them, continue to grow, and you will succeed. The pathways for actors, directors, and designers are unique in their own ways. But knowledge is power no matter what your discipline. Gather as much skill as you can and be a person that others like to work with. Life is short and we would prefer to work with people whose company we enjoy rather than those who may be brilliant but take out all the air in the room. Remember, you are there to solve the problem, not be the problem.

Theatre, film, and television director Craig Belknap is one of the rare directors who has managed to create a career in regional theatre, Hollywood, and academia (California Institute of the Arts). Over the years, I've had the privilege of sitting on the hard benches of Washington DC's Folger Theatre, the plush seats of Alabama Shakespeare Festival's Stage, and the dark screening rooms of Hollywood's private studio theatres to watch his productions. A gentle, yet determined, assertive, and seasoned professional, Mr. Belknap shares his secrets for success:

Work in all venues whenever and wherever you can, make contacts and stay in touch. For directors, until you run a theatre, always remember that you are a 'guest.' If you want to be asked back, do your homework, stay on schedule, provide a positive atmosphere, and collaborate! Research the production. Stay under budget! Egos and indecision must never, never enter on-stage or off!

Located in America's heartland, the Dallas Theater Center helped define the dramatic future of regional theatre. In a recent letter from Paul Baker, one of the pioneers of regional theatre (and a co-founder of the Dallas Theater Center), one begins to understand the demands of regional theatre. 'Are you willing to donate eighteen hours a day for years to learn your trade?' he asks. 'Are you willing to sacrifice your energy and all you value?'

Do it yourself!

Chicago has long been hailed as one of the most vibrant of America's theatre cities, and Joel G. Fink, professional director, casting director, and associate dean of the Chicago College of Performing Arts helps explain why:

If you are interested in regional theatre, take the time to discover what a particular theatre is doing now and if that is the work that you want to be doing. Of course, having lived in Chicago for the past decade, I have become used to groups of people with like artistic visions banding together to start their own theatre companies. Companies such as Steppenwolf, Lookingglass Theatre, Chicago Shakespeare Theater are all products of the Chicago mentality of 'do it yourself!'

Howard J. Millman's favorite saying is, 'Don't let the bastards get you down.' As former producing artistic director of Florida's Asolo Theatre Company, he urges 'those interested in regional theatre to believe in regional theatre for what it is, not a stepping stone for anything more. Let's all try to go back to the original concept of acting companies created specifically for our communities doing work designed for our audiences.'

Take responsibility (and stop that whispering)!

Dan McCleary, founder and artistic director of the Tennessee Shakespeare Company, offers a strong dose of reality and some historical perspective:

What's needed now is a strong sense of personal responsibility . . . the art of theatre, and its inherent creative risk, increasingly is giving way to the industry of theatre, and its inherent safety and fiscal assurance. As regional theatre creativity becomes industrial, artists and managers become increasingly specialized and enclosed, driving to achieve financial or employment objectives in their area of specialization without knowing how their creativity cooperates with others. The result is that there are few Renaissance women or men, fewer artist-managers (like Shakespeare and Burbage, for instance), fewer resident companies of artists, and, sadly, even fewer regional theatres that we can call our artistic homes. An artistic home might be described as a safe, inspired place to do and say dangerous, inspired things. As Shakespeare & Company's founder Tina Packer says, the function of theatre is to speak that which can't be spoken. It's usually hard, ugly, messy, and there's no getting it right. It's live art with live people, and it demands caretaking and responsibility: responsibility for fellow artists, for knowing budgets, for fundraising, for marketing, for cleaning, for the playwright, for the audience, for the community. My most recent experience at a large regional theatre in the South exemplified the direct opposite of all of the above. It was a dangerous place to speak freely and a dangerous place to act anything other than safely. The halls were filled with fear and notes in boxes and whispers. The stages were filled with shows that looked like each other, and a palpable malaise hung over the facility and filled the artists. It was a living example of the death of regional theatre. Thankfully, we know this is not the case in every theatre.

And in those theatres are usually people of responsibility; artist-managers who see the whole engine working, who care about their audience, who fill the office space and the stage with their humanity, and who take it upon themselves to be responsible for examining, questioning, and celebrating the human condition. Personal responsibility.

Is a university education or a graduate degree in theatre really necessary?

'Only two things are infinite, the universe and human stupidity, and I'm not sure about the former,' teased the wildly educated Albert Einstein.

A university education isn't for everyone and many directors, actors, playwrights, and craftspeople have succeeded in the theatre without a college degree. However, many would argue that a fine liberal arts background as an undergraduate student, combined with specific graduate training in your chosen field, will help you make friends and colleagues who develop into future professional collaborators and networking buddies.

If you decide to pursue the university route, consider the advice offered below by many of America's leading professionals, and do your research before going to an undergraduate school with a graduate program where all the best roles (on stage and off stage) go to the graduate students. Be savvy about researching graduate schools, applying for scholarships, and committing to training programs with connections to professional theatres that have made a financial investment and a training commitment to you (versus simply accepting your tuition payments and processing you through a series of prerequisite classes).

As the Emmy Award–winning producer for ABC's annual Academy Awards and producing director of Hollywood's The Geffen Playhouse, Gilbert Cates understands the theatre. He cites Joe Papp (founder of New York's Public Theater) as a key figure in American theatre because 'he dared to do what he thought was important. His reward was an audience of interested, earnest, and informed people.' Cates offers this advice:

Craft is Freedom . . . study, work hard, and don't accept defeat. I find university training an excellent background for theatre. Many graduate programs offer first-rate educations in the theatre. As past dean and

11

continuing faculty member of the University of California at Los Angeles, UCLA School of Theater Film and Television, I am a big proponent and advocate of university training. My own training included a BA and Master's at Syracuse University (1955 and 1965), and studies at the Neighborhood Playhouse.

Joel Fink, longtime director of the Chicago College of Performing Arts Theatre Conservatory, explains the value of professional training:

American actors today are faced with the greatest challenge of any actors in history. They are expected to have the craft and technique to handle works from all eras, all countries and all mediums. To make a living in the theatre today, actors are expected to have both a breadth and depth of skills and abilities. Actors today can't rely on inspiration or opportunities to learn their craft 'on the job.' Whether through professional training, internships, or other means, actors need the training to enter the profession with the ability to meet a wide range of artistic demands.

This is one reason why MFA training programs have proliferated in America. Where else will a young actor get to work on Shakespeare, Chekhov, Ibsen, the Greeks, Comedy of Manners, musicals . . . as well as gain experience in film and television technique? Fortunately, summer companies such as the Illinois Shakespeare Festival, the Colorado Shakespeare Festival, the Utah Shakespeare Festival, and other festivals in almost every state offer students opportunities to work with seasoned professionals on Shakespeare and other classic texts, while pursuing degrees.

The University of Delaware is well known and respected for its Professional Theatre Training Program. The director of the program is professional director and educator Sandy Robbins, who encourages aspiring regional theatre artists to:

Know the field. Travel and see everything you possibly can. Be aware of who is doing what where. Train at a conservatory that will equip you with the skills you will need and also provide entrée to the profession and introduce you in a meaningful way to those who hire.

Do not wait for opportunities; create them by making theatre wherever you are with whatever means you have. I think it is impossible to contribute to the kind of theatre I care about without knowing the literature and history of the theatre.

> *I think it crucial to develop the skills of acting and/or directing for the stage. The most efficient way to do this is to train at a conservatory.*

Finally, if it's the money that has you concerned, remember that scholarships are often available for financially needy and talented students, and note that there are a lot of terrific theatre professors at reasonably priced universities around America. Consider the words of Derek Bok (president of the not-so-reasonably priced Harvard University from 1971 to 1991): 'If you think education is expensive, try ignorance.'

Which university is the right university?

Making great contacts and networking through alumni, faculty, and staff connections is oftentimes one of the key reasons that parents, career counselors and theatre professionals advocate attending more 'high-profile' universities. Pulitzer Prize-winning playwright Robert Schenkkan addresses this issue:

> *I'm sure some training programs (professional or academic) are better than others and offer their graduates better connections and credits but I couldn't tell you who they are. And besides, they change drastically from year to year as people move from one program to the next. But certainly all regional theatres value talent and practical experience.*

Not surprisingly, as executive director of the University/Resident Theatre Association (U/RTA), Scott L. Steele has strong views on preparing for a career in regional theatre:

> *Those contemplating a career of any kind in regional theatre, whether in acting, directing, design or management, should pursue training on a professional, graduate level. People should take time off after college, and then invest in attending a great MFA training program. This may seem an obvious recommendation coming from an executive director of U/RTA, but the fact remains that graduate training provides the fundamental skills, helps develop the natural talent and intellect, and offers the specialized education, that are all necessary, along with luck, for a career in theatre. Of equal importance is that graduate training effectively provides the network of contemporary colleagues, as well as of accomplished professionals encountered during that training, which will, more than anything else, help a young professional to first gain work. Whether it is classmates starting a small theatre company somewhere, or a new administrator seeking an*

entry-level job with an established theatre, it is the relationships that are created over the three years of graduate training that make work happen. Perhaps 50 per cent of the value in graduate training is the rich resource it provides for building this network. It is true in most other professions, and is no less true in the field of theatre.

Education and training: liberal arts, conservatory, or both?

Kent Thompson, artistic director at the Denver Center Theatre Company, reviews the balance of broad academic training, life experience, and conservatory training:

> I always recommend a Bachelor of Arts degree from a liberal arts college rather than a BFA – I think the knowledge of the world that such a degree demands is very helpful in keeping the theatre professional connected to the world. Peter Zeisler always derided his staff at TCG if they didn't read the newspaper – there's a grain of truth in his criticism – theatre has to examine what it means to be human in the world today. You can't do that if you're disconnected or, worse, uninformed.
>
> For most theatre professionals, an advanced degree from a major training program or conservatory (preferably attached to a professional theatre) is the fastest way into the field. Such an experience will combine the classroom and independent study with practical work in the field. And provide you with lots of professional contacts in building your own network. Building and nurturing that network is the key to a successful career in professional theatre. Otherwise, find the theatre and the community you want to work in, apply for a job and work your way up.

The liberal arts are also high on the list of Ed Stern, producing artistic director of Cincinnati Playhouse in the Park:

> I am a firm believer in liberal arts training at the undergraduate level, as I love for actors and directors and designers to have as wide a range of knowledge as possible. Graduate school is a time to focus on acting, directing, or designing as a designated field of study. And get good training. Develop good discipline. The difficulty of entering a field teeming with actors, directors, and designers underscores the need for the finest training and discipline possible.

A re-creation of Shakespeare's historic indoor theatre, The Blackfriars Playhouse, may be found in the delightful hamlet of Staunton, Virginia, home to Shenandoah Shakespeare and the American Shakespeare Center. Embracing a 'we do it with the lights on' philosophy, executive director Ralph Alan Cohen believes that audiences 'should be in the show, not at the show.' He also hails the value of a more general university education: 'I still believe that a director has to have something to say and that something comes from a broad, liberal arts education.'

A liberal arts education is at the top of Charles Morey's list as well. As artistic director of Utah's prestigious Pioneer Theatre Company, Mr. Morey offers advice to students and parents:

> The best educated individuals make the best artists, artisans, and managers – not to mention colleagues. Go to a good college or university with a strong emphasis in the liberal arts. Do not go to an undergraduate conservatory program! (Parents, if you are reading this, do not allow your child to go to an undergraduate conservatory program! Refuse to pay for it.) Once you are enrolled in that good liberal arts program, major in theatre if you must, but take tons of literature, dramatic and otherwise. Study history, art, music, philosophy, psychology, maybe even the sciences. Then when you have given yourself a well-rounded liberal education and when you have convinced yourself that absolutely nothing else but a life in the theatre will make your existence bearable; then, work like hell to get into a good MFA program and when you're in it, work even harder.

In California, Marin Shakespeare Company managing director Lesley Schisgall Currier agrees:

> If all you've ever studied is acting, you will be far less interesting on stage. Travel, explore the world, have adventures . . . then you'll have something to create theatre about.

One of the few remaining classical repertory theatres in America is based in the historic Masonic Temple Building, Glendale, California. It has been hailed as Los Angeles' premier classical theatre, and its co-artistic directors, Julia Rodriguez and Geoff Elliott, offer this perspective on preparing for a career in theatre:

> The intensive conservatory atmosphere that we were happily a part of at ACT (in San Francisco) in the 1980s can't help but influence our answer – we feel it is essential for actors who are interested in pursuing serious

stage work to attempt to enroll in one of the several great conservatories in the country, organizations with working professionals on staff. We have watched countless actors over the years who, without the benefit of solid technique, find themselves at sea when faced with difficulties arising out of the creation of character and pursuit of passion-filled objective.

Florida's oldest nonprofit professional theatre, the Asolo Theatre Company, has a long-established Conservatory for Actor Training, affiliated with Florida State University (FSU). Richard G. Fallon, dean emeritus at FSU, was one of the Asolo's co-founders in 1960. He recommends that students 'prepare in university programs which have a relationship to a professional theatre company.' Dean Fallon also asks students to have a 'love – of yourself, those who work with you, the audience, the theatre, and your mission. You must have courage and dedication to see you through.'

Rehearsing *Hamlet* or reselling houses?

Professional director Theodore Herstand offers the following pointers:

Be prepared to struggle in your first years 'out there' after you've been graduated. Some don't have to struggle, but most do. If you can't take it, get yourself a good life selling houses. That way, you can afford to go to the theatre often and, perhaps, become a philanthropist who helps not-for-profit arts institutions.

The author of *Shakespeare's Friends*, Kate Pogue, sums it all up:

Regional theatre requires versatility, sensitivity to historical styles, and a commitment to a simple, hard-working, low-profile career as opposed to hope for fame and fortune. Actors need the most comprehensive vocal and physical training, and the broadest range of experience (personal and theatrical) they can find. They don't, however, have to go to the best and the biggest schools. At the undergraduate level they may be much better off at a small university, or local community college, where they can get decent training in all the theatre skills, and lots of onstage experience, saving their specialized training for the graduate level.

Discover me and save me from academia!

We've all heard the Hollywood stories of stars 'being discovered' at the local drugstore, on the beach, in the park, and through sheer serendipity. Is formal training, academic or otherwise, even necessary? 'Life is my college,' writes Louisa May Alcott. 'May I graduate well, and earn some honors!'

Although he holds an MFA from the University of California, Davis, Richard Rose, artistic director of Virginia's Barter Theatre, writes:

> *I am not an overall fan of the academic path, although it is the path we are currently following. I think education takes as much out of us as it gives us. Again, many of the artists of early regional theatre found their education and career paths in doing, not in studying.*

> *I think the most important aspect of training is learning every day and always striving to be better each and every moment. We have a saying here at Barter Theatre that 'Art equals learning.' If you want to call yourself an artist, you must learn always, first and foremost. We have found that those who succeed are not necessarily the most 'talented,' or the ones with the most 'potential.' Those who succeed in the long run in regional are the ones who strive to improve, never settle, never coast, and who have a real desire to learn. This has been a constant in my life. So, I don't care if you've gone to one of the elite universities, have a PhD, or if you are right off the street. Those who learn, succeed.*

> *So the necessary training or preparation is: 'Learn from everyone you meet, everyone you study, and every situation. Especially learn from your mistakes. They are your greatest teachers.'*

> *One of the problems with academic learning is that even those programs that give their students permission to fail do not necessarily teach their students success through failure. Largely because there are no consequences.*

Bernard Havard, producing artistic director of Philadelphia's Walnut Street Theatre, steers actors 'to develop yourself into a triple threat (acting, singing, dancing) in order to make the most of your options,' and advocates apprenticeships or internships as 'the most crucial element for those contemplating careers – it's a wonderful way to sort things out and gain the first rung on the ladder to success.'

Certainly, universities aren't for everyone and not every university does a great job of preparing students for careers in theatre. If you are going to invest the time, money, strength, and energy in a university program, make sure it's right for you and that you find a good match. One of Mario Puzo's characters in *The Godfather* offers this challenging question: 'You go to college to get stupid?'

And the beaches are great, too!

The graduate training process works for many. Stephen Rothman, chair of Theatre Arts at California State University, Los Angeles, offers this personal testimonial:

> *I had the unique experience of spending the last year of my MFA from Florida State at the Asolo Theatre full time. This was the crucial experience for me. After years of classroom training I was thrust for an entire year into a position/internship at a LORT theatre. Without that year my career would never have fast-tracked the way it did. This was a segue for me from training to doing it and it was what truly gave me a career.*

Decorum: on stage and off stage

Winston Churchill defined a gentleman as 'a man who is only rude when he intends to be.' Gil Lazier, longtime dean of Florida State University and the Asolo Theatre Conservatory, expresses similar sentiments:

> *It's really about attitude if you have the requisite talent and skill. You must be easy to work with – positive, optimistic and friendly. Otherwise, your first job could be your last. You need to make employers want to rehire you for the next gig. This work not only requires efficiency, creativity and skill, but also a high level of diplomacy, no matter what area is involved. You've got to get the job done with ease and good will in an intense environment. Be positive and honest. If you can't be positive and honest at the same time, be honest in the most positive way you can!*

Lynn Landis, former managing director of Philadelphia's The Wilma Theater, puts it more succinctly: 'Keep the drama on stage.'

Still, some people just like to shake things up! Berkeley Repertory Theatre managing director Susan Medak feels that her job is to 'challenge orthodoxy.' She explains that: 'To keep us from getting stale, my job is to make sure we aren't falling back on easy answers. At Berkeley Rep, our staff jokes that "Flexibility is a four letter word!" But in fact, when we "embrace flexibility," we make it possible for a broad range of artists to do their best work.'

'Never think the work isn't valued,' cautions Steven Woolf, artistic director of The Repertory Theatre of St. Louis. 'The chance to make art and investigate texts and themes is a privilege and a responsibility. Our work in our communities is part of the social fabric of our cities and vital to the society in our towns.'

As esteemed acting guru Stella Adler notes: 'Life beats down and crushes the soul, but art reminds you that you have one.'

The big picture:
what many universities fail to tell you

Certainly, there's no one way to train for a life in the theatre and there isn't a standard theatre curriculum that is taught in America's training institutions. Consider this book, *Everything You Need to Know About Working in the Theater that You Didn't Learn in Class*, and you will find some ingenious, effective tools that will help you throughout your career. 'The great difficulty in education,' writes George Santayana, 'is to get experience out of ideas.'

Get excited or excite yourself

'Visit the theatres you admire or are curious about,' insists Denver Center Theatre Company artistic director Kent Thompson. He adds:

> See their work, meet their artists and administrators. Find out what kind of theatre you want to work in. At the same time find a community that you can invest in personally and professionally, for these theatres work only with deep local roots and many on-going connections to the larger professional field. Find out what artists – playwrights, directors, actors – most excite you when you go to the theatre; then work with them or work at the theatres they frequent.

> Or start your own theatre.

> Always remain curious and always remain critical (that is, define your own aesthetic, your own vision of what theatre can become in twenty-first-century America.)

Be aggressive, say yes, do your homework, keep the faith!

Playwright Robert Schenkkan explains that aspiring regional theatre workers must 'pursue it aggressively' and remember that 'it's the people who run the theatre that matter; relationships are important.'

Former Syracuse Stage artistic director Robert Moss offers reliable advice, plain and simple:

> Say 'YES' as often as possible. See every play as if it's never been done before. Avoid the word 'just,' as in – 'it's just a living room.' Go to your heart more often than your brain for answers. When going to work at a regional theatre, try to understand it as an ongoing entity of which you will be a part. Go to its website before you arrive. Do some research. Be smart. Introduce yourself to the whole staff.

'Be familiar with the players,' asserts professional director, educator and National Theatre Conference president Jim O'Connor. He explains:

> One would hardly be prepared to be a physicist without the knowledge of past and present contributors to this discipline. The same should be expected of those who aspire for careers in the regional theatre. It is essential that one always be prepared with a number of interesting projects that might fit at particular theatres, and be prepared to actively present these proposals and have a good idea of personnel to implement them. Most important and certainly most difficult of all is to position oneself so that the work can be seen by artistic directors from the regional theatres.

'Keep the faith,' notes Barter Theatre artistic director Richard Rose. 'It is important work that regional theatres are doing . . . regional theatres are now the heart, soul, and, still, training ground for American theatre. My second piece of advice: don't give in. Success can lead to conservatism. Keep your ideals and boldly go where no one else is going. If you don't, who will?'

Much beloved and sorely missed theatre historian Vera Mowry Roberts offered three simple tips: 'First, be proficient in your art. Second, love people. Third, expect hard, long, work hours.'

And Mom said never to talk about politics or religion

'Like any career in the arts, it is important to know what's happening in the wider world (the arts as well as politics and economics). All of this impacts on our work,' asserts Repertory Theatre of St. Louis artistic director Steven Woolf. He explains:

> Whether it's interpretive in a new way of looking at a text or if you are an administrator trying to run and maintain a company, the more knowledge you have, the better equipped you are. If you are thinking about running a company, then knowing as much as you can about all the elements of the theatre is crucial – from design to construction to balance sheets to being able to stock the rest rooms with supplies. The more you know, the better everything works – on the artistic side, the technical side and the administrative side.

Okay, Superman, *Smalltown* is not *Smallville*!

'My advice, of course, is to work anywhere and everywhere,' counsels Ed Stern. 'Do not presume a theatre in Smalltown, USA, can only do small work. Certainly the day and age of simply waiting in New York to be "discovered in New York" is gone. The range of opportunities in regional theatre far outweighs the option of hoping for the occasional straight play just to be "seen" in New York City.'

'Be well educated. Be well trained. Work hard.' Obvious but often ignored advice from professional director and Pioneer Theater Company artistic director Charles Morey, who adds: 'Be the type of person with whom I would like to spend eight hours a day in a windowless rehearsal room. Be intensely disciplined in your work habits and work ethic. Your competition will have all those attributes listed above. And you probably have to locate yourself in one of those half-dozen cities in the country whence many if not most of the regional theatres hire.'

If I were a rich man!

For those interested in regional theatre work, 'Marry great wealth!' jokes Tom Markus, author of one of the best, most practical, and funniest books on the theatre, *An Actor Behaves: From Audition to Performance*. 'Otherwise,' he commands, 'find the strength in yourself to know that your rewards come from the work you do. The yuppie mantra says that the one with the most toys wins.

If your toys cost money, regional theatre is not for you. But if your toys are your experiences, your memories, the gifts of your labors that you give to your audiences, then you will die richer than Bill Gates.'

A professional director and longtime artistic director, Mr. Markus, admonishes aspiring theatre professionals to 'travel the world, as far and as often as you can. See how other people live, learn what they value, wonder at the myriad ways they make theatre. Travel in your mind – read, read, read. Go to museums. Go to concerts. Think. Think harder. Read. I have two mantras I always have posted above my desk. The first is my own (so far as I know): Take the work very seriously, but laugh at yourself. The second is Beckett's: 'No matter. Try again. Fail again. Fail better.'"

Take risks!

Jonathan Moscone, artistic director of the California Shakespeare Theater, echoes the sentiment: 'Take risks. Read. Go to museums, travel, experience as much of life as possible. Intern anywhere you can. It's the best first step into a career.'

The phenomenal producers and performers of Cirque du Soleil take risks onstage and offstage and, as a for-profit corporation, tour and perform throughout America and the world. Their production and performing team includes approximately 4,000 people from over 40 countries and generatates an estimated annual revenue of over $810 million – and it all started with creative risktaking and a dream.

Forget the risks, just learn your craft (and don't expect me to say thanks!)

'Craft, Craft, Craft, learn it, practice it, own it!' insists Alan Rust, director of *Connecticut's Professional Actor Training Program* at The Hartt School. 'You need a solid education to be able to embrace the broad scope of material that is explored in regional theatres,' adds Mr. Rust.

Marin Shakespeare managing director Lesley Schisgall Currier offers this bit of advice about working in the field:

> *Never expect gratitude. (We work so hard and very often end up feeling that our work is not recognized, rewarded or respected. Learning to find self-gratification in the work is a great gift you can give yourself. After all, despite how hard we work, we are extraordinarily fortunate to do what we do.)*

Treat your fellow theatre artists with respect. Returning phone calls, responding to (even unsolicited) scripts or résumés, caring about the often transitory artists without whom we cannot create collaborations, sharing knowledge, volunteering time to support the organizations that support our theatres – all these things are essential. The successful future of this young thing we call America's regional theatres depends not only on the longterm health and vitality of individual organizations, but also on continuing to learn to collaborate as a field to create viable career opportunities for artists, communicate our value, and become an essential part of the fabric of American life across the nation.

If I live in Denver, why do I have to go to New York to get cast in Denver? What, not anymore?

Emma Walton, co-founder of Sag Harbor's Bay Street Theatre in New York, offers extremely valuable advice on connecting with directors, and the ongoing reality of many regional theatres when it comes to casting: New York still rules! According to Walton:

Depending on whether their interests are creative or administrative, my advice to those interested in regional theatre work would change. At Bay Street, we cast almost exclusively out of New York City, so actors interested in working here need to have relationships with agents, casting directors, and directors in order to be submitted. Housing is a big issue for us, being located as we are in one of the most expensive resort communities in America – so if an actor or designer has local housing it's a big plus. Finally, though, we find that a lot of the actors, designers, stage managers, etc. that we employ have prior relationships with directors and are brought in by their request. So it's important to cultivate relationships with directors.

For administrative roles, it's another thing. In addition to experience in their specific field, it's critical for our staff members to be willing to multi-task, and to be team players. Any one of us is as likely to be found serving concessions one night, or painting a bathroom or replacing a lightbulb, as we are doing our more job-specific tasks . . . and anyone who isn't willing to get their hands dirty once in a while doesn't last long. It's not a line of work that offers a great deal of salary. It takes a small staff of very dedicated people who are interested in a different reward – a creative,

23

collaborative 'thinking outside the box' kind of life, with a spirit of fun about it – to make a small regional theatre like Bay Street survive and thrive.

I think anyone interested in making a life in regional theatre has to have a good deal of healthy perspective, and a willingness to place the good of the whole organization before any individual agendas or ambitions. Beyond that, I think to have had some practical theatre experience is critical – it's hard to be a good producer, or write a great, compelling press release about a show, or be a collaborative tech director etc., if you don't have a very clear understanding of what the creative process of making theatre entails. And the more experience the better – I worry about the kids coming out of college programs now who are so specialized they can't cross over from one department to another. Better to have been backstage, onstage, at the light board and sound board, in the box office – as much experience and understanding of all the components as possible. That's the only real way to develop the spirit of collaboration and the mutual respect that working in the theatre demands.

As you will discover when you review the theatre listings in this book, many theatres now cast in their own hometowns and invite potential employees to visit with them right there in their own regional cities (including Chicago, San Francisco, Minneapolis, Phoenix, Seattle, Omaha, and Los Angeles).

Beware the potential pitfalls

Theatre in America is a growing, changing, evolving beast of a profession and many of the 'innovations,' cost-cutting measures, and practices wreak havoc for employees, visiting artists, managers, and audiences. Financial realities and poor executive planning are sometimes the case, but oftentimes the concerns centre on employees who don't meet the basic expectations of their employers. 'The one sign I still have up says, "It ain't all bright lights and glamour,"' explains artistic director Steven Woolf.

Don't be pitiful!

Designer, educator, and consultant David Weiss doesn't mince words:

As for training, don't get me started. It is pitiful how little some of our so-called 'young artists' know these days. Play analysis? Who needs it? I have watched designers go through a full course of MFA training without ever understanding that ours is an art of collaboration and that it starts with the play. But what is worse, far worse, is that they cannot bring any true knowledge or experience to the table. They are almost unaware of the fine arts beyond the most conspicuous examples – the Mona Lisa? Sure, I've seen pictures of that. But do aspiring lighting designers, just as one example, have any understanding or appreciation of the magnificence of their art as expressed by Rembrandt, Rubens or Carravaggio, just to name a very few? Too often they do not. And it goes on from there into literature, history, geography, and the basic sciences – in other words, the liberal arts. Well, you know the rant as well as I do. Unfortunately, the problem starts all the way back in primary school these days.

Joint productions usually mean fewer people working

A growing trend during tough economic times is for theatres to share the cast, director, designers, etc., and move original productions between theatres as 'joint productions.' Jim O'Connor warns that 'there are fewer and fewer acting, directing, and design positions available as the composite number of individual productions on a national scale decreases due to the multiple stops of individual productions.'

Searching for Ibsen, Chekhov, Strindberg, and Shaw

It may be harder to find truly brilliant classical work on stage. Professional director and educator Sandy Robbins offers a bit of history:

It is my view that today we lack models of the kind of theatre that inspired me – we have few resident companies in this country and few, if any, truly distinguished companies performing the classics in rotating repertory. I was blessed to see many, many extraordinary performances and I believe that it is more necessary today than it was in the past to see a wide variety of theatre in this country and abroad so as to see performances that inspire.

Would you like fries with your Feydeau?

Kent Thompson talks about the challenges of a career in the theatre, and offers advice on artistic and personal survival:

The hardest thing about the first decade of your career in this profession is keeping yourself engaged and growing as a person and as an artist. This requires an investment in your own personal development as a person. And it requires an investment in the larger cultural, political and social life of the community that you're in. You may have to work as a waiter or temp or whatever, but go to theatre, work out in a gym, read, participate in sports, visit museums, travel the country, campaign for a political or social cause, write . . . do whatever will keep you alive as a person. And stay disciplined about developing your artistic discipline. Our artistic endeavors (whether we're a manager or an actor) always reveal how curious we have been as human beings, how much we have sought what life offers us, and how disciplined we have been in preparing ourselves for the rigors and practice of the art form.

The check is in the mail (not that it's about money)

Longtime Laguna Playhouse artistic director Andrew Barnicle lists more than one of the potential pitfalls in the business:

Advice: You can only be sure that you've got the part when you are standing on stage on opening night. Mantra: It's never about money, but it's always about money. Pithy quote – from Bernard Sahlins, founder of Chicago's Second City to his company before a New York opening: 'Just remember, guys, in New York City, if you're one in a million, there's thirteen o' yas.' Others: theatre, and especially casting, is not a democracy. Thank goodness. And the strongest personality in the room will direct the play.

A final note

According to Theater Communications Group's *Theatre Facts 2009*, theatres enhanced 'America's artistic legacy with 187,000 performances that attracted 30 million attendees; employing 128,200 administrative, artistic and production personnel; and contributing $1.9 billion to the economy.'

There may very well be a job or a career for you in American theatre. But how much of that payroll will trickle down to you? In Chicago, The Goodman Theater's executive director Roche Schulfer explains:

We have to find a way to improve the dismal economic situation for the American stage actor. Every producer in the country should make this issue a priority. At the same time, if we don't solve the problem of chronic undercapitalization in our industry, we can't do much for actors or other theatre professionals. We must do more to advocate with funding sources for multi-year support and other creative ways to provide for an infusion of capital to theatres that want to expand their artistic capacity.

In conclusion, do your research, hone your skills, network with potential employers, and see if this field is right for you.

Part 2

A brief history of theatre in America

Carrying the artistic torch

> *At a time when theatres were dark across America, plays*
> *began to be driven from the Atlantic to the Pacific, not*
> *only in city theatres, but in parks and hospitals, in Catholic*
> *convents and Baptist churches, in public schools and*
> *armories, in circus tents and universities, in prisons and*
> *reformatories, and in those distant and unfrequented*
> *camps where 350,000 of America's youth are learning*
> *all they know about life and art*
>
> Hallie Flanagan, Federal Theatre Project / WPA brief
> before the House of Representatives, 1938, page 3

An introduction to theatre in America

Why is it so important for current theatre practitioners to have a feel for the history of American theatre, and why is world theatre history a requirement (and often dreaded component) in virtually every college and university theatre program in America? Perhaps *Jurassic Park* novelist Michael Crichton says it best in his medieval romp, *Timeline*, when he notes that 'history is the most powerful intellectual tool society possesses.' Or, to quote Mark Hofflund, esteemed managing director of the Idaho Shakespeare Festival:

> *Typically, I find that our awareness (among theatre leaders) rarely goes*
> *back beyond our lifetimes and we only know about the things we invented.*
> *Yet, tying those inventions to our predecessors is richly rewarding and*
> *interesting. Invariably, it also ties us to existing movements whose*
> *relevance we may have discounted.*

At a recent Tony Award celebration of the best of Broadway at Radio City Music Hall, Tony Award-winner Norbert Leo Butz implored the audience to 'support regional theatre around the country' and paid tribute to San Diego's Old Globe Theatre, 'who gave us a home to create this play (*Dirty Rotten Scoundrels*).'

It is truly remarkable how quickly the tables have turned. Historically, of course, Broadway sparked the creative process and provided the playwrights, actors, dancers, singers, musicians, directors, designers, plays, and musicals through production in New York, through cast albums that made their ways into homes throughout America, and through touring productions to major cities, state-to-state throughout the United States. Today, the process is often reversed as regional theatres provide the artistic home and incubation period for many Broadway shows, including Pulitzer, Tony, and Drama Desk Award-winning plays and musicals.

Pulitzer Prize-winning playwright, Robert Schenkkan (*The Kentucky Cycle*) offers these insights:

> *I owe my career to regional theatre. With one exception, all my plays have first been produced in regional theatre before going to NYC. The regional theatre movement has kept theatre alive in this country. With Broadway and now even Off-Broadway too expensive to develop new work, as often as not it is in the regional theatre that new plays are being commissioned, written, developed, and produced.*

Even accomplished poet and former NEA Chair Dana Gioia notes that 'the growth of regional theatres has been the most important development in American theatre in the past forty years.'

Emma Walton, co-founder of New York's Bay Street Theatre, explains that regional theatres have 'more or less replaced the old "out-of-town tryout" period for a Broadway show – these days most Broadway shows were developed in the regions, at places like the Old Globe, Steppenwolf, Denver Center Theatre etc. These theatres afford the creative teams the opportunity to develop their material in a safer environment, using what they learn from audiences and local critics but protecting the show from the kind of national press that can kill a production before it makes a transfer.'

The regional theatre movement has evolved in surprising ways. Arts Orange County executive director Richard Stein offers an abbreviated history and advice for those who wish to work in the field:

The regional theatre in America has evolved from being a passionate
alternative to commercial New York theatre, to a foundation-driven, cookie-
cutter institutional formula heavily dependent upon government funding, to
an entrepreneurial quasi-commercial nonprofit hybrid struggling to survive
and attract audiences in an electronic age. To some, the heyday of the
regional theatre is long past, but I think what is emerging has the potential
to be a more democratic and pluralistic institution that more closely mirrors
our national character. It will be a sort of return to regional theatre's
roots and a rejection of its rigid, insular, and elitist adolescence . . .
Anyone who contemplates a career in regional theatre must be passionate
about the art and be able to communicate that passion to others.

So, if indeed regional theatre is returning to its artistic roots, an added bonus to reviewing the history of the movement is that it may very well provide insight into the future.

The vision of a nonprofit regional theatre

'Vision: the art of seeing things invisible.'
Jonathan Swift

Long before the beginning of what we now call the nonprofit theatre movement, theatre companies spanned the country as immigrants and settlers sought out entertainment options and, thanks to the industrialization of cities in the Eastern United States and expansion of the frontier, they had money to pay to fund their interests. Professional performances during and following the Revolutionary War included Thomas Wall's performances in Maryland (as early as 1781), and shows featuring comedians, musicians, and actors (many borrowed from the English theatre) were plentiful in Philadelphia in the late eighteenth and early nineteenth centuries. Philadelphia's Chestnut Street Theatre was designed by Inigo Richards and was considered one of the finest theatres in North America. Boston, New York and Charleston also emerged as major theatre centers in America in the 1790s.

As Americans moved West, so did the theatre. It wasn't unusual to find a collected works of Shakespeare packed next to the family Bible as settlers crossed the Mississippi River in search of a new home. From the early 1800s until the 1870s, once-itinerant actors found work, and a home, in for-profit resident repertory theatre companies. By the early nineteenth century, there were nearly two dozen resident theatre companies in America and by the middle of the century, there were over three dozen companies with emerging itinerant performers working in amphitheatres, touring plays, traveling circuses and related entertainments. New York's Park Theatre, Bowery Theatre, and Olympic Theatre are just a few of the theatres that were operating in the early to mid-1800s. Over the years, European classics, new American plays, specialty acts, minstrel shows, vaudeville and burlesque were all part of the boisterous repertory of a growing theatrical scene as the nation's pioneering spirit extended to theatre offerings from the mining camps of California to the 4,000-seat Bowery Theatre in New York.

By the late 1800s, New York was dominant as the theatrical center of America while over 200 touring companies (often traveling with 'star-power') were zigzagging the nation with such notables as Sarah Bernhardt, Henry Irving, and Edwin Booth. Negotiating tours outside of New York was a major headache for many commercial producers in smaller cities, since those working in America's hinterlands generally had to travel to New York to arrange seasons with an ever-changing series of questionable producers who often left them with artistic holes in their seasons and financial holes in their pockets. Perhaps foreshadowing the future of the American theatre and the Hollywood film industry, middlemen emerged as booking agents, small groups of producers sought control and 'The Syndicate' was born. The Syndicate offered artistic product but was restrictive and generally ruthless when theatre managers outside the system didn't buy in to their season choices. They controlled many of the most important venues and routes between America's large cities and by 1900 were in general control of the American theatre. Many local producers were shut out, uncooperative theatre artists were 'blackballed', and conservative star-studded productions were usually selected over artistic productions that weren't deemed likely to appeal to the masses.

Producer and playwright David Belasco eventually helped weaken the hold of the Syndicate on American theatre, and the Shubert brothers' rival chain of theatres pitted a corporate base to dilute the backdoor politics of the Syndicate's conglomeration of businessmen. Unfortunately, in the early to mid-twentieth century, the Shuberts monopolized the 'road tours' in much the same way as the Syndicate had. When they were forced by anti-trust legislation to sell many of their theatres, doors began to open for more individual producers. With an emphasis on flashy, large musicals and 'stars,' important playwrights and producers of less commercial dramas, classics, and new plays found it difficult to find an artistic home for their work on Broadway, on the road or throughout America. Suddenly, doors began to open for theatre entrepreneurs dedicated to more diverse seasons of drama – often featuring new voices in the American theatre.

In the decades that followed, economic and technological changes altered the theatre industry, creating a need and setting the stage for a new, nonprofit movement. In the 1920s, this new wave of theatres began springing up across the country. Its leaders were visionaries – artists, educators and community organizers. Their new theatres generally focused on the compelling nature of the plays and the dynamic and exciting process of theatre. Hundreds of nonprofit theatres suddenly surfaced in makeshift neighborhood theatres in small towns, midsize cities, and bustling metropolitan areas. Stephen Langley deftly chronicled the changes in these new nonprofit theatres that, instead of being led by profit-driven producers, were being governed by boards of trustees and artistic directors with 'their sights fixed on artistic rather than commercial goals' (Langley, *Theatre Management and Production in America*, p. 169).

The 1934 guidebook, *B'way Inc! The Theatre as a Business* is one of the earliest published books on theatre management in America. Its author, Morton Eustis, here offers a look at producing in America prior to the emergence of the nonprofit theatre movement:

> *Anyone who has money – or the ability to beg, or borrow it – can become a theatrical producer. Talent, background, theatre training, common or garden business sense, he need not have . . . to see his name in electric lights glimmering above that of the star and the play, he has only to take an option on a script, any script will do; engage a cast, director and technical staff; post a bond with Actors' Equity; sign a few standard contracts; rent a theatre, and order the curtain to be raised on another glamorous Broadway first night . . . producing a play can be a delightfully remunerative pastime.*
>
> Morton Eustis, *B'way Inc! The Theatre as a Business*, p. 18.

That same year, *Theatre Arts* editor Edith J. R. Isaacs wrote:

> *Any living theatre must have five essential qualities:*
>
> *It must have an entity, an organism that can be recognized, as you recognize a human being, by certain traits of character and of physical presence that are marks of a personal life.*

It must have permanence in some one or more of its fundamentals. It may be a permanence of place or of leadership, as in the Moscow Art Theatre, or the Vieux Colombier or the Neighborhood Playhouse; of repertory, of course, of company, or of idea, as in Meiningen or the Théâtre Libre or the Provincetown, or of any two or three of these combined; but they must have something that stands firm and rooted, something not too transitory, in that transitory world of the theatre where performances die as they live, each day, as a production is set up, played through and struck.

It must have the power of growth, of progress, both in its permanent and its impermanent factors, because times change and it must change with them . . .

It must bear within itself the power of generation, the element of renewal, a force that, having flowed out of its own inner strength and integrity, can bring back fresh strength from a newer, younger world.

And finally it must have a goal that is essentially a theatre goal. There is no reason under the sun why the leader of a fine theatre should not hope to gain money, or power, or preferment from the enterprise. But these are by-products of theatrical success, not essential theatre goals, which must always be in some way related to the performance of good plays by actors of talent, and the consequent development of the theatre's innate power of entertainment, edification, exaltation, escape, and social persuasion.

There has probably never been an organized theatre of importance that did not have, to some extent, these five qualities.

Isaacs, *Broadway, Inc!*, p. 191

Predating the regional theatre movement by almost three decades, these views of the American theatre are both wonderfully visionary and, in today's world, absolutely laughable. Producing a play as a 'delightfully remunerative pastime' is a concept that would elicit a chuckle from most Broadway producers, while non-profit theatre producers might be rolling in the aisles. Although Broadway has arguably been the longtime center of America's commercial theatrical universe, many would note that, today, America's true national theatre lies in the artistically, aesthetically, culturally, ethnically, socially, and politically diverse nonprofit resident theatres that are spread from coast to coast. This would no doubt please the many pioneers of the nonprofit theatre who were dedicated to artistic excellence and the production of creative work that was often being overlooked in favor of more financially promising commercial shows on Broadway.

The debates begin

'It is not an exaggeration to say that regional theatre saved American theatre,' explains Arthur Bartow, former artistic director of the undergraduate Department of Drama at New York's Tisch School of the Arts. According to Mr. Bartow:

> The regional theatre movement galvanized American theatre at a time when commercial theatre was at its nadir. It generated jobs for theatre artists and inspired universities to create professional training programs to supply qualified actors, designers, and directors to feed the burgeoning theatres. It exposed thousands of theatregoers to classical dramatic literature that had been neglected by commercial theatre. Later in the movement, the development of new and established playwrights was almost solely in the hands of regional theatres as commercial theatre shrank from the risk of producing new plays. Regional theatre created a national thirst for playgoing that fed not only nonprofit theatres but commercial theatres as well.

'Without the regional theatre movement, we'd all be living in New York competing for the five jobs available on Broadway, or, if we chose to live elsewhere, we'd be working at Walmart doing community theatre,' contends Pioneer Theatre Company artistic director Charles Morey. The regional theatre is 'Theater in America.'

'The regional theatre movement has, of course, transformed the landscape for theatre in America,' explains Ben Cameron, longtime executive director of the Theatre Communications Group (TCG). Mr. Cameron notes that 'theatres of all shapes and sizes, springing from diverse aesthetic and cultural traditions, now constitute a true theatre ecology in our country. Audience numbers from every source affirm the growing impact of this movement – audiences at an all-time high, and musical and nonmusical theatre the top two performing arts forms for public participation today.'

Scott L. Steele, executive director of the University/Resident Theatre Association (U/RTA) based in New York, weighs in with passion on the movement:

> The regional theatre movement did not just impact theatre in America. This movement created theatre in America. Good theatre outside the mainstream certainly existed prior to the development of regional or resident theatres, but it was a rather disparate group. The strength and growth that unity can provide came with the regional movement, as defined

in the fifties and sixties. Of course, I'm totally biased, having grown up in Washington, DC, with Arena Stage, The Washington Theatre Club (now extinct), and The Folger Theatre Group (now The Shakespeare Theatre).

Richard Rose, artistic director of Virginia's Barter Theatre, offers:

In the beginning, regional theatre served mostly to bring Broadway to the people, giving access to the shows created on Broadway and allowing audiences all over the nation to experience those shows. While places like the Barter and Cleveland and La Jolla did do a lot of new works and spawned many new authors, actors, designers, directors, etc. who went on to great careers, one could argue that regional theatre was, in the beginning, merely an outgrowth of summer stock: a place for actors (and other theatre artists) to work and hone their craft in anticipation of working on Broadway or in film. It was a training ground. Regional theatre was the 'farm team' to Broadway's 'major league.'

Gerald Freedman, professional director and dean of Drama at the North Carolina School of the Arts, explains that 'the regional theatre movement has evolved in a different manner than first conceived, as a kind of national theatre with numerous dispersed satellites. Individual regions would find their unique voice and birth ensemble companies of professional caliber to bring a steady stream of quality theatre, classics, current and new plays to enrich areas of the United States far from New York, Chicago, San Francisco. No longer would these outposts be dependent on touring companies with no regional roots.' He asks crucial questions: 'Without regional theatre, where would we train our young actors, directors, and designers? Where would our new playwrights find an outlet for their voice? Where would audiences experience the thrill of live performances in this time of mechanical reproductions?'

In no uncertain terms, noted author and professional director Tom Markus explains the potential influence and impact regional theatre can have on a community:

It has brought the life-nurturing experience of professional-quality live theatre to millions of Americans, improving the quality of their daily rounds by providing them with an alternative to foolish movies and more foolish television. It has given hope and enlightenment to our young people and confirmation and vitality to our old. It has infused our society with the wisdom of the great writers of the past and the insights of the promising writers of the future. It has placed artists in each community, living side by side with postmen, dentists, electricians, and stockbrokers. Without regional theatre, America would slide into ignorance and vulgarity.

Ted Herstand, professional director, historian, and Professor Emeritus at the University of Oklahoma, explains that 'regional theatre has provided a venue more conducive to new-play development than is found in the commercial theatre. In a very real sense, the National Theatre of America is the not-for-profit regional theatre. The commercial professional theatre is, more than ever before, dependent for whatever success it may have on the quality of regional theatre that feeds it people, plays, and productions.'

Longtime Florida State University/Asolo Theatre Conservatory dean Gil Lazier summarizes the overall impact of the regional theatre movement by noting that: 'It's fostered more good American playwrights by providing them with more venues for artistic development than New York ever could. It's given American actors a chance to have normal lives by becoming members of resident companies and receiving steady incomes so that they can have homes and families. It's permitted professional productions of classic plays, seldom seen in New York except through imports, thus keeping alive a repertoire of great theatre.'

Andrew Barnicle provides a bit of historical perspective:

It is crucial to remember that the national theatre of America has always been an organism in flux – in the 1830s every city had a resident rep company that supported traveling stars in a common repertoire of slightly rehearsed plays. The expansion of the railroads during the Civil War created the possibility of entire productions touring, scenery et al., which rendered the resident companies obsolete. The actors all moved to New York so they could go on the road. The monopolies of the Syndicate and others desultorily formulized touring shows until there was an overwhelming need for an art theatre movement, which eventually led to the small literary-minded regional theatres in the early twentieth century. This eventually resulted in the Off-Broadway and not-for-profit regional theatre movement. Now, ironically, the commercial producers are partnering with the not-for-profits. Who would have guessed?

Jim O'Connor, professional director and head of the MFA Directing program at the University of South Carolina, notes the historic importance of college and university theatres in the development of the American theatre:

The regional theatre movement along with the more widespread but less product-focused university theatre has been the major force in maintaining the viability and visibility of the art of theatre in the United States. While serving as the prime production archive of past cultures, the regional theatre has simultaneously served to produce the major new writers for theatre. Even a short review of the seasons of regional theatres will reveal that they are a combination of historically important scripts, new works written by resident or itinerant authors, and commercial works from Broadway, with the first two categories most prominent. During the past several decades, the flow of material has reversed from what had been the import from Broadway to the regional theatre to one from the regional theatre to Broadway.

A rose by any other name

'I dislike the term "regional theatre,"' notes Geffen Playhouse and longtime Academy Awards producer Gilbert Cates. 'I find it patronizing. The only regional theatre in America is on Broadway. The rest is American theatre.' The Goodman Theatre's savvy executive director, Roche Schulfer, concurs: 'I prefer the term "resident" to "regional" in referring to theatres that operate outside of the New York metropolitan area. I think that "regional" implies that a theatre serves a particular section of the country or that it is defined by its relationship to a specific geographic area, such as New York. "Resident," on the other hand, more accurately describes a theatre with an ongoing history in a community and a strong connection to local artists, audiences, and supporters.' Murray Ross of Colorado's Theatreworks also sees it this way: 'To my mind, "regional theatre" sounds like a minor-league franchise or branch . . . We don't think of ourselves as a regional theatre – just as a theatre . . . a good theatre not in the Broadway or West End region.' 'Just for the record, one could argue that New York (Broadway) is just a large regional theatre,' adds the Barter's Richard Rose.

Robert Moss, former artistic director of New York's Syracuse Stage, looks at the positive side: 'There are so many major theatre artists on Broadway who were brought up and nourished in the regions – it is a record we can be proud of.'

Still, however one labels the burgeoning growth of regional, resident, local, community, or 'home' theatres in America, it's clear that these theatres are changing the face of audiences and introducing many new faces as playwrights, actors, directors, and other theatre professionals. As Marin Shakespeare Company managing director Lesley Schisgall Currier explains: 'The regional theatre movement has added a new chapter to the history of theatre in America, providing myriad companies that serve the melting pot of communities and sub-communities throughout the 50 states. The most vital American theatre today is gestating not on Broadway, but in communities all over the nation where artists are finding their own voices, re-imagining the classics, providing creative opportunities for students of all ages, and making meaningful and entertaining theatre that forges long-lasting relationships with other individuals and organizations.'

Back to the beginnings: little theatre and community theatres

It is important to credit the many 'little theatres' and 'community theatres' that were a part of the American fabric long before the American regional theatre movement began to blossom fully in the 1960s. To quote professional designer and University of Virginia Professor Emeritus David W. Weiss, 'Keep in mind that long before anyone coined the phrase "regional theatre," there was some serious activity out in the boonies. It was called stock, of course, and it wasn't just in the summer.'

Writing about American drama during colonial times (and earlier), theatre historian Walter J. Meserve offers this perspective:

> If early attempts at dramatic literature were wild, one could surely describe the beginnings of an American theatre as stormy. Performances of plays were opposed by local and colonial governments and by certain religious groups. Bankruptcy was a common hazard for theatre managers. Playwrights were constantly subjected to abuse by theatre managers, actors, and the public . . .
>
> Just three hundred years ago, the first recorded play written in English in America, Ye Bare and Ye Cubb (written in 1665), was performed in Accomac, Virginia. During the intervening years, the advance of American drama to a position of world significance has been slow and painful.
>
> Meserve, *An Outline of American Drama*, pp. 1, 359

'On Tuesday I speak at Andover on "A Possible National Theater," my old theme, slightly changed,' writes Lady Gregory in a letter to Kenneth Macgowan, dated 17 January 1915, 'I am still full of the idea that one will be started in America – a tree with a root in every state.' And in his 1916 study, Arthur Edwin Krows writes:

> I welcome the various American experiments of little theatres, big theatres, open-air theatres, women's theatres, children's theatres, and the rest, for they signify a place for everything and everything in its place – with pleasure for all, varying scales of prices stabilized in each theatre, for development of clientele, and, above all, support of plays for which it would be impossible at the time to secure general public approval . . . Shakespeare's plays, which were written for theatres in the open air in the daytime, have proven admirable when performed in the open air (in America).
>
> Krows, *Play Production in America*, pp. 362–363

Kenneth Macgowan's *Footlights Across America: Towards a National Theater* traces the 'extent, nature and significance of the non-commercial theatre of America.' *Footlights* follows 14,000 miles of the author's travels helping to pinpoint the location of over 1,050 community and university theatres throughout the United States. He notes that George Pierce Baker of Yale University 'has listed 1,800 names of producing organizations' and that *Theatre Arts Monthly* 'has been in correspondence' with 1,000 groups (not counting the 6,000 high schools 'that produce as part of their class work anywhere from one bill of short plays to twenty-five bills of long and short, and 6,000 more high schools with dramatic clubs that give at least one play a year'). He writes:

> The history of the little theatre movement in America is a history of many things. It is a history of variegated efforts in acting, playwriting, direction, scene design, the organization of audiences, the financing and building of theatres. It is a history of amateur exhibitionism – the raw material of the stage – and of strongly talented artists who could make use of that material . . . It is, in short, a history of aesthetic, social, and economic change.
>
> Macgowan, *Footlights Across America*, p. 41

Boston's Toy Theatre (1912), Chicago's Little Theatre (1912), New York's Neighborhood Playhouse (1915), Massachusetts' Provincetown Players (1915), Ohio's Cleveland Play House (1915), New York's Washington Square Players (1918), California's Laguna Playhouse (1920), Chicago's Goodman Theatre (1925), and

California's Pasadena Playhouse (1925) were just a few of the more than 2,000 theatres established throughout America by the mid-1920s, according to Drama League of America and Theatre Communications Group records.

Two of these groups emerged from a group of actors, writers, and artists who were mounting informal shows at the Liberal Club, labeled as the center of intellectual life in New York's Greenwich Village. Theatre historian Jack Poggi tells the story:

> Out of these experiments two groups emerged, the Provincetown Players and the Washington Square Players. The two began to go in different directions. The Provincetown Players, more concerned with developing new writers, tried to preserve their freedom by remaining small and modest. The Washington Square Players, more concerned with improving production standards, expanded quickly and deliberately.
>
> Poggi, *Theatre in America*, p. 109

'Perhaps the happiest development of the 1920s was the success of the Theatre Guild of New York City . . . the founding fathers of the Guild were veterans of the defunct Washington Square Players,' writes Garff B. Wilson. Between 1920 and 1930, the Theatre Guild produced 67 plays including the works of Eugene O'Neill and Elmer Rice.

Writing about the growing professionalization of little theatres in the 1920s, Kenneth McGowan describes the 'definite professionalizing of the actors,' the cost of new productions, the salaries of directors, and 'somewhere in the neighborhood of twenty-five plays a year' performed at The Cleveland Play House in Ohio. He describes The Goodman Theatre in Chicago's 'handsome and finely equipped playhouse which the Goodmans built on the lake front', maintaining 'an entirely professional company of sixteen actors . . . nine new plays and two or three revivals, and the average run of about four weeks. All this – the school and its losses included – is done on a budget of $120,000.' In McGowan's travels to the Pasadena Community Playhouse in California, he discovered a company that 'caters to both a winter and a summer audience,' producing 28 plays and 322 performances a season, with a producing staff of 16, with 24 people 'in the work of administration,' and a budget over $145,000 (Macgowan, pp. 99–100).

Universities play a significant part in the regional theatre movement

Universities were expanding their dramatic activities as well in the late 1920s, and Macgowan found that 'not much less than 150 colleges have a course in the production of plays.' He concludes that 'universities have fed the new American theatre, sending playwrights to Broadway, and actors, directors, audiences, and ideals to the local theatres.' (Macgowan, p. 154).

In a Northwestern University thesis survey of 383 universities conducted by Miss Lucile Calvert in 1928–29, she found the following as the 'most active universities' who responded to her survey:

University	Annual Productions	Annual Performances
Carnegie Tech	20	128
Cornell	20	40–50
Northwestern	14	68
Iowa	14	40–50
Yale	13	34
North Carolina	6	130

Source: Macgowan, *Footlights Across America*, p. 110

'If one goes back to Norris Houghton's book *Advance from Broadway*, we discover that when he wandered around the country in the 1930s trying to get a handle on theatre in our country, he found mostly amateur theatre along with a fairly lively road business,' explains designer and longtime Institute of Outdoor Drama consultant David W. Weiss. 'There was plenty of community and college theatre that was of reasonably good quality but not much beyond that.' He adds: 'After the war, and largely because of the financial help made available from the Ford Foundation, the regional theatre as we know it now began to exist and thrive.'

Groundbreaking theatres and forceful leaders emerge

Eva Le Gallienne's Civic Repertory Theatre (1926) and the Group Theatre (1931) in New York were important artistic forces. Miss Le Gallienne, who presented an ambitious repertory of plays from 1926 to 1932, helped clarify the terminology we still use today:

> There was much confusion about just what repertory means . . .
> 'Repertory' derives from the Latin 'reperio,' 'to find again.' Its definition in
> the standard dictionary is 'a place where things are stored or gathered
> together' . . . A repertory theatre then, is a repository theatre, a theatre in
> which plays are gathered together and kept alive. Alternating performances
> of a wide range of plays is the only way to prolong their life. A permanent
> company is the only kind able to resume a play after months lapse from the
> current schedule without prohibitively arduous rehearsals . . . In other
> words, true repertory is the natural and normal form of the theatre.
> Steinberg, *The History of the Fourteenth Street Theater*, pp. 86–87

The mission of the Group Theatre, as reviewed by Harold Clurman in *The Fervent Years*, was 'to lead full lives disciplined by a unified moral and intellectual code that would direct them toward smiling goals of spiritual and material well-being.' The first directors included Mr. Clurman, Lee Strasberg, and Cheryl Crawford, and the actors included Elia Kazan, Stella Adler, Clifford Odets, Franchot Tone, J. Edward Bromberg, and Morris Carnovsky.

Important work was also being developed outside New York in Virginia's Barter Theatre (1933) and the Pittsburgh Playhouse (1933). The Barter Theatre's visionary Robert Porterfield attacked the Great Depression with the motto: 'With vegetables you cannot sell, you can buy a good laugh' as his theatre traded/bartered food and animals for theatre tickets.

As a means of battling unemployment, Hallie Flanagan Davis headed up the Federal Theatre Project in 1935 and employed over 10,000 people in 40 states in hundreds of productions. She labored to create an initiative based on economic necessity that would be uniquely American, involve government subsidy, and present the best theatre work of the day. In her landmark book, *Arena: The Story of the Federal Theatre*, Ms. Flanagan Davis explains that the Federal Theatre worked on performing projects where 'each region and eventually each state would have its unique, indigenous dramatic expression' (*Arena*, p. 371). In a 1938 report to the House of Representatives, she offered a history lesson in international arts support:

> *Government support of the theatre brings the United States into the best historic theatre tradition and into the best contemporary theatre practice. Four centuries before Christ, Athens believed that plays were worth paying for out of public money; today France, Germany, Norway, Sweden, Denmark, Russia, Italy and practically all other civilized countries appropriate money for the theatre.*

> Flanagan Davis, Federal Theatre Project/WPA brief
> before the House of Representatives, 1938 p. 1

Unfortunately, the Federal Theatre's progressive contributions to the cultural life of the nation ended on June 30, 1939, when it was killed by an act of Congress.

While the political and censorship battles were raging in Congress – in part over Mark Blitzstein's controversial play *The Cradle Will Rock*, the investigations of the Dies Committee on Un-American Activities, and charges that the Federal Theatre's activities were 'communistic' – theatre in the regions continued to flourish. In an April 5, 1940, address delivered by Frederick H. Koch at a 'Southern Regional Theatre Festival' (commemorating the founding of the Carolina Playmakers in 1918–19), Professor Koch reviewed much of the rich history of American theatre including 'Folk Drama,' 'The Negro Drama,' 'The Tenant Farm Drama,' 'Drama in Extension (schools outreach),' 'Plays of a Country Neighborhood (playwriting),' 'Mexican Folk Plays,' 'Carolina and Canada,' 'A Chinese Playmaker,' 'The Professional and the People's Theatre,' 'Communal Drama of American History' and 'Trouping (regional touring from the Carolinas to Boston, St. Louis, Dallas, Washington, DC, and to myriad other cities through 45 plays and 36 tours).

The University of North Carolina's George R. Coffman welcomed the 'Regional Theatre Festival' to the 'Drama in the South' convention (that included speeches by playwrights Clifford Odets and Paul Green and author Zora Neal Hurston) and proclaimed that 'critics and historians of American drama gave him [Professor Koch] first ranking as leader of a regional movement for native drama.' Even Orson Welles, founder of the Mercury Theatre and well-known Broadway and Hollywood actor-director, sent greetings, and wrote: 'It is groups like yours which stimulate and keep the American theatre alive.' Critics Brooks Atkinson and Stark Young sent greetings, along with philanthropist John D. Rockefeller, director Kenneth Macgowan, historian Allardyce Nicoll, and playwright Lynn Riggs.

In his address titled 'A Playwright's Credo,' playwright Clifford Odets tendered these words of advice to the assembled crowd:

> If America is to grow up in a creative sense the artist must realize how much he is like the life around him . . . America is a country of beginners, in the theatre as in many other things. I believe that here it is certainly fact – that the parochial, not the cosmopolitan, is the beginning of truth.
>
> 'A Playwright's Credo,' *The Carolina Play-Book*, p. 105

So, theatre certainly existed in the 'regions' long before what may eventually be known as the Golden Age of America's Regional Theatre when theatres were flourishing in the mid-twentieth century. However, it seems that for many current theatre professionals with short memories (or an abbreviated view of America's theatre history), the most important 'regional theatre movement' will always be tied to the founding of currently existing, generally thriving, and much-revered large institutions whose founders and ongoing leaders helped shape current production standards, theatrical architectural wonders, the collective bargaining of union contracts, and the artistic visions that currently spark twenty-first-century plays and productions.

The US outdoor drama movement

Exciting, invigorating, often epic productions featuring historic, adventurous moments from America's past, passionate moments of religious drama, or even rambunctious Shakespearean productions provided theatre in the regions long before the term 'regional theatre' was used to describe the nonprofit movement that was soon to follow. In Bulletin No. 42 in the *University of North Carolina Institute of Outdoor Drama* files, the 'Preliminary Guidelines for Outdoor Epic Drama' clarify the community partnership:

> Regional outdoor drama production as it exists in America today, regardless of whether the production is of an original historical play or established as a festival of classics, has almost entirely been developed by non-profit historical and cultural organizations which stress cooperation between local groups, foundations, education, and government.

With the help of the Federal Theatre Project, the Civilian Conservation Corps, and President Roosevelt's New Deal, the citizens of Roanoke Island, North Carolina, first produced Pulitzer Prize-winning playwright Paul Green's famed outdoor historical drama, *The Lost Colony*, in 1937. According to Scott J. Parker, former executive director of the Institute of Outdoor Drama (IOD), *The Lost Colony*, intended to run only one summer, was such a success that it continued each summer thereafter (except during World War II), and spawned the US Outdoor Drama movement, which currently numbers nearly 50 productions across America. Designed to preserve and celebrate the heritage of the country and to increase tourism, the historical plays are based on significant events and performed in amphitheatres on or near the sites where the events occurred.

Mark R. Sumner, Institute of Outdoor Drama executive director from 1964 to 1989, explains:

> *Green followed the success of* The Lost Colony *in 1937 with* The Common Glory *at Williamsburg, Virginia, in 1947, and Kermit Hunter, then a UNC graduate student, wrote his famed* Unto These Hills *in 1950 for the Cherokee Indian Reservation in the mountains.*

David W. Weiss offers this view of America at the time:

> *When Paul Green launched the first of his outdoor dramas,* The Lost Colony, *the world was a much simpler place. The simplicity of entertainment in those days, for children and adults, made going to an outdoor drama a highlight in vacation travel. It was alive! We went to an outdoor drama to see people who might have walked on the very spot we were looking at. And that was important because we also knew something about the historical events we were witnessing. There was truly a sense of pilgrimage, there was a reason we came to this place. We knew we would see history come to life. For decades the outdoor historical drama was an important part of summer travel. At a show one often heard people in the audience talking about other outdoor dramas they had seen. Families often planned the route of their vacation travel so that two or three dramas might be enjoyed.*

As an expert on outdoor drama, Mr. Sumner prophesied much of the future of the theatre (and the fears of theatre producers) in a 1973 fiftieth-anniversary program for the Carolina Dramatic Association:

> *Unless the whole field of outdoor theatrical endeavor keeps its eyes on constantly improving production and acting standards, it is also quite*

*possible that other and cheaper forms of entertainment through pay
television, video-cassette, and cable television will replace the outdoor
drama in the minds of the audience. New electronic devices for presenting
performances will bring more and more control to the hands of a few
individuals at the top of corporate entertainment structures.*

*Unless live theatrical forms can manage to hold huge segments of the
American public in regional theatres showing regional original material, we
may end up buying all our performing arts in electronic packages sold like
sausages in plastic tubing . . . The opportunities for imaginative directors,
paid positions for new performers, and the need for new writers and new
managers are great, as are the opportunities for increasing service to the
public . . . We have the opportunity to create a national drama as vital as
the festival of the ancient Greeks, where the awe of nature is real and
where live actors uphold the dignity of man.*

The Carolina Handbook, p. 41

The beginnings of the regional theatre movement

While the US Outdoor Drama movement was taking shape in small communities
throughout America, legendary theatre continued to surface and flourish in sometimes wonderful, sometimes bizarre, barely functional indoor spaces in New York
and throughout the country. The Cleveland Play House (1915), Laguna Playhouse
(1920), Arizona's Phoenix Theatre (1920), and Chicago's Goodman Theatre, (1925)
may have led the way, but the Oregon Shakespeare Festival (1935), San Diego's
Old Globe Theatre (1937), and New York City's The Mercury Theatre (1937) weren't
far behind.

'The 1930s were the great era for the proliferation of summer theatres of all
kinds,' explains Garff B. Wilson:

*They spread from coast to coast, varying from earnest amateur groups
performing in converted barns to professional companies presenting big-
name players in well-equipped playhouses. As an instrument to assist and
encourage the activities of the noncommercial theatres, the National
Theatre Conference (NTC) was founded in 1930 . . . Not directly related
to the noncommercial theatre but of great importance to the American*

stage was the establishment in 1926 by the Dramatists' Guild of the now
famous 'Minimum Basic Agreement,' which guaranteed to playwrights the
permanent ownership of their plays and a fair share of the profits derived
from them.

Mr. Wilson provides additional history:

In 1896, American performers had formed an association called the
Actors Society to protect their welfare. It had proved ineffective. In 1913
a new organization called Actors' Equity Association had been founded; for
six years it had tried futilely to obtain from managers and producers an
agreement which would guarantee actors a fair wage, no more than eight
performances a week and none on Sunday, a limitation on free rehearsal
time, certain travel benefits, and other protections against unreasonable
demands. Producers and managers had delayed, evaded, and refused.
Finally, in 1919 Actors' Equity had called a strike. It had closed almost
every playhouse on Broadway for four weeks and had ended in victory for
Actors' Equity. Now in 1926, seven years after the actors' strike, the
playwrights gained comparable protection under the Minimum Basic
Agreement. Thus ended the long exploitation of the American dramatist,
an ugly feature of the theatrical scene for almost two hundred years.

> Wilson, *Three Hundred Years of American Drama*
> *and Theatre*, pp. 375–76

Theatre support groups began to organize. Barnard Hewitt provides an overview
of theatre in America in the 1930s, 1940s, and 1950s:

Some individuals and groups attempted to find remedies for the theatre's
ills. Everyone was alarmed by the scarcity of good new plays, and efforts
were made to encourage the beginning playwright. The Bureau of New
Plays, headed by Theresa Helburn, in the thirties, and the New Dramatists'
Committee of the Dramatists' Guild, in the forties and fifties, provided
advice, criticism, and a kind of introduction to the profession.

In 1946 a group of producers, actors, playwrights, and critics, seeking
a united front for an attack on the whole theatre problem, organized and
set up offices as the American National Theatre and Academy (ANTA) . . .
It engaged in a great variety of activities, all well-intended and most of them
useful.

> Hewitt, *Theater USA*, p. 486

A brochure published by ANTA lists services ranging from job counseling and placement to information on international theatre matters, to speakers for conferences and meetings, to a variety of publications, and an annual national conference designed to bring together representatives of theatres to exchange ideas and information 'related to the development of the American Theatre.'

Theatres were continuing to sprout up in unlikely spots. Mr. Hewitt notes:

> Off-Broadway theatre had always existed, but not since the Washington Square Players, the Provincetown Playhouse, and the Greenwich Village theatres in the teens and early twenties had it commanded such attention from the public and the critics. This phenomenon was virtually limited to New York. Dallas, Texas, Washington, D.C., and perhaps one or two other large cities could boast resident companies long enough established to be called permanent, but attempts to establish them in Philadelphia and Chicago, for instance, had failed.

He concludes in a way that makes you wonder where he was hiding his crystal ball:

> If professional theatre Off-Broadway – and some of it deserved to be called 'professional' – continued to flourish, not merely within metropolitan New York but in other cities across the length and breadth of the land, the dream of ANTA and all other lovers of theatre would be realized – a genuine renaissance of living theatre in America.

Hewitt, *Theater USA*, pp. 486–87

In Hallie Flanagan's *Dynamo,* published in 1943, she discusses America's needs and the power of theatre in a way that resonates eerily with the America of recent years:

> America needs power, and because we are at war we think of this power in terms of men, money, and machines . . . We shall need as never before the energy that can create life, and this is the very pith and marrow of the theatre. The creation of life is the essence of all real theatre; it is the raison d'être of the theatre in the college. Such a theatre first finds and then releases youth's burning energy, an energy not only intellectual but biological, spiritual, and emotional, not to be ignored by processes concerned with the development of complete human beings.

Flanagan, *Dynamo*, pp. 3–4

While many theatre historians and critics were writing about the potential of America's theatre future, others were working to fulfill it. Actors Studio (1947), Dallas's Theatre '47 (founded by Margo Jones in 1947), Houston's Alley Theatre (founded by Nina Vance in 1947), Washington, DC's Arena Stage (founded in 1950 by Edward Mangum, Zelda Fichandler, and Thomas C. Fichandler), Circle in the Square (1951), Actors' Workshop in San Francisco (1952), Stratford Shakespeare Festival in Ontario, Canada (1953), New York Shakespeare Festival (1954), Milwaukee Repertory Theater (1954), Williamstown Theatre Festival (1955), and the American Shakespeare Festival in Stratford, Connecticut (1955) are just a few of the theatres established to produce new work and the classics during those years.

Why were these theatres so important? As Louis Kronenberger explained in the *Best Plays of 1954-55*, 'Real achievement, genuine stature, is indeed what Broadway fell short of most; what Broadway concerned itself with was seldom at a very high level.' Fortunately, there were regional theatres emerging to pick up the artistic slack. Regional theatre pioneer Margo Jones met Tennessee Williams in 1942, directed his plays at both the Pasadena Playhouse and Cleveland Play House, garnered a Rockefeller fellowship in 1944, incorporated the Dallas Civic Theater in 1945 (with Tennessee Williams and designer Jo Mielziner as board members), and opened the theatre under the name Theatre '47 in June 1947. She started the company with eight to nine Equity actors at salaries of 75 dollars per week and the theatre seated 198 in the audience (*The Handbook of Texas Online*, www.tsha.utexas.edu). Her words are prophetic: 'We must create the theatre of tomorrow today. What our country needs . . . is a resident professional theatre in every city with a population over one hundred thousand' (Jones, *Theatre-in-the-Round*, 1951, pp. 3–5). Dubbed 'the Texas Tornado' by Tennessee Williams, Margo Jones was a champion of many emerging playwrights and shared her vision and fervor with both Nina Vance and a very young Zelda Fichandler.

Nearby in Houston, Texas, the Alley Theatre's Nina Vance also started her theatre in 1947, with the $2.14 it cost to send 214 postcards to everyone she thought might want to get her theatre off the ground. Working in an 87-seat dance studio for the first two years, the Alley finally converted an old fan factory in 1949.

A year later in Washington, DC, Zelda Fichandler and co-founders rented an old movie house, raised $15,000, and started Arena Stage (originally as a commercial corporation and later reorganized as a nonprofit). In a January 2005 article for *American Theatre*, Zelda Fichandler reviewed her passion for the theatre:

I think the following is my 'why' for sustaining a life in the theatre for over half a century. It's about the audience: my friends and neighbors; the visitors of different colors; the despairing who lead tight, circumscribed lives; the rich and comfortable who in the dark may experience guilt and the rich and comfortable whose hunger can never be assuaged; the wide-eyed children in their one good dress; the lonely one in a single seat; the Masons in their funny hats; the cognizant and the non-knowing; the old who can forget about dying for a few hours; the egoists; the damned; the teenagers who under their bravado and with rings in every part of their anatomy yearn to be useful. The Audience, the terminus of all our work. God bless them all.

Out west in the 1940s, San Francisco drama critic Luther Nichols noted:

There were also strong indications that regional self-realization was being achieved in such semi-professional groups as the Workshop and Interplayers of San Francisco, and the Players' Ring, Stage Society, Hollywood Repertory Theater and Negro Ebony Showcase Theater in Southern California.

Cory, *The Dallas Theater Center*, p. 3

Other dates of great importance to the nonprofit theatre movement would include the commitment of the Ford Foundation to provide millions of dollars of philanthropic support to the arts (1957). In 1959, the Ford Foundation even developed three-year grants to help resident theatres create permanent companies – Arena Stage received $127,000, the Alley Theatre received $156,000, and San Francisco's Actors' Workshop, with directors Herbert Blau and Jules Irving, received $156,000.

Back in Dallas, a Cleveland Play House veteran, Beatrice Handel, teamed up with Robert D. Stecker and Paul Baker to create the Dallas Theater Center in 1959. In Paul Baker's own words:

For me, at least, the theatre is faith . . . It is the faith that each one of us must find this individual creative force and make it grow and take form. It is the faith that this individual creative force may be used to change and improve our lives and our perspective toward contemporary living. It is a faith developed out of experimentation and expenditure of every form of energy. It is the faith that must be expressed in action.

Cory, *The Dallas Theater Center*, p. 24

Broadway musicals spur regional theatre development

The 'golden age of musical comedy' on Broadway in the 1940s, 1950s, and 1960s (*Oklahoma!*, *Carousel*, *Annie Get Your Gun*, *Brigadoon*, and *Kiss Me Kate* in the 1940s through *Guys and Dolls*, *The King and I*, *Peter Pan*, *West Side Story*, *The Music Man*, *Gypsy*, and *My Fair Lady* in the 1950s, through *Camelot*, *Oliver!*, *Hello Dolly!*, *Fiddler on the Roof*, *Man of La Mancha*, and *Cabaret* in the 1960s) seemed to coincide with a decline in the production of classic and new American plays on the Great White Way due to financial and marketability concerns. New York ticket prices were spiraling due to the high cost of producing on Broadway. At the same time, many cities around America were beginning to hunger for their own 'arts teams.'

Acclaimed author Helen Sheehy, who captured the wit, soul, and story of Margo Jones in her marvelous biography *Margo*, discusses Broadway's aversion to risk in regard to the production of new plays: 'The fact is, Broadway as it existed in the 1940s and 1950s as a producing force . . . simply has not survived' (Sheehy, *Margo*, p. 270).

To the dismay of many American playwrights who were hoping for production on the Great White Way, more and more Broadway plays in the mid-to-late twentieth century were finding their roots in British imports and the new play development efforts of America's nonprofit theatres. To quote the late Peter Zeisler, longtime executive director of the Theatre Communications Group:

> *A very interesting thing happened in the fifties and the beginning of the sixties, sociological, really. After the war, cities throughout the country were really tired of relying on the Northeast to provide them with culture, and they wanted their own. At the same time, remember that in 1950 there was no professional baseball team west of St. Louis. There was no football team west of, I don't know where. Suddenly, to be big league, all these cities had to have their own, and among the things they had to have was a professional theatre. That was the mark of a big-league town. Look magazine had a series of most little cities in America, which were the big-league cities, and to be a big-league city you had to have a baseball team, you had to have a professional theatre. They all had symphonies, so that didn't count. That really started the not-for-profit theatre. Then, a few years later when the NEA started, the government started to recognize*

*theatres, not really support them, but recognize them – that really
changed the land.*

TCG Oral History Project, 2001

Partly fuelled by Broadway production concerns, the nonprofit theatre movement experienced unparalleled growth by the late 1950s and 1960s. Many theatres that would provide opportunities for new playwrights, employment for actors, training for eager students and astute leadership to shape the resident theatre movement, were emerging. Florida's Asolo Theatre Company (1960), Ohio's Cincinnati Playhouse in the Park (1960), Minnesota's The Children's Theatre Company, and the Utah Shakespeare Festival (1961) were a few of the early companies.

As the number of regional theatre operations continued to grow, there was a pressing need to communicate, collaborate, and share information among the many theatre leaders, especially those which set up shop far from the bright lights of Broadway. There was also a need for coordination that was articulated by corporations and foundations who were looking for ways to evaluate funding requests to support these emerging arts organizations. Fortunately, the Theatre Communications Group (TCG) was founded in 1961 and provided a national forum and communications network for the rapidly expanding nonprofit professional theatre field. W. McNeil Lowry, vice president of the Ford Foundation, declared the arts one of the foundation's five major priorities and encouraged the creation of an organization that would be championed by leaders in the theatre profession. He offered a three-year grant to create TCG, and the Ford Foundation was the sole supporter of the service group for a decade.

The Guthrie takes shape

In the meantime, Minnesota's Guthrie Theater began to take shape and was founded in 1963. The idea for the Guthrie Theater began when Sir Tyrone Guthrie, Oliver Rea, and Peter Zeisler decided that there were indeed options for staging theatre with integrity far from the lights, costs, and commercialism and critics of Broadway. To quote the theatre's twenty-fifth anniversary program:

*They wanted to create a theatre with a resident acting company that would
perform the classics in rotating repertory. Sir Tyrone Guthrie believed that
a company of actors performing the classics in rotating repertory would
form and nurture an artistic family; a family whose most important*

contribution would be the feeling of intimate companionship between audience and stage. In the end, it was this unique actor–audience relationship that has sustained the Guthrie as a prototype for an important new kind of theatre.

In order to make this dream come true, Guthrie and his colleagues knew their theatre had to be located far from the boom-or-bust psychology of Broadway. The Broadway atmosphere was conducive neither to producing the great worlds of literature, nor to cultivating the artists' talents, nor to nourishing an audience. The relationship the Guthrie wanted between audience and stage, artist and community, was in complete contrast to the commercial environment on Broadway.

This idea was introduced to the American public in a small paragraph on the drama page of the *New York Times* in 1959. 'Was any city outside of New York interested in providing a home to a new theatre?' asked Brooks Atkinson, theatre critic (Livingston, *The Guthrie Theater*, p. 1–2).

Again, Peter Zeisler adds his perspective to the shifting sands of the development of theatre in America:

The classic repertoire was really a great unknown to American actors. When we started the American Shakespeare Festival in Stratford, Connecticut, in '55, I interviewed over a thousand actors in New York for that first season. My first question was, 'What was the last Shakespeare play you've done professionally?' None of them had ever done Shakespeare professionally. A few had worked at the Old Globe in San Diego, but otherwise they hadn't done any Shakespeare since college. You can't scratch an actor now who hasn't done Shakespeare any number of times. There's a total change.

Once the Guthrie and a few other theatres started to examine the classic repertoire, actor training changed radically in this country. Before that, actor training consisted of learning how to sit on a sofa and hold a martini glass. There was no voice work, no movement work. It was all realistic modern drama. Suddenly, enormous physical demands were being made on actors. Suddenly it became necessary to have voice work and movement work in the training programs that there'd never been before. The not-for-profit theatre really started at Arena Stage in Washington, DC, and the Alley Theatre in Houston. But the Guthrie was the first large company. We played in rotating rep, which nobody else did; we had forty-

*seven Equity actors, unheard of in this country; and we were doing work
at a very high technical level. We had designs by Tanya Moiseiwitsch, one
of the premier designers in the world. That, I think, demonstrated that
you didn't have to be on 44th Street.*

TCG Oral History Project, 2001

An explosion in regional theatre

The continued growth of nonprofit theatres in America was nothing short of
startling. The same year that the Guthrie was founded (1963), Seattle Rep was
organizing on the West Coast; Center Stage was emerging in Baltimore, Maryland;
Trinity Repertory Company surfaced in Providence, Rhode Island; and the Goodspeed Opera House created a home in East Haddam, Connecticut. In 1964, the
Actors Theatre of Louisville began operations in Kentucky, Hartford Stage Company
began in Connecticut, the Missouri Repertory Theatre took up residence in Kansas
City, and both the PCPA Theaterfest and South Coast Repertory spearheaded
operations in California.

Between 1964 and 1974 at least 90 new nonprofit companies surfaced
nationwide and between 1975 and 1985 over 90 more companies jumped on
the bandwagon. To quote Garff B. Wilson:

> *The American dream of many centers of dramatic inspiration and activity
> came close to being realized during the 1960s. The decade was out-
> standing for the spectacular development of regional professional theatres
> and of university theatres . . . The development of regional professional
> companies has been generously supported by the private philanthropic
> foundations of the nation. Even more significant, perhaps, was the
> establishment of the National Foundation on the Arts and Humanities in
> the mid-1960s. After almost two hundred years, the federal government
> recognized its obligation to aid and encourage cultural activities . . . In
> 1965 the commitment was finally made and the foundation was estab-
> lished. It includes two groups, the National Endowment for the Arts (NEA)
> and the National Endowment for the Humanities (NEH).*

Wilson, Three Hundred Years
of American Drama and Theatre, p. 476

Activism, social change, and cultural diversity

Not surprisingly, many theatres promoting activist causes and celebrating the cultural diversity of a changing America surfaced in the 1960s. In California, Tim Dang's *East West Players* (1965) emphasized the Asian-Pacific American experience and Luis Valdez's *El Teatro Campesino* (1965) explored the 'curative, affirmative power of live performance,' imagining a 'worldwide cultural fusion of our times.' Philadelphia's Freedom Repertory Theatre (1966) produced plays from the rich African American canon, New York's INTAR Hispanic American Arts Center (1966) aimed to 'see Hispanic voices take their place in the forefront' of America's arts expression, and San Francisco's Magic Theatre embraced a 'phenomenal diversity of cultures and means of artistic expression.'

Two other dates of importance during this time period include the first League of Resident Theatres (LORT) and Actors' Equity Association contract (1966), and the creation of the now-defunct Foundation for the Extension and Development of the American Professional Theatre (FEDAPT) in 1967. FEDAPT assisted more than 700 performing arts companies over two decades and published comprehensive 'Monographs' and 'Workpapers' detailing the creative fundraising efforts, planning strategies, managerial relationships, season selection, board structuring, and overall 'problems and difficulties' of the not-for-profit theatre during a key growth period of the regional theatre movement. Frederic B. Vogel and Nello McDaniel served successively as executive directors of FEDAPT. According to Actors' Equity Association and ANTA lists, 40 resident Equity theatres from 22 states were operating in 1966–67.

Other theatres of historic significance to the regional theatre movement opened their doors in the 1960s, including Seattle's A Contemporary Theatre (1965), San Francisco's American Conservatory Theater (1965), New Haven's Long Wharf Theatre (1965), New York's Roundabout Theatre Company (1965), The Repertory Theater of St. Louis (1966), Yale Repertory Theatre (1966), Arizona Theatre Company (1967), Los Angeles's Mark Taper Forum (1967), Georgia's Alliance Theatre Company (1968), California's Berkeley Repertory Theatre (1968), Wisconsin's Madison Repertory Theatre (1969), and Washington, DC's The Shakespeare Theatre, founded in 1969 as the Folger Theatre.

'While the establishment of the theatre in the Lincoln Center has interested many people, the work of the Tyrone Guthrie Theater in Minneapolis and the increased number of workshop theatres and summer stock companies in various American cities are equally impressive,' wrote author Walter J. Meserve in 1965. 'College and university theatres now attract professional actors and actresses, who work with students in creating productions of taste and excellence. If there is a contemporary theatre movement at all, it is obviously designed to spread theatre throughout America.'

Children's theatre takes one giant step forward

Children's theatre, long a staple in community theatres, schools, and parks and recreation programs, took a major leap forward when The Children's Theatre Company was founded in 1961 in Minneapolis, Minnesota. Other significant companies followed, including St. Louis's Metro Theater Company (1973), Seattle Children's Theatre (1975), Tempe, Arizona's Childsplay (1977), Dallas Children's Theater (1984), and Bethesda, Maryland's Imagination Stage (1992). Seattle Children's Theatre former managing director Kevin Maifeld explains the children's theatre phenomenon:

> Our belief is to produce 'ageless' theatre so that a grandparent, parent, and child can attend and have an equally rewarding experience. When this happens, we open the magical world of theatre to a child and reinforce the importance of it to the parent and grandparent. We also believe in producing theatre at the highest professional level so that children seek quality in the future.

ASSITEJ/USA (now TYA/USA) is the International Association of Theater for Children and Young People. Founded in 1965, the organization's primary objective is to help develop professional theatre for young audiences and international exchange by sponsoring inter/national festivals and forums, aiding artist exchange, and providing publications to the theatre community.

Today, youth theatre is a major component of many nonprofit theatres. Many artistic directors who originally scoffed at the idea of 'kiddie theatre' and 'community outreach programs' seemed suddenly to shift their thinking when funding dried up for the arts but remained for 'educational programs.' While there are indeed artistic leaders with an inherent appreciation for youth theatre, the realities of funding and audience building inspired many others to address the broader cultural and educational needs of their home communities. Today, educational programs and children's theatre are well developed in many regional theatres, and are a key part of the mission statement for many professional theatres. Peter Brosius, artistic director of the Tony Award-winning The Children's Theatre Company in Minneapolis, explains:

> The field of theatre for young people is one of the most dynamic areas of the professional theatre. New theatres are being born every day. New multi-million dollar professional facilities to house professional theatre for young people are being created across the country.

Will regional theatre last?

Many theatres faced financial and organizational challenges and the word was still out on the future of the American regional theatre movement when Jack Poggi wrote *Theater in America, The Impact of Economic Forces, 1870–1967*:

> It's too early to tell whether the resident theatres will last. The fact that very few have closed since the movement began is encouraging. The fact that problems are accumulating faster than solutions can be found for them is discouraging. It is quite possible that the boom in resident theatres is a fad of a newly culture-conscious middle class . . . With all its weaknesses, the resident theatre movement has accomplished more for the theatre outside of New York in the last ten years than was accomplished in the preceding fifty.
>
> Poggi, Theater in America, pp. 240–41

Although Mr. Poggi felt that the days of the 'rugged individualist who sets out to build a theatre on his own appear to be over,' professional theatres continued to sprout up in unlikely spots throughout the 1970s, including Indianapolis's Indiana Repertory Theatre (1972), Anniston/Montgomery's Alabama Shakespeare Festival (1972), Rochester, New York's Geva Theatre (1972), Gainesville, Florida's The Hippodrome State Theatre (1973), Knoxville, Tennessee's Clarence Brown Theatre Company (1974), Minneapolis, Minnesota's Illusion Theater (1974), Pennsylvania's Pittsburgh Public Theater (1974), Kentucky's Roadside Theater (1974), and Little Rock's Arkansas Repertory Theatre (1976). Well-known 'actor-driven' nonprofit theatres also materialized during this period, including New York's The Wooster Group (1975), Chicago's Steppenwolf Theatre Company (1976), and Massachusetts's Shakespeare & Company (1978).

In 1976, Benjamin Mordecai, then producing director of the Indiana Repertory Theatre, offered these remarks at a Foundation for the Extension and Development of the American Professional Theatre (FEDAPT) gathering:

> They [Cincinnati Playhouse artistic director Word Baker, and Actors Theatre of Louisville artistic director Jon Jory] stated that anyone in this day and age who has intentions of opening a large-scale professional resident theatre has got to be out of his mind. The odds against its succeeding are extraordinary.
>
> Mordecai, Indiana Repertory Theatre, p. 5

In hopes of assisting other theatre entrepreneurs, Mr. Mordecai provided a brief list that captured Indiana Rep's formula for success. The list includes:

➢ An exceptional group of bright, talented people that were dedicated to accomplishment;

➢ A locale that was ready with an audience;

➢ Outstanding foundation and government support;

➢ A combination of an historic landmark and an inner-city location, which enhanced the appeal of the theatre;

➢ A good artistic product.

> Mordecai, Indiana Repertory Theatre, pp. 20–21

Perhaps the late Vera Mowry Roberts said it best: 'In my early days of traveling around the country as president of the American Theatre Association, students asked how they could make it in NYC. By the early 1980s, they were saying, "I'm going to make theatre where I am." Phenomenal.'

Jumping on the bandwagon

Despite the warnings and extraordinary odds against success, many larger American cities jumped on the bandwagon in the 1980s, hoping to round out the cultural opportunities and quality of life for their surrounding communities.

Colorado's Denver Center Theatre Company, Oregon's Portland Repertory Theater, California's San Jose Repertory Theatre, and Washington, DC's Woolly Mammoth Theatre Company all surfaced in 1980, while Boston's Huntington Theatre Company, California's Shakespeare Santa Cruz, New York's Ubu Repertory Theatre, and Los Angeles's West Coast Ensemble all followed two years later, in 1982.

Local heritage, Community Outreach and HIV

By this time, many theatres were rejecting the idea that they needed to recycle old Broadway hits or even attempt to mirror the commercial practices of popular New York theatres and touring shows. Instead, many theatres looked to their own communities and worked to tell the indigenous stories of their unique regions. Theatre at Lime Kiln (1984) tackled the heritage, culture, and history of its Virginia home with a small resident company. Ohio's Cleveland Public Theater (1983) was created to serve serious emerging theatre artists while confronting and examining 'the political and social milieu which shapes our lives.'

Societal issues certainly influenced the work and missions of promising non-profit theatres. New York's Irondale Ensemble Project (1983) established extensive outreach programs in New York City jails, while the Irondale AIDS Improv Team worked with NYC students on matters of safe sex and the facts of HIV infection. On the West Coast, Seattle's Alice B. Theatre (1984) emphasized providing a 'true clear voice' as a lesbian and gay theatre for all people.

There's more than one 'quiet crisis' in the arts

FEDAPT's 1989–1990 Annual Report, titled *Workpapers: The Quiet Crisis in the Arts*, by Nello McDaniel and George Thorn, addressed loud and forceful attacks on the National Endowment for the Arts and 'the quiet crisis' centring on mounting debt, organizational dysfunction, shrinking human resource pool, high turnover, and low morale of many in the ranks of struggling regional theatres. Over a dozen theatres had closed in the year prior to the report, which called for the development of 'new paradigms to lead and effect change for these new realities.'

New York's nonprofits offer Broadway alternatives

Certainly, many New York theatres were founded over the years to fill the void of actual plays on Broadway. Broadway's 1980s focused on blockbuster musicals (think *42nd Street, Barnum, Joseph and the Amazing Technicolor Dreamcoat, Nine, Cats, La Cage aux Folles, Les Misérables, Starlight Express, Into the Woods,* and *The Phantom of the Opera* and you get the general idea). New York's Primary Stages (1985) emerged to develop and produce new plays by American playwrights and the Atlantic Theater Company (founded by David Mamet and W. H. Macy in 1985) worked to produce 'affordable plays that speak to a new generation of theatregoers.'

While myriad smaller Off-Broadway and Off-Off Broadway theatres were surfacing in New York City, mega-institutions also offered Broadway alternatives. The Lincoln Center Theater (1985) gave a glorious home to new playwrights and audiences in search of American plays, and the Public Theater/New York Shakespeare Festival (founded by Joseph Papp three decades earlier) continued to 'put the voices and the experiences of all Americans' on stage.

Finding a home in regional theatre

In 1985, the Theatre Communications Group leaders organized discussions with artistic directors of America's institutional theatres and discovered, according to author Todd London in *The Artistic Home*, that 'the single most pressing concern . . . is to find ways of keeping the most talented artists in the theatre . . . as work in television and film continues to offer extraordinary compensation and celebrity.' Other areas for discussion included the creative and collaborative needs of artistic directors; desires for more institutional flexibility with subscriptions, scheduling, and rehearsal time; and the development of future audiences. Lloyd Richards, long-time dean of the Yale University School of Drama and artistic director of Yale Repertory Theatre, explained the groundbreaking discussions:

> *In 1985, a group of theatre trustees asked their own artistic directors a wonderfully explosive question: beyond money and survival, what do you want – what is your vision, and what will it take to get you there? . . . This collection of statements does reveal that the tremendous surge of artistic energy and daring which forged, established and validated the nonprofit theatre movement in this country more than twenty-five years ago still exists.*
>
> London, *The Artistic Home,* p. ix

63

As many of the larger 'institutional theatres' were contemplating their future plans, more adventurous, homegrown companies took root throughout America. Santa Monica, California's Cornerstone Theater Company (1986) commissioned multilingual plays and produced 'epic interactions between classic plays and a dozen rural towns.' Dayton, Ohio's The Human Race Theatre Company (1986) featured contemporary scripts introducing 'opposing ideas and concepts' within society, while Atlanta's Actor's Express (1988) produced plays 'like a stick of dynamite that holds within it the possibility of exploding our preconceptions of ourselves and the world around us.'

Arlington, Virginia's Signature Theatre (1990) balanced emotionally charged contemporary musicals and plays with school programs, The AIDS Project, a musical theatre series, an 'Emerging Playwrights' series, and a Cultural Exchange Night. In the Garage Theatre in Chelsea, Michigan, The Purple Rose Theatre Company (1991) declared its belief that 'there are creative and revelatory voices in America's heartland worth exploring and listening to,' and, back in Minneapolis, the Jungle Theater (1991) was formed as a playwrights' theatre.

Although a number of regional theatres ceased operations in the 1990s due to fundraising woes, the impact of various regional recessions, or leadership issues, over 100 new nonprofit professional theatres were established between 1992 and 2011, including New York's Tectonic Theatre Project (1992), Hailey, Idaho's Company of Fools (1992), Massachusetts's Barrington Stage Company (1994), Los Angeles's Geffen Playhouse (1994), New Mexico's Santa Fe Stages (1994), Austin, Texas's Rude Mechanicals (1995), Philadelphia's 1812 Productions (1997), Idaho's Boise Contemporary Theater (1997), Nevada Theatre Company (1997), Vermont's Northern Stage (1997), Boston Theatre Works (1998), Fort Myers's Florida Repertory Theatre (1998), Chicago's Congo Square Theatre (2000), Iowa's New Ground Theatre (2001), Hartford, Connecticut's HartBeat Ensemble (2002), Massachusetts' Actors' Shakespeare Project (2004), Arkansas' Theatre Squared (2005), Baltimore's Single Carrot Theatre (2005), Illinois' Night Blue Theatre (2006), New York's Chenango River Theatre (2007), Sonoma's Silver Moon Theatre (2008), Los Angeles' Rogue Machine Theatre (2008), Campbell/San Jose's Retro Dome (2009), Oakland's Inferno Theatre (2010), and Atlanta's New African Grove Theatre Company (2010).

Into the new millennium

Kent Thompson, recent Theatre Communications Group president and artistic director of the Denver Center Theatre Company, shares notes on how the development of regional theatre has created a pathway for future theatre artists to develop careers in the business and in related fields:

> *The regional theatre movement has impacted theatre in America in three significant ways:*
>
> 1. *Replacing Broadway and commercial theatre as the birthing place of new plays and musicals. It's hard to think up a major new musical or play that did not start its life in a regional theatre today. We are the research and development wing of theatre in America.*
>
> 2. *Creating a national network of professional theatre artists, managers, and craftspeople. Quite simply, the regional theatre movement has created the means for people to earn livelihoods in professional theatre across the United States. To live in and participate in the fuller life of the community. To buy a home or an apartment. To have a life in the theatre as a full-time profession.*
>
> 3. *The regional theatre movement remains the single most effective training ground for artists throughout the performing arts/entertainment worlds. Actors, playwrights, writers, technicians have all developed their careers in regional theatre. The skills they've learned and the experience they have earned have made them valuable and viable candidates for work in commercial theatre, television, film, theme parks and cruise ships, production companies, commercials, etc. This is a double-edged sword as it has led to a 'brain drain' from the regional theatre field.*

New York and Broadway today

New York and the commercial and nonprofit theatre community struggled through some tough economic times following the horrific trauma of 9/11, the catastrophic Wall Street scandals, and the heightened security and financial woes that followed. Not surprisingly, the resilience of Broadway audiences seeking solace from news related to high unemployment, wars in Iraq and Afghanistan, and government gridlock resulted in a flurry of exciting new work at the end of the new century's first decade. Culturally diverse stories and casts actually helped lead the way with *In the Heights*, *Fela*, *a West Side Story* revival, and *A Free Man of Color* garnishing awards and critical praise, while the troublesome *Spider Man Turn Off the Dark*, poignant *Billy Elliot*, juke-box musical *Jersey Boys*, and blockbusters *The Lion King* and *Wicked* settled in for long runs and weekly grosses up to and often over $1.5 million. Although long runs of contemporary plays are still scarce on Broadway, British imports (*The Pitmen Painters*, *Brief Encounter*), revivals/classics (*Driving Miss Daisy*, *The Merchant of Venice*) and a few wonderfully American plays and musicals (*Next to Normal*, *Bloody, Bloody Andrew Jackson*, *Lombardi*) did manage to sneak onto the Great White Way in 2010 to join the silliness of *Elf*, *The Addams Family Musical*, *The Pee-Wee Herman Show*, *Mary Poppins*, and *Mamma Mia!*.

Regional theatre today

So where is regional theatre in America today? In 2011, nonprofit theatres in America continue to emerge, struggle, flourish, and, hopefully, dig deep roots in their home communities. According to arts council and city arts service agencies, over 1,000 nonprofit theatres can be counted in four American cities alone: New York (400), San Francisco (300), Los Angeles (210), and Chicago (140).

One not-so-scientific but very twenty-first-century way of assessing the growth of American theatre is to research the number of entries that appear on the World Wide Web. If you follow America's favorite pastime and Google 'nonprofit theatre in America,' a mind-boggling 3,280,000 entries appear (which seems miniscule compared to the overwhelming 55,000,000 entries for 'Theatre in America'). The internet provides fascinating background research on regional theatre, but the best overview of the movement still emanates from the hearts and mouths of its artists.

'Theatre in America is a collective of bold, visionary artists and those dedicated to creating and supporting the creation of art,' maintains the Shakespeare Center Los Angeles' producing artistic director, Ben Donenberg. 'The regional theatre movement is a collective of one set of artists and supporters that contribute an important and meaningful component of the quiltwork.' Professional writer Iris Dorbian adds that regional theatre 'provides a wonderful, noncommercial option to the rampant, formulaic commercialism of Broadway.' Professional theatre, film, and television director and California Institute of the Arts faculty member Craig Belknap puts it another way: 'Unfortunately, for the most part, Broadway has become Las Vegas East. The regional theatre movement is where it's at. *Angels in America* and *The Kentucky Cycle* would never have gotten to New York without the regions.'

Stephen Rothman, chair of Theater Arts at California State University, Los Angeles, explains how regional theatre has opened up a whole new world of possibilities:

> *For my generation of artists who graduated from universities in the early 1970s, regional theatre has a tremendous impact as not only our segue from academia into having a first job but once there it became clear that there was now a place to spend your artistic life beyond Broadway and Hollywood. In other words, regional theatre opened up a whole new career path that did not exist before. It once was if you wanted a life in the theatre, that meant New York or LA – now you could have that life and live in your own home area, be that Sarasota, Florida, Cleveland, Ohio, or Seattle, Washington.*

'Regional theatre is the lifeblood of theatre in America,' note Jan and Griff Duncan, longtime producers of the Fullerton Civic Light Opera. 'It is the regional theatre that invests in the outreach programs so important in cultivating present and future audiences. National touring companies reap the benefits of this and if regional theatres should disappear, audiences would disappear in a few years as there would be no development in place. Regional theatre also involves the local public in the process and gives them a sense of satisfaction regarding the arts and the place they live.'

'The regional theatre movement has impacted all aspects of theatre in America, from playwriting and dramaturgy, to acting and directing and design,' adds longtime casting director and associate dean of the Chicago College of Performing Arts, Joel Fink. 'As the price of doing theatre in New York has skyrocketed, regional theatres have become the incubators for new theatre work and new theatre workers.' And Susan Medak, managing director of Berkeley Repertory Theatre, explains that:

> *The regional theatre movement spawned a generation of people outside of New York City who attend theatre with regularity, who see it as central to their lives, many of whom have chosen to make their own careers in the theatre. And I think that while generations of theatregoers in cities outside New York were raised on Theatre Guild tours which brought great artists and great plays to large theatres in major cities, the regional theatre*

movement spawned a sense of community pride in artists from their own communities and supported a repertoire that continues to be regionally specific. The entire sense of what 'theatre' is has gone from the limited nature of national tours to a sense that local theatre communities include everything from commercial tours to institutional companies to small storefront theatres.

Asolo Theatre's former producing artistic director Howard J. Millman agrees. 'The regional theatre movement has completely transformed theatre in America,' says Millman. 'It has taken the highest quality of artistic work from Broadway to most of the country. The great work of the American theatre now begins outside of New York. Regional theatre has created more work for all theatre artists around the country. The American public has become more sophisticated in its theatrical tastes and knowledge because of the regional theatre movement. We have moved from a commercial venture to the center of the cultural fabric of many American communities. Theatre is no longer "Show Business."'

So, what does this history and the regional theatre movement have to do with today's actors, directors, craftspeople, and audiences? To quote Shakespeare's Friends author Kate Pogue:

It placed theatre artistically on a par with symphony orchestras, art museums, ballet, and opera – a huge development in the attitude of the American public. It has offered stable career opportunities across the country to thousands of actors, directors, designers, technicians, managers, and front-of-house personnel. It has revived classic plays and created new plays, challenging the creativity of producers, writers, designers – and audiences.

For younger theatre practitioners it may be hard to understand the challenges and responsibility that are inherent in pursuing a career in regional theatre. John Quinlivan, managing director of the Geva Theatre Center, articulates the big picture: 'A sense of community is formed around each regional theatre. Each theatre is, in a sense, "owned" by that community. It is an awesome responsibility that we must all take very seriously.'

Sandy Robbins, freelance director for many professional theatres and director of the University of Delaware's Professional Theatre Training Program, adds:

The regional theatre movement has, for the majority of Americans, provided the only serious professional theatre available to them in or near where they live. I am one of many theatre professionals whose early theatre experiences were provided entirely by regional theatres. My view is that, while the range of quality in regional theatres varies enormously, it is nonetheless true that theatres like the Guthrie, Trinity Repertory, ACT, Ashland, and others maintained a high standard for a long enough duration of time to set an example of acting and directing that still influences those who saw or worked with them. This influence is then handed on to others who see the work of those under the influence of those early models.

Finally, the impact of these theatres has been and continues to be substantial on the development and production of new work that eventually gets to Broadway and Off-Broadway, and from there to the rest of humanity.

Bonding with home communities has emerged as a central theme for regional theatres eager to develop artistically and survive in a highly competitive American arts, entertainment, and tourism market. Edward Stern, producing artistic director at Cincinnati Playhouse in the Park, believes that 'the key element for me in regional theatre is how it empowers individual communities to create professional high-quality theatre. Touring companies cannot focus as regional theatres can on extensive education outreach programming. Theatre must do a better job of developing future audiences. Regional theatre can and should have that capability and focus. Moreover, regional theatres can do so many of the plays that never would tour into those individual communities.' Repertory Theater of St. Louis artistic director Steven Woolf concurs:

Theatre in America has been forever changed because of the regional theatre movement. Once audiences and communities began to understand and embrace their stake in professional theatre in their own towns, it became clear that Broadway was no longer really going to define artistic output in this country. Now, truly, Broadway is a great marketing machine and nothing carries a kind of shimmer like something called 'a Broadway show.' But it has been clear over the past twenty years or so that almost every play to find its way to Broadway has started in the regional theatres in this country. Now, musicals are working much the same way. So the development line has changed and the not-for-profit regional theatres are producing the work the commercial field wants. This is a major shift in the landscape in a very short amount of time. Ultimately the discerning views and artistic sensibilities of audiences outside of New York are really determining what the New York audiences are seeing. This is something that no one ever envisioned at the beginning of this movement.

Fred C. Adams, founder and executive producer emeritus of the Utah Shakespearean Festival (now Utah Shakespeare Festival), adds that 'a new vitality has found its way into the "formula"-driven Broadway scene. A vitality born of upstart regional theatres that were not afraid to try something new, or in some instances something really old. Look at *Angels in America* with its birth at the Eureka Theatre of San Francisco, or *Big River* from La Jolla. The August Wilson canon saw the light of day at Yale, and the Humana Festival has spawned many major pieces like *Crimes of the Heart.* American theatre, today, is its regional theatres, promoting new and exciting works or keeping the meaningful classics alive for our young promising actors to "cut their teeth" on.'

Today, over 700 member theatres and affiliate organizations are signed up as Theatre Communications Group members and there are more than 1,200 nonprofit theatres in America representing professional, community, youth, college, and university theatres. Many of the larger nonprofit theatres are featured in other areas of this book and each has contributed in significant ways to the development of theatre in America.

It is outside the scope of this book to try to catalogue all of America's regional theatres or the many leaders, pivotal players, and supporters of the nonprofit arts movement in America. Still, marvelous historical quotes and words of wisdom from many of the nation's theatre leaders (past and present) are to be found throughout and in the overviews of many of America's largest theatre companies. The summary in this chapter is intended simply to indicate the youth, ambitions, and needs of a resident theatre movement that has long been ill-defined and poorly compared to its mainstream, commercial counterpart, Broadway. In other areas of this book, you will find listings of nonprofit theatre associations guilds, contracts, and profiles of the Theatre Communications Group (TCG), League of Resident Theatres (LORT), Shakespeare Theatre Association of America (STAA), the Institute of Outdoor Drama (IOD), and many other key institutions that support America's theatres. You will also find information about the Broadway theatre and other commercial theatre operations.

What does the future hold?

'Regional theatres must continue to find ways to reinvent themselves so they can better serve the communities and audiences where they reside,' contends Utah Shakespeare Festival executive director R. Scott Phillips. He continues: 'A strong voice for new thoughts and ideas must prevail in America. I am convinced that regional theatre companies must be the leaders in contributing to that strong new voice.'

Regional theatres will have to be savvy, creative, flexible, entrepreneurial, and ferociously committed to a palpable artistic vision and strategic financial planning if the forward movement is to continue. The 'original, older' regional theatres are morphing, adapting, and reinventing themselves to survive the ever-changing funding, audience, and entertainment trends of the twenty-first century, and many start-up theatre companies are plunging in with a whole new set of dreams, ideals, hopes, and production plans. Perhaps it's too obvious to note that regional theatres are changing because America is changing – America's people, American cities, America's sense of security, and America's desires and needs are shifting as global technology, governance, population, politics, and economic realities shape the nation.

Recent American census population statistics suggest that the 'urban renaissance' that helped breathe new life into many cities at the end of the twentieth century seems to have stalled somewhat in the twenty-first. As real-estate prices have skyrocketed and then plunged in many major cities, American city planners are seeing a resurgence of interest in smaller communities. Looking to the future, it remains to be seen where the cultural growth and future homes of nonprofit theatres will develop. For example, virtually every Southern California community, regardless of size, has its own nonprofit theatre and many of the over 200 nonprofit Shakespeare festivals are located in the tiniest of towns, far from the bright lights of New York, Chicago, Los Angeles, or Seattle.

So, what does this mean for America's theatres? It means that the tremendous growth in many of America's smaller cities and suburbs may create opportunities for professional theatres eager to serve these new communities. It means that in a few of the larger cities where sky-high housing and theatre rental costs once were formidable, creative spaces may now open up for emerging theatre companies. No doubt, it also means that the larger cities that continue to grow (often as settling points for waves of immigrants, as in New York, Los Angeles, Phoenix,

Fort Worth, Houston, etc.) will spawn new theatres that address the desires and needs of a culturally diverse community.

Scott L. Steele, executive director of the University/Resident Theatre Association (U/RTA), offers another prediction:

> The next 'movement,' or framework, in which American theatre will grow will be found on campuses across the nation. Operating relationships between schools, and particularly graduate training programs, and professional theatres of diverse sizes and kinds will be the source of growth for current theatre companies, and the seedbed of future companies. This is not new. There are existing examples of such marriages. Nevertheless, it is a process that is gaining interest among theatre professionals, professional artists (who are also professional teachers), and academicians and administrators. Such relationships come in different formats and are not always easy to maintain, but the potential for mutually beneficial results is a powerful reason for making the commitment. One result, when such relationships enrich theatre production on campus, is that it might, just might, manage to harvest a part of the elusive 'new audience' that theatre is always seeking. And U/RTA, as the primary interface between professional theatre and the world of professional, graduate training, is already serving as a resource for this movement. Like a good matchmaker, U/RTA is encouraging the dialogue that can lead to programming and operating relationships. Future professionals should look at theatre–school relationships as invaluable resources. Such partnerships are going to be the focus of a lot of major activity, and will drive new and different theatre production in many places.

Looking to the future, longtime Utah Shakespeare Festival associate artistic director Kathleen F. Conlin expects that regional theatre will continue to 'decentralize theatre excellence, provide employment for numerous theatre artists, and inspire students throughout the country by offering internships and career entry while providing artistic presence for non-commercial plays – which will move on to commercial success.'

Cindy Melby Phaneuf, co-founder of the Nebraska Shakespeare Festival, predicts the growth trends will continue: 'There are only positives to working in regional theatre. There are more choices for directors and actors and designers. Playwrights and new plays can be nurtured with tender, loving care. Regional theatre provides the freedom to risk, to test the limits.'

The Goodman Theatre's longtime executive director, Roche Schulfer, offers a much briefer history and his own set of predictions:

What does the future hold? Overall, I think we are entering a new phase in the evolution of the resident theatre movement. Phase One was the founding mothers and fathers who came from the East and spread theatre across the country like Johnny Appleseed. Phase Two was the heyday of the not-for-profit–commercial producer collaboration, which by the mid-nineties turned Broadway into a showcase for the best in theatre from around the country.

The next phase will be about creating deeper roots in our respective communities. We are past the point of legendary founders and the obsession with Broadway megahits. We now have many theatres that are led by people who come from the community they serve (or somewhere other than New York City). In this new phase, artists, trustees, and staff have to work together to identify and promote the value and importance of theatre (and all the arts) in this precarious world. It has less to do with 'who is in charge' of a theatre and more to do with how we work together with mutual respect and trust to create quality art in our communities. This phase will be embodied by theatrical institutions with the highest standards of excellence and the deepest roots in their communities.

Whatever the future holds, it is clear that, collectively, the passion, power, and productivity of America's regional theatre has, by virtue of its mere existence, mainstream popularity, and creative roots, emerged as the national theatre of the United States of America. There's still a lot of excitement on Broadway, but as the first decade of the twenty-first century indicates, a lot of the Broadway thrills are emanating from the coast-to-coast artistic initiatives of America's regional theatres.

Part 3
Career planning

Career-planning needs

This book offers a 'self-education, self-help' guide, and your 'instructors' include some of the most knowledgeable professionals in the business. Still, if you are currently a student, there's nothing like working with someone who knows you, knows your work, and can offer specific, personalized counsel to supplement your research. A list of the types of assistance you might expect from your faculty or the career-planning professionals on your campus is included below. Talk to your faculty, search your school's website and phone directory for professional assistance, and ask each person and office you talk to if they have any samples, publications, or advice.

Check your institution for a career-planning office, placement office, internship office, mentoring program, job fair, study-abroad program, or counseling center that may offer tests, tools, and publications to help you.

Even if you're not a student, check out the libraries of neighboring colleges or universities for career information and services. Specifically, as an emerging professional, it is crucial to seek out assistance related to:

Arts résumés, photographs, and cover letters

Generic résumé skills won't work here – it must be a specialized workshop or individualized seminar focusing on résumés for actors, musicians, dancers, directors, designers, etc.

Interview and audition skills

Again, if these skills aren't being covered in your classes, seek out specially tailored workshops, training sessions or seminars specific to your area of interest: theatre auditions, dance auditions, design portfolio presentations, and actor auditions.

Time management for artists

Review the time- and life-management section of this book and develop a lifelong process that works for you.

Career counseling resources overview

Protect your budget by checking at your school library or the library in your institution's career center for theatre magazine subscriptions and job-search publications. Every serious university library and career center should have copies of *American Theatre*, *ARTSEARCH*, TCG's *Theatre Directory*, access to the online TCG profiles, and at least most of the books in the '10 Challenging Books to Power Your Acting Career' mentioned later.

Entrepreneurial assertive personal marketing

Every school and every library should have computers available for students and community members to research or conduct an internet job search. Check out the '10 Websites to Open Up Your Web World' detailed later in this book. Career counselors should be available to advise students on the targeted use of direct mail, agent mailings, and developing telephone/telemarketing skills, recommendations for employment and graduate school, and a network of mentors.

Financial survival tips: budgeting a career in the arts

Workshops or seminars that address the basic financial realities of a life in the arts (such as applying/budgeting for graduate schools, planning a move to New York or Los Angeles, standard arts tax deductions, etc.) should be developed in every serious theatre program.

Securing an agent and union basics

The basic strategies are generally outlined in most theatre career books and publications. '10 Pertinent Publications' (listed later in this book) is a great place to start. These should all be available for perusal in your school's library, career center, or departmental office.

Conquering performance anxiety

There are special counseling and therapeutic ways to counter, adapt, or overcome performance anxiety (auditions, public speaking, design presentations, director conferences, etc.), and your school's faculty or counseling staff may be of assistance if you suffer from this common concern.

Stress management

The theatre is a highly collaborative, often competitive field where unemployment runs rampant for actors, directors and designers. Check out the stress section in Part 6 ('12 Tips for Stress Reduction: Staying Fit for Life'), but seek help if your stress is impacting your health (and your choice of career).

Networking survival skills for theatre pros young and old

'He that won't be counseled can't be helped,' explained Ben Franklin, and in the spirit of 'counseling and sharing,' a group of artistic directors, managing directors, Equity actors, and non-Equity actors was asked to trade tips on surviving the highly competitive and financially perilous profession of theatre. The generally wise, occasionally wacky, sometimes anonymous tips include:

Why can't I be rich, famous, *and* happy?

Right out of school, try to take an audition trip across the country, schedule auditions in advance, and plan not only to see theatre and audition for it, but to see the country as well. A well-traveled actor is a smart actor. Also, my dad says, 'The goal in life is to be happy, not necessarily rich and famous.'

Cindy Gold, Equity Actress and Northwestern University Professor

Be a raging bull

I recall, while on National Tour with The Sound of Music, *seeing the tall, reedy fellow playing Max in the wings, preparing for an entrance, taking on the mannerisms of a raging bull, pawing the earth (the boards) with a twinkle in his eye. I invoke this memory/image to my students whenever I teach, because no matter how large or small the city or town on our tour, he prepped like a bull in the wings. Wherever you perform, do it with all your heart and all your might.*

Tad Ingram, Equity Actor/Broadway Original Cast of *Parade*

Look out – he's flatlining!

One of my favorite quotes is, 'It is not brain surgery. Let me make this production happen and get on with our lives.' I would also say that you will be most successful when you can comfortably admit that you don't know something and can still learn from someone else. As a leader of one of this country's regional theatres, I can say without hesitation that there is always room for continued learning.

R. Scott Phillips, Executive Director, Utah Shakespeare Festival

Recognize human behavior

I'm always saying to actors, 'Recognize human behavior.' I think that encompasses the entire human experience, but it also keeps a toehold in reality no matter what the situation. It has always been my experience as an audience member that the moment I see/hear something that doesn't seem psychologically possible, I check out of the moment. Even in the most extremely absurd situations, there is always a human being lurking beneath the lines and the circumstance. Only the desire to discover and present recognizable human behavior makes each moment rich and real.

Sidonie Garrett, Producing Artistic Director,
Heart of America Shakespeare Festival

Believe in instant karma

What goes around comes around. Treat others as you would like to be treated. Be kind and courteous. The tech person you step on today could be your producer/director tomorrow.

Avoid people who suck energy

These people only give you permission to procrastinate. You are not the person who is losing if you miss a few social gatherings in order to work.

To read or not to read?

That is the question. The only answer? Read as many plays as possible. Be familiar with all types of writing. The more familiar you are with a play, the better your audition will be. The better the audition, the better the part.

Leave your worries at the door!

Remember, the people you work with are not your therapists. Don't be so wrapped up in your personal problems that you let your frustrations impact your work.

Don't be a dropout!

My students are often eager to move on to the professional world, many times before finishing even their undergraduate degree, but they come back later and say how important their education is, and they are glad they finished their degrees. They have also noted how an advanced degree opens doors that had been closed.

Cindy Melby Phaneuf, Founder,
Nebraska Shakespeare Festival/
Isaacson Professor of Theatre, University of Nebraska, Omaha

Think twice before volunteering

Nobody likes an Equity Deputy. Actors consider it suspicious when an actor volunteers and it's tough if you get caught between your union and your theatre's management.

Respect the clock

Be on time. Punctuality shows that you respect and value a person's time. Being late is rude. Show up ready to work. Endure the process of auditions. Learn to reject the rejection before it rejects you.

Include time for yourself every day

Treat yourself to a walk, a trip to the local park, or a hot bath – you know, experience one of those international coffee moments that can change your life.

It's a small world after all

This is not an Orlando joke, even though I am near Disney World: 'It's a small world after all . . .' The regional theatre scene, though spread across the country, is a close-knit circle. Do your best work, always. Contribute to whatever theatre community you are in to the best of your best ability. The theatre world stays in touch with each other, especially the regional theatre artistic and managing directors. Your talent is important, but just as important is your attitude and positive energy.

Kate Ingram,
Orlando Shakespeare Festival/
Professor of Theatre, University of Central Florida

'We'll always have Utah!'

Falling for someone you work intimately with and for such a long time may be inevitable, especially in the veil of drama and 'make believe.' But rarely do these romances go beyond the run of the show.

Keep your pants on!

Never get too big for your britches. Be kind and considerate to everyone – you are part of an artistic team . . . today's stage manager may be tomorrow's director or producer.

David Heath, President, Heath Associates Inc.

Who died and made *you* king?

Nobody likes to hear a scolding 'Shh!' from another actor. Let the stage manager or director handle admonishing the parties involved. If they aren't present, remember that you catch more flies with honey and be diplomatic.

Who died and made *you* Elia Kazan?

Never, ever, ever, ever, ever direct another actor in your show.

Be kind to your dressers

Actors need to worship costume designers, staff, and dressers. They make or break how you look every day on stage.

Make Makita part of your Method

Offer to help with strike if it's not mandatory as part of your non-Equity contract. If it's mandatory, do not whine. Be a good sport. You will be remembered for what kind of person you are to work with, not the believability of your speech on Thursday night.

Know thyself

Avoid making life-changing decisions under stress, pressure, or on the spot. Make your decisions on your own time. Be clear in your own mind about what you want and what you are willing to do to get it – before you go in!

Stress check!

Don't panic. Stay organized and learn when to say 'no.'

Prepare for the worst, hope for the best

Go beyond basic preparation of the required or expected workload. Anticipate possible negative outcomes and have contingency plans.

Finally, a story of almost pure joy!

I'm going to be perfectly honest – sometimes I fantasize about going back to waiting tables. That's what I was doing five years ago, in my 'starving artist' period. I spent long hours on my feet, got no breaks during my shift, and had to endure a boss who had little respect for women. However, most nights I walked out of there with over a hundred dollars in my pocket, and left everything else at the door. There was no reason to think about the job outside the building; I had plenty of time for friends and other activities. As an emerging artist, I have a perfect blend of artistic responsibilities and classroom contact with K-12 children. I get to direct, and I get to teach. Sometimes I can't believe how lucky I got.

But, there are sacrifices, too. I had to take out a graduate school loan that far exceeds my yearly salary. I had to uproot myself to St. Louis, a place so far from my closest friends and family that I sometimes feel I'm stranded on a deserted island. I am the administrator, program designer, marketing specialist, graphic designer, registrar, grant writer, and lead teacher for nearly all our education programs, and it's exhausting. Because of my choices, I am thirty-something and still single, without children, and a long, long way from owning a home.

So, on the difficult days, I suffer a little bit of nostalgia for the old, carefree days of spare time and expendable income. But, then I remember that I am madly in love with my job, and madly in love with Theatre for Young Audiences. Joy is the reason I stay, and when Theatre for Young Audiences is at its most potent and meaningful, joy thrives. For now, the frequent experience of joy is enough reason for me to keep hanging on.

Emily Petkewich,
Former Education Director, Metro Theater Company

Uncredited tips by Krystal Allan, Brooke Aston, Evelyn Carol Case, Noelle Forestal, Kathy Hardoy, Amber Howard, James Hunt, Michelle Martinez, Melissa Maxwell, Erin McReynolds, Aleia Melville, Josh Miller, Justin Milley, and Pamela Woo.

Strategic time and life-management skills for savvy regional theatre artists

> ❝ *Listen, everyone is entitled to my opinion*
>
> Madonna

As anyone who has ever auditioned, acted, stage managed, crewed, directed, or produced a show knows, time management is really life management, people management, money management, and, all too often, stress management. Whether you are an extra in a movie, a spear-carrier in a Shakespeare play, a standup comic striving to land a movie, or a star at the largest regional theatre in town, this chapter will help you get organized and may even change your life.

Here you will find many tools that may help you organize your career, your romantic relationships, your family, and other aspects of your personal life. Still, you have to decide to use them. There are some tough life-management questions that only you can answer – questions that are crucial to your use of time management as a strategic tool. At the very least, time management calls for deciding who you are, where you want to be, how you want to get there, and then tackling your agenda with ferocity.

Ask the right questions!

For example, ask yourself: 'Where do I want to be at the end of this year (in terms of personal relationships? financial planning? work projects?) In five years? At retirement?' If you choose to plunge into time management as a strategic planning tool, these questions are your homework for the next two weeks.

Sometimes, there's just no reason to reinvent the wheel. When it comes to your life, you deserve to be treated with dignity, you have the opportunity to learn from the mistakes of others, and as Sondheim so sardonically maintains in *Assassins*, 'Everybody has the right to be happy.'

Now, work to set your goals and plot out how to achieve them. My suggestion is that you organize your strategy on your calendar. Goal setting is freeing – it can improve your personal relationships, enhance your business relationships, and wildly increase your productivity. Time management may indeed change your life! Aldous Huxley said, 'Ye shall know the truth and the truth shall make you mad!' Mad that you didn't get organized sooner.

Time and life management sometimes requires a different way of looking at yourself and the world. What time of day are you at peak performance? What tasks do you absolutely dread doing? Are you comfortable delegating? Do you have a quick temper? I'm not going to get into the 'Zen of Time Management,' but suffice to say that it is important that you know yourself and, as Shakespeare would say, 'to thine own self be true.'

Clarify what you value

Time management often leads to values clarification – knowing what is most important to you and why. Do you value your career over family? Are you a team player? How important is money and fame vs. job satisfaction and competency? For the harried artist, craftsperson, or administrator, time management involves assertiveness training, interpersonal skills, and organizational savvy. Passive artists tend to get run over and aggressive artists often alienate key collaborators, but assertive artists usually manage to achieve their goals without stepping on people or violating the rights of others. When clear values, a strategic mind, and an assertive character merge in the arts or business, artists are generally successful at finding a graceful approach to the ruthless pursuit of one's goals.

There are many different approaches to time, life, and office management; I'm going to share just one. It's the system I use and it's a combination of many systems and starts with setting aside part of one day – you could pick any day (perhaps on your next long plane trip or next Saturday) – during which you hide away, do some soul searching, and spell out your short- and long-range goals and how you plan to achieve them. Your findings don't have to be profound –

but they should be specific, should be in priority order, and should be attainable. Mine are listed on my to-do list as a constant reminder:

> Nurture family

> Exercise

> Publish

> Generate income

> Position for retirement

> Excel as a teacher/administrator/consultant

These items represent the most important things in my life, remind me that my career is not my entire life, and inspire me to do my best at work and at home.

Let's review this tool. At the top of any good to-do list are 'priority' projects. At the bottom of my list are 'to do today' tasks, which acknowledge the need to accomplish smaller timely tasks but don't allow me to stray too far from my first priority.

In the middle of this to-do list are the telephone numbers, account numbers, or other numbers I use most frequently and those I may need for an emergency. This saves tons of time searching through phone books, calling assistants or family members for telephone numbers, health insurance numbers, driver's license numbers, etc. It also means I have crucial numbers with me when I travel and I can leave my Rolodex and computers behind. For financial security, make sure you 'code' or 'disguise' confidential numbers!

Most important, this list is all on one sheet, corresponds to my working calendar and file system, is in priority order in regard to 'major tasks/minor tasks,' and can be updated on a daily basis in two minutes. This master list and my organizational planning calm me down, keep me from worrying, and propel me along each day. Ironically, they also allow me to be more spontaneous as surprise pockets of 'found time' inevitably surface as a result of a carefully organized schedule.

Let's look at a sample working calendar. I prefer a *Week At A Glance Professional Appointments* book for three major reasons:

> It allows users to break up the day into 15-minute segments;

> It is large enough to accommodate 8½ x 11 papers (the going size for most arts and business correspondence);

➢ It is large enough to be easily found, yet small enough to carry around discreetly.

Finally, to complete the 'time-management ensemble,' I heartily suggest a binder with a zipper that can hold a half-dozen computer disks, pens, pencils, a wallet, a calendar, a checkbook, and, most important, key files related to your priority to-do list, and a 'distribution folder,' a file folder where everything goes that needs to be mailed or given to someone else. The zippered binder, available in office supply and department stores everywhere, protects you from losing things and allows you to toss it in the back seat of your car with confidence.

Okay, enough about the tools that you can hold in your hand to make you feel better – let's talk about the strategies that use your brain power!

10 timely tips for savvy regional theatre artists

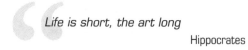

Life is short, the art long

Hippocrates

Timely Tip #1

Schedule the time it takes to prepare for an audition/interview/appointment, as well as the appointment, plus the time needed to follow up on the appointment. My experience is that this will cut your hurried, crisis-oriented scrambling in half. It will save you from running late for meetings, allow you to show respect for others by keeping your appointments on time, and enable you to complete projects at a time that is best for you – preferably when conversations and meetings are fresh on your mind.

> 'Decide exactly what you want to achieve. Do you want to help people, or do you want to be powerful?'
>
> Mario Cuomo

Timely Tip #2

Authorize, empower, and delegate partners to facilitate your time management. Don't complain, don't blame, don't shame – simply explain the importance of your time to your friends, your co-workers, and/or your family. Make it personal and let them know you will respect their time and their thoughts on how to maximize productivity. Enlist their support, understanding, and help – and use it.

> 'Progress may have been all right once, but it has gone on too long.'
>
> Ogden Nash

Timely Tip #3

Be proactive and maintain control over your schedule. Publish your goals, objectives, meetings, and remarkably tight schedule and put your goals on your calendar. Schedule blocks of time each week when you will work on your major goals. Schedule 90 minutes of 'do not disturb' time each day to tackle priority goals. 'Punch a hole' in tough projects by committing to a 10-minute outline that will get you started. If you need to get a haircut, put air in the tire of your car, pick up the children from daycare, or hide behind a *USA Today* and drink a café mocha – put it on your calendar! Make an appointment with an important person today: you!

> *Beware of the danger signals that flag problems: silence, secretiveness, or sudden outburst.*
>
> Sylvia Porter

Timely Tip #4

Walk the streets. By increasing visibility, you often serve as your own best agent by meeting people, stimulating your career through personal contact, and creating an awareness of what a great person you are. One friendly lunch, quick meeting, or warm handshake is worth a hundred generic letters and résumés that you spend hours typing, printing, and stuffing. You can head off many problems, inspire loyalty, show personal interest, and gain people's confidence through visibility and outreach. Go see other people's shows and let them know how much you enjoyed their work!

> *Always put off until tomorrow what you shouldn't do at all.*
>
> Anonymous

Timely Tip #5

Instruct your answering machine or service to take clear telephone messages with the full name, telephone number, date, time, and purpose of the call. Consider divulging your email on your answering machine or marketing materials to facilitate contact with people you want to be able to contact you. Plan on interruptions. Emergencies happen; just expect them and manage them. Don't let them derail your plans – the rule of the 'worst-case scenario' should be planned for and greeted with a calm sense of inevitability.

> *'There is never enough time, unless you're serving it.'*
>
> Malcolm Forbes

Timely Tip #6

Screen all calls and emails, and return phone calls and emails en masse at specified intervals each day at times that are convenient for you. This will eliminate two of the major time-wasters for most regional theatre artists and will put you in control of your 'email and phone life.' This also allows you to prepare and be ready for negotiations, concerns, and problems, and to gather the necessary data so that it is in front of you when you place the call or email. It also prevents ongoing disturbance of your work on priority goals and saves a lot of time (since it is more appropriate for you to quickly end a call that you initiated). A good voice-mail system or excellent answering machine is worth its weight in gold. Practice appropriate telephone etiquette and keep your phone messages professional.

A man with one watch knows what time it is. A man with two watches is never sure.

John Peer

Timely Tip #7

Write it down! Don't rely on your memory. Discipline yourself to jot down notes on important commitments or carry a small tape recorder that may be used for transcription later. Ask your friends and co-workers to commit important requests in writing or on email so that you have a record of them and don't forget about them.

I don't say we all ought to misbehave, but we ought to look as if we could.

Orson Welles

Timely Tip #8

Get the details on all rehearsals, production meetings, training sessions, or any other commitments that you have or make. Be aware of the who, what, where, when, and why of each commitment. This will hopefully keep you from wasting time looking for meetings or attending rehearsals, costume fittings, or photo calls that you don't really need to attend. Be on time for your commitments and don't bring surprises into meetings, rehearsals, or work sessions. Paraphrasing the former president of Avon Products: 'Bring me your problems early and you have a partner in solving the problems; bring them to me late (or surprise me with them), and you have a judge!'

You're never too old to do goofy stuff.

Ward Cleaver, *Leave It to Beaver*

Timely Tip #9

Get to know yourself. Goethe said, 'He who seizes the right moment, is the right man.' When are you at your best? When are your performing/writing/memorizing/welding/sewing skills ready for peak performance? When are your analytical skills clearly accessible? When do your creative skills tend to blossom? Matching your goals and tasks to your highs and lows will keep you from spinning your wheels and will help you make the most of your time. How do you procrastinate? (When I reach for my fourth cup of coffee and it's not yet 9 a.m., I know I'm avoiding the day. And when I rearrange my to-do list more than once a day, I know I'm in serious trouble)!

> *What one has to do usually can be done.*
>
> Anna Eleanor Roosevelt

Timely Tip #10

The future is now. Choose to spend time doing what you will remember 10 years from now and what you want other people to remember your doing. Learn to 'just say no' based on your own priorities and the priorities of your theatre. For example, I am often called on by my colleagues to sit on yet one more board or committee, or to deliver a speech or host a visiting VIP. Generally speaking, I usually sit down with the requesting party and review the priority projects I have selected or been previously assigned. We don't fight — Kafka reminds us that 'In a fight between you and the world, bet on the world.' Together, we explore options and usually tend to agree that my time is much better spent on previously assigned strategic planning, fundraising, community outreach, teaching, audience development, and/or writing assignments.

19 terrible distractions that erode productivity

> *We haven't the time to take our time*
>
> Eugene Ionesco

1 **Procrastination**

   Solution: Force yourself to get the job done and reward yourself for completing priority tasks.

2 **Overcommitment/poor delegation skills**

   Solution: Just say no, or if you feel it's impossible to say no, review your business or personal priorities with those closest to you and seek their help in establishing a reasonable schedule. Endeavor to work with people you respect and trust and give them the opportunity to shine by delegating responsibility.

3 **Perfection problems**

   Solution: Give each task your best shot for the amount of time you have to work on it and move on knowing you did your best under the circumstances.

4 **Endless firefighting**

   Solution: Plan for normal interruptions, deal with them quickly, and get back to work. Always finish thoughts before dealing with interruptions and quickly outline where you plan to go with a rehearsal, report, budget plan, or production requirement before you leave it.

5   **Shortsightedness/inflexibility**
    Solution: Don't be so wed to your schedule that you are unable to perceive and grab hold of opportunities that relate to your key life and career goals. Realize that change is inevitable and that, as Charles Kettering once said, 'If you have always done it that way, it is probably wrong.'

6   **Lack of preparation**
    Richard Nixon used to say, 'Always be prepared to negotiate, but never negotiate without being prepared.'
    Solution: To avoid straying from your work, and other distractions, bring to the table all the tools you need to finish the product.

7   **Not choosing the right place and the right time**
    Solution: Do easy tasks during high interruption times in your day and 'priority difficult tasks' at a site and during a time when interruptions are minimal.

8   **Open-door policies**
    An open door (at work or home) says, 'I am available to you and I'm not working on a priority project.' An open door for a short and consistent time per day may work for you, your friends, neighbors, co-workers, or employees who know they can catch you daily between 2 and 3 p.m.
    Solution: The aforementioned 'Walk the streets' tip allows you to choose the place of your accessibility much more efficiently than keeping your door open.

9   **The waiting game: losing time just hanging out**
    Tired or irritated by bank lines, traffic, or the grocery store?
    Solution: With your organizational binder, you have myriad projects just waiting for you! Save your mail to read when you are standing in lines or waiting for meetings to begin.

10 **Searching for addresses, telephone numbers, etc.**
    Solution: Type all your important numbers into your computer and reduce the type so they can easily be fit into and found in your notebook. This should include birthdays, anniversaries, holidays, etc. **Important note:** code any financial numbers to prevent theft.

11   Instant gratification syndrome
      Solution: Reward yourself only when priority projects are completed, and
      chastise yourself for dealing with little tasks just to get them off your list.

12   Listening and reacting to the squeaky wheel
      Solution: Reward individuals who respect your time and work plan, and
      penalize individuals who waste your time.

13   Bad attitude, fear of failure, jealousy, anger,
      Solution: Let go of the past, look to the future, forgive, forget, and seize the
      joy that is available to you. Inventory your strengths and blessings and be
      grateful for all you have accomplished. Consider seeking professional assist-
      ance and outside support for persistent emotional problems.

14   Mealtime madness
      So often, your prime time for working on priority projects is preempted by
      long, unproductive breakfast, lunch, or dinner engagements or meetings that
      don't challenge or relax or involve you for more than a few minutes.
      Solution: Avoid lunch dates and meal meetings that can drag on unpro-
      ductively for hours without any graceful means of escape. Delegate!

15   Busy work, reading contracts, proofreading . . .
      Solution: Read every word of any contracts you sign (including riders),
      proofread your own correspondence and edit materials appropriately. Save
      busy work for quiet TV or vegetation times, and for times when you are
      waiting for meetings to begin, when waiting in line, etc.

16   Handling the same projects, papers, and memos over and over
      and over and over and over and over and . . .
      Solution: Strive to handle each piece of paper just once before acting on
      it, delegating it, or trashing it. If you can't do this, put '#1' at the top of each
      new piece of paper that crosses your desk and add '#2,' '#3,' etc., each
      time you rehandle this paper. Resolve to complete the project, delegate the
      project, or toss the project the third time you handle it.

17 Handling correspondence on a piecemeal basis
Solution: Resolve to save up minor correspondence and respond to it all during preset times during the week. Utilize the fastest means of dispensing with bureaucratic correspondence (email, phone call, letter, Facebook, fax, etc.) and don't waiver. Delegate whenever possible.

18 The black hell of TV and Facebook and Twitter and MySpace and . . .
Solution: Use the time you must spend in front of a television or computer screen to review casting notices or job openings, catch up on sit-ups and push-ups, clean up your to-do list, or compose correspondence.

19 Reading junk mail
Solution: Don't do it (but be careful not to throw away important financial statements, residual checks, or timely bills!)

29 wonderful ways to seize control of your own life

1 **Enjoy the time off**
   Never fret, worry or fume about 'waiting' for anything. Consider the extra minutes a real gift that may be used to pursue activities you enjoy (such as reading a newspaper, sipping a cup of coffee, or working on your to-do list).

2 **You are special!**
   Take advantage of computer 'mail-merge' capabilities and social networking to keep in contact with friends and colleagues. Personalize letters but use a consistent body of text as appropriate. Facebook is easy but snail mail is still special.

3 **Way to go!**
   Send thank-you notes and congratulatory notes as a way of showing appreciation, nurturing subordinates, encouraging cooperation, and sharing credit. As one smart team player notes, 'It's amazing how much may be accomplished when we don't care who gets the credit.' Richard Nixon would say it in a different way: 'Always do as much for our friends as our adversaries would do for our enemies.'

4 **Teamwork pays off**
   When assembling a cast or work force, consider the whole ensemble along with the individual players.

5 **Massage time?**
   Avoid stressful situations or unpredictable traffic byways prior to rehearsals, performances, or important community meetings.

6   **Stay fit for life**

Reduce stress by exercising regularly, playing soothing music to drown out office distractions, dressing comfortably, and taking a break from the grind.

7   **A little perspective, please!**

Ask yourself, 'What will matter most to me, my family, and/or my colleagues a week from now? At the end of the year?'

8   **This is really important work!**

Consider ethical 'codes' when scheduling on your calendar. For example, 'stress-reduction management' could serve as a calendar listing for a basketball game, a picnic on the beach, a mid-afternoon nap, or time to finish a new play from *American Theatre*. 'Professional development hour' could be a code for listening to your favorite symphony or watching an important opera on video. Long-range planning provides the time and opportunity to read the latest journals and articles that shape your planning and learning process. The strategy is that an individual perusing your calendar will be more likely to barge in on your reading or attempt to usurp your picnic than to bother your 'stress reduction' or 'artistic planning' sessions.

9   **Lead by example**

Demand ethical standards and make sure you set the pace in the way you treat co-workers, board members, and janitorial staff. Columnist Ann Landers suggested that 'the standard by which you will be judged is how you treat the people who can't do anything for you.'

10   **Those dang dilemmas**

When faced with a difficult dilemma or a confusing ethical decision, ask yourself: 1) Is it legal? 2) Is it fair? 3) Does it fall within the guidelines of my theatre or business? 4) How would I feel if my decision were printed on the front page of my hometown newspaper tomorrow morning?

11   **Pick up the phone and talk to me!**

Surround yourself with positive-thinking, competent people. Here's a test. Call your home or office. How many rings before someone picks up? Does the individual who answers represent the professional image you want for your career? Does the person take careful messages? Is anyone even answering the phones or do you have an oftentimes frustrating voicemail system or poorly functioning answering machine? How can you be well organized if those individuals (or machines) who represent you aren't well trained and organized?

12 Way to go . . . and you're fired?

Help your director, guest director, stage manager, or staff build their personnel files and feel better about their work by sending short notes of congratulations or a thank-you note on their production work. Put good news in writing . . . deliver bad news in person!

13 Read the newspaper and follow up

A leadership and community outreach tip: scan theatre or arts publications and local newspapers and send notes of congratulations to directors, designers, or others who are positively reviewed. It's a very small world, and someone you congratulate today will most likely be interviewing or auditioning you next week.

14 Leave my family alone!

Instead of asking yourself, 'Is it fair or appropriate for me to assertively end this nonproductive meeting or cut off this rambling, inconsiderate individual who pushed their way into my house or office?,' ask yourself: 'Is it fair for me to deprive my children of their mother/father, my spouse/partner of my companionship, or my theatre of this crucial planning time because of this individual's lack of foresight or planning?'

15 Write it down, or just forget it!

Let those closest to you (spouse/partner, children, faculty, staff, etc.) know that you need key tasks and requests in writing, even scribbled on a Post-it. This saves you forgetting and having to deal with guilt and the wrath of others when you forget hasty requests screamed over balconies, on your way to work, in the hallways, when pulling out of the driveway, etc.

16   Watch where you grab me!

Remind individuals who 'grab you in hallways' that personal matters and personnel issues should be discussed behind closed doors and not in front of other company members and the world at large.

17   Don't put your clothes on, just pull them out!

Begin your morning the evening before. Pack up everything you need to take to work and put it in the same place each night. Pull out your clothes the night before and consider a programmable coffee maker.

18   Just file it under 't' for 'trash'

Experts insist we spend 20 to 30 per cent of our time looking for things. Toss out clothes you haven't worn in the last year, store everything in your desk that you haven't used in the past year, sift out files that are no longer necessary and move them out of your office (preferably into a garbage can).

19   But I spent 88 hours building this flat!

Work smarter, not harder. Remember that results count – not the time you spend on a project.

20   Welcome and get out now!

When interrupted in the office, do a half-standing, uncomfortable-looking crouch in front of your desk, and ask, 'What can I do for you?' Don't remain seated with a friendly smile – it's an invitation for the other party to sit down.

21   Why am I talking to you?

When you inadvertently end up on the phone with someone you have no interest in talking to, let the caller speak for a moment and quickly let him/her know you are 'in the middle of a project' or 'surrounded by people' and ask for the number so that the call may be returned. Then delegate it if you can.

22   Make memos count

When writing emails or memos, place your main point before your rationale, unless you feel your reader will disagree with you or lacks understanding of the issue and needs an explanation first. If you desire a response or a course of action, be specific and set a deadline. Never commit to letter, email, or memo form what should be discussed face to face.

23 Boo! Your letters are haunting you again!

Letters, emails, and memos should be used to confirm new plans or policy, not to surprise, irritate, or announce a new policy. Consider the consequences of the letters you write and understand that they may come back to haunt you.

Everybody gets so much information all day long that they lose their common sense.

Gertrude Stein

24 We are so good!

Consider writing an 'annual report letter' to your director or supervisor to list your key work-success stories, above-and-beyond-the-call-of-duty work, achievements, and progress. Being proactive enhances your image and saves valuable time defending your programs or work later. Keep it simple: short paragraphs and lists are fine. A personal annual report detailing your own achievements for your direct supervisor positions you more effectively for merit increases and future contract negotiations.

25 What would you do?

Always approach your supervisor with solutions, as well as with the problem. Ask those who report to you to do the same. As Richard Moran explains in *Never Confuse a Memo with Reality,* 'You are getting paid to think, not to whine.' Moran also advises, 'Don't get drunk at the company holiday party; never in your life say, "It's not my job," and always have an answer to the question, "What would I do if I lost my job tomorrow?"' I don't even want to begin to tell you the problems with alcohol I've seen at cast parties with the community present.

26 Here's what I want from you! Please?

Artists who bring out the best in people treat colleagues and employees with respect and dignity while communicating clear-cut expectations.

27   And you think you have storage problems now?

Take a world view and plan ahead. Stockpile birthday and Christmas/ Hanukkah/holiday presents in an empty closet, have generic greeting cards on hand, call stores and businesses before driving across town to find out they are closed, and stock up on groceries and office items you use a lot to save seemingly endless shopping trips. Use your assistant or a mail house to wrap and send mail and packages.

28   Could you repeat that?

Listen carefully! Time, energy, and massive frustration (for you and others) may be saved if you pay attention the first time. For example, have a pencil in hand when listening to telephone messages so you don't have to listen to the entire message just to retrieve the phone number. Writing down travel instructions will save you from missing appointment times or having to stop and call for new directions.

29   Don't you dare knock on my door!

Put a sign on your door that says 'In Conference,' 'Timely Work Session,' or 'Available 1–2 p.m. Today' to discourage interruptions.

Understanding human behavior is the key to successful work in the arts

Personal qualities/skills include being capable of striving in solitude and in community; a sense of independence; willingness to collaborate; readiness to accept work as it comes while seeking the ideal job; perseverance; networking; written and verbal communication skills; social skills . . . although you may work in a regional theatre, your knowledge and aesthetic should be informed by the national and global models of theatrical practice.
Kathleen F. Conlin, Utah Shakespeare Festival Director
and Professor, University of Illinois at Urbana-Champaign

The ridiculous rate of theatre unemployment coupled with the sheer ferocity of a life in the American theatre should be an obvious indicator of the need for careful and consistent organizational, life, and career planning. Producers and artistic directors are often amazed that the same individuals who spend many years and a small fortune on actor training, voice work, singing lessons, and dance training have trouble investing a few days and a modest amount of money to organize and/or polish their career skills. In a similar vein, actors are sometimes dumbfounded to discover that individuals who have risen to the executive ranks of arts organizations are sometimes rude, noncommunicative, poorly organized 'leaders' with unpolished people skills, erratic behavioral traits, and modest expertise in either the arts or organizational planning.

Professional trade publications brim with offers to train the perfect actor, to re-create lips, eyes, busts, thighs, chins, and cheeks, and then to snap the definitive photograph to mail to a brilliant agent list in hopes of securing the breakthrough audition. Unfortunately, few publications, support organizations, or universities train actors, directors, designers, production personnel, or administrators in the realities of the nonprofit world and the terrifying myriad tasks that they will be expected to accomplish the first year on the job. In the same way that young actors quickly grow to realize that the person with the cutest nose and thinnest thighs is not necessarily the one who wins the role, arts personnel in all areas soon discover that a prestigious school, an MBA, and a warm smile don't guarantee survival in the deficit-laden, tough-to-conquer world of the arts. Whether training actors, directors, or producers, it is clear that interpersonal communications skills, group-process understanding, and savvy strategic skills are every bit as important as training in acting, directing, design, and theatre history.

There's a reason that producers and artistic directors joke that the closest anyone comes to perfection is when they are applying for a job. Smart artists and executives know to take care with their cover letters, résumés, recommendations, and support materials. Experienced artists and administrators understand that nurturing directors, area heads, board members, or other potential employers is the most important step leading to an audition or an interview. So how does this nurturing process happen?

'Acting is a matter of giving away secrets,' hints actress Ellen Barkin. The same is true of the artist, craftsperson, or administrator's career-planning process – and in order to comprehend fully the rigors of the field, it is important to understand theatre psyches, performing egos, employer needs, and the changing trends in the ever-evolving American arts environment. Speaking for myself, even after thirty years of career planning, four college degrees, attending or conducting over 12,000 auditions, working as an executive search consultant for nonprofit clients, studying over 100,000 résumés, conducting countless personal interviews, and talking to many of America's arts leaders, only now am I beginning to grasp the intricacies of the process.

For over thirty years I have taught seminars at national conventions, in professional theatres, and on college campuses, titled 'Assertive Personal Marketing,' 'The Business of Acting,' and 'Introduction to Regional Theater.' Almost every session begins with counselor basics: teaching actors and administrators how to establish a rapport, make connections, and carry on a conversation outside the interview or audition. Seminar participants are prodded to risk establishing a more personal relationship by reaching out to potential employers with a sense of humor and disarmingly, honest, straightforward talk that is appropriate to the situation. To help with this, participants are encouraged to identify the basic traits that attract them to people. For example, when questioned about first impressions and friendships, many participants acknowledge that they tend to like people who are kind to them – flattery! In addition, 'warmth,' 'unselfishness,' 'friendliness,' and 'a giving, fun-loving personality' always top the 'people we like most' list.

With this in mind, doesn't it follow that harried, overworked producers, artistic directors, and production managers might admire and respect similar traits if they were communicated in a phone call, letter, or interview? Knowing this, doesn't it make sense to learn how to communicate positive personality traits through an enjoyable conversation and even rehearse, roleplay, or otherwise prepare for one of the most important parts of career building? Can you look someone straight in the eye, deliver a firm handshake, stand up straight, dress appropriately, make someone laugh, comfortably conduct a one-on-one interview, and participate in a group discussion? Do you understand the difference between assertive, passive, and aggressive behavior? Answer these questions and integrate them into your institutional leadership and career planning and you will stand out in any pool of artists.

The bane of one's existence in most arts environments centers on petty politics, gossip, and innuendo. Understanding that the kind of people producers and directors wish to work with have all the personality traits of a faithful dog may propel you to the front of the employment line. Individuals with integrity, honesty, loyalty, warmth, and a sensitivity to others stand out in a crowd. A strong sense of ethics offers a comprehensive personal framework for living a professional life worth living. Mark Twain said it best: 'Always do right . . . This will surprise some people and astonish the rest.'

Ego and a remarkably fatalistic attitude regarding employment are two major obstacles for many administrators. 'If I'm right for the job, they'll hire me,' explains one staff member. 'They know who I am and what I can do and if they don't want me, it's their loss,' complains another longtime regional theatre actor. These naive comments fail to acknowledge the incredibly busy and complex lives of most artistic directors, producers, and managing directors who respond favorably to friendly, consistent correspondence that reminds them that a potential employee is alive, still interested, and available.

Another artistic hiring roadblock is ignorance – simply not realizing that employers are human beings who may indeed have the sensibilities, interests, concerns, and motivations of other living, breathing, thinking, feeling creatures. Many perceive the job search as a humiliating battle that they usually lose, while others seize employment contacts as an opportunity to endear themselves to a director, production manager, artistic director, or fellow actor or stage manager, and, perhaps, even make a friend. Many directors and producers I know are quick to recall fondly the individual who remembers their opening night – or better yet, their daughter's birthday. Producers' desks are lined with the photographs of actors who stuck by them through a life crisis, sent a bottle of wine to celebrate a particularly brilliant review, or let them know how much they enjoyed their production (after the critics savaged it).

Of course, inspiring company members, strategic planning, and career sensitivity is more than sending birthday cards, nurturing egos, and making friends. A commitment to polishing personnel skills, understanding artistic needs, attaining communications basics, and contributing to company morale is a must for the savvy actor, director, craftsperson, designer, or administrator. Preparing the total career package and working to understand human nature and the forces that guide the actions of executives and nonprofit board members is exciting and rewarding work that will hopefully lead to an increased world perspective, personal satisfaction, and ongoing employment. Of course, if you are heading into theatre production areas such as production management, technical direction, costumes, props, scenery, or scene painting, many more doors and arms are open to embrace your entry into the field. For almost everyone else, it may be best to remember the words of Nelson Mandela: 'The greatest glory in living lies not in never falling, but in rising every time we fall.' The chapters that follow offer insights into the process of striving, rebounding, learning, and developing your career.

They say that time changes things, but you actually have to change them yourself.

Andy Warhol

Advice to regional theatre workers everywhere

16 wonderful ways to improve your life in the theatre

> One day Alice came to a fork in the road and saw a Cheshire cat in a tree. 'Which road do I take?' she asked. 'Where do you want to go?' was his response. 'I don't know,' Alice answered. 'Then,' said the cat, 'it doesn't matter.'
>
> Lewis Carroll

1 **Know where you want to go and stay positive**
Keep your eye on your goals, remember that you chose a creative but difficult profession, and approach your work with enthusiasm. Don't sabotage yourself! Henry Ford hit it on the head when he said, 'Whether you think you can or whether you think you can't, you're right.'

2 **Plan ahead for the people you love**
Don't forget you have a life as well a career to plan! Go ahead and plan something special for someone you love. Don't allow your life to turn into one big casting call or late-night rehearsal. Send flowers, book a reservation at that fabulous restaurant, or find a loved one something unique on eBay.

3 **Be a collaborator**
Whether you're a director, designer, assistant stage manager, or property assistant, you'll accomplish more if you nurture, inspire, motivate, empower, support, thank, and show you're a willing part of your theatre's team.

4   **Hide from the madness!**
Avoid stressful situations prior to performances, key meetings, or work sessions. Schedule aggravating situations and meetings with people at times that are best for you (and schedule time after the session to unwind and regain perspective). For example, if you're a stage manager, don't schedule a meeting with an angry actor just prior to opening night; if you're a director, separate salary negotiations and artistic discussions. Find the right time for every important job. Balzac said it best when he observed, 'Power is not revealed by striking hard or often, but by striking true.'

5   **Put the madness in perspective**
Try prioritizing these items: *Audition, Money, Chekhov, Chocolate, Health, Happiness, Mom.* Ask yourself, 'Where do my true priorities lie?'

6   **Ask for advice**
People may look to you for leadership and to promote 'ownership' or 'buy-in' for your theatre. When it is appropriate, consider asking your fellow workers or supervisor for advice or guidance or the benefit of their history with the organization. You don't have to take the advice, but people appreciate being asked. 'You ain't gonna learn what you don't wanna know,' says Jerry Garcia.

7   **Just say no to defensive behavior**
Stay open to constructive suggestions and graciously ignore the rude remarks of ignorant people. An old Indian proverb says, 'Call on God, but row away from the rocks.'

8   **Stay out of trouble**
Racist remarks, sexist behavior, crude gestures, off-color jokes, and obnoxious banter may be fascinating on stage in a Joe Orton play. They are less than fascinating and potentially devastating if they impact your working relationships with your peers, your employer, or your community.

9   Take risks

'Imagination will often carry us to worlds that never were. But without it we go nowhere,' counsels Carl Sagan. Remember why the nonprofit theatre movement was founded in the first place?

10   Put your personal stamp on your work

'Individuality is either the mark of a genius or the reverse. Mediocrity finds safety in standardization,' writes Frederick E. Crane. You don't have to be outrageous, just don't be consistently derivative.

11   Prove Emerson wrong

Pay attention to the people you love. The arts are demanding, but they don't need to rob you of your humanity. 'Art is a jealous mistress,' explains Ralph Waldo Emerson. 'If a man has a genius for painting, poetry, music, architecture, or philosophy, he makes a bad husband and an ill provider.' Prove Emerson wrong.

12   But when we get behind closed doors . . .

'Three may keep a secret if two of them are dead,' quipped Benjamin Franklin. Joking or not, old Ben certainly knew what he was talking about. Discuss salaries, grievances, and official business behind closed doors and not in front of other theatre folks and the world at large. Remember the Spanish proverb, 'Whoever gossips to you will gossip about you.'

13   Do a good deed today

Bring honor to your institution and satisfaction to your family as an ongoing 'good-deed doer.' Look around your company and change someone's life for the better. As a respected artist, you have the power to brighten days with a kind word, warm gesture, or expression of interest. Ben Jonson said it best: 'When a virtuous man is raised, it brings gladness to his friends, grief to his enemies, and glory to his posterity.'

14   Dream on!

Take time to daydream, stay healthy, sleep well, and give yourself a fighting chance to tackle your dreams! 'All men of action are dreamers,' explains James G. Huneker. Consider sporadic five-minute 'dream breaks' during the day.

15 **Focus on your vision and embrace the future**

'If art is to nourish the roots of our culture, society must set the artist free to follow his vision wherever it takes him,' notes John F. Kennedy. If you focus on your vision, you can free yourself from society's negativity and live a life in which you are true to your own spirit. Try it for a day, a week, a month, or a lifetime.

16 **Climb a mountain and see the world**

Take a world view and plan ahead. Take time each year to take stock of your life, pat yourself on the back for your progress and accomplishments, and thank those who have helped you along the way.

Doing the best at this moment puts you in the best place for the next moment.

Oprah Winfrey

5 tips for starting a new job

First impressions are essential in every field. Here are five proven suggestions for making a strong first impression (and a powerful ongoing impression) when starting a new job in the theatre.

1   When you start a new job, shake your producer's, director's, or boss's hand. Make it clear that you are excited about your work, loyal, trustworthy, industrious, and really happy to be working together on his or her agenda. Employers need to know that they can count on you.

2   Always arrive at work at least a half-hour to an hour early every day the first six months, and be the last person to leave the office. Be there on a weekend or a holiday if you can contribute in some significant (and, hopefully, visible) way. Be productive. Results count more than effort.

3   Leave a paper trail. Document your successes and failures. Let your successes be known with great subtlety. Own up to your failures and take responsibility . . . but don't dwell on them!

4   Asking for advice is a way of creating mentors, allies, and potential partners in your success. Be humble, quiet, and easygoing in your approach and generous with your gratitude. Write short, sincere thank-you notes.

5   Inspire . . . motivate . . . understand your boss and co-workers. What motivates them? What are their interests and career plans? Look at the big picture: their lives and your career.

A short cast of characters: people you need to know in the theatre

The artistic director and the artistic team

Certainly, the artistic director is the individual charged with crafting the vision, shaping seasons, hiring artistic personnel, and fully realizing the artistic mission of the institution. The title 'producing artistic director' typically means that the artistic director is also heavily involved in and essentially responsible for overall strategic decision-making and is heavily involved in the financial and fundraising aspects of the theatre.

In most nonprofit theatre operations, the following areas or individuals directly report to the artistic side of the institution (artistic director/producing artistic director, etc.):

- Directors

- Associate artistic directors

- Choreographers

- Musical direction (including composers, musicians, etc.)

- Designers (scenery, costumes, lights, sound, etc.)

- Actors

- Stage management

- Dramaturgy/literary management

- Production/technical direction (production manager, technical director, production crews, stage operations crews, etc.)

Since many of the standard theatre positions are outlined on the Sample Organizational Chart for Regional Theatres at the end of this chapter, I won't repeat them all here. However, four key individuals who have strong connections to both the artistic direction of the theatre and the management, budget, and income side of the theatre deserve special mention and clarification:

The managing director

The managing director of most professional theatres is generally charged with the financial, fundraising, marketing, and front-of-house and general day-to-day management of the theatre. Working in partnership with the artistic director, the managing director is often called on to take the lead in community relations, personnel management, media relations, budget planning, and board of trustee development and planning.

In most nonprofit theatre operations, the following areas directly report to the management side of the institution (executive director/managing director/general manager, etc.):

- Development (fundraising, advancement, unearned income)

- Marketing (audience development, sales, earned income)

- Finance (business management, accounting, contracts, financial reporting)

- Front of house (box office, house management, concessions, gift shops, etc.)

The production manager

The production manager of larger professional theatres works closely with the artistic director, directors, designers, and craftspeople, and usually supervises all production and technical areas of the theatre. On the management side, the production manager is also crucial in budgeting, personnel hiring and supervision, and financial controls. Aside from the expense of salaries and benefits, production (scenery, costumes, lights, sound, properties, etc.) tends to be the highest annual budget allocation. With these realities in mind, it is recommended that the production manager report to the artistic director on artistic matters and work closely with the managing director on financial and personnel matters. Technical directors and costume, scenery, lighting, makeup, stage operations, and other technical and production crews and personnel are typically considered production staff.

The company manager

Company managers are most often involved with the coordination and implementation of travel, housing, and contract commitments with an emphasis on meeting union agreements with the Actors' Equity Association (AEA), the Stage Directors and Choreographers Society (SDC), United Scenic Artists (USA), and other out-of-town independent contractors. In many theatres, the company manager is also encouraged to assist with company communications and morale, and special events for the company. Since the bulk of the work is usually artist-related (even though the day-to-days are largely management oriented), it's recommended that the company manager maintain very strong ties and reporting responsibilities to both the artistic and management sides of the theatre.

The director of education

The director of education is often called on to conduct artistic research, tie productions to educational outreach efforts, and represent the artistic side of the theatre. At the same time, the director of education is often considered a pivotal player in group ticket sales, consumer relations, and the development of earned income. With these dual responsibilities, it's recommended that the director of education nurture strong relationships and report to both the artistic and management sides of the theatre.

Sample Organizational Chart

The Sample Organizational Chart on the following spread offers an overview of areas of responsibility and general reporting lines for most regional theatres.

Sample Organizational Chart
for Regional Theatres

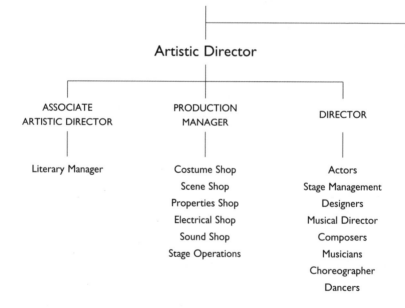

BOARD OF TRUSTEES

Board of Trustee Committees

(Executive Committee, Finance/Legal Committee, Nominating/Recruitment
Committee, Fund-raising Coordination Committee, Governmental Relations
Committee, Marketing/Volunteers Committee, Strategic Planning Committee)

Artistic Director

ASSOCIATE ARTISTIC DIRECTOR	PRODUCTION MANAGER	DIRECTOR
Literary Manager	Costume Shop	Actors
	Scene Shop	Stage Management
	Properties Shop	Designers
	Electrical Shop	Musical Director
	Sound Shop	Composers
	Stage Operations	Musicians
		Choreographer
		Dancers

Managing Director

GENERAL MANAGER/ FINANCE DIRECTOR	MARKETING DIRECTOR	DEVELOPMENT/ FUND-RAISING DIRECTOR
Finance	Audience Development	Annual Campaign
Box Office	Media	Grants
Front of House	Sales	Corporate
Office	Public Relations	Foundation
Facilities	Touring/Outreach	Volunteers
	Publications	Endowment

NOTES:

1 It's recommended that the artistic director and managing director both have strong ties and reporting lines to the production manager, company manager, and education director to protect both artistic and fiscal integrity.

2 Volunteers deserve top-level support.

Part 5

The American theatre employment universe

100+ prime sources

Information equals power

In a mad fit of institutional dedication and loyalty, I once auditioned 700 actors in three days when I was on the Board of Directors of the Southeastern Theatre Conference. This may seem like a bizarre way to get to know actors but, believe it or not, hundreds of artistic leaders subject themselves to this craziness (and worse) on an annual basis!

My advice is to attend auditions, interviews and conferences, get to know the business, consult many 'experts' (whether it be through publications, personal interviews, or discussions with your career mentors), and turn yourself into an expert on *your* life and career! This will empower you to make your own informed decisions and take responsibility for the decisions you make and the life you create.

The truth (and more) is out there

There was a time when job seeking and career building seemed a mysterious enterprise. Today, thanks to the sweeping communications potential of the World Wide Web, the efficiency and availability of email, and the clarity of theatre, social networking, and arts service organization websites, the information is generally out there if one knows where to start.

Certainly, the major publications of the industry are useful tools and so much career information is accessible on each publication's website, as well as on local newsstands (or in local bookstores). Spend time paging through these publications or surfing these websites and you'll be rewarded with timely job-search information, hiring tips, interview suggestions, audition and photography advice, networking guidance, agent submission details, professional development opportunities, arts advocacy lessons, class and training endorsements, and a whole host of other information that may be absolutely useful or sheer propaganda.

Thousands of publications and websites offer theatre information – way too many to mention or list in this book. However, here are a few of my favorites on which you will find hundreds of resources that will help you narrow to your specific field of interest.

10 pertinent publications

American Theatre

www.tcg.org

American Theatre is the national monthly magazine for the American professional not-for-profit theatre, informing readers about groundbreaking international work, providing state-by-state listings of professional theatre seasons, and offering ongoing reports and surveys of the field. Masterfully edited by Jim O'Quinn, with must-read musings by Theatre Communications Group (TCG) executive directors, *American Theatre* should be required reading for every theatre professional and serious high school, college, and university theatre student. Check the website to delve in and to track down subscription information.

ARTSEARCH

www.tcg.org

Also published by the Theatre Communications Group, *ARTSEARCH* is a fabulous regional theatre resource and provides the opportunity for online job hunting for full-time, part-time, seasonal, year-round, and internship opportunities, from entry level to upper management. Listings include openings in administration, artistic, production, design, career development and education in theatres, performing arts centres, summer festivals, universities, arts councils, and related arts organizations. Check out the website for a subscription to access the printable pdf and online information.

Back Stage East and Back Stage West
www.backstage.com

This site makes it possible to access content from *Back Stage East* (New York/ national/international theatre news) and *Back Stage West* (Southern California emphasis), including exclusive online content, advance casting notices before they appear in print, and regional casting notices for every state in the US, not to mention from Canada and worldwide. Subscriptions range in price. Check the website for details. Weekly editions are available in bookstores and newsstands nationwide and offer job notices, theatre reviews, advice columns, savvy career information, and a host of other practical information. The production charts, casting ads, and updated theatre addresses and contact information are worth the price of a subscription.

Dramatics
www.edta.org

Dramatics is the Educational Theatre Association's magazine for theatre students and teachers containing practical articles on acting, directing, design, and other facets of theatre; sage advice from working professionals; new plays; and book reviews. Two special issues each year offer directories of college theatre programs (December) and summer theatre work and study opportunities (February). Check the website to delve in or for subscription information.

Live Design
www.livedesignonline.com

Live Design offers a comprehensive look at the art and technology of show business with sound, lighting, scenery, production, and design articles; listings of Broadway master classes in production; industry resources; and articles related to unions and service organizations, including the United States Institute for Theater Technology (USITT) news. Check the website to explore or for subscription information.

The Hollywood Reporter

www.hollywoodreporter.com

The Hollywood Reporter is a longtime entertainment industry information source focusing on film, television, and digital media, and is an excellent resource for theatre folk looking to expand their horizons. Subscriptions range in price. Check the website for details.

Quarto

www.staaonline.org

At last count, there were over 200 Shakespeare festivals in America; *Quarto* offers practical advice on working in the field and a host of other ongoing features including 'Weird William,' 'Shakespearean Snippets,' and 'Seasons of Shakespeare.' Published by the Shakespeare Theatre Association (STA), *Quarto* is available to STA associate members. Check the website for membership information.

Stage Directions

www.stage-directions.com

Stage Directions magazine focuses on production planning and implementation; theatre resources; theatre book, CD, and play reviews; theatre profiles; and many other areas of the theatre. Check the website to delve in or for subscription information.

Theater Magazine and Technical Brief

www.drama.yale.edu

Theater Magazine is described by playwright Tony Kushner as 'an indispensable publication for anyone seriously concerned with the art of theatre in the world today.' The magazine focuses 'primarily, but not exclusively, on experimental theatre – American and international – and theatre that touches on political and cultural debates.' Check out the website for subscription information or back issues.

Technical Brief, a publication of the Yale School of Drama Technical Design and Production Department, is a self-proclaimed 'indispensable publication for technical managers in theatre. Written by professionals for professionals, its purpose is simple: communication.' Check the website for subscription information.

Variety

www.variety.com

Variety has covered film, television, international entertainment, and myriad other areas of show business since 1905. *Variety* prides itself on 'timely, credible and straightforward news and analysis.' Check the website to investigate or for subscription information.

10 websites to open up your web world

Introduction

With over half a billion members (at last count), most of the world has caught on to the power of Facebook for career networking, event planning, theatre blogging and just keeping up with friends and colleagues. Here are a few more theatre-specific websites to open up your worldwide web world:

Amazon
www.amazon.com

Everyone knows this website, but few understand what a great resource it can be for theatre professionals. The site offers quick script mailings and 'how to' book purchases, out-of-print books and theatre biographies, inexpensive used books, sections where theatre books and magazines are rated, and quick links to what books theatre people are buying. Check it out!

TheaterMania
www.theatermania.com

The TheaterMania website invites you to browse a database of over 3,000 theatres and 7,000 productions including Broadway, Off-Broadway, Off-Off-Broadway, and regional theatre productions as well as links to theatre tickets.

BackstageJobs
BackstageJobs.com
This free job-listing service for behind-the-scenes positions in the 'live entertainment industry' strives to detail information on 'everything but acting.'

Culturevulture
www.culturevulture.net
This 'somewhat haphazard and pronouncedly idiosyncratic sharing of matters cultural' lists theatres and productions throughout the US.

Curtain Rising
www.curtainrising.com
Curtain Rising offers 8,100 links to live theatre, organizing the connections by touring companies, cities, states, Shakespeare festivals, and live theatre around the world. A quick, dandy resource!

Playbill
www.playbill.com
Playbill magazine has served theatre audiences since 1884. Today its website offers listings for Broadway, Off-Broadway, regional, tours, London, summer stock, international news, ongoing features and statistics, and job listings. Check the website to delve in or for member services.

Broadway.com
www.broadway.com
Broadway.com offers overviews of Broadway plays, ticket links, photos, travel packages, video clips and 'Broadway Buzz' features on Broadway personalities.

StageAgent
www.stageagent.com

Focusing on dramas, musicals, and operas, StageAgent is a web service dedicated to performers and producers, and endeavors to provide 'useful information for the people who make theatre magic happen.' For more information, email info@stageagent.com or check out the website.

Artslynx International Arts Resource
www.artslynx.org

This site lists marvelous links to acting, design, drama therapy, fight direction, education, production, stage management, and technical theatre websites.

Backstage Employment Network
www.plsnbookshelf.com/classifieds/

The website for the Backstage Employment Network is a subsidiary of three trade magazines – *Projection, Lights and Staging News; FRONT of HOUSE;* and *Stage Directions* – and bills itself as 'an active employment community targeted for the live entertainment industry,' including 'entertainment production technologists, practitioners, and educators.'

10 challenging books to power your acting career

Acting for the Camera: Revised Edition
by Tony Barr
Regional theatre may be the place to work, but film and television is a way to make money to subsidize your classical repertory career. The *Los Angeles Times* calls Tony Barr's writings 'A first-class book for the beginner and refreshing review for any pro.' (New York: Harper Perennial, 1997.)

Acting Professionally: Raw Facts about Careers in Acting
by Robert Cohen and James Calleri
A straightforward guide to the business of acting, offering counsel on actor training approaches, career positioning, finding an agent, auditioning, interviewing, and making long-range career decisions. (New York: Palgrave-Macmillan, 2009.)

An Actor Behaves: From Audition to Performance
by Tom Markus
The title says it all, and producer/director Tom Markus has a witty, wonderful way of speaking the truth, spinning a yarn, and sharing a life in the theatre. (New York: Samuel French, 1992.)

An Actor Succeeds
by Terrance Hines and Suzanne Vaughan
Interviews with casting directors, writers, managers, accountants, publicists, agents, and attorneys make this a unique book full of actor tools and specialized advice. (New York: Samuel French, 1990.)

Audition: Everything an Actor Needs to Know to Get the Part
by Michael Shurtleff

Over twenty years old and still useful! (New York: Walker & Company, 2003.)

Auditioning: An Actor-Friendly Guide
by Joanna Merlin

Award-winning casting director, actor, and educator Joanna Merlin covers acting choices, the audition space, and comprehensive instruction on how actors can improve their auditions – this is my students' favorite! With a foreword by Harold Prince. (New York: Vintage, 2001.)

Acting in Film: An Actor's Take on Movie Making
by Michael Caine

Movies are being made all over America – maybe even near a regional theatre in your neighborhood! This popular film actor's overview on the movies is worth reading if you are contemplating a trip to Hollywood or anywhere where movies are made. Also available as a CD. (New York: Applause, 2000.)

Respect for Acting
by Uta Hagen

Uta Hagen's profound book offers readers insights into the passion, joy, and craft of acting. (New York: Wiley, 2008.)

Sanford Meisner on Acting
by Sanford Meisner

A founding member of the Actors Studio (with Lee Strasberg, Stella Adler, and Harold Clurman), Meisner developed his own unique lessons based on his understandings of Stanislavski, and influenced theatre training in profound ways. (New York: Vintage, 1987.)

The Back Stage Actor's Handbook: Fourth Edition
compiled and edited by Sherry Eaker

Subtitled 'The How-To and Who-To Contact Reference for Actors, Singers, and Dancers.' Longtime *Back Stage* editor Sherry Eaker draws on her vast network of writers and her immense personal experience to cover everything from résumés, headshots, negotiations, voice-overs, jingles, soaps, radio drama, commercials, children's theatre, cabarets, stand-up comedy, film, theme parks, showcases, touring, and most every other area of the theatre. (New York: Back Stage Books, 2004.)

15 quirky books on working in New York City and beyond

The Cheap Bastard's Guide to New York City: A Native New Yorker's Secrets of Living the Good Life – for Free!, 4th Edition by Rob Grader
Globe Pequot, 2008.

The New York Agent Book: How to Get the Agent You Need for the Career You Want by K. Callan
Sweden Press, 2008.

Frommer's NYC Free & Dirt Cheap (Frommer's Free & Dirt Cheap), 3rd Edition by Ethan Wolff
Frommers, 2008.

Working Together in Theatre, Collaboration and Leadership by Robert Cohen
New York: Palgrave Macmillan, 2011.

Acting: Make It Your Business. How to Avoid Mistakes and Achieve Success as a Working Actor by Paul Russell
New York: Back Stage Books, 2008.

The Intent to Live: Achieving Your True Potential as an Actor by Larry Moss
Bantam, 2005.

An Agent Tells All by Tony Martinez
Hit Team Publishing, 2005.

The Power of the Actor by Ivana Chubbuck
Gotham, 2005.

**Self-Management for Actors: Getting Down to (Show)
Business, 3rd Edition** by Bonnie Gillespie
Cricket Feet Publishing, 2008.

**An Actor Prepares . . . to Live in New York City: How to Live
Like a Star before You Become One** by Craig Wroe
New York: Proscenium Publishers, 2003.

An Actor's Guide: Making It in New York City by Glenn Alterman.
New York: Allworth Press, 2002.

**How to be a Working Actor, 5th Edition: The Insider's Guide
to Finding Jobs in Theater, Film, and Television** by Mari Lyn Henry
New York: Back Stage Books, 2007.

**Acting Is Everything: An Actor's Guidebook for a Successful
Career in Los Angeles, Expanded Gold, 11th Edition** by Judy Kerr
September Publishing, 2006.

Making it on Broadway: Actors' Tales of Climbing to the Top
by David Wienir and Jody Langel
Allworth Press, 2004.

10 bountiful books on directing, design, producing and production

A Director Prepares: Seven Essays on Art and Theater
by Anne Bogart

A thought-provoking treatise on creating theatre, by the artistic director of the SITI Company, an ensemble-based theatre company that the author founded with Tadashi Suzuki. (New York: Routledge, 2001.)

A Sense of Direction by William Ball

This may be out of print, but it's worth tracking down on the used book market. It is indeed a rare book as it represents the life's work of one of America's theatre pioneers: William Ball, founder and general director of the acclaimed American Conservatory Theater (ACT) in San Francisco. (New York: Drama Book Publishers, 1984.)

Backwards and Forwards:
A Technical Manual for Reading Plays by David Ball

Simply put, reading this short text will help you to analyze scripts, understand playwrights, and succeed as a director, actor, or producer. (Carbondale, Illinois: Southern Illinois University Press, 1998.)

How to Run a Theater, 2nd Edition by Jim Volz

'Required reading for anyone working in the field of arts management – be they artists or managers,' writes actress-choreographer-educator-manager Suzanne Celentano in the international *Arts Management Network Newsletter*. TCG's Ben Cameron called it, 'A joy!' and artistic directors, managers and critics have hailed the chapters on boards of trustees, audience development, life management and fundraising. (London: Methuen Drama, 2011.)

Life is a Contact Sport: Ten Great Career Strategies that Work by Ken Kragan and Jefferson Graham

Personal manager, television producer, talent adviser, and supreme negotiator, Ken Kragen has been called 'the most successful behind-the-scenes operator in show business.' This book outlines his strategies for career success, and it's brilliant. (New York: William Morrow, 1994.)

Management and the Arts by William J. Byrnes

This book offers an excellent overview of how the arts are structured, with marvelous tools for budgeting, fundraising, financial management, personnel management, and arts organization, with career-planning advice and examples. (Burlington, Massachusetts: Focal Press, 2008.)

My Life in Art by Konstantin Sergeevich Stanislavski

This wise book penned by one of the theatre's great men ranks right up there with the author's three other books that should be on your bookshelf for ongoing reference: *An Actor Prepares, Building a Character,* and *Creating a Role*. (New York: Theatre Arts Books, 2004.)

The Artistic Home: Discussions with Artistic Directors of America's Institutional Theatres by Todd London

First published in 1988, *The Artistic Home* still packs a punch and offers a giant dose of artistic empowerment, institutional vision, and theatre history. (New York: Theatre Communications Group, 1988.)

The Dramatic Imagination: Reflections and Speculations on the Art of Theatre by Robert Edmond Jones

This is the man who helped countless theatre artists discover the importance of theatrical design. Scenery and lighting would never be the same. (New York: Theatre Arts Books, 2004.)

The Empty Space. A Book About the Theatre: Deadly, Holy, Rough, Immediate by Peter Brook

Brook's 1968 book is a theatre classic. Read it and find out why – it might change the way you view the theatre. (New York: Touchstone, 1996.)

10 largest American cities in order of size

If you are planning a career in the theatre, doesn't it make sense to go where the people are . . . or at least where there are potential audiences? If only it were that easy! With that strategy, no one would ever have created a theatre in the tiny towns of Ashland, Oregon (Oregon Shakespeare Festival); Stratford, Canada (The Stratford Festival); or the midsize city of Montgomery, Alabama (Alabama Shakespeare Festival), where over a million people attended productions last year! Marvelous theatres have turned up in unlikely places (Hailey, Idaho; Creede, Colorado; West Liberty, Ohio; Jackson, Mississippi; Anchorage, Alaska; Skokie, Illinois; and Fish Creek, Wisconsin – to name a few.)

The US population increase between 1990 and 2000 was the largest in American history, with the West growing the fastest and the South reaching 100 million people. All states increased in population, Nevada most rapidly (thanks to Las Vegas) – and the majority of Americans were living in the ten most populous states.

The 2000 census* counted 281.4 million people in the United States, a 13.2 per cent increase from the 1990 census population of 248.7 million. Eight of the ten largest cities in 2000 gained population in the 1990s (while Philadelphia and Detroit declined in size). New York remained the country's largest city with over 8 million people. Phoenix is hot in more ways than one – up by 34 per cent over the decade.

* **Source:** Census Bureau, July 1, 2004, *Estimates*

City and State	Population April 1, 1990	Population April 1, 2000	Number Change	% Change
New York, NY	7,322,564	8,008,278	685,714	9.4
Los Angeles, CA	3,485,398	3,694,820	209,422	6
Chicago, IL	2,783,726	2,896,016	112,290	4
Houston, TX	1,630,553	1,953,631	323,078	19.8
Philadelphia, PA	1,585,577	1,517,550	−68,027	−4.3
Phoenix, AZ	983,403	1,321,045	337,642	34.3
San Diego, CA	1,110,549	1,223,400	112,851	10.2
Dallas, TX	1,006,877	1,188,580	181,703	18
San Antonio, TX	935,933	1,144,646	208,713	22.3
Detroit, MI	1,027,974	951,270	−76,704	−7.5

Source: US Census Bureau, Census 2000; 1990 Census, *Population and Housing Unit Counts*, United States (1990 CPH-2-1).

The 1990s was the first decade since the 1930s that New York City led city population growth. Los Angeles had been leader in each decade from the 1940s to the 1990s (except for the 1970s, when Houston reigned supreme).

In 2005, San Jose replaced Detroit in the top ten and San Antonio outgrew Dallas to claim the eighth largest city spot. As a June 29, 2005, *USA Today* report indicates, key factors in recent city growth trends are changing immigration patterns (big-city housing costs are no longer a bargain) and 'high housing costs in cosmopolitan cities that have almost no vacant land for construction.' Conversely, 'smaller, less glamorous places have plenty of room to grow.'

New York, NY

There's nowhere on earth quite like the Big Apple, and it's hard to know where to start if you decide on New York City as your home base. With that in mind, I am including many tried and true sources for planning your New York experience. The theatre industry in New York is constantly changing and these news sites, job sites, casting sites, job-seeker tools and direct links to many of the most up-to-date employment resources will help you stay on top of trends and opportunities.

15 quick links and websites to put you in touch with Broadway, Off-Broadway and beyond

1   **www.tdf.org (TKTS Discount Theatre Booths in New York)**

To quote from the mission site: 'Theatre Development Fund, a not-for-profit organization, was created with the conviction that the live theatrical arts afford a unique expression of the human condition that must be sustained and nurtured. TDF's twofold mission is to identify and provide support, including financial assistance, to theatrical works of artistic merit, and to encourage and enable diverse audiences to attend live theatre and dance in all their venues.' Most people know TDF through their TKTS discount theatre booths located in Times Square, downtown Brooklyn or South Street Seaport. TKTS discount booths offer tickets to Broadway and Off-Broadway musicals and plays at up to 50% off (plus a $4.00 per ticket service charge). For operating hours and listings, check out the website. Note that there is a special 'plays only' line at the TKTS in Times Square, located 'under the red steps' in Father Duffy Square on Broadway and 47th Street. Happily, TDF is more than TKTS, so check out the website for all the resources it provides.

2.   **www.actorsequity.org/NewsMedia/newslinks.asp**

This is a terrific quick-link website to key media and websites important to New York actors, directors, designers and all personnel available through the Actors' Equity Association website. It provides links to significant Broadway websites as well as Canadian and London sites including *Theatre Land, Theatre Canada, Talkin' Broadway, TheatreMania, Direct from Broadway, Albemarle of London, Internet Broadway Database,* and all the longtime publications and websites (Backstage.com, Variety.com, ShowBusinessWeekly. com, American Theatre Magazine/www.tcg.org, BroadwayLeague.com, Off Broadwayonline.com, Broadway.com Show Business, Playbill, American Theater Web, NYTheatre.com, online.Performink.com and more.

3. **www.backstage.com & http://casting.backstage.com/jobseekerx**

   Many of the websites already mentioned offer an abundance of free advice, access to articles on the business, job listings, interviews, and job-search tools, but some services are 'members only' and come at a price. Only you can decide if these services will be worth it for you. They can represent a serious investment for the frugal job seeker. For example, subscribing to *Back Stage's Call Sheet Online* and *Backstage.com* services or access to the print and online version of *Backstage* costs around $200 for 12 months of service. I worked for over a decade for *Back Stage* in New York and I was always impressed with the integrity, artistry and dedication of the writers and editors. To check out their services, go to www.backstage.com or directly to http://casting.backstage.com/jobseekerx which provides multiple paid services (monthly access for full services are around $20 per month) and some free ideas on how to manage your job search. You can search entertainment-industry job notices for film, TV, and theatre casting calls, modeling auditions, crew calls and various jobs in the performing arts, including work for singers, writers, dancers, comedians, writers, filmmakers, and more. To quote the website, '*Back Stage* helps actors, performers, and behind-the-scenes talent excel in their careers by providing trustworthy and up-to-date casting/job notices, industry news, interviews, and advice. The Back Stage Casting Center assists casting directors, directors, producers, talent coordinators, agents, and managers publish casting and job notices, promote auditions, and find the best talent around, across the world. And the Back Stage Career Center/Actor's Toolbox helps actors, performers, and models manage their acting résumés, headshots, and audio/video reels online, in our searchable talent database.'

4. **www.theatricalindex.com**

   Theatrical Index is a weekly publication that has been a useful resource to theatre professionals for over forty years. Subscribers include producers, managers, media, actors, directors, banks, attorneys, lawyers, and others connected to the theatre industry. The editors endeavor to provide timely, personal service. 'Need to know if the producers of next season's big show have hired a stage manager yet?' asks the website writer. 'We can help you find out. If you don't see it in the *Index*, give us a call and we'll track it down.'

The publication focuses on current and future Broadway and Off-Broadway shows, road tours, regional productions, and special attractions. Price Berkley started what has been called 'The Bible' of the American theatre on November 9, 1964.

5. **www.showbusinessweekly.com**
    Show Business is a weekly trade paper for New York City's performing arts industry. Since 1941, *Show Business* has helped actors, singers and dancers in the performing arts and now provides direct access to important audition and casting notices. The publication's 'Cityshoot' section is a comprehensive listing of independent and studio films in development and production in New York and details who is filming what, when, and where to make contact. Recent stories provided help on finding an apartment, avoiding scams aimed at actors and the industry, and making a living as a playwright.

6. **www.playbill.com**
    Free membership in the *Playbill Club* offers theatre discounts ranging from 10% to 50% on Broadway, Off-Broadway, and opera tickets, as well as restaurant and hotel expenses. Playbill.com includes the latest New York news, current listings for Broadway, Off-Broadway, and regional productions, and news features about working in the theatre. The site's casting and job listings have assisted thousands of past job seekers with jobs ranging from receptionists to actors, from education program directors to props assistants, and from dancers to company and general managers.

7. **www.nytheatre.com**
    This website offers guides to the overall New York City theatre experience including Broadway, Off-Broadway and Off-Off Broadway. It lists what's happening around town regarding plays, musicals, physical theatre, cabaret, comedy, for kids and families, gay and lesbian, indie theatre, plays by women, stars on stage, late-night programs. and more.

8. **http://nymag.com/arts/theatre**
    This newsy magazine-style website offers advice, trends, interviews, breaking news, calendar listings. and such useful articles as 'Ten Ways to Score Broadway Tix' and 'Theatre on a Shoestring.'

9. **www.Broadway.com**

   This website ranks the most popular Broadway shows, details the 'Latest Broadway Buzz,' and offers direct links to hotels, last-minute deals, interviews, video clips, polls, quizzes and comprehensive listings for Broadway, Off-Broadway, and London theatre productions.

10. **http://curtainup.com**

    Online since 1996, *CurtainUp* is a useful theatre magazine of reviews, news, annotated listings, and features with a handy review archive and listings for everywhere from the Berkshires to Broadway and from London to California.

11. **www.talkinbroadway.com**

    Talkin' Broadway offers a marvelous section on Broadway history, Broadway and Off-Broadway theatre discussions, cast recording news, Tony Awards links, shopping, restaurant, book and theatre reviews.

12. **www.dramabookshop.com**

    For theatre lovers, the Drama Book Shop has long been one of New York's most engaging bookstores, hangouts, and sources for information about working in the New York theatre and beyond. The website offers links to New York casting sources, casting blogs and tools for the profession (books, CDs, DVDs, agent and casting director information, dialect tapes, etc.)

13. **http://broadwayworld.com**

    BroadwayWorld.com combines ticket links to Broadway, Off-Broadway, tours and London shows, a media room with the latest CDs, DVDs, and books, links to theatre in every major city in America, message boards for New York, London and students, hotel and restaurant finders, audition notices, classified ads, and a special section on stage to screen news.

14. **www.1auditions.com/audition.html**

    This diverse site offers hundreds of actor, dancer, model, commercial, television, and film audition opportunities in New York, Hollywood and many places in between that are searchable by location and keyword. There is no charge for viewing the auditions, but the site asks that you become a free member (which also provides many tools for actors and models including a free website, email, auditions calendar and more than 20,000 free resources such as listings for agents, casting directors, coaches, and photographers), and that you notify them if you land an audition or casting so that they can mention it on their site.

15. **www.stagedooraccess.com**

Billing itself as 'Your Online Virtual Agent,' *StageDoorAccess.com* offers an audition calendar, a hot topics section that talks about Equity, non-Equity choices, headshots, résumés, agents, casting directors, finding acting coaches and voice teachers and more. The actor toolbox includes YouTube videos, a message board, and many other resources. Much of the website information is free, but special services have monthly fees.

Final note on New York City

If these sites don't answer your questions, head to the bookstore and pick up a few of the '10 Challenging Books to Power Your Acting Career' or '10 Handy Books to Consider Before Moving to New York' included earlier in this book – or Google 'Broadway Theatre' and you'll have your choice of over 41,500,000 other websites.

Los Angeles, California

There's an amazing array and seemingly endless stream of world premieres, experimental theatre, reinvented classical theatre, musical theatre, and straight-forward drama on Los Angeles stages. Over 200 theatres are operating at any given time in the Los Angeles area. Unfortunately, only a few pay a living wage and a lot of the theatre is miserable, although many hold out the promise of résumé-building, professional development, Hollywood networking, and/or sitcom heaven. There are institutional theatres (The Geffen Playhouse, Mark Taper Forum, Pasadena Playhouse, Ahmanson, etc.) and there are 'membership theatres' (nearly four dozen theatres whose company members generally pay dues for special services and to defray producing expenses.) These include The Antaeus Company, Company of Angels, Knightsbridge Theatre, Theatre Banshee, Sacred Fools Theater Company, Son of Semele Ensemble, and Theatre of Note, to name a few. Helping to sort through the morass of theatres is the LA Stage Alliance (www.lastagealliance.com), which ably serves the Los Angeles performing arts community by increasing advocacy, awareness, and audience attendance on behalf of the 200-plus performing arts organizations in Los Angeles County. The organization has advocacy and ticket services and offers student and individual memberships. Member organizations span the distance from Ventura to La Mirada, California.

Chicago, Illinois

The Midwest seems to have opened its arms and embraced aspiring theatre producers, actors, and craftspeople, as more than 250 theatres representing a wide range of artistic ambitions and play-filled dreams exist in the Chicago area. There are the giants in town (the Goodman Theatre, Chicago Shakespeare Theater on the Navy Pier, the Court Theatre, Northlight Theatre, Victory Gardens Theater, Steppenwolf Theatre Company, etc.) But smaller theatres are a great adventure and you might want to put Dog and Pony, About Face, Hypocrites, Aguijon, Annoy-ance, Infusion and Tuta theatres on your list! Founded in 1979, the League of Chicago Theatres (www.chicagoplays.com) works to promote awareness and visibility for live theatre in the Chicago area and 'provides services that strengthen the operations of more than 190 member theatres.' There's an excellent 'Industry Professionals' section with jobs, auditions, blogs and even a Wiki space. A handy site with a nifty theatre map, half-price theatre links, video previews and an auditions and jobs listings section is Theatre in Chicago (www.theatreinchicago. com). Performink Online also provides news, auditions, classified ads, calendar listings and more on the theatre industry in Chicago (online.performink.com) and Chicago Reader (www.chicagoreader.com) is a good source for theatre news and general job listings and volunteer opportunities. All of these resources can serve as a good starting point for your research and potential move to the Windy City.

One of Chicago's most successful producers, the Goodman Theatre's Roche Schulfer, explains it this way:

> In Chicago, people not only believe that the arts are the fabric of society, they put their money where their mouth is as audience members, patrons, and advocates. All of that makes Chicago a great place to start a new theatre company. Relatively speaking, space, audiences, press coverage, and money are available. The League of Chicago Theatres has created a very collaborative atmosphere among local producers. This is particularly true because the membership embraces Equity, non-Equity, not-for-profit, commercial, and educational theatres. As a result more and more young people are coming to Chicago to start theatres. Some may last only a few years but the long-term success stories are well known: Steppenwolf, Victory Gardens and Chicago Shakespeare among many others were created out of whole cloth by the imagination of artists.

Houston, Texas

The big oil city of Houston has diversified over the years and the arts have generally prospered. The Houston Theater District website (downtownhouston. org/district/theatre) offers links to performance calendars and the big guys in town, including the Alley Theatre, Theatre Under the Stars, the Houston Grand Opera, Broadway Across America, and Uniquely Houston (dedicated to nurturing small and mid-sized arts groups including theatres). Theatreport (www. theatreport.com) is a useful online theatre service with free registration, area theatre news, a theatre directory, newsletters, polls, and forums to help you get the scoop from area residents and professionals. Along with the Alley and the large musical theatres, The Houston Shakespeare Festival, Stages Repertory Theater, The Ensemble Theater, Main Street Theater, A.D. Players, Radio Music Theater, The Company Onstage, Country Playhouse, Theater Southwest, and Theater Suburbia offer diverse employment or, at least, interview or audition opportunities.

Philadelphia, Pennsylvania

The 'City of Brotherly Love' features more than Independence Hall, the Liberty Bell, over 90 museums, colonial churches, row houses, the 76ers, and history simply oozing from the streets. It may be hard to focus on just your career in Philadelphia, but the best place to start might be the Theatre Alliance of Greater Philadelphia (www.theatrealliance.org) as it provides member programs and services and lists jobs, auditions, discount tickets, and area news. You can also email questions to info@theatrealliance.org. And check out the Greater Philadelphia Cultural Alliance at www.philaculture.org.

If you really want to plunge in, you can pick up Irvin R. Glazer's record of 813 theatres constructed in Philadelphia since 1724, *Philadelphia Theatres, A–Z*, but for a look at what's happening today, stick with the Theatre Alliance or the Philadelphia Theatre website at www.philadelphia.com/theater. The Walnut Street Theatre, the Wilma Theater, the Philadelphia Theatre Company, the Arden Theatre Company, and the Prince Music Theater may offer the best audition and employment bets, but there's plenty of other theatre in and around town, including Act II Playhouse, Brat Productions, Azuka Theatre Collective, Bristol Riverside Theatre, 1812 Productions, Freedom Repertory Theatre, McCarter Theatre Center for the Performing Arts, People's Light and Theatre Company, The Philadelphia Shakespeare Festival, Philadelphia Theatre Company, Pig Iron Theatre Company, Random Acts of Theater, Inc., Society Hill Playhouse, and Venture Theatre.

Phoenix, Arizona

It's more than one of the fastest-growing retirement centres in the United States! While discovering Phoenix's pioneering beginnings at the Museum of History, the fabulous Native American exhibits at the Heard Museum, and the must-see Museo Chicano, you can be planning your next career move before you take the educational 'First Friday Art Walk.' The Arizona Commission on the Arts (www.azarts.gov) has a well-organized website and support system that lists opportunities, tools, programs, theatres, and arts organizations in the state (including Phoenix, of course), and links to all of the theatre websites. You can also email info@azarts.gov.

The unique and well-respected Arizona Theatre Company, founded in 1966, certainly leads the way as a major LORT theatre (profiled elsewhere in this book), while the Actors Theatre of Phoenix (founded in 1985) 'strives to be a major voice in the cultural conversation of the Valley of the Sun,' and the Phoenix Theatre (1920) describes itself as 'the oldest arts institution in the State of Arizona and one of the oldest continuously operating arts organizations in the country.' There are also the Arizona Jewish Theatre Company, the Arizona Opera Company, the Black Theatre Troupe, Inc., the Great Arizona Puppet Theater, and the Improbable Theatre Company, with more theatres on the horizon.

San Diego, California

There's a reason that San Diego is the seventh-largest city in America. It's hard to resist the sun, the beaches, the culture, the museums, the zoo, and the easygoing lifestyle of southern California. The venerable theatre The Old Globe, built for $20,000 as part of the California Pacific International Exposition in Balboa Park, has been around since 1935 and is profiled elsewhere in this book. San Diego Repertory Theatre, founded in 1976, is also a major theatre force in the city. Located in historic Horton Plaza, the company operates two theatres as a multi-cultural, multi-disciplinary arts complex. Two strong sources of information are the San Diego Performing Arts League (www.sandiegoperforms.com) and the SD Theatre Scene (www.sdtheatrescene.com). The latter lists auditions and employment opportunities, and offers a 'Who's Who in San Diego Theatre,' play listings, theatre listings, and a host of other handy information and contacts for fifty or so theatre companies, including the Asian American Rep, Center Stage Players, Cygnet Theatre, Lamb's Players Theatre, N Park Vaudeville, OnStage Playhouse, Peter Pan Jr. Theater, Playwrights Project, and Poorplayers Theatre. Of course, the award-winning La Jolla Playhouse is just up the coast. If you are contemplating a move to or a career in San Diego, check out www.sandiegoplaybill.com, which lists over 100 theatres stretching from Carlsbad to Oceanside and beyond.

San Antonio, Texas

A crossroads for the Wild West and a fascinating blending of Native Americans, Germans, Old Mexico, and the Deep South, San Antonio welcomes nearly 20 million annual visitors for the culture, the River Walk, the food, the Spurs, the missions, the largest Mexican marketplace outside Mexico (in Market Square), and, of course, The Alamo. The gorgeous Majestic Theatre, built in 1929, and the Charline McCombs Empire Theatre, built in 1913 (with arts roots dating back to 1879), are used as Broadway tour houses, etc. The website, www.sahearts.com, lists services, arts groups, calendars, and other information pertinent to your research.

Area theatres include the Actor's Theatre of San Antonio at the Woodlawn Theatre, Harlequin Dinner Theatre, Sheldon Vexler Theatre, Jump-Start Performance Co., The Magik Children's Theatre, San Antonio Living History Association, San Pedro Playhouse, Spotlight Theatre and Arts Group, and Steven Stoli's Playhouse. The San Antonio Theatre Coalition (www.satheatre.com) will be a terrific asset if you are considering San Antonio, sharing audition information, season listings, maps to theatres, and a lot of other information. Check out the website or email satheatre@satheatre.com. The website provides detailed information and links to more than thirty member theatres.

Dallas, Texas

Currently the ninth-largest city in America, Dallas is #1 in Texas as a visitor destination spot, and the 384 square miles of rolling prairie have been developed into a sophisticated, cosmopolitan Southwest wonder. Margo Jones started her theatre here and helped launch the whole regional theatre movement. She wanted it to always stay current, so the theatre's name changed annually (Theatre '47, Theatre '48, Theatre '49 – get the picture?). Read 'A Brief History of Theatre in America' on page 29 for the longer story! The Dallas Theater Center and Dallas Children's Theater are the old stalwarts and are descibed elsewhere in this book. The Kitchen Dog Theatre, founded in 1990, and the Undermain Theatre, founded in 1984, have had a local impact, while Dallas is also home to a surprising array of new theatres, including three companies that have surfaced in the new millennium: Uptown Players (2001), Contemporary Theatre of Dallas (2002), and Second Thought Theatre (2003).

A great place to start your research is The Dallas Theatre League (www.dallastheatreleague.com), a professional association of all kinds of theatres. It encourages 'cooperation between theatres and artists to promote common interests and better business methods; as well as to celebrate the expansive diversity of the Dallas Theater community.' The League provides information on health insurance, performance calendars, theatre companies, and direct links to more than 30 theatres, including Rover Dramawerks, Lyric Stage, Shakespeare Festival of Dallas, Echo Theatre, Pegasus Theatre and Wing Span Theatre Company.

San Jose, California

It's not a bedroom community for San Francisco anymore. San Jose is a charming, progressive, coffeehouse-on-every-corner California city that's overshadowed by the Silicon Valley folks who have driven up housing prices astronomically. The computer boom has propelled San Jose into number 10 on the 2005 census list and it's a great city (if you can afford to live there.) Founded in 1980, the San Jose Repertory Theatre is wonderfully placed between the edge of downtown and the university. To research other theatres, Arts Council Silicon Valley (www.artscouncil.org) is a fine resource, listing more than 130 small- to midsize arts organizations and artists countywide. There's also the Artsopolis website (www.artsopolis.com), which bills itself as 'All Arts. Online. Anytime.' It's definitely worth a look.

San Jose area theatres include the Children's Musical Theater San Jose, City Lights Theater Company, Dimension Performing Arts, Easy Street Theatre Company, Teatro Visión, and Tabard Theatre Company, to name a few of the 90 or so in the area.

10 of the friendliest American theatre cities for your consideration

First of all, let's note that this is a wildly subjective list and that, as the regional theatre history section of this book points out, great theatre can happen virtually anywhere. Your best opportunities may be in the theatres closest to your home, while your heart may yearn for theatre companies in more exotic American cities such as Boulder, Colorado; Honolulu, Hawaii; Sedona, Arizona; Lenox, Massachusetts; Hilton Head Island, South Carolina; or Horse Cave, Kentucky! The important point is to research the American theatre, keep your options open, and network like crazy. Here's a start on your research.

Atlanta, Georgia

Atlanta is generally the epitome of Southern hospitality, but don't let all the graciousness lull you – the ever-evolving downtown area can be dangerous, traffic snarls to a crawl during busy times of day, and all that fried food can wreak havoc with your cholesterol count. Still, the home of *Gone with the Wind* boasts affordable housing and a diverse and ambitious theatre scene. The Atlanta Coalition of Performing Arts (www.atlantaperforms.com) comprises nearly 150 groups and almost 400 individual members. The website lists job openings, training programs, auditions, events, and performances.

The Alliance Theatre Company (detailed in Part 5 of this book) is the major LORT theatre in town, while Georgia Shakespeare Festival, 7 Stages, The Shakespeare Tavern, Actor's Express, the Academy Theatre, Dad's Garage Theatre Company, the New Jomandi Productions, and Theatrical Outfit all have substantive and impressive artistic histories and visions. All told, in the area are over 80 theatre operations, a lot of community theatre, interesting family theatre, thriving university theatre, and a compelling spectrum of culturally diverse theatres.

Austin, Texas

Forbes Magazine has listed Austin as the third-best place for singles in America; *Men's Journal* deemed it the fourth-smartest city in America, Child.com listed it twenty-seventh in the 'best cities for families' category, and Sperlings *BestPlaces* put Austin thirty-second in its list of the top fiscally fit places to live. How can you go wrong? Austin is the state capital of Texas and dang proud of it!

So where do you go to find out about the theatre scene? The Austin Creative Alliance (www.austincreativealliance.org) is a nonprofit arts service group that's been helping theatres and theatre folks since 1974. It provides marketing, ticketing, career information, and email updates to members, and hosts Austin's premiere theatre industry awards event: the annual B. Iden Payne Awards.

The Rude Mechanicals may be the best known of the Austin groups but there are many others, including Austin Cabaret Theater, Austin Playhouse, Austin Scottish Rite Theater, ScriptWorks, Austin Shakespeare Festival, Austin Theater Alliance, Biscuits & Gravy Productions, Blue Theatre, Hyde Park Theatre, One World Theater, Oracle Theatre Company, Salvage Vanguard Theater, Theater Action Project, and the Zachary Scott Theater Center to name a few. To help with your research, About Austin Texas (www.austin.about.com/od/theatre) is a good way to get a feel for the area.

Boston, Massachusetts, and surrounding areas

With so many historical stories of adventure on the streets of Boston, it's a wonder anyone goes to the theatre. With the Boston Harbor, immigrant trails, freedom trails, the Black Heritage Trail, live renditions of the Battle of Bunker Hill, battleships, and over 100 museums and attractions, you may have to work a bit to discover Boston's quality stages (such as Huntington Theatre Company and The Lyric Stage Company of Boston) or nearby stages in Cambridge (including Harvard's American Repertory Theatre). The world-renowned Williamstown Theatre Festival, founded in 1954, is also nearby, The Berkshire Theatre Festival has provided fond theatre memories for Stockbridge visitors since 1928, and The Monomoy Theatre has been producing in Chatham/Cape Cod for over fifty years.

StageSource (www.stagesource.org), the Alliance of Theatre Artists and Producers, is definitely worth checking out, as it hosts regional auditions and job expos, posts position openings, provides group health insurance for freelance theatre artists, maintains headshot/résumé files, and publishes a fine resource guide to the theatre community of Greater Boston. In the Alliance's own words, 'Theatre, film and casting companies get access to thousands of theatre artists and to support services, audience development, advocacy . . . Theatre performers, directors, playwrights, designers, technicians, and administrators get access to programs for professional and aspiring theatre artists including access to job information, networking, resources, and more!' Since 1975, ArtsBoston (www.artsboston. org), a nonprofit audience development organization, has served as a collective voice for Boston's diverse arts community and growing audiences. ArtsBoston lists over 90 theatres on its website, ranging from ACT Roxbury, Apollonaire Theatre Company, and Actors' Shakespeare Project to Boston Playwrights' Theatre, Centre Stage Theatre, and the Underground Railway Theater.

Denver, Colorado

Colorado is a heavenly spot for hiking, climbing, fishing, and sports, but is it really a place to pursue a career in the theatre? You bet! The Denver Center Theatre Company is the Tony Award-winner in town, but much more is to be found in the Great Denver Area, which includes Arvada, Boulder, Golden, Fort Collins, Westminster, and a multitude of growing communities that share the gorgeous backdrop of the Rocky Mountains. There are dozens of companies to approach, including the kooky Buntport Theatre, Curious Theatre Company, Impulse Theatre, Paragon Theatre, Su Teatro, The Bug Theatre, Arvada Center for the Arts and Humanities Theatre, and the Germinal Stage.

The *Denver Post*'s theatre news (www.denverpost.com/theater) is clever, comprehensive, and enjoyable to read, and should be a part of your research if you plan to make the Rocky Mountain area your new home. Denver area theatre receives a nice overview on the Denver.com website (www.denver.com/theater), while Colorado Arts Net (www.coloradoarts.net) lists dozens of theatres in the metropolitan Denver/Boulder/Evergreen area, providing addresses, phone numbers, and direct links to websites. It is a very helpful and comprehensive site. Finally, Artslynx Colorado (www.artslynx.org/colorado) provides instant access to over 130 arts groups in Colorado and can save you tons of research time. Boulder, Colorado, is just down the road and home to the Colorado Shakespeare Festival, the Upstart Crow Theater Company, and others.

Minneapolis, Minnesota

If you travel to Minneapolis, you might think that you're in the New York of the Midwest – it's cold in the winter and the people talk funny! No, no, I mean the great selection of theatres, the four distinct seasons, the terrific shopping (the Mall of America), and the beauty of the city. Minneapolis.org (www.minneapolis.org) offers a fine overview on theatre in the land of the lakes, noting that the city has more than 30 venues and nearly 100 theatre groups. The mighty Guthrie Theater and much-revered The Children's Theatre Company reign in Minneapolis, but few folk realize how many other theatres grace the Minneapolis–St. Paul area.

Curtain Rising (www.curtainrising.com), a national website, offers a good starter list of 70 or more theatres in the Minneapolis area. These include Cromulent Shakespeare Company, Great American History Theatre, Gremlin Theatre, GTC Dramatic Dialogues, Illusion Theater, The Jungle Theatre, Minnesota Fringe Theater and Performance Festival, Minnesota Jewish Theater, Mixed Blood Theatre Company, Pangea World Theatre, Penumbra Theatre, Teatro del Pueblo, Theater Latte Da, Theater Mu, and Theatre Unbound. The City of Minneapolis Arts Commission helps foster the development of the arts and lists arts options and theatre links at www.ci.minneapolis.mn.us/leisure.

Orange County, California

If you're independently wealthy or don't mind living with four, five, or six of your best buddies, Orange County is a ripe spot for homegrown theatre nestled between the ocean, the mountains and the quickly vanishing orange groves, strawberry farms, and horse ranches. The median housing prices are among the highest in the nation, you must have a car to survive, and the area has more than its fair share of earthquakes, fires, and mudslides. Still, if you can find a spot with one of America's premier theatres, South Coast Repertory (Costa Mesa), or with one of America's most savvy producing theatres, the Laguna Playhouse (Laguna Beach), you might be able to make ends meet. Otherwise, artistic and production opportunities abound in the myriad 99-seat and smaller theatres where few get paid but most everyone is mightily entertained.

The industrious Arts Orange County (www.artsoc.org) will help open up communications to the theatres with directories, workshops, advocacy, and a friendly, caring core of diligent, determined, and intelligent executives. There's the

Vanguard Theatre, The Maverick Theatre, and Hunger Artists Theatre Company, Fullerton Civic Light Opera and others in Fullerton, Grand Central Theatre and the Monkey Wrench Collective in Santa Ana, Shakespeare Orange County in Garden Grove, and over 50 other producing theatres in the county. Many artists make ends meet working at Disneyland, Knotts Berry Farm, or one of the other higher-budget entertainment venues in the area and create their own work at a friendly neighborhood theatre during their down time.

Orlando, Florida

This area blossomed when Walt Disney World emerged and a host of other entertainment parks, arts-related businesses, and theatre people followed (along with traffic, pollution, rising real estate, and crime). Still, despite the heat and humidity, Orlando is a quick drive to the Gulf of Mexico and the Atlantic Ocean, and an ever-growing home to myriad theatre groups including the very hot Orlando–UCF Shakespeare Festival and The Orlando Repertory Theatre. Of course, the remarkable Cirque du Soleil, the reliable Disney folks, Busch Gardens, Cypress Gardens, Universal Studios Florida, Gatorland, and all the other entertainment parks offer opportunities in a vast array of performance and related fields, and the cost of living in Florida is still reasonable.

Definitely, the best place to start is the Central Florida Performing Arts Alliance (www.artsandculturalalliance.org) which represents individuals, theatres, and businesses, and creates publications, provides facilities, organizes workshops, and advocates on behalf of the arts. The Alliance also lists grant opportunities, workshops and classes, job announcements and casting calls, and produces Unified Auditions to attract artistic and casting directors from around Central Florida. There are over 80 theatre operations of various sizes in Central Florida including the Winter Park Playhouse, Moonlight Players, LA Acting Workshop, Celebration Players, Empty Spaces, Burry Man Productions, Mad Cow Theatre Company, Titusville Playhouse, Women Playwrights Initiative, and Kangagirl Productions.

The Orlando International Fringe Theatre Festival, modeled after Edinburgh, Scotland's famous festival, typically involves over 50 companies offering 'Ten Days of Theatre, Art, Music, and Madness!' The Orlando, Florida, Guide (www.orlando floridaguide.com) also offers a theatre section and terrific links to all the wonders of the city and state.

San Francisco, California

There's an unrivaled fusion of culture, art, theatre, and thrilling American history in San Francisco that is much more than Alcatraz, Chinatown, the American Conservatory Theater, and the Golden Gate Bridge.

San Francisco's nonprofit Theatre Bay Area (TBA) has been telling the story for three decades and it is a good place to start your research. TBA's mission is to unite, strengthen, and promote theatre in the region and it serves more than 300 member theatre companies and 2,900 individual members in the San Francisco Bay Area and Northern California. Check out the website (www.theatrebayarea. org) and the remarkable theatre scene that surrounds one of America's most exhilarating (and expensive) cities. Of course there are theatres with a rich history, including the Magic Theatre, Inc., founded in 1967, A Traveling Jewish Theatre, founded in 1979, and nearby Berkeley Repertory Theatre, founded in 1968. The San Francisco Shakespeare Festival and California Shakespeare Theater are also major forces. Berkeley Rep, the American Conservatory Theatre, California Shakespeare, and San Francisco Shakespeare are all featured in Part 5 of this book, and the website will open the doors to the hundreds of other avant-garde, musical, contemporary, classic, and comedy stages.

Seattle, Washington

There was a time it seemed that everyone in the theatre (outside of New York anyway) wanted to move to Seattle or Chicago to launch their regional theatre careers. Dozens of exciting new theatres were opening, rent and real estate were reasonable, and, with all the rehearsals and performances, prospective theatre professionals thought that they would barely notice the rain. Actually, given the lakes, mountains, ocean, Starbucks, and native beauty of the area, who cares about a little rain? Soon, however, the massive influx of Californians sent real estate sky-high, the actor migration to Seattle resulted in many out-of-work performers, the harsh economics threatened the financial status of many performing arts groups, and today the city may only be a great place to live versus a mind-blowing, theatrical dream world. The best way for you to check out this wet and wonderful world is to hit SeattleActor.com (www.seattleactor.com), a well-managed and attractive website that offers audition information, actor tips, theatre links, advice on the area, reviews, and other convenient information. 'From auditions to reviews, photographers to voice teachers, SeattleActor.com strives to make the most of all of the resources available on the web,' states the website – and does it astonishingly well! Also, for everyone in the business, the City of Seattle's Office of Cultural Affairs (www2.seattle.gov/arts) is worth perusing. Its website links to theatres and forums, and discusses arts funding and workshops. Seattle Shakespeare Company's Stephanie Shine encourages actors to go to Theatre Puget Sound (www.tpsonline.org) for bi-annual unified audition information.

Finally, Seattle Performs (www.seattleperforms.com) lists daily performances, reviews, and good links to over 100 Seattle producers and presenters, including the prestigious ACT Theatre, historic Seattle Repertory Theatre, spunky Seattle Shakespeare Company, dedicated Intiman Theatre, delightful Seattle Children's Theatre, and many others, ranging from the Book-It Repertory Theatre to Macha Monkey Productions and Printers Devil Theatre. Other companies to watch out for are The 5th Avenue Theatre Association, the Village Theatre in Issaquah, Washington Ensemble Theatre, and Theater Schmeater.

Washington, DC

Of course, you could spend the better part of a lifetime simply learning about the theatre and related arts by visiting the National Theatre Archive, the Smithsonian, the Kennedy Center for the Performing Arts, Ford's Theatre, the Washington Area Archive of the Performing Arts, and other historical sites in the area. This is one proud, wild, busy city with a very active and engaged theatre community led by some of the best artists and producers in the business. Fortunately, there are helpful groups to assist you in researching or getting settled in Washington, DC, and one of the best is WashingtonDC.com (www.washingtondc.com/theatre), which has helpful listings of everything in the city, including the theatre. Both this website and the DC Registry (www.dcregistry.com/theatre.html) offer quick links to many area theatres. Established in 1982, the League of Washington Theatres (www. lowt.org) is an association of nonprofit professional theatres for the Washington metropolitan area. It supports theatre and helps create audience awareness and appreciation. The league lists annual auditions and training opportunities, and provides many useful links to the community. The Arena Stage and the Shakespeare Theatre Company generally garner the most attention and theatre awards and have a rich history (detailed later in this book) to back up all the kudos. Still, there's the African Continuum Theatre Co., the GALA Hispanic Theatre, Theater J, the Round House Theatre, the Folger Theatre, The Studio Theatre, the Woolly Mammoth Theatre Company, The Signature Theatre, and over 50 other theatres to research in the nation's capital.

10 service organisations

ALLIANCE FOR INCLUSION IN THE ARTS
(formerly the Non-Traditional Casting Project)
1560 Broadway, Suite #709, New York, NY 10036
Phone: (212) 730-4750. Fax: (212) 730-4820
Email: info@inclusioninthearts.org
www.inclusioninthearts.org
Founded in 1986, Alliance for Inclusion in the Arts is a national nonprofit advocacy organization that strives to address and provide solutions to the problems of racism and exclusion in theatre, film, and television. Its mission is to serve as an expert advocacy and educational resource for full inclusion, focusing on issues of race, culture, ethnicity, and disability. The Alliance continues to effect change by providing assistance with casting, the adoption of inclusive casting language, the use of preferred terminology, audition accessibility issues, roundtables, and resource events. Its staff serves as consultants to the arts and entertainment fields nationwide.

AMERICAN ALLIANCE FOR THEATRE & EDUCATION (AATE)
7979 Old Georgetown Road, 10th Floor, Bethesda, MD 20814
Phone: (301) 951-7977. Fax: (240) 235-7108
Email: info@aate.com
www.aate.com
Theatre educators and theatre artists are well served by the American Alliance for Theatre & Education (AATE), the leading national professional organization for those who use drama in the classroom. Perhaps the best feature of the site for employment seekers is the resources page that details links to influential arts organizations, funding opportunities, playwriting information, professional theatre for youth, professional training and universities, and more.

THE AMERICAN THEATRE WING (ATW)

570 Seventh Avenue, New York, NY 10018

Phone: (212) 765-0606. Fax: (212) 307-1910

Email: mailbox@americantheatrewing.org

www.americantheatrewing.org

ATW is dedicated to supporting excellence and education in theatre and, among its many activities, supports scholarship programs, theatrically related radio and television programs, a theatre intern group, video archives of theatre seminars and discussions, and the annual presentation of the Tony Awards.

ASSOCIATION FOR THEATRE IN HIGHER EDUCATION (ATHE)

P.O. Box 1290, Boulder, CO 80306-1290

Phone: (888) 284-3737, (303) 530-2167. Fax: (303) 530-2168

Email: info@athe.org

www.athe.org

The Association for Theatre in Higher Education is an organization of 1,800 or so individuals and institutions that, in its own words, 'provides vision and leadership for the profession and promotes excellence in theatre education.'

Membership benefits include the online newsletter *ATHENEWS,* the quarterly *Theatre Journal,* and a semiannual journal, *Theatre Topics.* Members of ATHE can also join one or more of 23 focus groups to communicate with other members with similar interests. An annual conference brings everyone together for professional development, workshops, seminars, and myriad sessions of import- ance to the field.

THE DRAMA LEAGUE

520 Eighth Avenue, Third Floor, Suite 320, New York, NY 10018

Phone: (212) 244-9494, outside NYC (877) NYC-PLAY. Fax: (212) 244-9191

Email: audienceproject@dramaleague.org

www.dramaleague.org

With over 3,000 members, The Drama League is, in its own words, 'a service organization for theatre lovers interested in enhancing their understanding and experience of live theatre, and . . . an unparalleled training program for emerging theatre artists.' Member benefits include discounted Broadway, Off-Broadway, and regional theatre tickets, and workshops and seminars with leading figures in the theatre. The League supports new initiatives for young artists through The Directors Project, 'encouraging and training young talents while providing much-needed exposure and essential connections to the professional theatrical community.'

LEAGUE OF HISTORIC AMERICAN THEATRES

334 N. Charles Street, 2nd Floor, Baltimore, MD 21201
Phone: (410) 659-9533, toll-free (877) 627-0833. Fax: (410) 837-9664
Email: info@lhat.org
www.lhat.org
The League of Historic American Theatres (LHAT) has been around since 1976, and is made up of a marvelous group of folk who 'appreciate the cultural and architectural heritage of historic theatres and who work locally and nationally to rehabilitate them.' Theatre operators, managers, preservation activists, architects, structural engineers, design and acoustical consultants, urban planners, restorationists, booking and artist management firms, fundraising consultants, and others are involved, and the website offers insights into the historic theatres that produce around America. Some services, such as the membership list/directory, are benefits available only to dues-paying members, but other services are available to all. If you are seeking a career in theatre management, the LHAT Job Bank may be the perfect resource for you and you can view posted listings without cost. Check the website for details.

NATIONAL ALLIANCE FOR MUSICAL THEATRE (NAMT)

520 Eighth Avenue, #301, New York, NY 10018
Phone: (212) 714-6668. Fax: (212) 714-0469
Email: info@namt.org
www.namt.org
Founded in 1985, NAMT is a national service organization dedicated to musical theatre, with a membership that includes theatre institutions, universities, and independent producers. In its own words, NAMT advances musical theatre by 'nurturing the creation, development, production, presentation and recognition of new musicals and classics; providing a forum for the sharing of resources and information relating to professional musical theatre through communications, networking and programming; and, advocating for the imagination, diversity, and joy unique to musical theatre.'

NEW DRAMATISTS

424 West 44th Street, New York, NY 10036-5298

Phone: (212) 757-6960. Fax: (212) 265-4738

Email: newdramatists@newdramatists.org

www.newdramatists.org

Founded in 1949 and located in the heart of New York City's Theatre District, New Dramatists is, in its own words, 'the nation's oldest nonprofit center for the development of talented playwrights.' A membership organization devoted to cultivating the work of playwrights, New Dramatists provides career support, offers play readings, and develops workshops to help members 'fulfill their potential and make lasting contributions to the theatre.' Over 600 writers have benefited from more than five decades of support. In 2001, the American Theatre Wing and the League of American Theatres and Producers awarded New Dramatists with a special Tony honor for its work. New Dramatists offers playwrights a home base and self-guided laboratory for seven years, free of charge. In the company's own words: 'The playwright company is made up of emerging and mid-career writers who collectively embody an artistic, cultural, ethnic, and geographic diversity rarely found in the American theatre.'

New Dramatists has over 50 current resident playwrights and provides services ranging from the Scriptshare program (which links playwrights with theatres and film companies across the country) to a variety of international exchange programs that foster communication with theatre communities around the world. The many past members who have received Tony Awards for writing include John Patrick in 1954 for *The Teahouse of the August Moon*, Joseph Masteroff in 1967 for *Cabaret*, August Wilson in 1987 for *Fences*, and John Patrick Shanley in 2005 for *Doubt*. Among other alumni are Israel Horovitz, John Guare, William Inge, Lanford Wilson, Suzan-Lori Parks, Paula Vogel, Donald Margulies, Nilo Cruz, and Doug Wright.

Membership applications and additional information about New Dramatists is available online at www.newdramatists.org.

New Dramatists offers full and part-time internships that are provided with small weekly stipends. College credit may be available. Check the website for details.

THEATRE FOR YOUNG AUDIENCES/USA

2936 N. Southport Avenue 3rd Floor, Chicago, IL 60657

Phone: (703) 403-5820. Fax: (773) 529-2693

Email: info@tyausa.org

www.assitej-usa.org

Formerly United States Center for the International Association of Theater for Children and Young People, Theatre for Young Audiences/USA is a national service organization that, in its own words, promotes 'the power of professional theatre for young audiences through excellence, collaboration and innovation across cultural and international boundaries.' The website lists the latest news, links, and information about its member theatres.

UNITED STATES INSTITUTE FOR THEATRE TECHNOLOGY (USITT)

315 South Crouse Avenue, Suite 200, Syracuse, NY 13210

Phone: (800) 938-7488. Fax: (866) 398-7488

Email: info@office.usitt.org

www.usitt.org

Founded in 1960, USITT celebrated its fiftieth anniversary in 2010 as the association of design, production, and technology professionals in the performing arts and entertainment industry. USITT's mission is, in its own words, 'to actively promote the advancement of the knowledge and skills of its members.' The membership hails from the United States, Canada, and 40 other countries and includes scenery, costume, sound, and lighting designers; scenery, costume, sound, and lighting technicians; properties, makeup, and special effects craftpersons; stagehands, architects, theatrical consultants, acousticians, and performing arts educators; and staff and performing arts manufacturers, suppliers, and distributors.

The USITT Annual Conference and Stage Expo attracts over 4,000 people to a different host city each year and generally offers more than 175 sessions featuring design, technology, costume, sound, architecture, management, engineering, and production. Of particular note from a career-planning point of view, the conference offers professional development workshops and a Theatre Conference Employment Service linking employers and applicants by providing computerized job listings, posting of résumés, and scheduled interviews. Also, portfolio reviews provide members with the opportunity to meet individually with professionals in their fields to discuss their portfolios, résumés, and careers with separate sessions for scenery, lighting, costume design, costume technology, props, and technical production. Other marvelous programs include the Stage Management Mentor Project, the Student Volunteer Program, the Tech Olympics, Tech Expo and Stage Expo, and a Young Designers Forum. Check out the comprehensive website for conference information and member services.

10 regional/national audition and job sites

CALIFORNIA EDUCATIONAL THEATRE ASSOCIATION (CETA)

www.cetoweb.org

For 65 years, CETA has provided opportunities in theatre production, teaching and scholarship, and for over 25 years has held auditions and interviews that include professional theatres, colleges and universities. This annual audition and interview opportunity for students pursuing a career in theatre, television, and film is 'a next step for actors and designers to meet casting directors, agents, graduate programs and theatres.' Long associated with the Kennedy Center/American College Theatre Festival (KCACTF), CETA's auditions, interview and scholarship opportunities are all listed on the website along with detailed information about the annual conference. Note that the website, www.cetoweb.org, is for three of the California Educational Theatre Organizations: CETA, the Drama Teachers Association of Southern California (DTASC), and the California State Thespians (CST).

FLORIDA PROFESSIONAL THEATRES ASSOCIATION

P.O. Box 2922, West Palm Beach, FL 33402-2922

Phone: 561-848-6231. Fax: 561-848-7291

www.fpta.net

This statewide service organization represents professional theatre, entertainment, and production companies, as well as individual theatre professionals, by coordinating annual statewide auditions for professional companies looking to hire Equity and non-Equity actors and conducting professional workshops for actors and staffs of professional companies. FPTA also puts together a professional theatre directory, maintains job-bank files and résumé files on theatre professionals, and provides other benefits. State auditions typically include over a dozen companies, among them the Actors' Playhouse (Coral Gables), American Stage (St. Petersburg), Asolo Theatre Company (Sarasota), Caldwell Theatre Company (Boca Raton), Florida Repertory Theatre (Fort Myers), Florida Stage (West Palm Beach), Gorilla Theatre (Tampa), Hippodrome State Theatre (Gainesville), Tampa Bay Performing Arts Center (Tampa), and The Schoolhouse Theater (Sanibel Island).

INSTITUTE FOR OUTDOOR DRAMA (IOD)
NATIONAL OUTDOOR DRAMA AUDITIONS

Institute of Outdoor Drama, East Carolina University College of Fine Arts and Communication, 310 Erwin Building, Greenville, NC 27858-4353

Phone: 252-328-5363. Fax: 252-328-0968

Email: outdoor@ecu.edu

http://outdoordrama.unc.edu

More than 33 original plays throughout the country (based on historical events and performed where they occurred) employ 3,000 actors, singers, dancers, and technicians each summer, and these auditions are a way to discover them all. The Institute of Outdoor Drama (see the IOD section on page 352) sponsors the only combined auditions bringing outdoor historical dramas, performers, and technicians to one place. Around 10 outdoor historical dramas from across the country typically hold annual auditions through the IOD. These are open to anyone 18 or older with previous theatre experience. Jobs generally require a commitment of 9 to 12 weeks, including approximately 2 weeks of rehearsal. Although most jobs are non-union, some companies will hire union actors. Outdoor historical drama is rich in opportunities for performers and technicians to hone their skills. The productions need the expertise of stunt or combat professionals, pyrotechnicians, horseback riders, historians, and others. Staff skilled in design, installation, and maintenance of equipment for sound, electronic vocal reinforcement, special effects, and lighting are also in demand. Companies that have attended in the past include North Carolina's Horn in the West, The Lost Colony, The Sword of Peace and Unto These Hills; Kentucky's The Stephen Foster Story; Ohio's Tecumseh! and Trumpet in the Land; and West Virginia's Hatfields and McCoys and Honey in the Rock. Check the website for additional information and applications.

MIDWEST THEATRE AUDITIONS (MWTA)

470 E. Lockwood Avenue, St. Louis, MO 63119

mwta@webster.edu

The MWTA auditions are Equity and non-Equity combined auditions that typically attract over 600 actors and 100 design/tech/stage management interviewees to the three-day session. Somewhere between 50 and 70 theatre companies attend the annual meeting and past attendees have included everyone from the Utah Shakespeare Festival, Wisconsin's Milwaukee Repertory Theater, and Kentucky's Stephen Foster Story to Montana's Bigfork Summer Playhouse, South Dakota's Black Hills Playhouse, Ohio's Cedar Point Live Entertainment, and Montana's Missoula Children's Theatre.

NEW ENGLAND THEATRE CONFERENCE (NETC)

215 Knob Hill Drive, Hamden, CT 06518

Phone: (617) 851-8535. Fax: (203) 288-5938

Email: mail@netconline.org

www.netconline.org

The New England Theatre Conference serves Connecticut, Maine, Massachusetts, New Hampshire, Rhode Island, and Vermont. It provides professional services, career development, and recognition awards; and nurtures and promotes new theatre activity. Boston drama critic Elliot Norton founded NETC in 1952. Recently, 700 performers auditioned for 60 or so companies at the annual conference. NETC publications include the quarterly NETC News, the scholarly *New England Theatre Journal*, mailing lists, and an *Annual Directory and Resource Book*.

NORTHWEST DRAMA CONFERENCE

www.kcactf.org/7

The Northwest Drama Conference encourages the highest possible standards of theatre throughout the Pacific Northwest and facilitates the interchange of theatre groups, persons and ideas through an annual conference. Check the website for annual information on and downloadable applications about the conference.

ROCKY MOUNTAIN THEATRE ASSOCIATION

www.rmta.net

Star Trek's William Shatner and *All in the Family*'s Carroll O'Connor are just two of the Rocky Mountain Theatre Association members who have gone on to fame and fortune. The RMTA region includes Colorado, Idaho, Montana, Utah, and Wyoming, and represents over 30 organizations, including high schools, colleges, universities, and theatrical businesses. There are around 1,000 members. Founded in 1951, RMTA is one of the oldest regional theatre organizations in America. Students, artists, theatre professionals, and others gather annually at Festivention, a convention that includes workshops, performances, competitions, scholarships, employment opportunities, and informal gatherings. Also, RMTA Scholarship Auditions are conducted for college and university scholarships, while RMTA Employment Auditions are for professional summer stock positions at theatres throughout the Rocky Mountain region. (Check the website for state contacts, addresses, phone numbers, and email addresses.)

SOUTHEASTERN THEATRE CONFERENCE (SETC)

P.O. Box 9868, Greensboro, NC 27429

Phone: (336) 272-3645. Fax: (336) 272-8810

Email: setc@setc.org

www.setc.org

SETC is the regional theatre organization for the Southeastern US, with a membership of 4,000. It hosts the largest theatre convention in the United States, with over 4,000 attendees at the annual March convention. SETC sponsors professional auditions every spring and fall for actors, singers, and dancers. More than 1,000 companies seek performers for both summer and year-round roles at the Spring Convention, where approximately 900 actors audition. Attendees also interview for other theatre positions, attend workshops and theatre festivals, and network with peers, university leaders, and industry professionals. Over the years, this has been a grand place for professionals and university students to seek jobs in all areas of theatre, including acting, production, management, summer internships, and apprenticeships.

Founded in 1949, SETC's member states include Alabama, Florida, Georgia, Kentucky, Mississippi, North Carolina, South Carolina, Tennessee, Virginia, and West

Virginia, but participants in the auditions and activities journey from throughout America and overseas. Many professional companies return annually, including representatives from the Actors Theatre of Louisville, Alabama Shakespeare Festival, Barter Theatre, Berkshire Theatre Festival, and Georgia Shakespeare Festival to Big Fork Summer Playhouse, Williamstown Theatre Festival, Springer Opera House, North Carolina Shakespeare Festival, Naples Dinner Theatre, Walt Disney Entertainment, Universal Japan, Blue Man Group, Dixie Stampede, The Lost Colony, Mill Mountain Theatre, Santa Fe Opera, Trumpet in the Land, and Missoula Children's Theatre.

The Fall Professional Auditions in September offer employment opportunities at over 30 theatre companies for 250 to 300 auditionees. The website provides helpful, instant links to the member companies so you can look them over prior to auditions or interviews. SETC's endowment funds sponsor approximately $15,000 annually in academic scholarships for theatre students. Membership in SETC includes *Southern Theatre,* a quarterly magazine; and *Job Contact Bulletin,* a web posting of technical, academic, administrative and design positions.

STRAWHAT AUDITIONS

#315, 1771 Post Road East, Westport, CT 06880
Email: info@strawhat-auditions.com
www.strawhat-auditions.com
StrawHat assists non-Equity actors and production personnel 'looking to start and continue their professional careers in the theatre.' The StrawHat Auditions are held in New York every spring and over 750 actors and production personnel usually attend, while staff from more than 40 theatres conduct interviews and auditions. Actors audition for summer seasons while potential production personnel have their résumés posted online for phone or onsite interviews. In the company's own words, over one million visitors have checked out www.strawhat-auditions.com 'to learn more about summer stock theatres, review the thousands of actor and technical résumés on our site and to take advantage of casting and information services. The theatres that attend the auditions produce everything from melodrama to plays, history fairs to musicals. Most are summer stock theatres, but some are regionals that run almost year round.' Check the website for registration fees, services and additional information.

UNIFIED PROFESSIONAL THEATRE AUDITIONS (UPTA)

51 S. Cooper Street, Memphis, TN 38104

Phone: (901) 725-0776. Fax: (901) 272-7530

Email: upta@upta.org

www.upta.org

Recently, 939 registered actors and production personnel and 99 companies registered for the annual UPTA auditions that 'offer you access to quality, paying theatres, as well as offering theatres access to quality talent.' Michael Detroit, UPTA's audition coordinator, notes that 'UPTA is a set of auditions and interviews organized for actors, production personnel, and producers so that the greatest number of quality actors and production personnel who are available year-round can be seen by quality professional theatre companies. These auditions are national in scope.' The theatres that attend are offering paid year-round employment, paid jobbed-in employment, or paid internships. Note the word 'paid'! For the regular auditions, actors need to be available for employment throughout the year and meet at least one of the audition requirements (postgraduate degree, Equity or EMC Program member, previous attendee, or endorsement from UPTA or TCG member). For the pre-professional auditions, actors must have an undergraduate degree by a certain date, be available for year-round work, and have their registration signed by their university department chair.

Production personnel must be available for employment throughout the year and meet the same requirements as the actors (except substituting Equity stage manager for Equity/EMC member). See the website for the complete details, requirements, testimonials, and application forms. The conference is held at the longstanding (since 1969) Playhouse on the Square in Memphis, Tennessee. Past company members include everyone from the Alaska Cabin Nite Dinner Theatre, Arkansas Repertory Theatre, Minnesota's Chanhassen Dinner Theatres, and New York's Disney Theatrical Productions to Ohio's Johnny Appleseed Outdoor Drama, Montana's Missoula Children's Theatre, Colorado's Rocky Mountain Repertory Theatre, and Blowing Rock, North Carolina's Tweetsie Railroad, Inc.

10 city and surrounding area websites

Your geographical needs, interests, and plans will determine which of the websites listed below will be of use to you. The websites detail services, programs, auditions, and interviews offered by each organization. The theatre artists, educators, craftspeople, and administrators who comprise these groups have all gotten their acts together and found collaborative ways to organize their careers as well as their productions!

Atlanta Coalition of Performing Arts (Georgia)
www.atlantaperforms.com

Greater AustinCreative Alliance
www.austincreativealliance.org

Baltimore Theatre Alliance (Maryland)
www.baltimoreperforms.org

Central Florida Performing Arts Aliance
www.artsandculturalalliance.org

Cleveland Theater Collective (Ohio)
www.clevelandtheater.com

Illinois Theatre Association
www.illinoistheatre.org

League of Washington Theatres (Washington, DC)
www.lowt.org

New Jersey Theatre Alliance
www.njtheatrealliance.com

Ohio Theatre Alliance
www.ohiotheatrealliance.org

Sacramento Area Regional Theatre Alliance (California)
www.sarta.com

Theatre Alliance of Greater Philadelphia (Pennsylvania)
www.theatrealliance.org

Theatre Auditions in Wisconsin
www.dcs.wisc.edu/LSA/theatre/auditions.htm

Theatre Bay Area (California)
www.theatrebayarea.org

10 unions/alliances/ societies/guilds/agencies

ACTORS' EQUITY ASSOCIATION (AEA)
National Headquarters/Eastern Region
165 West 46th Street, New York, NY 10036
Phone: (212) 869-8530. Fax: (212) 719-9815
www.actorsequity.org

Orlando
10319 Orangewood Boulevard, Orlando, FL 32821
Phone: (407) 345-8600. Fax: (407) 345-1522

The Central Region/Chicago
125 S. Clark Street, Suite 1500, Chicago, IL 60603
Phone: (312) 641-0393; Auditions: (877) 232-1913, ext 815
Fax: (312) 641-6365

The Western Region/Hollywood
6755 Hollywood Boulevard, 5th Floor, Hollywood, CA 90028
Phone: (323) 978-8080. Fax: (323) 978-8081

Actors' Equity Association is the labor union representing more than 45,000 American actors and stage managers working in the professional theatre. In its own words, 'Equity has negotiated minimum wages and working conditions, administered contracts, and enforced the provisions of our various agreements with theatrical employers across the country' for over 90 years. 'The time-honored Equity card is the symbol of a commitment to a theatrical career and represents the highest standards and responsibilities of professionalism. Those who choose to become members implicitly pledge to represent the theatre, the union, and themselves, with integrity and dignity.' From the AEA website you can download a free brochure that describes benefits, membership, and services, or you can write to any of the above addresses. The website also provides applications, contract information, and explanations of three of the most misunderstood big-city agreements, under which actors are paid 'stipends' vs. 'salary.' These Actors' Equity Association showcase agreements include the 'Los Angeles 99-Seat Plan' agreement for smaller LA County Equity–approved theatres that stage no more than six performances a week with unsalaried actors. New York City's 'Basic Showcase Code' allows Equity actors to participate in approved productions without salary if the total production budget is limited to $20,000 and performances are limited to twelve within a four-week period. Tickets are limited to $15 and seating is limited to 99. The 'Seasonal Showcase Code' in New York City is for nonprofit theatres with ticket prices limited to $19, seating limited to 99 seats, and varying stipends. Most of AEA's efforts are focused on collective bargaining and negotiating appropriate salary and working conditions that simply wouldn't have been possible without the diligent work of the Equity management and membership.

AMERICAN FEDERATION OF TELEVISION AND RADIO ARTISTS (AFTRA)
National Office – New York
260 Madison Avenue, New York, NY 10016-2401
Phone: (212) 532-0800. Fax: (212) 532-2242

National Office – Los Angeles
5757 Wilshire Boulevard, Ninth Floor, Los Angeles, CA 90036-0800
Phone: (323) 634-8100. Fax: (323) 634-8194

Membership Department
Phone: (866) 855-5191
Email: membership@aftra.com
www.aftra.org

The American Federation of Television and Radio Artists (AFTRA) represents almost 80,000 performers, journalists, and other artists, as the national labor union for those working in the entertainment and news media. According to AFTRA publications, its 'scope of representation covers broadcast, public and cable television (news, sports and weather, drama and comedy, soaps, talk and variety shows, documentaries, children's programming, reality and game shows); radio (news, commercials, hosted programs); sound recordings (CDs, singles, Broadway cast albums, audio books); non-broadcast and industrial material as well as internet and digital programming.' AFTRA's membership includes a wide array of performers and talent, among them, pop, rock, country, classical, folk, jazz, comedy, Latin, hip hop, rap, and R&B artists; and others in television and radio advertising, non-broadcast video, audio books and messaging, and individuals who provide their skills for developing technologies such as interactive games and internet resources. The union negotiates and enforces over 300 collective bargaining agreements that guarantee minimum salaries, safe working conditions, and health and retirement benefits. The website directs professional performers or broadcasters who wish to join AFTRA to their local offices or to the national membership department at (866) 855-5191, or by email at membership@aftra.com to find out about AFTRA, the services it provides, and how to join.

AMERICAN GUILD OF MUSICAL ARTISTS (AGMA)
1430 Broadway, 14th Floor, New York, NY 10018
Phone: (212) 265-3687. Fax: (212) 262-9088
Email: agma@musicalartists.org
www.musicalartists.org
In its own words, AGMA is 'the labor organization that represents the men and women who create America's operatic, choral and dance heritage,' including the soloist, chorister, dancer/choreographer, and stage manager/stage director. Audition notices for members are published on the website and available from the AGMA Hotline.

AMERICAN GUILD OF VARIETY ARTISTS (AGVA)
363 Seventh Avenue, 17th Floor, New York, NY 10001
Phone: (212) 675-1003. Fax: (212) 633-0097
Email: info@agvausa.com
www.agvausa.com
AGVA represents live performers in variety shows, touring productions, and theme parks, and certain performers in Broadway, Off-Broadway, and cabaret productions, as well as various live performers in variety shows and touring productions.

THE DRAMATISTS GUILD OF AMERICA, INC.

1501 Broadway, Suite 701, New York, NY 10036

Phone: (212) 398-9366. Fax: (212) 944-0420

www.dramatistsguild.com

Over 6,000 dramatic writers are members of The Dramatists Guild of America, the professional association of playwrights, composers, and lyricists. The DGA has categories of membership that include active members, associate members, and student members, with a wide array of benefits and services including contract negotiation advice, access to the business affairs office (with model contracts and agreements), and subscription to *The Dramatist*, the bi-monthly DGA magazine. The members list is a virtual 'who's who' in American theatre.

INTERNATIONAL ALLIANCE OF THEATRICAL STAGE EMPLOYEES (IATSE)

1430 Broadway, 20th Floor, New York, NY 10018

Phone: (212) 730-1770. Fax: (212) 730-7809

www.iatse-intl.org

IATSE is the labor union representing technicians, artisans, and craftspersons in the entertainment industry, including live theatre, motion picture and television production, and trade shows. In its own words:

> The International Alliance of Theatrical Stage Employees, Moving Picture Technicians, Artists and Allied Crafts of the United States, its Territories and Canada was originally chartered by the American Federation of Labor as the National Alliance of Theatrical Stage Employees in 1893. Our name has evolved over the course of 110 years of geographic and craft expansion as well as technological advancement. The current title, adopted in 1995, more accurately reflects the full scope of our activities in the entertainment industry.

> Since the birth of our organization, the stage hands and projectionists have been joined by a great variety of other craftspersons in the numerous branches of the entertainment industry, including motion picture and television production, product demonstration and industrial shows, conventions, facility maintenance, casinos, audio visual, and computer graphics.

NATIONAL ENDOWMENT FOR THE ARTS

The Nancy Hanks Center, 1100 Pennsylvania Avenue, NW, Washington, DC 20506

Phone: (202) 682-5400

www.arts.gov

The NEA has awarded more than 120,000 grants to artists and arts organizations throughout America. The recent 'Shakespeare in American Communities' project marked the largest theatrical tour of Shakespeare in US history. A public agency dedicated to supporting excellence in the arts, the NEA strives to bring the arts to all Americans and provide leadership in arts education. Undergraduate and graduate students and other volunteers may apply for ongoing NEA Internships. Guidelines and application forms for grants and internships are available online.

SCREEN ACTORS GUILD (SAG)

National Contact Information – Hollywood

5757 Wilshire Blvd., Los Angeles, CA 90036-3600

Phone: (323) 954-1600, main switchboard; (323) 549-6648 for deaf performers only: TTY/TTD; 1-800-SAG-0767 for SAG Members outside Los Angeles

Email: saginfo@sag.org

www.sag.org

New York

360 Madison Avenue, 12th Floor, New York, NY 10017

Phone: (212) 944-1030, main switchboard; (212) 944-6715 for deaf performers only: TTY/TTD

In the union's own words, 'Screen Actors Guild is the nation's premier labor union representing actors. Established in 1933, SAG has a rich history in the American labor movement, from standing up to studios to break long-term engagement contracts in the 1940s to fighting for artists' rights amid the digital revolution of the twenty-first century. With 20 branches nationwide, SAG represents nearly 120,000 actors in film, television, industrials, commercials and music videos. The Guild exists to enhance actors' working conditions, compensation and benefits and to be a powerful, unified voice on behalf of artists' rights. SAG is a proud affiliate of the AFL-CIO.'

STAGE DIRECTORS AND CHOREOGRAPHERS SOCIETY (SDC)

1501 Broadway, Suite 1701, New York, NY 10036-5653

Phone: (800) 541-5204; in NYC (212) 391-1070. Fax: (212) 302-6195

Email: info@sdcweb.org

www.sdcweb.org

SDC represents members throughout the US and abroad and is a national independent labor union. SDC has jurisdiction over the employment of directors and choreographers working in Broadway and national tours, Off-Broadway, Off-Off-Broadway, resident theatre/LORT, resident summer stock companies/Council of Resident Stock Theatres (CORST), summer stock and civic light opera, Council of Stock Theatres (COST), Dinner Theatres (DTA), Regional Music Theatre (RMT), Outdoor Musical Stock (OMS), and non-Equity tours. In its own words, SDC 'also provides a special contract to protect members who wish to work for theatres not covered by one of the above mentioned Collectively Bargained Agreements.'

UNITED SCENIC ARTISTS, Local USA 829

29 West 38th Street, 15th Floor, New York, NY 10018

Phone: (212) 581-0300. Fax: (212) 977-2011

Email: usa829@usa829.org

www.usa829.org

USA is the union for designers and artists in the entertainment industry. It has offices in New York, Chicago, Los Angeles, Miami, and New England. According to Larry Robinson, USA-829 historian, the American Society of Scenic Painters, formed in 1891, 'had as its members the foremost scenic designers and artists of the United States,' and in 1918 became United Scenic Artists, Local 829. Collectively bargained agreements include Broadway, LORT, opera and dance, film, television, and special projects.

Part 6

American theatre's major employers

totalling over **1,000** theatre companies

99+ major
American theatres

including League of Resident Theatres (LORT) theatres, non-LORT theatres operating under special agreements, and other notable professional theatres throughout the United States

Many of the most prestigious and artistically ambitious nonprofit professional theatres in the US belong to a national association called the League of Resident Theatres (LORT), and operate under LORT contracts. For various reasons, other large professional theatres operate under special agreements with the unions. LORT companies are listed alphabetically; companies with special agreements are listed in the section that follows; and both types are combined in the alphabetized section of select company profiles. Many more Equity regional theatres operate under Small Professional Theatre contracts (SPT) or Letters of Agreement (LOA), and many of these theatres can be found elsewhere in this book.

League of Resident Theatres (LORT)

1501 Broadway, Suite 2401, New York, NY 10036

Phone: (212) 944-1501, ext. 19. Fax: (212) 768-078

LORT Counsel: Harry H. Weintraub, Esq.

General inquiries: Stephanie Drotar, LORT Management Associate

Email: stephanie@lort.org

www.lort.org

The League of Resident Theatres includes numerous Tony Award-winning companies. Through the member institutions, it includes many of the playwrights, producers, artists, managers, and company members who have created and sustained theatre throughout the United States, as well as the creative forces which continue to drive the future of the American theatre.

LORT is the largest professional theatre association of its kind in the United States, with over 75 member theatres located in every major market in the US, including 29 states and the District of Columbia. LORT theatres collectively issue more Equity contracts to actors than Broadway and commercial tours combined. LORT administers the primary national not-for-profit collective bargaining agreements with Actors' Equity Association (AEA), Stage Directors & Choreographers Society (SDC), and United Scenic Artists (USA), and also deals directly with personnel and management issues involving theatre staff, artists, and craftspeople. LORT members communicate collectively via LORT Counsel's office in New York.

LORT is also a forum for sharing information regarding all aspects of theatre. Semi-annual meetings provide opportunities for LORT members to study, discuss, and exchange information on such non-labor management issues as development, marketing, public relations, education, and technology, as well as providing a forum for developing professional relationships. LORT is also committed to the continued training of current and future LORT Managers. All individual LORT member websites may be accessed through links found at the LORT website: www.lort.org.

The principle objectives of LORT, as stated in its by-laws, are:

* To promote the general welfare of resident theatres in the United States and its territories;

* To promote community interest in and support of resident theatres;

* To encourage and promote sound communications and relations between and among resident theatres in the United States and between resident theatres and the public;

* To afford resident theatres an opportunity to act for their common purpose and interest;

* To act in the interest and on behalf of its members in labor relations and related matters:

    * To serve as bargaining agent for its members in bargaining collectively with unions representing employees of its members;

* To establish and maintain stable and equitable labor relations between its members and unions representing employees of its members;

* To provide guidance and assistance to its members in administering collective bargaining agreements;

* If requested by a member, to handle disputes between members and their employees and/or union representatives; and

* To represent LORT members before government agencies on problems of labor relations.

* To carry on all lawful activities which may directly or indirectly contribute to the accomplishment of such purposes; and

* To communicate with the Federal Government through the National Endowment for the Arts and the American Arts Alliance and to keep those agencies apprised of the needs and status of LORT's membership.

Membership requirements

The following criteria must be met for new membership into LORT:

* The theatre must be incorporated as a nonprofit IRS-approved organization.

* Each self-produced production must be rehearsed for a minimum of three weeks.

* The theatre must have a playing season of twelve weeks or more.

* The theatre will operate under a LORT–Equity contract.

LORT counsel Harry H. Weintraub, Esq. is one of America's unsung theatre heroes and a gentleman who has helped many of America's theatre producers and artists in their quest to produce at the highest levels of the theatre. He helps guide and advise the LORT Executive Committee, which is made up of elected officials from the executive ranks of the membership.

LORT member theatres

Theatre	City	State
ACT THEATRE	Seattle	WA
ACTORS THEATRE OF LOUISVILLE	Louisville	KY
ALABAMA SHAKESPEARE FESTIVAL	Montgomery	AL
ALLEY THEATRE	Houston	TX
ALLIANCE THEATRE	Atlanta	GA
AMERICAN CONSERVATORY THEATER	San Francisco	CA
AMERICAN REPERTORY THEATRE	Cambridge	MA
ARDEN THEATRE COMPANY	Philadelphia	PA
ARENA STAGE	Washington	DC
ARIZONA THEATRE COMPANY	Tucson/Phoenix	AZ
ARKANSAS REPERTORY THEATRE	Little Rock	AR
ASOLO REPERTORY THEATRE	Sarasota	FL
BARTER THEATRE	Abingdon	VA
BERKELEY REPERTORY THEATRE	Berkeley	CA
BERKSHIRE THEATRE FESTIVAL	Stockbridge	MA
CAPITAL REPERTORY THEATRE	Albany	NY
CENTERSTAGE	Baltimore	MD
CENTER THEATRE GROUP	Los Angeles	CA
THE CINCINNATI PLAYHOUSE IN THE PARK	Cincinnati	OH
CITY THEATRE COMPANY	Pittsburgh	PA
CLARENCE BROWN THEATRE COMPANY	Knoxville	TN
THE CLEVELAND PLAY HOUSE	Cleveland	OH
COURT THEATRE	Chicago	IL
DALLAS THEATER CENTER	Dallas	TX
DELAWARE THEATRE COMPANY	Wilmington	DE
DENVER CENTER THEATRE COMPANY	Denver	CO
FLORIDA STAGE	Manalapan	FL
FLORIDA STUDIO THEATRE	Sarasota	FL
FORD'S THEATRE	Washington	DC
GEFFEN PLAYHOUSE	Los Angeles	CA
GEORGE STREET PLAYHOUSE	New Brunswick	NJ
GEORGIA SHAKESPEARE	Atlanta	GA

GEVA THEATRE CENTER	Rochester	NY
THE GOODMAN THEATRE	Chicago	IL
GOODSPEED MUSICALS	East Haddam	CT
GREAT LAKES THEATER FESTIVAL	Cleveland	OH
THE GUTHRIE THEATER	Minneapolis	MN
HARTFORD STAGE COMPANY	Hartford	CT
HUNTINGTON THEATRE COMPANY	Boston	MA
INDIANA REPERTORY THEATRE	Indianapolis	IN
INTIMAN THEATRE	Seattle	WA
KANSAS CITY REPERTORY THEATRE	Kansas City	MO
LAGUNA PLAYHOUSE	Laguna Beach	CA
LA JOLLA PLAYHOUSE	La Jolla	CA
LINCOLN CENTER THEATER	New York	NY
LONG WHARF THEATRE	New Haven	CT
MALTZ JUPITER THEATRE	Jupiter	FL
MANHATTAN THEATRE CLUB	New York	NY
MARIN THEATRE COMPANY	Mill Valley	CA
MCCARTER THEATRE	Princeton	NJ
MERRIMACK REPERTORY THEATRE	Merrimack	MA
MILWAUKEE REPERTORY THEATER	Milwaukee	WI
NORTHLIGHT THEATRE	Skokie	IL
THE OLD GLOBE	San Diego	CA
PASADENA PLAYHOUSE	Pasadena	CA
THE PEOPLE'S LIGHT AND THEATRE COMPANY	Philadelphia	PA
THE PHILADELPHIA THEATRE COMPANY	Philadelphia	PA
PITTSBURGH PUBLIC THEATER	Pittsburgh	PA
PLAYMAKERS REPERTORY COMPANY	Chapel Hill	NC
PORTLAND CENTER STAGE	Portland	OR
PORTLAND STAGE COMPANY	Portland	ME
PRINCE MUSIC THEATER	Philadelphia	PA
THE REPERTORY THEATER OF ST. LOUIS	St. Louis	MO
ROUNDABOUT THEATRE COMPANY	New York	NY
ROUND HOUSE THEATRE	Bethesda	MD
SAN JOSE REPERTORY THEATRE	San Jose	CA
SEATTLE REPERTORY THEATRE	Seattle	WA

SHAKESPEARE THEATRE COMPANY	Washington	DC
SIGNATURE THEATRE COMPANY	Arlington	VA
SOUTH COAST REPERTORY	Costa Mesa	CA
STUDIO ARENA THEATRE	Buffalo	NY
SYRACUSE STAGE	Syracuse	NY
THEATRE FOR A NEW AUDIENCE	New York	NY
THEATREWORKS	Palo Alto	CA
TRINITY REPERTORY COMPANY	Providence	RI
VIRGINIA STAGE COMPANY	Norfolk	VA
THE WILMA THEATER	Philadelphia	PA
TWO RIVER THEATRE COMPANY	Red Bank	NJ
YALE REPERTORY THEATRE	New Haven	CT

20+ select theatres operating under special LORT contracts

ARVADA CENTER FOR THE ARTS	Arvada	CO
BAY STREET THEATRE	Sag Harbor	NY
BERKSHIRE THEATRE FESTIVAL	Stockbridge	MA
CALIFORNIA SHAKESPEARE FESTIVAL THEATER	Berkeley	CA
CONTEMPORARY AMERICAN THEATER FESTIVAL	Shepherdstown	WV
EUGENE O'NEILL THEATER CENTER	Waterford	CT
FULTON THEATRE	Lancaster	PA
MEADOW BROOK THEATRE ENSEMBLE	Rochester	MI
NEW YORK SHAKESPEARE FESTIVAL	New York	NY
NORTH CAROLINA SHAKESPEARE FESTIVAL	Highpoint	NC
NORTHERN STAGE	White River Junction	VT
OREGON SHAKESPEARE FESTIVAL	Ashland	OR
PEARL THEATRE COMPANY	New York	NY
PIONEER THEATRE COMPANY	Salt Lake City	UT
RIVERSIDE THEATRE	Vero Beach	FL
THE SHAKESPEARE CENTER LOS ANGELES	Los Angeles	CA
SHAKESPEARE THEATRE OF NEW JERSEY	Madison	NJ
THE SITI COMPANY	New York	NY

UTAH SHAKESPEARE FESTIVAL	Cedar City	UT
WALNUT STREET THEATRE	Philadelphia	PA
WESTON PLAYHOUSE	Weston	VT

15 notable theatres operating under various other contracts (including past Equity contracts)

THE ACTING COMPANY	New York	NY
AMERICAN PLAYERS THEATRE	Spring Green	WI
ARROW ROCK LYCEUM THEATRE	Arrow Rock	MO
BUSHFIRE THEATRE OF PERFORMING ARTS	Philadelphia	PA
THE CHILDREN'S THEATRE COMPANY	Minneapolis	MN
FREEDOM REPERTORY THEATRE	Philadelphia	PA
THE HUMAN RACE THEATRE COMPANY	Dayton	OH
MILL MOUNTAIN THEATRE	Roanoke	VA
THE NEW HARMONY THEATRE	New Harmony/	
	Evansville	IN
ORLANDO-UCF SHAKESPEARE FESTIVAL	Orlando	FL
THE PHOENIX THEATRE	Indianapolis	IN
THE PUBLIC THEATER/		
NEW YORK SHAKESPEARE FESTIVAL	New York	NY
THE SAN FRANCISCO SHAKESPEARE FESTIVAL	San Francisco	CA
SEATTLE CHILDREN'S THEATRE	Seattle	WA
SEVEN ANGELS THEATRE	Waterbury	CT

THE ACTING COMPANY

P.O. Box 898, New York, NY 10108-0898

630 Ninth Avenue, Suite 214, New York, NY 10036

Administration: (212) 258-3111. Fax: (212) 258-3299

Email: mail@theactingcompany.org

www.theactingcompany.org

Perhaps the *New York Times* says it most succinctly: 'The Acting Company endures as the major touring classical theatre in the United States.' For three decades and nearly 100 productions, The Acting Company has been touring and teaching in America's cities with a touring repertory of classical productions, enjoyable young actors, and teaching artists. The company generally tours to over 50 cities and 70,000 patrons (including more than 25,000 students). The company was founded in 1972 by John Houseman and current producing director Margot Harley with members of the first graduating class of Juilliard's Drama Division. Company alumni include Kevin Kline and Patti LuPone, and past honors include the Obie Award and two Tony Award nominations.

General employment opportunities, internships

Check the website for audition and employment opportunities or email: mail@theactingcompany.org. The Acting Company often needs development, marketing, and production interns and there's a direct link on the website.

ACT THEATRE

A Contemporary Theatre, Kreielsheimer Place, 700 Union Street,

Seattle, WA 98101-4037

Administration: (206) 292-7660. Box Office: (206) 292-7676. Fax: (206) 292-7670

Email act@acttheatre.org

www.acttheatre.org

There's more than great coffee, computers, and the Seattle Repertory Theatre in Seattle. Despite some tough financial times, ACT has managed to hold on to a loyal and dedicated subscriber base, produce the work of many emerging play-wrights, and garner numerous awards including Shubert, NEA, AT&T, and Kennedy Center recognition. ACT was established in 1965 by Gregory and Jean Falls as the first theatre dedicated to new plays in Seattle. After a $30 million renovation in

1996, ACT Theatre opened as Kreielsheimer Place, a blossoming cultural center with four performance spaces, administrative offices, rehearsal spaces, and scene and costume shops. ACT's mission of 'presenting great contemporary stories told through the voices of the uniquely talented community of Seattle actors, designers and artisans' has resulted in artistic productions of the highest caliber and the staging of more than 80 contemporary plays at Kreielsheimer Place including the work of Philip Glass, Donald Margulies, Randy Newman, Joyce Carol Oates, Neil Simon, Stephen Sondheim, Lanford Wilson, David Hare, and Theresa Rebeck.

Career opportunities overview

ACT Theatre posts historical information, a season overview, and information regarding job opportunities, internship programs, auditions, and playwright submissions on its website: www.acttheatre.org.

Casting

ACT holds general auditions for the first 30 non-Equity actors to sign up for the first Thursday of each month. Only one audition is allowed each actor in a six-month period. To participate, actors may schedule an appointment in person, in advance, by coming to the box office lobby of ACT at 700 Union Street, bringing a headshot and résumé. Check out the website for more details. The theatre requests that you not call to schedule or cancel an appointment. To be included in ACT's Actor database, mail one headshot and résumé along with a cover letter to: Casting/ACT Theatre, 700 Union Street, Seattle, WA 98101-4037.

Script submissions

ACT accepts scripts solicited by the literary manager or artistic director and scripts sent by agents and/or other theatre professionals. Northwest playwrights can submit a synopsis of their play and a ten-page sample of their work. ACT does not accept unsolicited scripts. Scripts for The Women Playwrights and FringeACT Festivals are considered through nomination only.

Internships

ACT's internship program 'is committed to fostering the growth and development of dedicated students of theatre in the Seattle area,' offering unpaid internships year-round in development, marketing, literary, and artistic areas. Internship application packets should include a résumé, cover letter highlighting your interest in and prior experience with ACT, and two letters of recommendation. Application materials may be sent via email to act@acttheatre.org or by mail to: ACT Theatre, Internships, 700 Union Street, Seattle, WA 98101-4037. See the website for more instructions.

ACTORS THEATRE OF LOUISVILLE

316 West Main Street, Louisville, KY 40202-4218
Administration: (502) 584-1265. Box office: (502) 584-1205 or (800) 4ATL-TIX.
Fax: (502) 561-3300
www.actorstheatre.org

The Kentucky Derby may have a lock on the equestrian crowd, but when it comes to new plays, theatre critics and artistic leaders love Actors Theatre of Louisville. Actors Theatre was created in 1964 and designated the State Theatre of Kentucky ten years later. In 1976, then-producing director Jon Jory started the internationally celebrated Humana Festival, and for 35 years Actors Theatre of Louisville and Humana Festival have been household names for professional theatre folk. Today, artistic director Marc Masterson leads the company, which, in its own words, 'provides insight into the human experience through live theatre that invigorates minds and emotions,' while its 'vision is to build a home for inspired collaboration where great art sets new standards in excellence that will shape the future of the American theatre. We seek discovery by embracing the artistic spirit in everything we do. We will build a better community by bringing people together to partici- pate in the power of collective imagination.' Annually, nearly 500 performances of about 20 plays lure more than 200,000 audience members to this phenomenon.

Originally housed in a tiny loft (formally the Gypsy Tea Room) and later a railroad station, the theatre eventually settled in a merging of the old Bank of Louisville and the adjacent Myers-Thompson Display Building. The 633-seat Pamela Brown Auditorium opened in 1972 and the 159-seat Victor Jory Theatre opened in 1973. In 1994, a $12.5 million expansion and renovation project included the new 318-seat Bingham Theatre. The venues are funky, the city is welcoming and the combination has produced more than 400 Humana Festival plays that have been celebrated in theatres throughout America. Humana Festival premieres include the Pulitzer Prize-winning plays *Dinner with Friends* (Donald Margulies), *Crimes of the Heart* (Beth Henley), and *The Gin Game* (D.L. Coburn). In 1980, Actors Theatre became the fifth company to receive the Regional Theatre Tony Award. Actors Theatre's international touring program has included more than 1,500 invitational performances in more than 29 cities in 15 foreign countries.

Auditions and interviews

Equity auditions are held in New York, Chicago, or Los Angeles. Auditions are arranged through agent submissions, and scheduled by a casting director in one of those cities. Actors are encouraged to send a photo and résumé to Casting, Actors Theatre, 316 West Main Street, Louisville, KY 40202-4218.

Local auditions include annual open calls for actors of all ages and are held in order to meet actors from the Louisville community. These auditions are generally not for specific roles in productions, but for introductory purposes. To schedule an appointment, call (502) 584-1265 ext. 3005.

General auditions for Equity actors from the region and across the nation are generally held in Louisville twice a year. For details, send a self-addressed stamped envelope to Casting, Actors Theatre of Louisville, 316 West Main Street, Louisville, KY 40202-4218. For a general audition, prepare two monologues of no more than four minutes in combined length. See ActorsTheatre.org for specifics.

Apprentice/internships

The theatre offers an apprentice/intern training program designed to help recent college graduates make the transition from academic to professional theatre. This competitive program results in excellent employment placement for its talented participants. The apprentices, an ensemble of 22 actors, attend regular classes in movement, scene study, text analysis, and audition technique. Apprentices participate in master classes with distinguished artists and administrators, who include agents and casting directors, visiting guest directors, and actors. Apprentices also observe rehearsals, perform in projects throughout the season and work with technical and stage management staff as crew support on mainstage productions. The apprentice season concludes with an acting showcase for industry professionals at the Humana Festival of New American Plays. Additional information can be found at ActorsTheatre.org.

Other internships

Professional interns work directly with department managers and staff, receiving hands-on training in artistic, administrative and production areas of the theatre. Internships are available on a full-time seasonal basis (late August to late May) with possible exceptions on a project or summer intern basis. These are positions that give practical experience and educational guidance in the intern's desired field.

Interns are selected by application and interview. It is possible to arrange course credit with the intern's academic institution. Internship areas include apprentice/ intern company administration, arts administration/company management, public relations, marketing, graphic design, costumes, development, festival manage- ment, lighting, literary management, properties, scenic artistry, sound design, stage management, directing and technical direction.

ALABAMA SHAKESPEARE FESTIVAL

One Festival Drive, Montgomery, AL 36117
Administration: (334) 271-5300. Box office: (334) 271-5353
or toll free (800) 841-4ASF (4273)
Email: info@asf.net
www.asf.net

Shakespeare, Southern writers, and rotating repertory in the Heart of Dixie? The Alabama Shakespeare Festival (ASF), located in the state capital, Montgomery, is the sixth-largest Shakespeare festival in the world and attracts more than 300,000 annual visitors from all 50 states and over 60 countries.

ASF was founded by Martin Platt in 1972 as a summer theatre festival in an old high-school auditorium with no air-conditioning. It blossomed into a 250-acre park and a new two-theatre, 100,000 square-foot, $21.5 million complex in 1985. ASF operates year-round, producing over a dozen productions and 400 annual performances in the 750-seat Festival Stage and 225-seat Octagon.

The Southern Writers' Project (SWP) was founded as an exploration of the South's rich cultural heritage and is dedicated to creating a theatrical voice for Southern writers and topics. Geoffrey Sherman, ASF's producing artistic director, 'is delighted to work with a company that is devoted, as I am, to producing theatrical classics as well as new works. I am dedicated to leading this theatre in continued service to Montgomery, the surrounding community, and all of Alabama,' says

Sherman. 'ASF is one of the best theatres in the country! Every element of the theatre from technical support through design and performance is superb!'

Script submissions
The Southern Writers' Project accepts original scripts and adaptations, not professionally produced, that meet certain criteria posted on the website. Submissions that meet these criteria are considered for the Southern Writers' Project Festival of New Plays, an annual weekend of readings of new work. These plays are then considered for production in subsequent ASF seasons.

Casting, general employment opportunities, internships
Casting, employment, and internship information may be obtained by writing the theatre, emailing info@asf.net, or through the website, www.asf.net.

ALLEY THEATRE
615 Texas Avenue, Houston, TX 77002
Administration: (713) 228-9341. Box office: (713) 220-5700. Fax: (713) 222-6542
Email: webmaster@alleytheatre.org
www.alleytheatre.org

Some legends seem too good to be true, but the Alley Theatre's beginnings have been retold in so many historical documents and LORT conference bar rooms that they deserve a quick synopsis. In 1947, high-school teacher and regional theatre pioneer Nina Vance mailed 214 penny postcards asking, 'Do you want a new theatre for Houston?' Over 100 friends, neighbors, and interested parties gathered in an 87-seat dance studio hidden at the end of an alley . . . Such were the beginnings of the Alley Theatre. Don't believe it? Call me and I'll send you a copy of the postcard! Today, the Alley is one of the few companies in the US that still maintains a resident acting company and tours nationally and internationally.

Recipient of the 1996 Regional Theatre Tony Award, the Alley now performs year-round as a professional resident theatre company in its two-theatre complex in downtown Houston. The Alley has also toured 40 American cities and abroad and has nurtured relationships with exceptional theatre luminaries. Three Alley productions debuted on Broadway in the 1990s: Tennessee Williams's rediscovered Not About Nightingales, and Frank Wildhorn's The Civil War and Jekyll and Hyde.

These creative relationships are tied to Gregory Boyd's arrival as artistic director in 1989. Boyd has produced more than 150 productions at the Alley, including two productions in one season at the Venice Biennale and at New York's Lincoln Center. Dean Gladden was appointed managing director in 2006.

The 824-seat Hubbard Stage and the 'up to 310-seat' Neuhaus Stage are home to 'a wide range of plays, embracing classic, new, and neglected plays.' The Alley has grown tremendously from its humble beginnings and the complex now houses its own costume, scenic and properties, and lighting and sound departments, rehearsal studios, and administrative offices. The Alley maintains a company of more than 100 individuals.

General employment opportunities

The Alley Theatre does not accept unsolicited résumés, and résumés are only accepted for specific job openings. Job openings are usually advertised on the company's website, in the *Houston Chronicle*, or in TCG's *ARTSEARCH*. Check the website for current information
.

Casting/production positions

The Alley Theatre maintains a resident company of actors. When casting productions, the Alley looks first to its company to fill key roles, then auditions on an as-needed basis. The Alley announces auditions on its website as well as through the local media. It maintains a database of select actors seen in auditions or in performance in the past two years. The staff does not keep or return unsolicited headshots and résumés of actors that it has not seen in audition or in performance. For production positions, write to: Production Manager, Alley Theatre, 615 Texas Avenue, Houston TX, 77002. Apply by email or fax: (713) 228-0527. The theatre does not accept phone calls for positions.

Internships

The Alley Theatre's internship program provides college- and graduate school-level students the chance to participate in and observe a professional theatre environment and meet regularly to share experiences and learn about other areas of the theatre. Applicants to the program must be at least 18 years old and have a minimum of 12 hours of college credit. Intern applicants should possess basic computer literacy, excellent teamwork and communication skills, initiative, and flexibility. The Alley doesn't offer internships in design, acting, or directing, although students are encouraged to learn about these areas from their experience in any of the other Alley internships. Intern applications are available online at www.alley theatre.org. Internships at the Alley are non-paying, although other employee perks exist such as free parking and complimentary tickets to Alley productions.

Production internships are available in costumes, lighting and sound, production management, properties, scenery (carpentry and painting), and stage management. Theatre administration internships are available in company management, development, education and community outreach, marketing, and dramaturgy/artistic office.

ALLIANCE THEATRE COMPANY

1280 Peachtree Street NE, Atlanta, GA 30309

Administration: (404) 733-4650. Box office: (404) 733-5000. Fax: (404) 733-4625

Email: allianceinfo@woodruffcenter.org

www.alliancetheatre.org

If Atlanta's many innovative theatres have their say, the South will indeed rise again! Home to many American premieres, the Alliance Theatre Company's mission 'sets the highest artistic standards, creating the powerful experience of shared theatre for diverse people.' Pearl Cleage's *Blues for an Alabama Sky*, Sandra Deer's *So Long on Lonely Street*, and Alfred Uhry's *The Last Night of Ballyhoo* all premiered at the Alliance.

As a resident of the Robert W. Woodruff Arts Center in Atlanta, the Alliance Theatre produces ten productions annually, with performances in the 750-seat Alliance Stage and the 200-seat Hertz Stage, and Theatre for Young Audiences offerings in the 14th Street Playhouse. Richard Dreyfuss, Paul Winfield, Morgan Freeman, and Jane Alexander all appeared on the Alliance Theatre stage. National foundations including the Shubert Foundation, the National Endowment for the Arts, and the Lila Wallace Reader's Digest Fund awarded major funding to the Alliance. The theatre celebrated its 30th anniversary in 1998–99 with the world premiere of Elton John and Tim Rice's *Elaborate Lives: The Legend of Aida*, produced by special arrangement with Walt Disney Theatrical Productions. Current artistic director Susan V. Booth has a strong commitment to the creation of new works for the American theatre, coupled with fresh explorations of classical works.

Casting

Check the website for audition information as it is updated often. The Alliance generally holds two invited casting calls for each of its Alliance Stage and Hertz Stage productions – the first in Atlanta and the second in New York. Additional calls are conducted in other cities on an as-needed basis. Alliance Children's Theatre productions usually feature adult actors and are cast solely out of Atlanta. All open calls held in Atlanta are listed on the Alliance Audition Information Phone Line at (404) 733-4622 and on the Atlanta Coalition of Performing Arts (ACPA) Hotline at (770) 521-8338. New York calls are based primarily on agent submissions through New York casting agencies. Open calls are listed in *Backstage*. The Alliance Theatre participates in the ACPA Unified General Auditions held each spring in Atlanta. For information call ACPA at (770) 521-8338. Actors living in the Atlanta area are encouraged to send headshots and résumés to: Casting Director, Alliance Theatre, 1280 Peachtree Street NE, Atlanta, GA 30309.

Script submissions

The Alliance Theatre accepts submission of full scripts only from literary agents (professional representation). Please note that lawyers and law firms do not qualify as 'professional representation' at this venue. Due to the high volume of submissions and the theatre's desire to respond with care and relative promptness to each one, it is not able to accept unsolicited full manuscripts directly from authors. Playwrights without professional representation may submit a one-page synopsis telling the play's entire story and listing any past productions, a complete list of characters, and up to ten pages of sample dialogue. See the website for additional information or contact the Alliance Theatre Literary Department, by emailing ATCLiterary@woodruffcenter.org or writing to: Alliance Theatre Literary Department, 1280 Peachtree Street NE, Atlanta, GA 30309.

Internships

The Alliance Theatre offers many exciting internship opportunities in acting, administration, artistic, education, literary, and production.

General employment opportunities

Located in midtown Atlanta, Woodruff Arts Center employs over 500 people, is in the heart of Atlanta's Arts District, and includes the Alliance Theatre Company, High

Museum of Art, Atlanta Symphony Orchestra, 14th Street Playhouse and the Atlanta College of Art. More information is available through the Woodruff Center Job Hotline on (404) 733-4323.

ACT/AMERICAN CONSERVATORY THEATER

30 Grant Avenue, Sixth Floor, San Francisco, CA 94108-5800

Administration: (415) 834-3200. Box office: (415) 749-2ACT. Fax: (415) 433-2711

Email: casting – ghubbard@act-sf.org; MFA Program – mfa@act-sf.org;

Summer Training Congress – studioact@act-sf.org

www.act-sfbay.org

So many of America's current artistic leaders and acting company members still point to the American Conservatory Theater's early inspiration as the driving force for their careers in the theatre. Founded in 1965 by William Ball, ACT opened its first San Francisco season at the Geary Theater in 1967.

Many performances were broadcast nationally on PBS, the theatre was awarded the prestigious Regional Theatre Tony Award for outstanding theatre performance and training in 1979, and in 1996 ACT's efforts to develop creative talent for the theatre were recognized with the prestigious Jujamcyn Theaters Award. Today, under the leadership of artistic director Carey Perloff, 'American Conservatory Theater nurtures the art of live theatre through dynamic productions, intensive actor training in its conservatory, and an ongoing dialogue with its community.' The conservatory serves over 1,800 students every year and Danny Glover, Annette Bening, Denzel Washington, Benjamin Bratt, and Winona Ryder are among former students. To quote ACT materials, 'With its commitment to excellence in actor training and to the relationship between training, performance, and audience, the ACT Master of Fine Arts Program has moved to the forefront of America's actor training programs, while serving as the creative engine of the company at large.'

Casting

The casting office at ACT casts ACT's mainstage and second-stage shows, as well as new-play development workshops and readings throughout the season. The staff holds yearly general auditions for Equity actors on a show-by-show basis by invitation only. Check the website for more complete information, but ACT looks for actors 'with significant classical training and performing experience.' ACT works under LORT A and LORT D contracts with Actors' Equity. ACT reps attend both the Equity and non-Equity portions of the Theater Bay Area (TBA) general auditions, which are held yearly in the Bay Area during the winter. For more information about TBA's auditions, call (415) 430-1140 or visit its website at www.theatrebay area.org. Auditions in New York and Los Angeles are also scheduled. Audition announcements are listed on the website and on the Actors' Equity website. Local auditions are also listed in *Theater Bay Area* magazine and on the local Equity hotline; out-of-town auditions are listed in such publications as *Back Stage East* and *Back Stage West*. Casting of actors 18 years old and under is coordinated through ACT's Young Conservatory, which can be reached at (415) 439-2444. ACT accepts submissions of headshots and résumés via mail only (no emails): Casting Office, American Conservatory Theater, 30 Grant Avenue, Sixth floor, San Francisco, CA 94108-5800.

General employment opportunities
Check the website or contact: ACT, Attn: Human Resources, 30 Grant Avenue, San Francisco, CA 94108-5800 or via email at hr@act-sf.org.

Internships
ACT's internship program provides advanced training in both theatre production and administration. ACT interns have access to a variety of benefits designed to integrate them into the artistic life of the company. A monthly series of intern round tables with guest speakers provides an overview of the creative work throughout the organization. The two general categories of ACT internships include artistic and administrative internships and production department internships.

AMERICAN PLAYERS THEATRE
P.O. Box 819, Spring Green, WI 53588
Administration: (608) 588-7401. Box office: (608) 588-2361. Fax: (608) 588-7085
Email: aptmaster@americanplayers.org
www.americanplayers.org
American Players Theatre is a grand, classical theatre in a lovely natural amphitheatre on 110 acres of woods and meadow just off the Wisconsin River in Spring Green, Wisconsin. The 1,148-seat venue is committed to the plays of Shakespeare

and other works ranging from the Greeks to British comedies. When in full production, the company comprises approximately two dozen actors and 120 other staff who produce five plays in rotating repertory. Founded in 1979, the theatre notes that 'our first obligation is to tell a gripping story, our next is to make dramatic poetry the necessary and unpretentious expression of those intimate and otherwise inexpressible moments of human consciousness that great plays explore.'

Casting, general employment opportunities

Generally, APT assembles 13 to 15 Equity actors and 14 to 16 non-union actors (including four to six interns). Actors must have classical experience and/or a deep appreciation for poetic text. Interested actors should submit a photo and résumé in October to be considered for the following season. Auditions are held November through January with the season completely cast by February 1 (except for interns). Specific dates and locations are posted in the fall and APT generally auditions in Chicago, Milwaukee, and New York. Check the website for more details. APT hopes to have its full production staff hired by March each year and a variety of production positions are often open.

AMERICAN REPERTORY THEATRE

Loeb Drama Center, Harvard University, 64 Brattle Street, Cambridge, MA 02138
Administration: (617) 495-2668. Box office: (617) 547-8300. Fax: (617) 495-1705
Email: information@amrep.org
www.amrep.org

The American Repertory Theatre (ART) is a complex combination of a resident acting company and an international training conservatory, operating in association with Harvard University. Recipient of a Pulitzer Prize, a Regional Theatre Tony Award, and a Jujamcyn Award, ART has performed in over 81 cities in 22 states since 1980, and internationally in 21 cities in 16 countries on four continents. Founded in 1980 by Robert Brustein and Robert J. Orchard, ART is in residence at Harvard University's Loeb Drama Center. Diane Paulus is the Artistic Director. ART presents a varied repertoire that includes new plays, progressive productions of classical texts, and collaborations between artists from many disciplines. It is also a training ground for young artists. The theatre's artistic staff teaches undergraduate classes in acting, directing, dramatic literature, design, and playwriting at Harvard, and in 1987 it founded the Institute for Advanced Theater Training. In conjunction with the Moscow Art Theatre School, the institute provides world-class training for graduate-level actors, directors, and dramaturgs.

ART's American and world premieres include works by Christopher Durang, Elizabeth Egloff, Jules Feiffer, Dario Fo, Carlos Fuentes, Philip Glass, David Mamet, Marsha Norman, Han Ong, David Rabe, Paula Vogel, Derek Walcott, Naomi Wallace, and Robert Wilson.

Casting

The American Repertory Theatre is a LORT B theatre. The company's website generally lists Boston Equity Principal auditions for each season. Most recent instructions were to prepare two contrasting two-minute monologues, one contemporary and one classical, and to bring a picture and résumé stapled together. Call (617) 496-2000 ext. 8840 to schedule an appointment. The address for mailing résumés is: Artistic Coordinator, American Repertory Theatre, 64 Brattle Street, Cambridge, MA 02138. There is a separate application/audition process for the Institute for Advanced Theater Training. See the institute home page on ART's website for the specifics.

General employment opportunities

Staff positions, when available, are posted via the Harvard University website at http://jobs.harvard.edu. On that page, select 'American Repertory Theatre (Loeb)' from the list of 'Institutions.'

Internships

ART internships are open to any interested person and are directed toward undergraduate and graduate students as well as young professionals. College credit is available for certain internships through the intern's sponsoring institution. Administrative internships are often available in these areas: artistic, box office, financial, fundraising, house management, literary, marketing/PR, and production. Production internships are available in stage management, crew, scene, shop, paint, costumes, props, lighting, and sound.

ARDEN THEATRE COMPANY

40 N. 2nd Street, Philadelphia, PA 19106

Administrative: (215) 922-8900. Box office: (215) 922-1122. Fax: (215) 922-7011

Email: info@ardentheatre.org

www.ardentheatre.org

The Arden Theatre Company is, in its own words, 'dedicated to bringing to life the greatest stories by the greatest storytellers of all time. We draw from any source that is inherently dramatic and theatrical – fiction, nonfiction, poetry, music, and drama. The Arden presents programs for the diverse greater Philadelphia community that arouse, provoke, illuminate, and inspire.'

The Arden has produced over 24 world premieres, has a full-time paid staff of around 30, boasts the second-highest attendance among Philadelphia's nonprofit producing theatres, and has a budget of around $3 million. Founded in 1988 by Terrence J. Nolen, Amy Murphy, and Aaron Posner, the Arden began producing at the 70-seat Walnut Street Theatre Studio, later co-founded the St. Stephen's Performing Arts Center to provide the company with a larger theatre, and in 1995 purchased a 50,000-square-foot building in Philadelphia's Old City neighborhood. This building includes the 175-seat Arcadia Stage and the 360-seat F. Otto Haas Stage. The Arden operates under an agreement between LORT and Actors' Equity Association. The scenic, costume, lighting, and sound designers in LORT theatres are represented by United Scenic Artists Local USA-829, IATSE.

Casting

The Arden's casting representatives participate in the annual Equity and non-Equity Theatre Alliance of Greater Philadelphia auditions. Additional Arden auditions are held throughout the year by invitation only. To be considered for an upcoming role, please submit your headshot and résumé for attention of: Casting, Arden Theatre Company, 40 North Second Street, Philadelphia, PA 19106. Materials sent via email will not be opened.

Script submissions

The Arden accepts agent submissions and professional recommendations. Playwrights without agents must submit plays following these guidelines: 'Send 20 pages of sample dialogue, a synopsis and character breakdown, the play's production and workshop history, and the playwright/creative team biographies via email to dsmeal@ardentheatre.org. The theatre does not accept unsolicited scripts and only materials submitted as indicated above will be given consideration. See the website for additional details.'

General employment opportunities
The Arden accepts résumés and letters of introduction, sent to: Human Resources, Arden Theatre Company, 40 North Second Street, Philadelphia, PA 19106. Fax: (215) 922-7011. Email: jobs@ardentheatre.org.

Apprentices
The Arden's Professional Apprentice (APA) program provides work in every aspect of the Arden's operations, including artistic direction, marketing, box office, development, production (load-in/strike, run crew, prop/set/costume building, etc.), stage management, finance, and general management. Graduates of the apprentice program include the founders of several new Philadelphia-based theatre companies, a Grammy Award-winning singer/songwriter, and an NEA/TCG Career Development Directors Fellow.

Internships
Internships at the Arden are designed to provide insight and hands-on experience for a specific technical or administrative area of the theatre. Intern applicants should send a copy of their current résumé, including two references, a cover letter discussing their specific areas of interest, and available time commitments to: Internships, Arden Theatre Company, 40 North Second Street, Philadelphia, PA 19106. Email: jobs@ardentheatre.org.

ARENA STAGE
1101 Sixth Street, SW, Washington, DC 20024
Administration: (202) 554-9066. Box office: (202) 488-3300. Fax: (202) 488-4056
Email: arena@arenastage.org
www.arenastage.org
Entering the Arena Stage complex, one can sense the excitement of the audience and experience the sublime history of one of America's most dynamic cultural institutions. Arena Stage is a theatre of firsts – the first regional theatre to transfer a production to Broadway, the first invited by the US State Department to tour behind the Iron Curtain, and the first to receive a Tony Award. Founded in 1950

by Edward Mangum, Zelda Fichandler, and Thomas C. Fichandler, Arena Stage is one of America's oldest, most revered theatre companies. The mission of Arena Stage, in the words of artistic director Molly Smith, is 'to produce huge plays of all that is passionate, exuberant, profound, deep, and dangerous in the American spirit. We are interested in plays of the Americas – North and South – with a special emphasis on living writers. On occasion we may dip into the European canon or other bodies of work for contrast, but for now we are interested in plays associated with American themes, history, culture, and literary traditions.'

From humble beginnings in a former movie house (The Hippodrome Theatre), 1950–55, to the converted hospitality hall of the Old Heurich Brewery in 1956–61, Arena Stage emerged as an industry leader. By the time the company mounted its first production in its new Arena Stage in 1961, Zelda Fichandler's vision and leadership were already the stuff of legend. She helped set the pace for the American regional theatre and contributed to the field for 40 seasons (through 1991) as Arena Stage's producing director.

Today, in the theatre's words, 'Our legacy of world-class productions includes vast epics, charged dramas, rousing musicals, and probing profiles. From the monumental to the developmental, we've helped build the canon of American theatre.'

Casting

Submit to: Casting Director, Arena Stage, 1101 Sixth Street, SW, Washington, DC 20024. Audition requests are evaluated 'based on training and experience and résumés will become permanent in our casting files and should only be updated upon request or if there are additions to credits, or a new photo.' Additional information is available on the website.

Script submissions

Arena Stage only accepts scripts directly from writers with 'bona fide professional representation.' The literary manager does accept queries from writers without representation in the form of a cover letter, résumé, one-page synopsis, and (no more than) ten consecutive pages of sample dialogue. Mail these submissions to: Literary Manager, Arena Stage, 1101 Sixth Street, SW, Washington, DC 20024.

General employment opportunities

Check the theatre website at www.arenastage.org for information.

ARIZONA THEATRE COMPANY

P.O. Box 1631, Tucson, AZ 85702

Administration/Phoenix: (602) 256-6899. Administration/Tucson: (520) 884-8210.

Box Office/Phoenix: (602) 256-6995. Box Office/Tucson: (520) 622-2823.

Fax/Phoenix: (602) 256-7399. Fax/Tucson: (520) 628-9129

Email: info@arizonatheatre.org

www.arizonatheatre.org

This is indeed a tale of two cities! The Arizona Theatre Company is unique among LORT theatres in that it operates at the Temple of Music and Art in Tucson and in the Herberger Theater Center in Phoenix, playing to about 150,000 annually. The Santa Rita Hotel in Tucson, Arizona, provided a home, and Sandy Rosenthal led the way for the Arizona Civic Theatre's first production in 1967. Five years later, in 1972, the troupe developed into a professional company and was soon attracting a number of America's most sought-after directors and managers (including Mark Lamos, David Hawkanson, and Jessica Andrews). Christened the Arizona Theatre Company in 1978, it added a Phoenix presence with productions of *Vanities* and *Equus*, produced full seasons in both cities in 1983–84, was commended by President Ronald Reagan for innovative operations, and was deemed the State Theatre of Arizona in 1990.

Today, according to artistic director David Ira Goldstein, ATC 'seeks to honor the diversity, intelligence and good will of our audience through producing a wide-ranging repertoire of both new and classic works.' The company has attracted new plays and world premieres while developing significant relationships with American playwrights.

Casting

Arizona Theatre Company holds general season auditions for Equity and non-Equity actors in Tucson and Phoenix. Consult the website for dates and details. Appointments are required and audition announcements can usually be downloaded from the site. ATC also conducts production-specific auditions throughout the year in various cities including New York, Los Angeles, Seattle, and San Francisco. Headshots and résumés may be mailed to: Attention: Casting, Arizona Theatre Company, P.O. Box 1631, Tucson, Arizona 85702. Do not email headshots or résumés.

Script submissions

ATC accepts unsolicited play submissions from Arizona writers only. In the submission, Arizona writers must include the full play script, a production history, if any, a brief autobiography of the playwright, and a stamped self-addressed envelope for a reply.

Submissions from out of state must include a synopsis of the play, ten pages of sample dialogue, a production history, if any, a brief autobiography of the playwright, and a stamped self-addressed envelope for a reply. Send all submissions for the attention of: Literary Department, Arizona Theatre Company, P.O. Box 1631, Tucson, Arizona 85702.

Internships

ATC's internship program provides students with training in both theatre administration and production. Many interns have gone on to become successful staff members at Arizona Theatre Company and other professional theatres throughout the country, including the Alley Theatre, Huntington Theatre Company, and Chicago Shakespeare Theater. Administration internships are available in theatre management, artistic, development, marketing/public relations, and company management. Production internships are available in costumes, props, electrics/lighting, sound, scenic, stage management, scenic painting, and production management. See the website for more specifics. Students must be enrolled in a course of study and receive college credit throughout the duration of the internship in order to participate in the professional internship program.

To apply or to request additional information regarding ATC's professional internship program, mail a résumé and letter of interest to: Arizona Theatre Company, Professional Internship Program, P.O. Box 1631, Tucson, AZ 85702.

ARKANSAS REPERTORY THEATRE COMPANY – THE REP

601 Main Street, P.O. Box 110, Little Rock, AR 72201
Administration: (866) 378-0445. Box office: (501) 378-0405 or toll free (866) 684-3737. Fax: (501) 378-0012
Email: info@therep.org
www.therep.org
Bill and Hillary Clinton used to live just round the corner from this ambitious, engaging company and even turned up in the audience from time to time. Cliff

Fannin Baker founded the The Rep in 1976 and dazzled crowds with passionate storytelling and artistic standards that often rivaled the best in American theatre. Today, in its own words, Arkansas Repertory Theatre 'exists to create a diverse body of theatrical work . . . with a focus on dramatic storytelling that illuminates the human journey. The Rep entertains, engages, and enriches local and regional audiences of all ages and backgrounds.' The Rep moved into a new downtown performing arts center in 1988 and was one of the few companies that toured both regionally and nationally. Producing artistic director Robert Hupp heads the company, which operates under an AEA Letter of Agreement.

Casting, general employment opportunities, internships
Arkansas Rep's website, www.therep.org, lists audition sites and positions that are currently open. Additional information is available via email at info@therep.org.

ARROW ROCK LYCEUM THEATRE
P.O. Box 14, Arrow Rock, MO 65320
Administration: (660) 837-3311. Fax: (660) 837-3112
Email: lyceumtheatre@lyceumtheatre.org
www.lyceumtheatre.org
A small white church stands up on the hill on Main Street in Arrow Rock, Missouri, and it's listed as a National Historic Landmark. The 130-year-old church is also billed as 'the oldest professional regional theatre in Missouri' and home to the Arrow Rock Lyceum Theatre. Quin Gresham is the artistic director and the theatre produces musicals and plays for five months out of every year. Check the website for employment and audition information. A recent expansion included a 408-seat air-conditioned venue for the 40-year-old company.

ARVADA CENTER FOR THE ARTS AND HUMANITIES THEATRE
6901 Wadsworth Boulevard, Arvada, CO 80003-9985
Box office/administration: (720) 898-7200. Fax: (720) 898-7204
www.arvadacenter.org
Dedicated on July 4, 1976, the Arvada Center for the Arts and Humanities has grown to become one of the largest cultural attractions in the Denver metro area. It is

home to an Equity theatre, features four shows in the Main Stage theatre and three shows in the Black Box theatre. It also produces highly acclaimed children's theatre. The Arvada Center often wins best musical awards from the Colorado Theater Guild. Gene Sobczak is the executive director and Rod Lansberry the artistic producer.

General employment opportunities
The Arvada Center is a division of the City of Arvada, and all job postings are listed on the city's job line, at http://arvada.org/city-jobs/.

ASOLO REPERTORY THEATRE
5555 North Tamiami Trail, Sarasota, FL 34243
Administration: (941) 351-9010. Box office: (941) 351-8000 or toll free (800) 361-8388. Fax: (941) 351-5796
Email: asolo@asolo.org
www.asolorep.org

Asolo Repertory Theatre's long, rich history has almost fairytale beginnings. In the 1950s, circus leader John Ringling moved a gorgeous eighteenth-century court theatre from Asolo, Italy, to Sarasota, Florida. This building provided a summer home to a Florida State University company in 1960 and the seasonal event (founded by Eberle Thomas, Robert Strane, Richard G. Fallon, and Arthur Dorlag) became known as the Asolo Theatre Festival. In 1966, the company became a year-round, professional LORT Theatre, and in 1973 the entire graduate actor-training program from Florida State University was shifted from the main campus in Tallahassee to Sarasota. The FSU/Asolo Conservatory for Actor Training was born and America's theatre world was almost instantly a better place.

Following 30 years in the historic Asolo Theatre, the acclaimed Asolo Rep moved into the stunning, palm tree-laden FSU Center in 1990, where it began performing in the delightful 500-seat Harold E. and Esther M. Mertz Theatre – a former opera house built in 1903 in Dunfermline, Scotland. The theatre, which had been rescued from a planned razing, was shipped in crates over the ocean and reconstructed piece by piece within the FSU Center. In 1994, the 161-seat Jane B. Cook Theatre was built for the performance of the Conservatory season and for smaller Asolo Rep productions.

In 2006, the Asolo Theatre Company was renamed Asolo Repertory Theatre. This new name was chosen to reflect more accurately their status as one of the only rotating repertory theatres in the country. Asolo Rep and the Conservatory still perform in the FSU Center on two stages, the Mertz and the Cook Theatres, and occasionally both companies perform select shows in the historic Asolo Theatre reopened on the Ringling Museum campus. In the theatre's own words, 'Asolo Repertory Theatre is Florida's premier professional theatre and one of the most important cultural forces in the Southeastern United States.

As a center for theatrical excellence, Asolo Rep crafts the highest quality productions of classical, contemporary and newly commissioned work all performed in the rarest form of rotating repertory. Featuring an accomplished resident company – complemented by distinguished guest artists – Asolo Rep offers audiences a unique and dynamic theatre experience. Under the leadership of producing artistic director Michael Donald Edwards and managing director Linda DiGabriele, this world-class institution has taken a bold step toward the future, building landmark partnerships and collaborations which will add to its success for generations.

About the FSU/Asolo Conservatory

The Florida State University/Asolo Conservatory for Actor Training is a three-year graduate program culminating in a Master of Fine Arts degree. Students are provided with rigorous training in a professional theatre environment. The program combines classroom work of the highest caliber with guest artist workshops and professional production experience. Only 12 students are chosen each year from the thousands who audition in four cities nationwide for the FSU/Asolo Conservatory. Upon graduation, all students are eligible to join Actors' Equity Association and enter the ranks of this country's most highly regarded professional artists. Graduates of the program have appeared on and off Broadway, in regional theatres, in feature films and on television. The program was initiated by the Florida State University School of Theatre in Tallahassee in 1968 and moved to Sarasota five years later to establish a permanent relationship with the Asolo Repertory Theatre.

The FSU/Asolo Conservatory for Actor Training is a member of the University/Resident Theatre Association, Inc. (U/RTA) and is accredited by the National Association of Schools of Theatre.

Casting

Asolo Rep generally holds auditions in Sarasota between May and July for the upcoming season. Asolo Rep also attends the May Florida Professional Theatre Association (www.fpta.net) and the Florida West Coast Theatre Alliance auditions. The dates for FPTA and FWCTA will be announced by those organizations. For Asolo Rep Sarasota auditions, check the website, local newspapers, and other media for updated information.

General employment opportunities, internships, and application information for the Conservatory

Check the website www.asolorep.org or contact: Personnel, Asolo Repertory Theatre, 5555 N. Tamiami Trail, Sarasota, FL 34243; email asolo@asolorep.org.

BARTER THEATRE

127 West Main Street, Abingdon, VA 24210
Mailing address: P.O. Box 867, Abingdon, VA 24212
Administration: (276) 628-2281. Box office: (276) 628-3991. Fax: (276) 619-3335
Email: barterinfo@bartertheatre.com
www.bartertheatre.com

'Imagine a live hog or a dead rattlesnake for the price of admission. We are a theatre of curiosity. And endurance.' So reads the introduction to the Barter Theatre and it's no wonder! The Barter is one of America's oldest theatres and its remarkable beginnings are an integral part of early American theatre history lore. Actor Robert Porterfield attacked the Depression head on when he arrived in southwest Virginia with an audience development approach that would make subscription guru Danny Newman proud. Bartering farm produce for play tickets seemed a logical way to make ends meet, and on June 10, 1933, Barter Theatre opened its doors, charging 40 cents or the equivalent in vegetables, milk, eggs, pigs, chickens, or whatever might be found for trade. To quote Barter historians, 'At the end of the first season, the Barter Company cleared $4.35 in cash, two barrels of jelly, and a collective weight gain of over 300 pounds. Today, at least one performance a year celebrates the Barter heritage by accepting donations for an area food bank.'

The Barter is a founding member of LORT, a charter member of TCG, and was a major force behind the creation of ANTA, the American National Theatre Association. In 1946, the Barter was designated the State Theatre of Virginia, and in 1948, the company was awarded the Tony Award for Regional Theatre. The Barter is home to two theatres, the Barter Theatre (507 seats) and the more intimate Barter Stage II (167 seats). One of artistic director Richard Rose's favorite quotes is from John Eldredge's *Wild at Heart*: 'Don't ask what the world needs. Ask yourself what makes you come alive, and go do that, because what the world needs is people who have come alive.'

Casting

Barter Theatre generally employs a resident company of actors year-round. The company is made up of eight to ten Equity actors and six to seven non-Equity actors (Player Company). Usually Barter Theatre holds local auditions once a year, almost always during the month of December. To attend one of the local auditions, call (276) 619-3338 or consult the website sometime near the middle of November to schedule an audition in December. These auditions usually take place over the course of two days. Also, Barter Theatre occasionally casts in New York City using Paul Russell Casting, is represented at the LORT auditions every year, and at Unified Professional Theatre Auditions and Southeastern Theatre Conference. Résumés may also be sent to: Associate Director, Barter Theatre, P.O. Box 867, Abingdon, VA 24212-0867.

Intern/apprentice auditions

Those interested in Barter's Player Company or the Barter Intern/Apprentice program should check the website for a contact name and number, or send their résumés to: The Barter Player Company Artistic Director, Barter Theatre, P.O. Box 867, Abingdon, VA 24212-0867.

General employment opportunities

Open positions are posted on the company website.

Internships

For information on other internships, contact: The Barter Player Company Artistic Director, Barter Theatre, P.O. Box 867, Abingdon, VA 24212-0867

BAY STREET THEATRE

P.O. Box 810, Sag Harbor, NY 11963

Administration: (631) 725-0818. Box office: (631) 725-9500. Fax: (631) 725-0906

Email: mail@baystreet.org

www.baystreet.org

Sybil Christopher is the artistic director for this 299-seat professional theatre on the Long Wharf in Sag Harbor. Founded in 1991, Bay Street is dedicated to 'presenting new, classic, and contemporary works of the highest professional quality, which challenge as well as entertain, speak to our diverse community, and champion the human spirit. It is our mission to create an artistic haven, where an extended family of established and emerging artists may flourish in an atmosphere free from commercial pressures.' Bay Street operates from March through December, and many of its past premieres or shows in development have moved to Broadway, Off-Broadway, or other venues, including Swingtime Canteen and Three Hotels. Year-round programs include play readings, cabarets, performances and programs for young people, an internship program, acting and playwriting workshops, and the Young Playwrights Festival.

Casting, script submissions, general employment opportunities

Bay Street Theatre accepts scripts by agent submission only. Casting is by agent submission to the casting director for each production. Check the website for audition information, internship overviews, and part-time and full-time positions.

BERKELEY REPERTORY THEATRE

2025 Addison Street, Berkeley, CA 94704

Administration: (510) 647-2900. Box office: (510) 647-2949 or toll free (888) 427-8849. Fax: (510) 647-2976

Email: info@berkeleyrep.org

www.berkeleyrep.org

Berkeley Rep School of Theatre

The Nevo Education Center, 2071 Addison Street

Mailing address: 2025 Addison Street, Berkeley, CA 94704

Administration: (510) 647-2972. Fax: (510) 647-2979

Email: school@berkeleyrep.org

Berkeley, California, in the mid-1960s was the place to be and Berkeley Repertory Theatre founder Michael Leibert made the most of the converted storefront theatre he established in 1968 as the East Bay's first resident professional theatre. In 1980, the company moved into a new complex in downtown Berkeley. Sharon Ott succeeded Leibert in 1984 and Tony Taccone took the helm in 1997. Susan Medak has been managing director since 1990. Recipient of the 1997 Regional Theatre Tony Award, Berkeley Rep has attracted the world's most prestigious theatre artists, including Tony Kushner, Mabou Mines, Anna Deavere Smith, Tadashi Suzuki, Culture Clash, Theatre de la Jeune Lune, George C. Wolfe, and Mary Zimmerman, and has produced premieres of plays by Neal Bell, Philip Kan Gotanda, Lillian Groag, Naomi Iizuka, Heather McDonald, and José Rivera, to name a few.

In 2001, the company added the Roda Theatre, a 600-seat proscenium space to the already existing 400-seat thrust stage. A theatre school in the adjacent Nevo Education Center opened soon after. In the company's own words:

> Berkeley Repertory Theatre seeks to set a national standard for ambitious programming, engagement with its audiences, and leadership within the community in which it resides. We endeavor to create a diverse body of work that expresses a rigorous, embracing aesthetic and reflects the highest artistic standards, and seek to maintain an environment in which talented artists can do their best work. We strive to engage our audiences in an ongoing dialogue of ideas, and encourage lifelong learning as a core community value. Through productions, outreach and education, Berkeley Rep aspires to use theatre as a means to challenge, thrill and galvanize what is best in the human spirit.

Casting

Berkeley Rep is a LORT B theatre. It hires Equity actors and, every once in a while, local non-union actors for large-cast shows. Actors are hired on a show-by-show basis during the season and auditions for individual shows are by invitation only. Auditions are held annually in the late spring and are announced on the Actors' Equity hotline and the Theater Bay Area hotline and magazine. Berkeley Rep also attends the Theater Bay Area general auditions, which are usually held in February. Out-of-town Equity actors who may be visiting the Bay Area are seen on the third Monday of every month. Members of Equity who plan to be in the Bay Area and would like to schedule auditions should check the website for instructions.

Script submissions

Berkeley Rep accepts script submissions only from writers, agents, and theatre artists with whom it has an existing professional relationship. Berkeley Rep is not able to accept unsolicited scripts. The only exception to this policy is for writers whose permanent address is within the Bay Area. Those scripts will be read and assessed. To quote the theatre's materials: 'To determine the kinds of plays in which Berkeley Rep has an interest, you might profitably consult the history page of our website. We are attracted to plays that explore the complexity of contemporary society, that demand the theatre as their form of expression, and that compel our audience toward a significant examination of how and why we live our lives as we do. We are partial toward work in which the language is used for expressing multifaceted ideas in a complex way rather than simply as a vehicle for human psychology.'

Internships

Interns accepted into the program generally begin work in August or September and conclude their residency in June or July. See the website for more information. Internships in artistic and administrative areas include assisting the artistic director, working with the casting director, development and fundraising, education, graphics/web/publications, literary/dramaturgy, company/theatre management, and marketing/box office. Production internships include stage management, production management, scenic construction, scenic art, sound, lighting/electrics, properties, and costumes. Applications are accepted no earlier than January 1 and materials must be received by April 1 for positions beginning the following August. Application forms and additional information are available on the website. All materials should be submitted to: Berkeley Repertory Theatre, Attention Internship Coordinator, 2025 Addison Street, Berkeley, CA 94704.

BERKSHIRE THEATRE FESTIVAL

P.O. Box 797, Stockbridge, MA 01262
Administration: (413) 298-5536. Box office: (413) 298-5576. Fax: (413) 298-3368
Email: info@berkshiretheatre.org
www.berkshiretheatre.org
The Berkshire Theatre Festival is one of the oldest and most respected in the United States. Artistic and executive director Kate Maguire notes that 'the theatre's

access to its past translates into a vivid sense of what it means to be a participant in today's diverse and ofttimes unsettling world.' Between Memorial Day and Labor Day, Berkshire Theatre Festival generally produces four Equity main-stage productions, four to five Unicorn Theatre productions, and one BTF PLAYS! production for young audiences.

Designed and constructed by Stanford White, the Stockbridge Casino opened in 1888 and soon emerged as the center of social and cultural life in Stockbridge. Membership declined in the early 1900s and by 1927 the casino faced demolition. Mabel Choate, the wealthy daughter of one of the casino's founders, bought it for $2,000 and sold it to a group known as the Three Arts Society. Reborn as the Berkshire Playhouse, the 415-seat theatre opened in 1928 with *The Cradle Song*, starring Eva Le Gallienne. Forty-odd years later, the Three Arts Society sold the Playhouse, which was renamed the Berkshire Theatre Festival. The theatre is listed on the National Register of Historic Places.

In the 1970s, the Unicorn Theatre was created as a second stage. In the company's own words, the Berkshire Theatre Festival's mission 'is to sustain, promote, and produce theatre for the community through performance and educational activities. BTF remains dedicated to producing theatre that recognizes its venerable past as well as providing a home for the next generation of the American theatre's creative artists.'

General employment opportunities

BTF is in the far western corner of Massachusetts in the heart of the Berkshires. Résumés are reviewed between December and April and production positions that are often available include assistant to the production manager, Equity stage managers, non-Equity stage managers, technical director, assistant technical director, master carpenter, carpenters, scenic charge, painters, prop master, props, prop artisan, costume shop manager, assistant costume shop manager, drapers, first hand, stitchers, wardrobe supervisors, master electricians, electricians, sound engineer, and assistant sound engineer. Administrative positions include box office clerks, company manager, assistant company manager, and house managers. To apply, check the website for updated information and send a cover letter, résumé, and three references to: General Manager, Berkshire Theatre Festival, P.O. Box 797, Stockbridge, MA 01262.

Apprentices

Descriptions and an application are available on the company website and should be mailed with a cover letter, résumé, and three references to: Administrative Director of Education, Summer Performance Training Program, Berkshire Theatre Festival, P.O. Box 797, Stockbridge, MA 01262-0797. Candidates range in age from 18 to 25 and are interested in pursuing a career in theatre.

The program runs from June to September, is tuition based, and the fee covers room and board. Students may apply for financial assistance from the Betsey McKearnan Scholarship Fund. The program includes training in acting, voice, movement, strength building, and various styles of text work with an emphasis on ensemble work. College credit is available. Apprentices are encouraged to participate at all levels of production, sharing both backstage and onstage responsibilities.

Internships

Each season the Berkshire Theatre Festival offers between 20 and 25 internships. Length of internship varies from three to four months, depending on the position and intern's availability. However, generally from mid-May to Labor Day, interns will work on four main stage Equity productions and four productions on the Larry Vaber Stage in the Unicorn Theatre. Room and board are included. Internships are often available in public relations, marketing, development, accounting, company management, audience services, and general administration. Production internships are often available in scenic art, carpentry, props, costumes, electrics, sound, stage management, general production, and production management.

BUSHFIRE THEATRE OF PERFORMING ARTS

224 South 52nd Street, Philadelphia, PA 19139
Administration: (215) 747-9230. Box office: (215) 747-9230. Fax: (215) 747-9236
Email: thebushfire@verizon.net
www.bushfiretheatre.org

The Bushfire Theatre Company was founded by a group of actors interested in creating theatre opportunities for African American actors. In 1977, Al Simpkins developed the Bushfire Theatre of Performing Arts to produce theatre 'that depicts the African-American experience.' This work includes a wide-ranging repertory of original work, dramas, comedies and musicals. An old vaudeville theatre, The Locust, was renovated into a working theatre and the company has also developed other spaces to make room for a café, the SanKofa Puppet Theatre, a Children's Literary Club, reception spaces, and offices. The complex includes a 419-seat mainstage theatre, a 90-seat workshop space, and a 90-seat café theatre.

CALIFORNIA SHAKESPEARE THEATER

701 Heinz Avenue, Berkeley, CA 94710

Administration: (510) 548-3422. Box office: (510) 548-9666. Fax: (510) 843-9921

Email: info@calshakes.org

www.calshakes.org

Founded in 1974, California Shakespeare Theater is a fully professional, critically acclaimed theatre known for its innovative Shakespeare productions and other re-imagined classics. Its home, the Bruns Amphitheater, located in the East Bay hills between Berkeley and Orinda, was recently named 'one of the most beautiful outdoor performing spaces in America' by the *Wall Street Journal*. Under the leadership of artistic director Jonathan Moscone and managing director Susie Falk, 'Cal Shakes' makes boldly imagined and deeply entertaining interpretations of Shakespeare and the classics; provides in-depth, far-reaching artistic learning programs for learners of all ages; and brings disparate communities together around the creation of new American plays that reflect the cultural diversity of the Bay Area.

Casting, general employment opportunities

The theatre posts information regarding jobs and auditions on its website and makes audition information available through *Back Stage West* and the *Theater Bay Area* magazine. To be included in the actor database, mail one headshot and résumé along with a cover letter to: Casting/California Shakespeare Theater, 701 Heinz Avenue, Berkeley, CA 94710.

Apprenticeships

The theatre offers year-round apprenticeships in the administrative offices and production apprenticeships during the season. See the website or email the theatre for details.

CAPITAL REPERTORY THEATRE

111 North Pearl Street, Albany, NY 12207

Administration: (518) 462-4531. Box office: (518) 445-7469. Fax: (518) 465-0213

Email: officeassistant@capitalrep.org

www.capitalrep.org

Founded in 1980 by Michael Van Landingham and Oakley Hall III, Capital Rep is a LORT company working in the Market Theatre, a 254-seat thrust stage. Located near New York City, the theatre attracts quality artists and takes great pride in its ambitious production history and connection to its community.

In the company's own words, 'The mission of Capital Repertory Theatre is to create a meaningful theatre generated from an authentic link to the community. Capital Repertory Theatre serves as a safehouse for the cultural lives of both artists and the community at large. It fosters the belief that the theatre must serve as an advocate and caretaker of the common threads that bind the American culture together in a world that is defined more and more by diversity. Capital Repertory Theatre strives to bring to life those works that speak to our common cultural heritage as well as new work that expands our perceptions of ourselves and explores new horizons of thought through the medium of theatre.'

Capital Rep producing artistic director Maggie Mancinelli-Cahill notes that 'the theatre must have an authentic connection to its community to be meaningful. As an advocate and caretaker of a culture defined more and more by diversity, Capital Repertory Theatre strives to bring to life works that speak to the commonality of our heritage. Rather than be bound by any specific aesthetic agenda, the theatre at its best entertains, cajoles, and inspires; it enlists its community by providing a wide scope of work drawn from classics, vintage comedy, and drama, as well as from new horizons of human thought and expression. It recognizes the mind and imagination as its most powerful ally.'

General employment opportunities

Capital Rep posts openings on its website. Production and stage management apprentice applicants should contact the production manager for job descriptions and more details about positions: Production Manager, Capital Repertory Theatre, 111 North Pearl Street, Albany, NY 12207; email to prodmgmt@capitalrep.org.

CENTERSTAGE

700 North Calvert Street, Baltimore, MD 21202

Administration: (410) 986-4000. Box office: (410) 332-0033. Fax: (410) 539-3912

Email: info@centerstage.org

www.centerstage.org

Baltimore's leading theatre was founded in 1963 by a community arts committee and operates under a LORT contract in the 541-seat Pearlstone Theatre and 150- to 350-seat Head Theatre. Playing to more than 100,000 annual audience members, this award-winning theatre resides in Baltimore's historic Mt. Vernon Cultural District. In the theatre's own words:

> Centerstage is an artistically driven institution, producing and developing an eclectic repertory in collaboration with leading theatre artists for a diverse audience, interested in challenging, bold, thought-provoking work. Values central to our mission are the centrality of the artistic vision to all institutional decision making, a rigorous pursuit of excellence in all we do, the courage to take risks, and a commitment to diversity. Simply put, artistry – in service both to our artists and our audiences – is Centerstage's top priority.

Artistic director Irene Lewis, set to leave at the end of the 2011 season, leads a company that is 'collectively committed to developing and producing the broadest possible range of theatre.' Centerstage's annual program typically includes a six-play main-stage season that encompasses 're-imagined classical work, new plays, and a music theatre piece.' 'First Look' is a developmental workshop series designed to nurture the artist and to expose audiences to the early stages of new plays. Three 'First Look' readings of plays commissioned by Centerstage, and two additional work-shopped plays, have led to subsequent main-stage productions: Warren Leight's *No Foreigners Beyond This Point* and Lynn Nottage's *Intimate Apparel* (2002–03), James Magruder's version of Molière's *The Miser* (2003–04), Thomas Gibbons's *Permanent Collection* (2004–05), and Motti Lerner's *The Murder of Isaac* (2005–06).

Casting

Centerstage generally auditions local actors twice a year, at general auditions held by the theatre each fall and as part of the Baltimore Theatre Alliance (BTA) area-wide auditions held in June. For more information on the BTA auditions, visit www.baltimoreperforms.org or call (410) 662-9945. Centerstage also participates in annual general Actors' Equity auditions in New York City (posted with AEA). For additional information or questions, check the website or send an email.

Script submissions, new play commissions

Centerstage presents new works on the main stage and has worked with many of America's most exciting emerging playwrights. The company has 'a revitalized play commissioning program' as well as 'First Look', a workshop/play-reading series. The 'First Look' series offers each script a week-long workshop with professional actors and directors, with a reading for the general public.

Internships

Theatre production, arts administration, and dramatic literature are all internship areas and full-time interns must commit to an entire season at Centerstage (usually August/September to May/June). Academic credit is available but arrangements must be made by the intern. Interns may be able to supplement internship stipends by working in the box office, as a child wrangler, or as a bartender in one of the theatre's three cafés. Production interns are usually in electrics, props, scenic art, sound, stage management, costume, or carpentry; and administrative and artistic interns are usually in audience development, company management, development, community programs, front of house, publications, and dramaturgy. To apply for an internship at Centerstage, see the website for the internship form and send it via mail to: Internship Coordinator, Centerstage, 700 North Calvert Street, Baltimore, MD 21202 or via fax to (410) 986-4091. Review the website for other information and options.

CENTER THEATRE GROUP: AHMANSON THEATRE, MARK TAPER FORUM, KIRK DOUGLAS THEATRE

Company Offices at the Music Center Annex,
601 W. Temple Street, Los Angeles, CA 90012
Administration and box office: (213) 628-2772. Fax: (213) 972-4360
Email: taper_manager@ctgla.org
www.centertheatregroup.org

Mark Taper Forum & Ahmanson Theatre at the Music Center
135 N. Grand Avenue, Los Angeles, CA 90012

Kirk Douglas Theatre, 9820 Washington Blvd., Culver City, CA 90232

Center Theatre Group is the umbrella for the Mark Taper Forum, Ahmanson Theatre, and Kirk Douglas Theatre. The group's identity will always be linked to the groundbreaking regional theatre entrepreneur Gordon Davidson, who founded the Mark Taper Forum in 1967 and worked for decades to develop the intimate Kirk Douglas Theatre before handing over the reins to Michael Ritchie in 2005. Mr. Davidson talked of 'enlightening, amazing, challenging, and entertaining our audience' and predicted that the 'future of Mark Taper Forum lies in the pursuit of artistic excellence, aesthetic daring, and community service.' Indeed, Mr. Davidson helped pave the way for America regional theatres. In discussing his first season as artistic director, Michael Ritchie hinted at his future priorities: 'I'm pleased that this – my first season at the Taper – represents what I think is best about an entertaining season of theatre: a wide range of compelling stories to tell, a broad spectrum of theatrical styles in which to tell these stories, and the creativity and artistry of the playwrights, directors, actors, and designers who serve as our guides through these stories.'

According to its historical documents, the Center Theatre Group 'exists to nurture artists by placing the creative process at the foundation of its commitment and by initiating programming that identifies, encourages, and supports these artists and the development of new work; to expose theatre to a wide range of audiences; to enlighten young people, by encouraging their appreciation of theatregoing as a lifelong experience; and to provide artists and a diverse community an unparalleled educational and emotional encounter for generations to come.'

The Music Center opened in 1964 and has been the home for the Mark Taper Forum, Ahmanson Theatre, Los Angeles Opera, Los Angeles Philharmonic, and the Los Angeles Master Chorale. CTG/Ahmanson Theatre productions have garnered Tony Awards and the 1990 Pulitzer Prize for Drama (August Wilson's *The Piano Lesson*). The Mark Taper Forum Pulitzer Prize-winning productions include *The Shadow Box* by Michael Cristofer in 1977, *The Kentucky Cycle* by Robert Schenkkan in 1991, and *Angels in America Part One – Millennium Approaches* by Tony Kushner in 1992. It has also been celebrated with a host of Tony Awards, including the Regional Theatre Award in 1977.

Casting, general employment opportunities
It's probably best to check the website for updates to this process as recent artistic changes have been sweeping through the company.

Script submissions

At press time, the company requested a brief description of the work and from five to ten sample pages along with a résumé, audio tape, and/or reviews. Playwrights may also want to check in with the Literary Department, Mark Taper Forum, 135 N. Grand Avenue, Los Angeles, CA 90012.

THE CHILDREN'S THEATRE COMPANY

2400 Third Avenue South, Minneapolis, MN 55404-3597
Administration: (612) 874-0500. Box office: (612) 874-0400. Fax: (612) 874-8119
Email: info@childrenstheatre.org
www.childrenstheatre.org

Hailed as America's flagship theatre for young people and families, CTC is a nationally respected, award-winning institution founded in 1965. In the institution's own words, 'The Children's Theatre Company exists to create extraordinary theatre experiences that educate, challenge, and inspire young people.' Artistic director Peter C. Brosius joined CTC in 1997. The company produces six mainstage shows annually. These productions include original plays, classic tales, and work from around the globe. Winner of the 2003 Regional Theatre Tony Award, CTC is the first theatre for young people to receive this honor. CTC's production of *A Year with Frog and Toad* received substantial critical acclaim and was nominated for three Tony Awards. Leading playwrights who have worked at the theatre include Kevin Kling, Kari Margolis, Carlyle Brown, Ruth MacKenzie, Nilo Cruz, Jeffrey Hatcher, and Kia Corthron. CTC is based on a campus in south Minneapolis along with the Minneapolis Institute of Arts and the Minneapolis College of Art and Design. It operates on a budget of over $10 million in a 60,000-square-foot facility built in 1974 and has a 746-seat performance space. CTC operates under an AEA Special Agreement contract.

Casting, general employment opportunities, internships

Casting, employment, and internship information may be obtained by writing the theatre, emailing info@childrenstheatre.org, or through the website.

CINCINNATI PLAYHOUSE IN THE PARK

962 Mt. Adams Circle, Cincinnati, OH 45202-1593

Mailing address: P.O. Box 6537, Cincinnati, Ohio 45206-0537

Administration: (513) 345-2242. Box office: (513) 421-3888, (800) 582-3208 (toll-free in Ohio, Kentucky and Indiana). Fax: (513) 345-2254

Email: administration@cincyplay.com

www.cincyplay.com

Perched high on a hill near the rambling Ohio River, the Cincinnati Playhouse in the Park overlooks downtown Cincinnati and thrives as a professional regional theatre that combines artistic excellence and wide-ranging productions for diverse audiences. Producing artistic director Edward Stern, who joined the Playhouse in 1992, rejuvenated the subscriber base, provided a warm home and midwestern hospitality for artists and emerging playwrights, and led his company to a Regional Theatre Tony Award in 2004, as well as a 2007 Tony Award for Best Revival of a Musical, *Company.* 'Theatre must do a better job of developing future audiences,' advises Mr. Stern, who is certainly doing his part, producing nearly year-round to more than 200,000 people. The 626-seat Robert S. Marx Theatre and the 225-seat Thompson Shelterhouse are surrounded by Eden Park.

Meyer Levin's *Compulsion,* directed by David Marlin Jones, the theatre's first artistic director, opened the then 166-seat Shelterhouse theatre in 1960. Over the years, everyone from Scott Bakula, Roscoe Lee Browne, Patty Duke, Bonnie Franklin, and Swoosie Kurtz to Cleavon Little, Donna McKechnie, Estelle Parsons, Anthony Perkins, Charlotte Rae, Lynn Redgrave, Mercedes Ruehl, Susan Stroman, Daniel J. Travanti, Cicely Tyson, and Henry Winkler have touched audiences with their work. The Robert S. Marx Theatre opened in 1968, enabling the theatre to produce in two spaces. In 1973, Harold Scott joined the Playhouse as the first African American artistic director in the history of American regional theatre.

To quote Playhouse historical materials:

> The Playhouse always has contributed to the national stage. Ever since the US premiere of Henry Livings' Eh? in 1966, which subsequently played to great success Off-Broadway, the American theatre has benefited greatly from the vision and craftsmanship now synonymous with the Playhouse. Among its many other premieres are Caravaggio in 1971, directed and produced by Word Baker; Sing Hallelujah!, which enjoyed huge acclaim when it moved to Off-Broadway's Village Gate in 1987; Tapestry: The

Music of Carole King *(1988), which ran Off-Broadway five years later; and* The Notebook of Trigorin *(1996), a newly discovered work by Tennessee Williams which garnered international attention.*

Over the past two decades, the Playhouse has typically produced at least one world premiere production each season, including *In Walks Ed* by Keith Glover in 1997 (nominated for the Pulitzer Prize) and *The Love Song of J. Robert Oppenheimer* by Carson Kreitzer, honored as the runner-up for the 2004 American Theatre Critics/Steinberg New Play Award. Edward Stern and executive director Buzz Ward head a company of more than 70 people, not to mention a board of about 54 trustees, nearly 1,000 volunteers, and more than 15,000 season subscribers. Sadly, the remarkable Edward Stern has announced his retirement effective at the end of the 2011 season.

Casting

The Cincinnati Playhouse in the Park generally participates in the League of Cincinnati Theatres Unified Auditions. For more information or to download an application, visit www.leagueofcincytheatres.com. Check the website or information line for additional audition information.

The Macy's New Play Prize for Young Audiences

A commission fee is granted to the winner of the Macy's New Play Prize for Young Audiences. The play will receive a full production as part of the Playhouse's outreach program. The play should be 50 to 55 minutes in length, written for an audience of elementary, middle, or high-school students, able to tour in a van, and be suitable for a cast of three to five actors (actors can play multiple roles). No musicals. The play cannot have been produced previously. See the website for other guidelines and information.

CITY THEATRE COMPANY

1300 Bingham Street, Pittsburgh, PA 15203
Administration: (412) 431-4400. Box office: (412) 431-CITY. Fax: (412) 431-5535
Email: theatre@citytheatrecompany.org
www.citytheatrecompany.org
City Theatre Company specializes in new plays and has developed work by such national playwrights as Adam Rapp, Christopher Durang, and Jeffrey Hatcher. City

Theatre's mission is 'to provide an artistic home for the development and production of contemporary plays of substance and ideas that engage and challenge a diverse audience.' A 270-seat mainstage and the 100-seat Lester Hamburg Studio are the two key performance spaces and, in 2004, City Theatre purchased a former steel rolling plant for development into parking and other creative uses.

City Theatre opened in 1975 as the City Players sharing its renovated performance space with the newly formed Pittsburgh Public Theater. Unfortunately, by 1978, Pittsburgh Public Theater's schedule necessitated its occupying the space year-round, and the City Players soon moved into a residency with the University of Pittsburgh's Theater's Arts Department and changed its name to the City Theatre. They continued touring, as well as working with the newly formed Three Rivers Shakespeare Festival. The company restructured in 1981, and in 1987 the troupe found a new complex on Pittsburgh's South Side: the former Bingham United Methodist Church. In 1991, the renovated space became City Theatre's new home. In 2001, Tracy Brigden became artistic director. Typically, City Theatre produces seven plays along with 'Momentum': new plays at different stages (a new works festival), and the Young Playwrights Festival (seventh- to twelfth-grade playwrights from the region).

Casting

For casting information, check out the website, set up an appointment at casting @citytheatrecompany.org, and be aware of the audition policies: 'General Equity and non-Equity auditions for City Theatre are held in June. If you are an actor visiting or moving to the Pittsburgh area, and would like to audition, appointments are available at the discretion of the artistic staff.' Headshots and résumé submissions are accepted throughout the year. Send a headshot and résumé to: Attention: Casting, City Theatre, 1300 Bingham Street, Pittsburgh PA 15203.

Script submissions

City Theatre Company commissions new plays, though commissioned playwrights are not chosen through a formal submission or application process. The company approaches writers it has an interest in but 'we are always seeking unproduced work, and we accept full-length original plays, adaptations, translations, musicals, and solo plays.' City Theatre Company does not accept unsolicited scripts, nor does it accept submissions by email. For consideration, playwrights should mail a query letter, along with a résumé, a complete synopsis of the play, a character breakdown, a 15- to 20-page dialogue sample (and demo cassette or CD for musicals), and the development and production history of the play to: Literary Manager and Dramaturg, City Theatre Company, 1300 Bingham Street, Pittsburgh, PA 15203. See the website for additional information.

CLARENCE BROWN THEATRE

206 McClung Tower, Knoxville, TN 37996
Administration: (865) 974-6011. Box office: (865) 974-5161. Fax: (865) 974-4867
Email: cbt@utk.edu
www.clarencebrowntheatre.com

This theatre was founded by Anthony Quayle and Ralph G. Allen on the campus of the University of Tennessee in 1974. The university's historical records document theatre on campus 'as early as 1840.' Unfortunately, there weren't any decent facilities on campus for play production and, over the years, the program improvised with use of the university's Ayres Hall, Tyson House, the downtown Bijou Theatre, Tyson Junior High School, and, in the summer of 1951, a tent (named the Carousel Theatre because of its arena design).

The summer experiment was very successful, and it became clear that a permanent theatre could fill community and university needs. Plans were made, and in December 1951, UT trustees approved the financing for a building designed on the basis of the Carousel tent. During the next two decades the Carousel Theatre program expanded to include 13 productions with attendance in excess of 70,000 people. The Children's Carousel, a series of plays for schoolchildren, began in 1953. The tremendous success of 'Kiddie Carousel,' as it was frequently called, is credited by many with helping to create a strong theatre audience in Knoxville.

In 1973, Clarence Brown and his wife, Marian Spies Brown, donated $12 million as a permanent endowment fund to guarantee a high level of support for professional theatre and theatre study. Using this support and NEA grants, Ralph Allen and Sir Anthony Quayle founded the Clarence Brown Theatre Company and toured throughout the Southeast with a 1976 production of *Rip Van Winkle* (starring Quayle and directed by Joshua Logan), even touring to Washington, DC's

Kennedy Center. Over the years, Zoe Caldwell, Dame Judith Anderson, Mary Martin, Earl Hyman, and Eva Le Gallienne joined the company, and Ralph Allen's Broadway hit *Sugar Babies* was developed at the theatre.

In the 1980s, Thomas Cooke instituted an international exchange and the department hosted and co-sponsored the International Theatre Festival, world premieres, and an actor training conference with attendees from more than 17 countries. The producing artistic director of the theatre is Calvin MacLean.

Casting, script submissions, general employment opportunities
Check the website for audition details or call (865) 974-6725 for additional information.

THE CLEVELAND PLAY HOUSE
8500 Euclid Avenue, Cleveland, OH 44106
Administration: (216) 795-7000. Box office: (216) 795-7000 x4. Fax: (216) 795-7005
www.clevelandplayhouse.com
One of my favorite regional theatre moments was standing outside the historic, monumental Cleveland Play House complex in the 1980s and watching a group of LORT leaders and regional theatre founders (including the joyous and irascible Peter Zeisler) try to hail a taxi after dark in Cleveland, Ohio! Being a good Ohio boy, I was the guy who 'was volunteered' to go out and explain the ways of the Midwest (meaning you had to call for a taxi in Ohio) to this group of big-city producers.

Considered one of the oldest of America's regional theatres (founded in 1915 by Raymond O'Neill), the Cleveland Play House has been key to developing new works for the American theatre while producing a wide-ranging repertoire 'celebrating the creative impulse of the artist,' and creating educational programs for the community. Distinguished artistic director Michael Bloom produces the classics and original work in the 548-seat Kenyon C. Bolton Theatre, the 499-seat Drury Theatre, the 138-seat Charles S. Brooks Theatre, and the 124-seat Studio One. The mission of the Cleveland Play House is 'To inspire, stimulate and entertain diverse audiences in Northeast Ohio by producing plays and theatre education programs of the highest professional standards.'

Casting

The Cleveland Play House generally conducts an open call in the spring for all union and non-union actors from the local area. Check the website for specific information. Following the open call, individuals may be called in to read for specific productions during the course of the season. For actors outside the Cleveland area, the theatre uses Paul Fouquet of Elissa Myers Casting, 333 West 52nd Street, #1008, New York, NY 10019. Actors from out of town who are passing through may call for a general audition, depending on staff availability. All interested actors may send a picture-résumé to: Casting, Cleveland Play House, 8500 Euclid Avenue, Cleveland, OH 44120.

General employment opportunities, internships

Check the website, www.clevelandplayhouse.com.

Script submissions

The Cleveland Play House is committed to commissioning plays, developing them in a 'Next Stage' festival, and producing them on the main stage. The Next Stage Festival generally includes six to eight playwrights, including members of the Playwrights' Unit (a group of Cleveland-area playwrights who meet in a supportive environment to receive constructive criticism and encouragement) and early-career writers who have submitted their work to the director of New Play Development during the course of the previous year. While the Cleveland Play House does not accept unsolicited manuscripts, it does accept a synopsis and ten-page sample. See the website for details. Send your proposal to: Attention: Play Submissions, The Cleveland Play House, 8500 Euclid Avenue, Cleveland, OH 44106-0189.

COCONUT GROVE PLAYHOUSE

3500 Main Highway, Miami, FL 33133

www.cgplayhouse.com

To quote the theatre's website, 'While the . . . season is currently on hold, many exciting things continue to happen in the life of the Playhouse. This is thanks to its committed leaders and the team of professionals who have continued to work daily to keep professional, regional theatre alive at the Playhouse. The momentum is strong and the future is promising. As time moves on, we will post news updates about the Playhouse future, so check back with us soon! Should you have any questions or concerns, please email to saveourplayhouse@aol.com.'

CONTEMPORARY AMERICAN THEATER FESTIVAL AT SHEPHERD UNIVERSITY

P.O. Box 429, Shepherdstown, WV 25443

Administration/box office: (800) 999-CATF or (304) 876-3473. Fax: (304) 876-5443

Email: info@catf.org

www.catf2.org

The Contemporary American Theater Festival is, in its own words, 'dedicated to producing and developing new American theatre.' Producing director Ed Herendeen founded the company in 1991 and has produced over a dozen world premieres and commissioned a number of new plays for staging in historic Shepherdstown, West Virginia. The festival also hosts special events including 'Under the Tent' lectures. Over the years, playwrights Lee Blessing and Keith Glover have worked on new shows with the festival.

General employment opportunities, apprenticeships, internships

The festival lists openings on the website and often hires for a two-month period (June and July). CATF also provides intern- and apprenticeships in all areas of the theatre. These positions are usually listed on the website in December.

Script submissions

The festival generally accepts agent submissions only. To submit a play for consideration, send a one-page synopsis and your biography to: Play Submissions, Contemporary American Theatre Festival, P.O. Box 429, Shepherdstown, WV 25443.

COURT THEATRE

5535 S. Ellis Avenue, Chicago, IL 60637

Administration: (773) 702-7005. Box office: (773) 753-4472. Fax: (773) 834-1897

Email: info@courttheatre.org

www.courttheatre.org

For over 50 years, the Court Theatre has been reinventing the classics with a long line of impressive artists and directors. Between September and June, the theatre generally stages five productions in the 250-seat theatre located on the University of Chicago campus, for around 35,000 patrons. The theatre also plays to 4,000 area students through its high school matinee and in-school residencies programs. Charles Newell has been artistic director of Court Theatre since 1994. He has directed more than 20 productions and embraced the mission of 'discovering the power of classic theatre' along with the vision 'to be the nationally celebrated professional center of excellence for classic theatre at the University of Chicago.' The theatre states its top three strategic goals as being to 'produce provocative, emotive, disciplined, and irreverent classic theatre that attracts national recognition; define and create an environment that is a locus for the finest classic theatre artists; and create opportunities for artists to develop skills in classic theatre that draw the best early-career and established artists to Court.'

Casting
Send headshot-résumé and inquiries to: Casting Director, Court Theatre, 5535 S. Ellis Avenue, Chicago, IL 60637. Non-Equity general auditions are generally listed on the theatre website along with Actors' Equity national and local generals. Watch the Equity website for information or contact info@courttheatre.org.

General employment opportunities
Check the website, www.courttheatre.org.

Internships
Paid theatre internships exist for University of Chicago students in casting, dramaturgy, directing, production management, theatre administration, arts education, development, box office, marketing, and front-of-house management. Descriptions and application guidelines are available on the website.

DALLAS THEATER CENTER
2400 Flora Street, Dallas, TX 75201
Administration: (214) 526-8210. Box office: (214) 880-0202. Fax: (214) 521-7666
Email: info@dallastheatercenter.org
www.dallastheatercenter.org
Frank Lloyd Wright designed the theatre; the brilliant Paul Baker established the company and stayed for 23 years; Texas-native Adrian Hall left an indelible mark;

Ken Bryant embraced the community; Richard Hamburger led the way for years; and Kevin Moriarty is the new artistic director. Committed to reinterpreting the classics, the Dallas Theater Center produces old plays, contemporary plays, and premieres, endeavoring to 'create communal experiences that inspire new ways of thinking and living.' The company ambitiously seeks to nurture and help shape the future of the American theatre. The 466-seat Kalita Humphreys Theater has a thrust stage that melds with the trees on a steep slope above Turtle Creek, while the 500-seat Arts District Theater provides a flexible space.

Casting
Dallas Theater Center general auditions are posted on the website. Headshots and résumés may be submitted by mail at any time to: Casting, Dallas Theater Center, 3636 Turtle Creek Blvd., Dallas, TX 75219.

General employment opportunities
Specific employment opportunities are listed on the website in great detail. The theatre's production department occasionally requires qualified short-term people for scenic construction, costume construction, electrics load-ins, sound load-ins, etc. If this interests you, send your résumé with a cover letter expressing your field(s) of expertise and interest to: Production Manager. Dallas Theater Center, 3636 Turtle Creek Blvd., Dallas, TX 75219-5598.

DELAWARE THEATRE COMPANY
200 Water Street, Wilmington, DE 19801-5048
Administration: (302) 594-1104. Box office: (302) 594-1100. Fax: (302) 594-1107
Email: dtc@delawaretheatre.org
www.delawaretheatre.org
Here's a company that originally produced in an old firehouse before building and moving into its current location on Wilmington's Riverfront in 1985. Mixing the classics with contemporary and new work, the Delaware Theatre Company recruits heavily from New York and throughout the nation. The annual audience of around 40,000 enjoys productions in the theatre's 389-seat proscenium stage. Founded in 1979 by Cleveland Morris and Peter DeLaurier, DTC is the Brandywine Valley's only resident professional theatre.

In its own words, the Delaware Theatre Company 'is a cultural, educational and community-service organization whose purpose is to create theatre of the highest professional quality in Delaware and thereby enrich the cultural life of the area.' Producing director Anne Marie Cammarato has helped the theatre become a critical part of the community's plans to revitalize Wilmington's waterfront and pioneer a master cultural-tourism plan for the Brandywine Valley.

DTC's award-winning educational programs include the Delaware Young Playwrights Festival, theatre classes, a summer theatre camp, and valuable programs using theatre to combat teen addictions and the spread of HIV/AIDS among adolescents, as well as specialized programs for at-risk children who are mentally challenged, hearing-impaired, chronically ill, autistic, incarcerated, and/or who live in group homes.

Casting, general employment opportunities

Casting for actors is conducted by Delaware Theatre Company through its general call and by casting agents. Notices are submitted to breakdown services and posted on the website. Send pictures and résumés to: The Associate Artistic Director, Delaware Theatre Company, 200 Water Street, Wilmington, DE 19801. Other positions are posted on the very well-organized employment section of the company website.

DENVER CENTER THEATRE COMPANY

1101 13th Street, Denver, CO 80204
Administration: (303) 893-4000. Box office: (303) 893-4100 or toll free (800) 641-1222. Fax: (303) 825-2117
Email: feedback@dcpa.org
www.denvercenter.org

One of my favorite theatre moments was watching a spaceship fly on to the stage during artistic director Edward Payson Call's Denver Center production of Shakespeare's *The Tempest* in the early 1980s. A lot of theatrics have taken place in the Rocky Mountains since that time and DCTC has led the way. Founded in 1979 by Donald R. Seawell, the Denver Center Theatre Company celebrated its 25th anniversary, 77 world premieres, and a Tony Award before welcoming artistic director Kent Thompson to the mile-high city in 2005. The four stages in the Helen Bonfils

Theatre Complex include the 778-seat thrust Stage Theatre, the 450-seat Space Theatre in the round, the 250-seat proscenium Ricketson Theatre, and the smaller thrust 200-seat Jones Theatre. DCTC world premieres include *Quilters* (six Tony nominations), *The Immigrant* (both as 1986 play and 2002 new musical), *Black Elk Speaks*, *It Ain't Nothin' but the Blues* (four Tony Award nominations), *Tantalus* (critically acclaimed in its Denver world premiere and six-city United Kingdom tour), and *The Laramie Project.*

Casting, general employment opportunities, internships
Audition and job information is posted on the website and internship opportunities are available in Denver Center Media (film production), the Denver Center Theatre Company, development, graphic design, the National Center for Voice and Speech, public affairs, and public relations.

FLORIDA STAGE
701 Okeechobee Blvd., Suite 300, West Palm Beach, FL 33401
Administration: (561) 585-3404. Box office: (561) 585-3433 (inside Palm Beach County), (800) 514-3837 (outside Palm Beach County). Fax: (561) 588-4708
Email: info@floridastage.org
www.floridastage.org
Florida Stage's mission is 'to engage its audiences through the presentation of a literature of the theatre that deals with issues, ideas, and the innovative use of language, structure, and style' and 'welcomes and encourages each audience member to meet its work with intellect and imagination.' The company is committed to providing a 'creative working environment that nurtures theatre professionals from Florida and across the United States, and promotes the highest levels of artistic quality and achievement.'

The theatre was founded as the Learning Stage in 1985 by actor/director Louis Tyrrell, now producing director. In 1991, the company moved to Manalapan and became the Pope Theatre Company, and in 1997 changed its name to Florida Stage. In 2010, the company moved to West Palm Beach to the Rinker Playhouse at the Kravis Center for the Performing Arts and into a new home in a 255-seat theatre. The company has produced over 15 world premieres including works by William Mastrosimone, Peter Sagal, Nilo Cruz, and Lee Blessing.

Casting

Florida Stage holds general auditions each year for professional actors during the summer months, and callbacks throughout the season as needed. For more information, check out the website and postings on the Actors' Equity Hotline for South Florida. Florida Stage also attends the annual Florida Professional Theatre Association auditions in the early fall. Equity actors visiting the area can call the theatre and the company 'will make every effort to arrange an audition during your stay in South Florida.'

Script submissions

Florida Stage no longer accepts unsolicited play submissions. Agents are asked to email Florida Stage before submitting. Playwrights are asked to work through agents and not submit directly.

Internships

Hands-on training is offered in the areas of administration, costumes, stage management, and in general technical areas. Interns work with Florida Stage professionals as crew, shop labor, and staff assistants. Administration interns are concentrated in the areas of company management, dramaturgy, and general administration. Internships span the production season (October–June). For more information, contact the production manager.

FLORIDA STUDIO THEATRE

1241 North Palm Avenue, Sarasota, FL 34236
Administration: (941) 366-9017. Box office: (941) 366-9000. Fax: (941) 955-4137
Email info@floridastudiotheatre.org
www.floridastudiotheatre.org
Florida Studio Theatre (FST) produces world premieres and contemporary works and has been in operation in Sarasota since 1973. Richard Hopkins has been the artistic director since 1980 and has helped build the theatre into a $4 million operation with 20,000 subscribers, the largest subscription base of any theatre of its size in the country. FST operates three theatres including the 173-seat Keating Mainstage Theatre, the 160-seat Gompertz Theatre and the 109-seat Goldstein Cabaret Theatre.

FST is comprised of six main programs: Mainstage, Cabaret, the Gompertz Theatre, Education, Touring, and New Play Development. The Education wing offers over 20 classes weekly, and FST's touring company reaches over 60,000 students annually in the Southeastern United States and beyond. Through these programs, FST inspires children to write plays for their annual Young Playwrights Festival.

The New Play Development Program receives 8,000 new plays a year from established, emerging, and young writers.   Many new scripts developed through this program reach the Mainstage and Cabaret Theatre stages. Over the years, FST has grown from a small touring company to an institution with three theatres and four buildings, over 45 full-time employees, and 120 guest artists annually.

Casting, hiring and internship opportunities

Florida Studio Theatre holds auditions for projects throughout the season. Anyone interested in auditioning should send photo and résumé (including address and phone number) to: Casting and Hiring Coordinator, Florida Studio Theatre, 1241 N. Palm Avenue, Sarasota, FL 34236-5602. If you have any other questions, please contact James Ashford at (941) 366-9017 or via email: jashford@floridastudio theatre.org. For internship information, check out: www.floridastudiotheatre.org.

FORD'S THEATRE

511 10th Street, NW, Washington, DC 20004
Administration: (202) 638-2941. Box office: (202) 347-4833. Fax: (202) 347-6269
Email: onstage@fordstheatre.org
www.fordstheatre.org

Ford's Theatre, John Wilkes Booth, and Abraham Lincoln will always be darkly linked in America's history, but the theatre itself stands today as a symbol of President Lincoln's love of the performing arts, and is an American treasure visited by schoolchildren and visitors worldwide. Under the leadership of director Paul R. Tetreault, Ford's Theatre has been recognized for the superior quality of its artistic programming. From the nationally acclaimed *Big River* to the world premieres of *Meet John Doe* and *The Heavens Are Hung in Black*, Ford's Theatre is making its mark on the American theatre landscape. For its accomplishment, the organiz-ation was honored in 2008 with the National Medal of Arts. Ford's Theatre and museum underwent a major renovation wherein accessibility to all levels of the building was improved, a new lobby and entrance was added and the stage was reconstructed to allow for improved lighting and sound capabilities.

General employment opportunities and internships
Employment and internship opportunities are posted on the company website.

FREEDOM REPERTORY THEATRE
1346 North Broad Street, Philadelphia, PA 19121
Administration: (215) 765-2793. Box office: (215) 978-8497. Fax: (215) 765-4191
www.freedomtheatre.org
Rooted in the African American tradition, this North Philadelphia institution is 'dedicated to achieving artistic excellence in professional theatre and performing arts training.' The theatre's home is an historic mansion that once belonged to actor Edwin Forrest. Founded in 1966 by John Allen, the theatre's producing artistic director is Walter Dallas. The 299-seat theatre has attracted a remarkable array of artists, including Grover Washington, Jr., August Wilson, Ntozake Shange, and Lynn Nottage. Freedom Repertory also serves 'as a learning laboratory and a model of excellence' for the Performing Arts Training Program which has provided over 10,000 students with 'a safe, challenging environment in which to learn acting, dance, and vocal arts.' Freedom Rep produces four annual productions each year in the John E. Allen, Jr. Theatre.

General employment opportunities, apprenticeships, internships
Check the website at www.freedomtheatre.org or call the theatre for additional information.

GEFFEN PLAYHOUSE
10886 Le Conte Avenue, Los Angeles, CA 90024-3021
Administration: (310) 208-6500. Box office: (310) 208-5454. Fax: (310) 208-0341
Email: boxoffice@geffenplayhouse.com
www.geffenplayhouse.com
The warm and intimate main stage of the Geffen Playhouse is a grand spot to experience contemporary plays and the classics, while the new Audrey Skirball-

Kenis Theater at the Geffen Playhouse is set to house and develop new works for Los Angeles. The Geffen's ambitious ten-year project of producing a 'Festival of American Originals' is underway and audiences continue to flock to the cutting-edge work produced on the fringe of the UCLA campus. Past artists read like a 'who's who' of the theatre, including Marcel Marceau, Uta Hagen, David Hyde Pierce, Frank Langella, Steve Martin, John Mahoney, Jason Alexander, Peter Falk, Debbie Allen, Annette Bening, Donald Margulies, Neil Simon, and many more. The experienced duo of producing director Gilbert Cates and artistic director Randall Arney have established the Geffen as one of Los Angeles's premier theatres.

Casting, general employment opportunities, internships
Check the website or drop a note to the Geffen for updated employment information.

GEORGE STREET PLAYHOUSE
9 Livingston Avenue, New Brunswick, NJ 08901
Administration: (732) 846-2895. Box office: (732) 246-7717. Fax: (732) 247-9151
www.georgestplayhouse.org
In 2003, *American Theatre* magazine noted that three of the top fifteen plays produced in America's regional theatres were developed at the George Street Playhouse. That's a great start to the twenty-first century! Founded in 1974 by Eric Krebs and currently helmed by artistic director David Saint, George Street Play-house is committed to the production of new and established plays.

The Playhouse serves an audience of approximately 140,000 through a Main Stage Series (in a 367-seat proscenium/thrust stage), education, and outreach initiatives with a staff of approximately 50 artists, technicians, and administrators. The mission of George Street Playhouse is 'to enrich people's lives by producing world-class theatre' and the Playhouse seeks to produce the 'highest quality of intellectually and emotionally challenging new works, re-imagined classics, and educational programming that speak with relevance to society; to serve as a vital cultural institution in New Jersey and a creative force nationally; to positively shape and be shaped by the diverse character of our community; and to create a nurturing home for the highest level of professional in the arts.'

Casting

George Street currently uses McCorkle Casting, Ltd. for Equity-actor casting needs. For non-Equity actors, auditions are held at the annual New Jersey Theatre Alliance Combined Auditions. Contact the Alliance for more information or visit its website at www.njtheatrealliance.org. Check the George Street website for updates.

Script submissions

George Street doesn't accept unsolicited scripts but will consider 'inquiry packets' which contain a synopsis of a play, a character breakdown, set requirements and sample pages (no more than ten) along with a self-addressed envelope. Check the website for specific information. Mail inquiry packets to: Attention: Literary Associate, George Street Playhouse, 9 Livingston Avenue, New Brunswick, NJ 08901.

Summer academy internships and teachers

Academy interns provide teaching assistance and administrative support to instructors, teaching a wide variety of theatre classes and performance programs to students ranging in age from 5 to 17. Bachelor's degree preferred (minimum of one year of college required) with a background in theatre, education or a related field. Theatre teachers teach acting skills, direct projects, and act as summer counselors. Teachers work Monday through Friday, 8:30 a.m. to 4:30 p.m. Theatre teaching experience is recommended, with a degree in theatre, education, or related fields. Check the website for additional information. To apply, send a cover letter, résumé, and contact information for three references to: Director of Education, George Street Playhouse, 9 Livingston Ave., New Brunswick, NJ 08901 or fax to 732-247-9151.

General employment opportunities, internships

Open positions are detailed on the company website.

GEORGIA SHAKESPEARE FESTIVAL

4484 Peachtree Road, NE, Atlanta, GA 30319
Administration: (404) 504-3400. Box office: (404) 264-0020. Fax: (404) 504-3414
Email (audition information): companymanager@gashakespeare.org;
(general information): boxoffice@gashakespeare.org
www.gashakespeare.org

This is one terrific theatre company and it's come a long way since the days of performing in a large circus tent. In its own words:

> *Georgia Shakespeare Festival exists to delight and inspire audiences with the excitement, mystery, and fun of live theatre. While William Shakespeare shall be our primary playwright, we shall also explore other perspectives, stimulating and enduring authors. Georgia Shakespeare Festival, a not-for-profit organization, shall unite local and national artists to produce for our audience a lively and imaginative Festival. An integral part of the Festival's purpose shall be to provide educational opportunities for our audiences, young and old alike, through pre- and post-production activities. We shall be committed to the theatre as a viable profession and shall utilize an apprentice program for both actors and technicians to further the education of aspiring theatre professionals. The Festival shall be managed within a sound and stable plan.*

Founded in 1986, Georgia Shakespeare Festival is one of the oldest and most active Shakespeare Festivals in the Southeast. Producing artistic director and co-founder Richard Garner leads the company with passion and finesse. GSF performs in the lovely 509-seat Conant Performing Arts Center, surrounded by a forest and the vibrant Oglethorpe University campus community, modeled after England's Oxford University. GSF's mainstage season runs from June through November.

Casting, general employment opportunities, internships
Check the website and write the theatre for information.

GEVA THEATRE CENTER
75 Woodbury Boulevard, Rochester, NY 14607
Administration: (585) 232-1366. Box office: (585) 232-4382. Fax: (585) 232-4031
Email: gevatalk@gevatheatre.org
www.gevatheatre.org
Founded in 1972, Geva attracts over 174,000 patrons annually to the 552-seat Elaine P. Wilson main stage. Productions range from musicals to reinvigorated American and world classics. The Ron & Donna Fielding Nextstage, Geva's 180-seat second stage, features contemporary theatre and is home to Geva Comedy Improv. Geva Theatre Center offers educational, outreach, and literary programs

'designed to enrich and deepen the theatregoing experience for our current audience and provide access and affordable theatre to the Rochester community including thousands of area students.' Geva is also committed to developing new plays and playwrights and nurturing 'audiences and artists of the next generation.' Mark Cuddy is the artistic director.

Casting

Geva's casting is coordinated by casting director Paul Fouquet in New York City. Address all résumés/headshots to his attention at: Elissa Myers Casting, 333 West 52nd Street, Suite 1008, New York, NY 10019. Geva Theatre Center also holds general auditions for Equity members, plus non-Equity adults and children. Check the website for updates.

Script submissions

American Voices New Play Readings are one-day workshops (three per season) of previously unproduced scripts with little or no development history. After rehearsal, the script is presented in a public reading followed by a talkback with the playwright. 'Hibernatus Interruptus: A Winter Festival of New Plays' is Geva Theatre Center's annual, two-week new play workshop cluster. Geva selects and/or commissions two to four new and/or unproduced plays, tailors the length and focus of each workshop to the playwright's needs, and usually presents the works in progress as staged readings, followed by talkbacks with the playwrights. Unproduced scripts submitted to Geva are considered for the new play programs listed above. Geva does not accept unsolicited scripts from writers without professional representation. Geva welcomes submission inquiries, including cover letter, synopsis, résumé or production history, and ten sample pages of dialogue, which may be sent to: New Plays Coordinator, Geva Theatre Center, 75 Woodbury Blvd., Rochester, NY 14607. Other playwright opportunities and specifics on submissions are listed on the website or by emailing gevatalk@gevatheatre.org.

General employment opportunities

Check out the website or write to the theatre for employment and intern opportunities.

GOODMAN THEATRE

170 N. Dearborn Street, Chicago, IL 60601-3205

Administration: (312) 443-3811. Box office: (312) 443-3800. Fax: (312) 443-7448

Email: info@goodman-theatre.org

www.goodman-theatre.org

The rich and vibrant history of the Goodman Theatre, may be traced back to 1925 when it was founded as a tribute to playwright Kenneth Sawyer Goodman. Originally a repertory company and drama school connected to the Art Institute of Chicago, the theatre took a giant leap forward 75 years later in 2000, when the company moved from the old Goodman to its glorious new 170,000-square-foot home in the heart of Chicago's North Loop. The 856-seat Albert Ivar Goodman Theatre's inaugural show, August Wilson's *King Hedley II,* was followed by Alan Ayckbourn's *Garden* in the flexible 335- to 467-seat Owen Bruner Goodman Theatre. Artistic director Robert Falls and executive director Roche Schulfer have led the Goodman artistic collective (including Frank Galati, Mary Zimmerman, and Regina Taylor) to the Regional Theatre Tony Award, to Broadway productions, and to myriad world premieres (including notable works by David Mamet, August Wilson, and Rebecca Gilman).

Casting

The Goodman casts primarily Chicago-based actors. Auditions for specific productions throughout the season are by invitation only. If you have interest in a particular production, mail your picture, résumé, and letter of interest for the attention of the Casting Director at the Goodman Theatre.

The Goodman holds general auditions each year in the summer months. Once Equity general audition dates have been announced, Equity performers can either make an appointment in person at the Equity Office or call the Chicago Equity audition hotline. Non-Equity performers should request an audition in writing by sending one picture, résumé (with address and phone number), and stamped, self-addressed envelope. Written requests should be postmarked between May 1 and July 15. Do not call the Goodman to schedule an audition. See the website for additional information. Actors planning on moving to the Chicago area may send in a picture and résumé upon arrival and try to set up a general audition appointment. For more specific questions, contact the Casting Office at (312) 443-3817 or email CastingInfo@goodman-theatre.org.

Script submissions

The Goodman does not accept unsolicited manuscripts from playwrights. Only an agent may submit unsolicited scripts. The Goodman requests that playwrights without agents first send the following: a professional résumé, a professional letter of recommendation, a brief synopsis, an optional ten-page dialogue sample, and a self-addressed stamped envelope. Allow six to eight weeks for submissions to be read and processed. The literary department will contact you if it wishes to solicit the full manuscript. Materials should be sent to: Literary Manager, Goodman Theatre, 170 North Dearborn Street, Chicago, IL 60601.

Internships

The Goodman Theatre Internship Program is for qualified college students and recent college graduates who are preparing for careers in professional theatre. Goodman interns have the opportunity to refine their practical and critical thinking skills through close interaction with Goodman staff and artists, and through independent exploration of Chicago's legendarily large and diverse theatre community. Internships are offered in the following areas: casting, costumes, development, dramaturgy, education and community programs, general management, literary management, marketing/PR/press, production management, sound, and stage management. Stipends are available for all internships. Stage management interns are also eligible to receive Equity membership points. The awarding of academic credit is at the discretion of the intern's college or university. Internship applications and information are detailed on the website.

General employment opportunities

Check the website and address inquiries to: Human Resource Manager, Goodman Theatre, 170 N. Dearborn St., Chicago, IL 60601 or fax: (312) 553-7234.

GOODSPEED MUSICALS

Norma Terris Theatre, 33 North Main Street, Chester, CT 06412
Mailing address: P.O. Box A, East Haddam, CT 06423
Administration: (860) 873-8664. Box office: (860) 873-8668. Fax: (860) 873-2329
Email: info@goodspeed.org
www.goodspeed.org

So many grand musicals have been shaped and produced at the Goodspeed Opera House since Goodspeed Musicals was formed in 1959 to restore the nineteenth-century Goodspeed Opera House. Professional theatre resurfaced in 1963 and artistic director Michael P. Price, who joined Goodspeed in 1968, has spent over four decades building the theatre's international reputation for production, preservation and advancement of musical theatre and the development of new works. Over 25 world premieres have been staged in the Norma Terris Theatre, located in Chester, Connecticut. From April through December, Goodspeed produces three musicals at the Opera House in East Haddam, and three new musicals at the Terris Theatre. Sixteen Goodspeed productions have transferred to Broadway, receiving more than a dozen Tony Awards. William Goodspeed built the Opera House in 1876 for his bank and shipping operations and to provide a home for theatre.

Script submissions
Goodspeed Musicals does not accept unsolicited submissions of new musicals and only accepts submissions from agents and professional recommendations. Materials from agents should be forwarded to: Producing Associate and Literary Manager, Goodspeed Musicals, Box A, East Haddam, CT 06423. No phone calls, please.

General employment opportunities
Casting and employment opportunity inquiries may be addressed to the theatre, and production applications and internship requests may be submitted on the company website (www.goodspeed.org). There may be opportunities not published there, but the website is a good place to start.

GREAT LAKES THEATER (SHAKESPEARE) FESTIVAL
1501 Euclid Avenue, Suite 300, Cleveland, OH 44115
Administration: (216) 241-5490. Box office: (216) 241-6000. Fax: (216) 241-6315
Email: mail@greatlakestheater.org
www.greatlakestheater.org
Shakespeare provided the earliest roots for this grand old theatre, and great plays of all cultures and time periods currently find their way to the 550-seat Hanna Theatre. Founded in 1962, the mission of Great Lakes Theater Festival has evolved

and includes bringing 'the pleasure, power, and relevance of classic theatre to the widest possible audience' and 'the occasional mounting of new works that complement the classical repertoire.' In its own words, this Cleveland theatre company endeavors 'to share such vibrant experiences with people across all age groups, creeds, racial and ethnic groups, and socioeconomic backgrounds.'

In 1961, English professor and Shakespeare director Arthur Lithgow (actor John Lithgow's dad), who had founded a Shakespeare theatre a decade earlier at Yellow Springs' Antioch College, was invited to produce in the Lakewood City Auditorium. On July 11, 1962, the Great Lakes Shakespeare Festival opened. Lawrence Carra, Vincent Dowling, Gerald Freedman, and James Bundy all followed as artistic directors and made their marks on the theatre. Mr. Freedman brought Hal Holbrook, Olympia Dukakis, Jean Stapleton, Piper Laurie, and others to the Ohio stage. Producing artistic director Charles Fee joined the company in 2002, bringing a renewed vision for staging the classics. He currently produces five annual shows at the theatre.

Casting

Great Lakes Theater Festival and the Cleveland Play House conduct an open call for all union and non-union actors each year. The auditions are by appointment. To make an appointment to audition, call (216) 795-7000 ext. 967. Check the website for additional information.

Auditions for actor/teachers

Great Lakes Theater Festival also auditions for non-Equity actor/teachers for its School Residency Program; actors of all cultural backgrounds are encouraged to audition for full-time, seasonal, paid positions.

Requirements include an undergraduate degree in any discipline, as well as previous stage experience or actor training. Teaching experience or prior work with elementary, junior high, or high-school age students is a plus, but not required. Applicants must have use of a reliable automobile. Check the website for additional information.

Internships

Internships are generally available in production and company management, stage management, costuming and wardrobe, properties, and set construction.

Internships are full-time, paid positions. To be eligible, you must be an entering, current, or graduating college student. Start and end dates are flexible. To apply, provide a cover letter and résumé to Great Lakes Theater Festival. Check the website for deadlines and additional information. Send your letter to: Production Internships, Great Lakes Theater Festival, 1501 Euclid Avenue, Suite 300, Cleveland, OH 44115.

GUTHRIE THEATER

818 South 2nd Street, Minneapolis, MN 55415

Administration: (612) 225-6000. Box office: (612) 377-2224 or toll free (877) 447-8243. Fax: (612) 225-6004

Email: management@guthrietheater.org

www.guthrietheater.org

The Guthrie Theater is one of the revered 'grandfathers' of the American theatre movement which, in its own words, 'sees itself as a leader in American theatre with both a national and international reputation.' The Guthrie dates back to 1959 when Sir Tyrone Guthrie, Oliver Rea, and Peter Zeisler decided to create a theatre with a resident acting company that was different from their Broadway experience. The company was formed in 1963 with the vision that actors performing the classics in rotating repertory would develop into an artistic family and that this intimacy would create a marvelous relationship between actors and audience members; and this is what happened during the early years. Actor George Grizzard (who played the title role in the opening season's *Hamlet*) tells marvelous stories of the opening season that included such noted actors as Jessica Tandy, Zoe Caldwell, and Hume Cronyn. Legendary artistic directors Douglas Campbell, Michael Langham, Alvin Epstein, Liviu Ciulei, and Garland Wright followed over the years. Current artistic director Joe Dowling, long associated with Ireland's Abbey Theatre, pursues the Guthrie Theater's mission to serve 'as a vital artistic resource for the people of Minnesota and the region . . . to celebrate, through theatrical performances, the common humanity binding us all together. The theatre is devoted to the traditional classical repertoire that has sustained us since our foundation and to the exploration of new works from diverse cultures and traditions.'

Today, the Guthrie employs more than 900 people each year. On June 24, 2006, the Guthrie opened a new multistage theatre center on the banks of the

Mississippi River, including three stages: a classic thrust stage for the grand-scale classics of the centuries, a proscenium stage for the more intimate classics of this century, and a studio theatre to nurture new plays.

Casting

Most of the casting for Guthrie Theater productions is done locally, although some out-of-town actors are hired for almost every Guthrie production. The majority of out-of-town casting is arranged through the Guthrie's New York City representative, McCorkle Casting, 575 Eighth Avenue, 18th Floor, New York, NY 10018.

Auditions for specific productions are held in Minneapolis and in New York as needed throughout the year. Actors based in the Twin Cities area should make a habit of checking the Guthrie's website as well as www.minnesotaplaylist.com or www.callboard.org. When holding open auditions, the Guthrie usually places notices in the audition section of those media outlets. The annual Twin Cities general auditions are usually scheduled in the spring. Occasionally, Guthrie auditions are held in other major cities (such as Los Angeles, Seattle, and Chicago).

Actors who wish to submit their pictures and résumés are welcome to send them via regular mail to: Casting: Guthrie Theater, 818 2nd Street South, Minneapolis, MN 55415.

Script submissions

The Guthrie Theater no longer accepts unsolicited scripts from any source and does not request scripts based on reading synopses or sample dialogue. Unsolicited scripts are recycled.

General employment opportunites

Check the Guthrie Theater's website at www.guthrietheater.org for position openings and instructions on how to apply.

Internships

The Guthrie Theater internship program provides college students and recent graduates an opportunity to engage in hands-on professional theatre training from Guthrie staff, artists and craftspeople. An internship with the Guthrie is a valuable supplement and follow-up to a strong theatrical education. Internships at the Guthrie are unpaid; however, interns receive other employee perks such as professional development opportunities, complimentary Guthrie tickets, invitations to meet-and-greets, staff meetings and more.

To apply for an internship, visit the internship page of the Guthrie website (www.guthrietheater.org/opportunities/internships) for information on deadlines and submit the online application and requested materials. Depending on the needs of the theatre, internships may be offered in any of the following areas: company development, company management, costumes, development, directing, dramaturgy/literary, education, information systems, lighting, marketing, multimedia communications, props, public relations, sound, stage management, and technical production. The theatre does not offer internships in acting.

HARTFORD STAGE COMPANY

50 Church Street, Hartford, CT 06103
Administration: (860) 525-5601. Box office: (860) 527-5151. Fax: (860) 244-0183
Email: administration@hartfordstage.org
www.hartfordstage.org
Hartford Stage is a Regional Theatre Tony Award-winner, a Margo Jones Award-winner for Development of New Works, and the proud owner of OBIE awards, a New York Critics Circle Award, a Dramatists Guild/CBS Award, and an Elliot Norton Award. Jacques Cartier founded the theatre in 1963 in an old grocery store warehouse and opened it with *Othello* in 1964. Paul Weidner took over in 1968, moving the company to the 489-seat John W. Huntington Theater. Mark Lamos became artistic director in 1980, bringing international recognition to Hartford Stage during his 17 seasons. Michael Wilson came on board in 1998 and announced his resignation in 2010. He developed the Tennessee Williams Marathon, the annual 'Brand: NEW' festival, and Summer Stage. Hartford Stage has given over 50 plays their world or American premieres, including works by Theresa Rebeck, José Rivera, Christopher Durang, Horton Foote, Eve Ensler, Edward Albee, Alfred Uhry, Beth Henley, Edwin Sànchez, and Tennessee Williams.

Casting

General Equity and non-Equity auditions for each season are held in late July/early August. Children's auditions (ages six to thirteen) are held separately in early October. Additional auditions are held on an as-needed basis throughout the year.

Notice of all auditions are posted on the website with specific instructions for making an appointment. Actors are welcome to send a headshot and résumé at any time during the year to: Casting, Hartford Stage, 50 Church Street, Hartford, CT 06103. No phone calls.

Script submissions

Hartford Stage accepts scripts by agent submission or professional recommendation only. Response time is usually several months. The theatre does not accept unsolicited material for review.

General employment opportunities

Full-time, part-time, and seasonal opportunities exist from time to time in various areas of the theatre. Available positions are often updated on the website and are generally advertised in *The Hartford Courant* and *ARTSEARCH*. To be considered for employment at Hartford Stage, send a résumé and cover letter to: Hartford Stage, 50 Church Street, Hartford, CT 06103, or stop by the box office at the same address to fill out an application.

THE HUMAN RACE THEATRE COMPANY

126 North Main Street, Suite 300, Dayton, OH 45402-1710
Administration: (937) 461-3823. Box office: (937) 228-3630 or toll free (888) 228-3630. Fax: (937) 461-7223
Email: contact@humanracetheatre.org
www.humanracetheatre.org
The Human Race Theatre Company is one of Dayton, Ohio's many welcome surprises, as the Eichelberger Loft Season of The Human Race provides audiences with edgy contemporary plays, new works, and American classics. The Musical Theatre Workshop offers original work or seldom-performed musicals, while the company's education and outreach programs are ambitious, exciting, and important to the Miami Valley community. The company makes its home in the Metropolitan Arts Center in downtown Dayton and produces one show a year for the Victoria Theatre's Broadway Series. Youth training programs, including Adventures in Theatre classes, residencies, in-school tours, youth summer stock, and Theatre in Context allow the company to connect with over 30,000 students and teachers

annually. In the troupe's own words, 'The Human Race Theatre Company works to affect the conscience of our community, to see our audiences as our partner in the creative experience, to provide a platform for our artists to evolve and explore, and to be an educational resource for our community. As our name suggests, we present universal themes that explore the human condition and startle us into a renewed awareness of ourselves.' Kevin Moore is the executive director.

Casting

The Human Race holds general auditions in the spring and early summer in Dayton and Chicago. Specific dates and locations are announced in April. At these auditions, the company is usually casting roles for the Eichelberger Loft Season of The Human Race (typically a combination of plays and musicals), one production in the Victoria Theatre's Broadway Series, an in-school tour production. and at least one Musical Theatre Workshop production. The Human Race works under a Small Professional Theatre contract in the Loft Theatre, a 219-seat thrust stage. Other employment opportunities and internships are listed on the website when available.

HUNTINGTON THEATRE COMPANY

264 Huntington Avenue, Boston, MA 02115-4606
Administration: (617) 266-7900. Box office: (617) 266-0800. Fax: (617) 353-8300
Email: jobs@huntingtontheatre.org
www.huntingtontheatre.org

Founded in 1982, the Huntington Theatre Company is now over two decades old, still enjoying its residence at Boston University, and continuing to grow with artistic director Peter DuBois at the helm. The company works in both the 890-seat Boston University Theatre and the Stanford Calderwood Pavilion at the Boston Center for the Arts (which houses the 360-seat Virginia Wimberly Theatre and the 200-seat Nancy and Edward Roberts Studio Theatre). Over 17,000 subscribers attest to the artistic quality of the company, which has received three Tony Award nominations for Broadway transfers. The Huntington has produced nearly 50 New England, American, or world premieres, including works by Tom Stoppard, Brian Friel, Christopher Durang, Donald Margulies, and Horton Foote. The Breaking

Ground Festival of new play readings and the Stanford Calderwood Fund for New American Plays are part of the Huntington's efforts to commission and develop new works from emerging and established writers.

Casting

The Huntington holds general casting sessions. Send résumés to: Casting, Huntington Theatre Company, 252 Huntington Avenue, Boston, MA 02115-4606.

Script submissions

The Huntington Theatre Company does not generally accept unsolicited submissions from writers without agents but will accept unsolicited submissions from agencies in the United States, Canada, and the UK. In efforts to support the work of area writers, the literary department will accept unsolicited scripts from playwrights without agents who are residents of the Greater Boston region. For these purposes, the Boston region includes all of Massachusetts and Rhode Island. See the website for additional information.

General employment opportunities

Check the website for opportunities, email jobs@huntingtontheatre.org or check with: Personnel Administrator, Huntington Theatre Company, 264 Huntington Avenue, Boston, MA 02115.

INDIANA REPERTORY THEATRE

140 West Washington Street, Indianapolis, IN 46204
Administration: (317) 635-5277. Box office: (317) 635-5252. Fax: (317) 236-0767
Email: indianarep@indianarep.com
www.irtlive.com

The Indiana Repertory Theatre (IRT) is a gem that in its own words, 'values live theatre as an entertaining and educational event created by professional artists especially for our audience. We believe theatre provides a unique opportunity for audiences and artists to share experiences that can be enjoyable, uplifting, thought-provoking, even life-changing. The IRT is the place that creates and perpetuates programs to make these experiences available to all segments of our community.'

Founded by Edward Stern, Gregory Poggi, and Benjamin Mordecai in 1972 and designated the State of Indiana's 'Theatre Laureate' in 1991, the historic Indiana Theatre is a cultural landmark now led by artistic director Janet Allen. IRT is the only fully professional resident not-for-profit theatre in the state, attracts audiences of over 139,000 annually, and plays to more than 49,000 students from 59 of Indiana's 92 counties. Generally, a staff of more than 100 seasonal and year-round employees creates nine productions in the 1927 Indiana Theatre, which houses the 607-seat Mainstage, 269-seat Upperstage, and 150-seat Cabaret theatres.

Casting
General auditions are conducted every year in May or early June for Equity and experienced non-Equity actors. IRT also auditions actors on a show-by-show basis by invitation only in Indianapolis, Chicago, and New York. IRT encourages actors to send a cover letter, headshot, and résumé to: Casting, IRT, 140 West Washington Street, Indianapolis, IN 46204. Check the website for dates, times and procedures.

Script submissions
Submit plays to the Resident Dramaturg, Indiana Repertory Theatre, 140 West Washington Street, Indianapolis, IN 46204.

General employment opportunities
Check the website for general hiring information and submit applications and résumés to: Human Resources, Indiana Repertory Theatre, 140 West Washington Street, Indianapolis, IN 46204.

Internships
IRT doesn't have a formal internship program, but informal internships are available in most production areas. Internships are unpaid, are for students only, and must be taken for credit. Interested students should check the website for details.

INTIMAN THEATRE

201 Mercer Street, Seattle, WA 98109

Mailing address: P.O. Box 19760, Seattle, WA 98109

Administration: (206) 269-1901. Box office: (206) 269-1900. Fax: (206) 436-7895

Email: intiman@intiman.org

www.intiman.org

One of the best theatres in the Pacific Northwest is the Intiman, founded in 1972, and committed to developing new work, including the world premiere of Joan Holden's *Nickel and Dimed* and the Tony Award-winning musical *The Light in the Piazza*, by Craig Lucas and Adam Guettel. Under the leadership of artistic director Kate Whoriskey, Intiman produces classics and contemporary plays. In its own words, 'Intiman's legacy is defined by the boldest vision in the production of classics and new plays. It is rich with talent and amazing people – artists who have made their homes in Seattle and nationally recognized artists, all of whom are dedicated to engaging our community in conversation, and to having an impact on our culture locally and nationally.'

Casting

Intiman Theatre's season runs from March through December. Intiman holds two days of Equity local auditions per year. Equity generals are listed on the local Equity Hotline at (888) 266-1731, extension 19; on the Equity website at www.actors equity.org; and on the Theatre Puget Sound (TPS) website at www.tpsonline.org.

Intiman participates in the annual general auditions for both Equity and non-Equity actors organized by TPS. For more information, check out the website. Intiman maintain an active file of both local and out-of-town actors based on those auditions. More specific information about general auditions, as well as auditions for specific shows, can be found on Intiman's Actor Info-line, (206) 269-1901 extension 129, or on Seattle 's Equity hotline, (888) 266-1731, extension 19. Intiman Theatre is an equal opportunity employer and actors of all cultural backgrounds and abilities are encouraged to audition.

Script submissions

The Intiman accepts work from literary agents or by the recommendation of an artistic director, literary manager, or dramaturg affiliated with a professional theatre. No unsolicited manuscripts are accepted. Check the website for more specifics. The best submission time is from October through March.

General employment opportunities

Check the website for general employment information.

KANSAS CITY REPERTORY THEATRE

4949 Cherry Street, Kansas City, MO 64110 (Spencer Theatre)

One H and R Block Way, Kansas City, MO 64105-1905

Administration: (816) 235-2727. Box office: (816) 235-2700. Fax: (816) 235-5367

Email: info@kcrep.org

www.kcrep.org

Kansas City Repertory Theatre produces a full season of plays and events in Spencer Theatre at the James C. Olson Performing Arts Center on the campus of the University of Missouri – Kansas City, where the Rep is the professional theatre in residence, and also at Copaken Stage, located in downtown Kansas City. The theatre serves approximately 100,000 patrons annually and employs more than 250 professional artists, technicians and administrators. Each year, about 10,000 students from schools in the two-state region attend educational matinee performances and participate in classroom programming and workshops. Under the artistic leadership of Eric Rosen, Kansas City Rep's creative vision supports new works, musicals, and classics of literature that are diverse, literate, and timely. Rosen is only the fourth artistic director in the Rep's 46-year history, following Peter Altman (producing artistic director 2000-07), George Keathley (artistic director 1985-2000), and founder Dr. Patricia McIlrath, who guided the theatre from 1964 until she retired in 1985.

Casting

The Rep selects both Actors' Equity and non-Equity actors through the audition process. Contact the theatre's artistic office for information about auditions: Kansas City Repertory Theatre, 4949 Cherry Street, Kansas City, MO 64110, or (816) 235-2727. Notices for general audition are posted at www.KCRep.org and on the Equity Hotline (913) 248-8228.

General employment opportunities/internships

Check the website for openings.

LAGUNA PLAYHOUSE

Moulton Theater, 606 Laguna Canyon Road, Laguna Beach, CA 92652
Mailing address: P.O. Box 1747, Laguna Beach, CA 92652
Administration: (949) 497-2787. Box office: (949) 497-2787. Fax: (949) 497-6948
Email: box_office@lagunaplayhouse.com
www.lagunaplayhouse.com

Just around the corner from the Pacific Ocean, this ambitious theatre has a grand history and a network of professional artists to shape the future. It all started in a living room in 1920, when a group of Laguna Beach citizens sat down to establish a local theatre. From private homes and storefronts, the Laguna Playhouse has blossomed into an impressive professional theatre with ongoing West Coast, American, and world premieres playing to over 110,000 patrons. In 1924, at a cost of $5,000, the Playhouse was built on Ocean Avenue. It was used to entertain the soldiers and was dressed up for USO dances during World War II. In 1969, the theatre's current home, the Moulton Theatre, opened on Laguna Canyon Road. In the theatre's own words: 'We will maintain The Laguna Playhouse as a long-standing cultural and educational force on the regional and national theatre landscape. We will reflect and serve our community. We will actively engage artists and audiences through enlightened programming of the highest quality. We will develop future theatre artists and audiences through education programs for adults and youth.' Longtime artistic director Andrew Barnicle announced his resignation in 2010 and a search for new artistic leadership was underway in 2011.

Casting

Actors seeking roles in mainstage season productions are invited to submit a photo and résumé to Casting, Laguna Playhouse, P.O. Box 4049, Laguna Beach, CA 92652. Most productions are cast through agent submissions. Since the Laguna Playhouse operates under a LORT contract, few roles are cast with non-Equity performers. However, all actors are welcome to submit résumés. Audition information for adult and youth roles in the Youth Theatre season is posted under the 'Education' section of the website.

Script submissions

Scripts may be submitted to Laguna Playhouse, P.O. Box 4049, Laguna Beach, CA 92652. The Playhouse does not encourage unsolicited manuscripts, and the review process may take up to one year.

General employment opportunities, internships
Check the website for employment openings and internships.

LA JOLLA PLAYHOUSE
P.O. Box 12039, La Jolla, CA 92039
Administration: (858) 550-1070. Box office: (858) 550-1010. Fax: (858) 550-1075
Email: information@ljp.org
www.lajollaplayhouse.org

A number of Broadway shows were created at the La Jolla Playhouse (including The Who's *Tommy* and *Big River*), and artistic director Christopher Ashley believes in advancing theatre 'as an art form and as a vital social, moral, and political platform by providing unfettered creative opportunities for the leading artists of today and tomorrow.' In the theatre's own words, 'With our youthful spirit and eclectic, artist-driven approach we will continue to cultivate a local and national following with an insatiable appetite for audacious and diverse work.' The Playhouse produces a main-stage season of six to eight new plays, classics, and musicals, many of which are world premieres, and supports the creation of new work through its 'Page to Stage' play development program, which includes commissions, readings, and workshops. Tony Award nominee Ashley and the Playhouse have staged over 60 world premieres and 35 American or West Coast premieres. The theatre received the 1993 Regional Theatre Tony Award. La Jolla Playhouse was founded in 1947 by Gregory Peck, Dorothy McGuire, and Mel Ferrer, and revived in 1983 under the leadership of Des McAnuff, who served as artistic director from 1983 to 1994 and again from 2001 to 2007. McAnuff was succeeded by Michael Greif, who served as artistic director from 1995 to 1999. The theatre is currently led by artistic director Christopher Ashley and managing director Michael S. Rosenberg. The Playhouse is in residence on the University of California, San Diego campus.

Casting, script submissions, general employment opportunities
Check the website for ongoing information.

Internship program
The Playhouse offers full-time and part-time internships over a minimum of 12 weeks. The program runs all year, but can be extended or adjusted according to

availability and departmental need. There is no stipend. Positions generally include public relations, graphics, general management, company management, costumes, fundraising/special events, artistic, literary/dramaturgy, education, and outreach programs, production management, props, run/wardrobe crew, scene shop, scenic artist, stage management, and operations. Positions are not offered in directing or acting. College credit is available. An application, personal statement, résumé, and two letters of recommendation must be received prior to consideration. An online internship application should also be completed and sent to: La Jolla Playhouse, Attn: Internship Program, P.O. Box 12039, La Jolla, CA 92039.

LINCOLN CENTER THEATER

The Vivian Beaumont and Mitzi E. Newhouse Theaters,
150 West 65th Street, New York, NY 10023
Administration: (212) 362-7600. Box office: customerservice@lct.org or telecharge:
(212) 239-6210. Fax: (212) 873-0761
Email: info@lct.org
www.lct.org

Founded by John D. Rockefeller, Lincoln Center is currently led by chairman J. Tomilson Hill, artistic director Andre Bishop and executive producer Bernard Gersten. Lincoln Center has produced myriad award-winning plays for millions of audience members at the Vivian Beaumont Theater, the Mitzi E. Newhouse Theater, and other venues.

John D. Rockefeller's mandate that 'the arts are not for the privileged few, but for the many' still thrives as the Lincoln Center Theater makes every effort to 'keep admission prices low and its doors open to all.' Ongoing activities include the literary journal, *Lincoln Center Theater Review*; the Playwrights Program; the Directors Lab; Open Stages, an arts-in-education program operated in cooperation with New York City public schools; and the Platform Series of free conversations with LCT artists. The complex includes the 1,100-seat Vivian Beaumont Theater and the 299-seat Mitzi E. Newhouse Theater. Since 1985, the not-for-profit company Lincoln Center Theater has operated the Beaumont and Newhouse, producing world premieres and classics, including *Marie Christine, Parade, Juan Darien, Arcadia, Contact, A New Brain, Pride's Crossing, Hapgood, The Sisters Rosensweig,* and *The Substance of Fire.*

Casting, script submissions, general employment opportunities
Check the website and email the theatre at info@lct.org for ongoing information.

LONG WHARF THEATRE

222 Sargent Drive, New Haven, CT 06511
Administration: (203) 787-4284. Box office: (203) 787-4282 or toll free (800)
782-8497. Fax: (203) 776-2287
Email: info@longwharf.org
www.longwharf.org

Many great plays have found a home at the Long Wharf Theatre since two Yale
University alumni created the institution in 1965. Jon Jory and Harlan Kleiman
opened the theatre with Arthur Miller's *The Crucible*. The venue was constructed
in an old warehouse and named for the Long Wharf port along New Haven
Harbor. Over four decades later, the Tony Award-winning company boasts an
annual audience exceeding 100,000 and, in its own words, produces 'imaginative
revivals of classics and modern plays, rediscoveries of neglected works, and a
variety of world and American premieres.' Broadway or Off-Broadway transfers
include *Wit* (1999 Pulitzer Prize), *Hughie*, *Broken Glass*, *The Gin Game*, *Streamers*,
American Buffalo, *Requiem for a Heavyweight*, and *Quartermaine's Terms*. Gordon
Edelstein is the artistic director.

Casting

Long Wharf Theatre works under a LORT/AEA contract and the union determines
the number of non-Equity actors in any production. Equity auditions are held in
New York, Chicago, or Los Angeles, depending on the needs of the production,
and auditions are arranged through agent submissions, and scheduled by a
casting director in each city. Actors may send a photo and résumé to: Casting,
Long Wharf Theatre, 222 Sargent Drive, New Haven, CT 06511.

Script submissions

Long Wharf Theatre only accepts scripts received via agent submission or professional recommendation and does not accept unsolicited scripts.

General employment opportunities

Check the website and email the theatre at info@longwharf.org for ongoing information. Freelance production artists are often in demand. The Long Wharf Theatre posts employment opportunities for experienced theatre professionals. Check the website or send queries to: Human Resources, Long Wharf Theatre, 222 Sargent Drive, New Haven, CT 06511.

Internships

Internships offer recent college graduates and early-career professionals the opportunity to work extensively in their area of interest in a professional regional theatre. Internship benefits include seminars and workshops led by guest artists and theatre professionals, complimentary tickets to all Long Wharf productions, and the opportunity to attend other Connecticut theatres and special events, a weekly housing stipend, and affordable housing available through Long Wharf. Full-time, full-season internships are available, as well as part-time and semester-long internships. College credit may be arranged with academic institutions. Application forms are online, or email internships@longwharf.org for additional information.

MALTZ JUPITER THEATRE

1001 E. Indiantown Road, Jupiter, FL 33477
Administration: (561) 743-2666. Box office: (561) 575-2223 or toll free (800) 445-1666
Email: info@jupitertheatre.org
www.jupitertheatre.org

With productions ranging from world premieres to musicals to contemporary plays, the theatre accomplished a dramatic $10 million renovation, and opened as a 550-seat, nonprofit community-based regional theatre. In six years, the Maltz Jupiter Theatre (MJT) has become one of Florida's pre-eminent professional theatres, committed to performance, production, and education through its collaborations with local and national artists. Under the leadership of artistic director Andrew Kato and managing director Tricia Trimble, MJT has received multiple Carbonell Awards, South Florida's highest honor for artistic excellence, and has increased its subscription base to more than 7,100. The theatre's programs include a Conservatory of Performing Arts, which serves students in after-school, weekend, and summer programs. A MacArthur Fund grant helped the theatre create the Emerging Artists Series in Musical Theatre Playwriting.

Casting, general employment opportunities, internships
Check the website for general employment information or email info@jupiter theatre.org.

MANHATTAN THEATRE CLUB

311 West 43rd Street, 8th floor, New York, NY 10036
Administration: (212) 399-3000. Fax: (212) 399-4329
Email: questions@mtc-nyc.org
www.mtc-nyc.org

MTC/Biltmore Theatre

261 West 47th Street, New York, NY 10036

Stages I and II at NY City Center

131 West 55th Street, New York, NY 10019
Box office: CityTix (212) 581-1212; Telecharge (212) 239-6200

The revered Manhattan Theatre Club is, in its own words, 'the creative and artistic home for America's most gifted theatrical artists, producing works of the highest quality by both established and emerging American and international play-wrights.' Manhattan Theatre Club nurtures and develops new and emerging talent in playwriting, musical composition, directing, acting, and design. Artistic director Lynne Meadow and executive producer Barry Grove have developed the theatre from an Off-Off Broadway showcase into one of the country's leading theatre institutions.

Founded in 1970, MTC has 20,000 subscribers and produces seven plays a year in Broadway's restored Biltmore Theatre on West 47th Street and at the historic City Center complex on West 55th Street. The company's three performance spaces include the 650-seat Biltmore Theatre and City Center's 299-seat Stage I and 150-seat Stage II. MTC's many awards include eleven Tony Awards and three Pulitzer Prizes.

Casting

MTC accepts both agent and personal submissions. Individuals and agents should submit headshots and résumés along with a letter of interest. All submissions can be sent to: Manhattan Theatre Club, Attn: Casting, 311 West 43rd Street, 8th Floor, New York, NY 10036.

Directing fellowships

Manhattan Theatre Club offers directing fellowships for each of the Biltmore (Broadway), Stage I and Stage II (Off-Broadway) shows. These fellows are selected by letter-résumé submission and work closely with MTC staff and directors in assisting with the staging of each production. Experienced individuals should send a letter of interest and current résumé to: MTC: Directing Fellows, Manhattan Theatre Club, 311 West 43rd Street, Eighth Floor, New York, NY 10036, or to directingfellows@mtc-nyc.org.

Script submissions

The literary department at MTC accepts only agent submissions for full-length plays. MTC does not accept unsolicited scripts, but interested parties can fax or mail MTC announcements of local readings and productions.

General employment opportunities, internships

Check the website for detailed production opportunities and artistic, business, casting, development, special events, education, executive producer, general management, information technology, marketing, literary, and production internships. Interns are provided a weekly stipend, free tickets to all MTC productions, invitations to readings of new plays and exciting special events, and free and discounted ticket offers to other companies' Broadway and Off-Broadway performances. Check the website for details and the MTC intern application form.

MARIN THEATRE COMPANY

397 Miller Avenue, Mill Valley, CA 94941-2885
Administration: (415) 388-5200. Box office: (415) 388-5208. Fax: (415) 388-0768
Email: info@marintheatre.org
www.marintheatre.org

This company packs a double-wallop with Jasson Minadakis as artistic director and Ryan Rilette as producing director in the San Francisco Bay Area's best mid-sized theatre and the leading professional theatre in the North Bay. MTC produces 'provocative plays by passionate playwrights' in two intimate theatres – a 231-seat proscenium and a 99-seat thrust. MTC is committed to the development and production of new plays by American playwrights, with a comprehensive New Play Program that includes world premieres, playwriting awards, new play readings and workshops, and a leadership position in the National New Play Network. The company also creates meaningful educational programs, including theatre for young audiences, that perform in the theatre and tours to schools throughout Marin. Teachers in the classroom, a summer camp, student matinees, free tickets for teachers, and internships are just a few of the educational programs that serve more than 6,000 students each year.

Casting, hiring, and internship opportunities

Checkout www.marintheatre.org for information and contact names for casting, hiring, internships and educational program opportunities.

McCARTER THEATRE CENTER

91 University Place, Princeton, NJ 08540
Administration: (609) 258-6500. Tickets and general inquiries: (609) 258-2787 or (888) ARTSWEB. Fax: (609) 497-0369
Email: admin@mccarter.org
www.mccarter.org

Emily Mann has led the Tony Award-winning McCarter Theatre with her unique vision 'to create a theatre of testimony, engaged in a dialogue with the world around it, paying tribute to the enduring power of the human spirit and scope of the imagination.' Over 20 new plays and adaptations have had their world or American premieres at the McCarter since 1991 and more than 200,000 audience members journey to the theatre annually. Recipient of the 1994 Tony Award for Outstanding Regional Theatre, McCarter's five-play Theatre Series is supplemented by broad-based outreach activities, including programs for students, the elderly, and persons with disabilities. The building was constructed in 1929 to provide a permanent home for Princeton University's Triangle Club. Daniel Seltzer founded the theatre in 1972, and it is currently is supported by nearly 15,000 subscribers.

Casting

Productions are cast through Alan Filderman Casting, The Bernard Telsey Agency, and Elissa Myers Casting in New York. Check the McCarter website for agency addresses. McCarter also participates in general audition calls required by Actors' Equity contract, and in the New Jersey Theatre Alliance lottery auditions: (973) 593-0189; www.njtheatrealliance.com. For casting inquiries email: casting@mccarter.org. For non-Equity casting for the annual *A Christmas Carol*, send picture and résumé to: McCarter Theatre, Attn. Christmas Carol Casting, 91 University Place, Princeton, NJ 08540, or email picture and résumé to casting@mccarter.org. Check the website for additional information on children's casting for boys and girls ages 5 to 13.

Script submissions

The McCarter accepts full-length scripts sent by agents or established theatre professionals (director, artistic director, literary manager) who are familiar with the work produced at McCarter. The McCarter does not accept unsolicited scripts or email submissions. All letters of inquiry should be sent to: McCarter Theatre, Attn: Literary Manager, 91 University Place, Princeton, NJ 08540.

General employment opportunities

Check the website for specific positions and send résumés to: McCarter Theatre Center for the Performing Arts, 91 University Place, Princeton, NJ 08540. Résumés are also accepted for freelance scenic artists, costume/wardrobe staff, and stage technicians with professional experience. Shop overhire is generally on a per-show basis. Stage work varies throughout the season: mostly one- to three-day electrics and scenery load-ins; occasional three-week-run crew positions. Send letter, résumé, and references to the Production Manager, fax them to (609) 497-0369, or email to production@mccarter.org.

MERRIMACK REPERTORY THEATRE

50 East Merrimack Street, Lowell, MA 01852
Administration: (978) 654-7550. Box office: (978) 654-4678. Fax: (978) 654-7575
Email: info@merrimackrep.org
www.merrimackrep.org

Founded in 1979 by John Briggs, Mark Kaufman, D.J. Maloney, and Barbara Abrahamian, Merrimack Rep is one of only three League of Resident Theatres

(LORT) members in eastern Massachusetts. Located in historic downtown Lowell, the theatre has an active September through May production season as well as a Young Artists at Play summer program and educational and community outreach programs.

Casting

Send photos and résumés to: Casting, Merrimack Repertory Theatre, 50 East Merrimack Street, Lowell, MA 01852. No phone calls.

Internship opportunities

Internships at MRT are open to students with a serious interest in pursing a career in professional theatre. For information or an application to MRT's internship program, email artadmin@merrimackrep.org. Internships are available in stage management, electrics, carpentry, dramaturgy, education/outreach, youth theatre (summer only), arts management, box office management, business management, development, and public relations.

MILL MOUNTAIN THEATRE

One Market Square SE, Second Floor, Roanoke, VA 24011-1437
Administration: (540) 342-5749
Email: mmtmail@millmountain.org
www.millmountain.org

The Mill Mountain Theatre was founded in 1964, and according to its website, is 'currently being reinvented' and is focusing on its conservatory program. Check the MMT website for employment volunteer and audition information.

MILWAUKEE REPERTORY THEATER

108 E. Wells Street, Milwaukee, WI 53202
Administration: (414) 224-1761. Box office: (414) 224-9490. Fax: (414) 224-9097
Email: mailrep@milwaukeerep.com
www.milwaukeerep.com

In 1954, Milwaukee native Mary John founded the Fred Miller Theater on Oakland Avenue (named after the head of Miller Brewing Company). The company produced Broadway's current hits, often with star performers. A resident acting company and expanded repertoire (including the classics and new works) followed a 1963 reorganization as the Milwaukee Repertory Theater, and in 1968 a move to a 504-seat theatre in downtown Milwaukee. In 1987, the company moved to a new complex, across from Milwaukee's City Hall. The converted power plant is an artistic fortress and houses three theatres: the Quadracci Powerhouse, seating 720, the 218-seat flexible Stiemke, and the Stackner Cabaret (a 118-seat full-service restaurant and bar). The Rep has a history of international collaboration, maintains a resident acting company, and runs many community programs. Mark Clements is the artistic director.

Casting, general employment opportunities
Check the company website for opportunities and job listings.

Internships
The Rep works with about 15 acting, directing, and literary interns who join the company full-time. Brochures and applications are available on the company website. Interns in the artistic department devote their time entirely to acting, directing, or dramaturgy.

THE NEW HARMONY THEATRE
University of Southern Indiana, 8600 University Boulevard, Evansville,
IN 47712-3596
Administration: (812) 682-3115. Box office (toll free): (877) NHT-SHOW.
Fax: (812) 464-0029
Email: nhtheatre@usi.edu
www.usi.edu/nh
New Harmony, Indiana, is a spiritual sanctuary that once thrived as a haven for international scientists, scholars, and educators who 'sought equality in communal living.' Tucked away on the banks of the Wabash River in southwestern Indiana, historic New Harmony is home to the New Harmony Theatre (NHT), produced by the University of Southern Indiana and operating under a special LORT agreement. Founded in 1987, the theatre itself is located on 419 Tavern Street and generally operates in the summer, producing contemporary plays, classics, and musicals. The artistic director is Lenny Leibowitz.

Casting, general employment opportunities

NHT conducts a national search for theatre professionals. Casting occurs in New York and Los Angeles, at the Southeastern Theatre Conference, and regionally. Designers and technicians are hired chiefly in New York and Chicago, through national conferences, and distinguished colleges. Details for auditions and employment opportunities are generally listed on the website or can be obtained by emailing nhtheatre@usi.edu.

NORTHLIGHT THEATRE

9501 Skokie Blvd., Skokie, IL 60077
Administration: (847) 679-9501. Box office: (847) 673-6300. Fax: (847) 679-1879
Email: bjjones@northlight.org
www.northlight.org

With a budget near $3 million and attendance approaching 75,000, the Northlight Theatre continues to grow its overall community following a move from Evanston to Skokie (both Chicago suburbs). In its own words, Northlight 'presents life-affirming theatrical works which reflect and challenge the values and beliefs of the community it serves and involves community members, young and old, in the theatrical experience.' Over the more than 30 years since its founding by Greg Kandel in 1974, the theatre has produced over 150 plays, including more than 30 world premieres, and has received a bunch of Chicago's prestigious Joseph Jefferson Awards. Artistic director B.J. Jones notes that Northlight continues 'to balance artistic risk with engaging and pleasurable evenings in the theatre' and invites audiences to come to the theatre 'ready to think, to feel, to be challenged, and to enjoy. In return we will offer you thought-provoking, emotionally engaging work, flecked with humor and rich with the familiar ache of the human experience.' Northlight produces musicals, classics, world premieres – and, adds B.J. Jones, 'freshly minted work from the New York and world stage.'

Casting

Northlight Theatre casts primarily from actors based in the Chicago area. Casting actors from outside this area depends specifically upon the demands of each individual production. General Equity auditions are held once a year and listings are made on the Northlight website, in *PerformInk*, and via the Equity Hotline. General auditions are usually held in early summer for non-Equity performers.

Announcements for non-Equity general auditions are made on the Northlight website and in *PerformInk*. Submit a headshot and résumé with your phone number, c/o Casting, Northlight Theatre, 9501 Skokie Blvd., Skokie, IL 60077. No calls.

General employment opportunities
Check the website for detailed employment information and openings.

Internships
Northlight Theatre offers a variety of internships to qualified applicants with an interest in professional theatre and not-for-profit management. Internships are available in the artistic, administrative, and technical/production areas of the theatre. Check the website for specifics. Internships are generally non-salaried and typically part-time for three months (summer), four months (fall), or five months (winter/spring). Stage management internships are for approximately eight to ten weeks per production and stage management interns may be eligible for stipend positions.

Script submissions
Northlight does not accept unsolicited manuscripts. To have their scripts considered, playwrights should first send Northlight a letter of inquiry with a synopsis of the play and a few sample pages (a scene or less). Include a brief description of any unusual staging requirements, a cast breakdown, and any other such relevant information. If reviews of the play are available (workshop or full production) enclose these as well. Enclose a stamped, self-addressed envelope in order to have your materials returned. Check the website for more detailed information. Northlight does accept submissions from bona-fide literary agents and these should be sent to: Dramaturg and Literary Manager, Northlight Theatre, 9501 Skokie Blvd., Skokie, IL 60077.

THE OLD GLOBE
P.O. Box 122171, San Diego, CA 92112-2171
Administration: (619) 231-1941. Box office: (619) 234-5623. Fax: (619) 231-5879
Email: mailus@theoldglobe.org
www.theoldglobe.org

The Old Globe is the theatre many students and professionals dream of, with its beautiful inside and outside venues in a glorious park, surrounded by a world-class zoo and the Pacific Ocean, and productions that capture America's imagination ranging from musical premieres to Shakespeare. Emerging from the California-Pacific International Exposition in Balboa Park in 1935, The Old Globe now boasts a subscription base of over 40,000 and a reputation for terrific, audience-engaging theatre. Louis G. Spisto is the executive director.

The Old Globe premieres of *Dirty Rotten Scoundrels*, *Hairspray*, *The Full Monty*, *Damn Yankees*, *Into the Woods*, *Joe Turner's Come and Gone*, *Rumors*, *The Piano Lesson*, and *Two Trains Running* (to mention a few) all went on to Broadway productions and both the theatre and former artistic director Jack O'Brien garnered well-deserved Tony Awards.

Casting
Check the website for information and make casting inquiries to: Casting Director, The Old Globe, P.O. Box 122171, San Diego, CA 92112-2171.

Script submissions
Submissions are accepted year-round from agents and by invitation only. No unsolicited scripts; rather, send a synopsis, dialogue sample, and letter of inquiry to: The Old Globe, Artistic Dept., P.O. Box 122171, San Diego, CA 92112.

General employment opportunities
Check the website for opportunities and details and send a cover letter and résumé to: Human Resources, The Old Globe, P.O. Box 122171, San Diego, CA 92112-2171 or email: HR@TheOldGlobe.org.

Internships
While The Old Globe does not offer a formal internship program, individual departments sometimes have openings for non-paid interns for various projects. Old Globe materials encourage students to 'contact the director of the area in which you wish to volunteer your services.' Check the website for staff lists. The Old Globe occasionally accepts applications for internships in stage management, involving interns in daily rehearsals, technical rehearsals, production meetings, and understudy rehearsals. The stage management internship is a full-time

commitment, six days a week. A typical internship would last eight weeks, though the length of internship could be adapted to fit school schedules. Interns are considered company members and receive perks such as complimentary tickets and free entrance to Balboa Park attractions. For stage management internships, send a cover letter, résumé, and two letters of recommendation to: Internships, c/o Production Stage Manager, The Old Globe, P.O. Box 122171, San Diego, CA 92112-2171, or check the website for other options.

OREGON SHAKESPEARE FESTIVAL

15 S. Pioneer Street, Ashland, OR 97520
Administration: (541) 482-2111. Box office: (541) 482-4331. Fax: (541) 482-0446
Email: administration@osfashland.org
www.osfashland.org

The Tony Award-winning Oregon Shakespeare Festival (OSF) is the USA's largest nonprofit theatre and employs approximately 600 theatre professionals (around 375 full-time). OSF produces 11 plays in three theatres (four by Shakespeare and seven by classic and contemporary playwrights). Recent audiences have exceeded 400,000 patrons, with a budget exceeding $26 million. The artistic director is Bill Rauch, a 20-year veteran of the Cornerstone Theater Company. In his own words:

> When I first directed Handler at OSF in 2002, I sensed that I had found
> a new artistic home. Each successive artistic adventure in Ashland has
> continued to deepen that conviction. I've taken risks in every project that
> I've undertaken at the Festival, and those risks have been rewarded by the
> response of a literate and passionate audience. I am moved by the sheer
> eclecticism of the programming – Shakespeare and other classics,
> contemporary work, and brand new plays commissioned for our company.
> I am energized by the scale of the operation: the largest audience and
> acting company in the country, eleven plays, three stunningly different
> theatre spaces, a wide range of educational programs. There is invaluable
> legacy and history, including individuals with 20, 30, even 50 years of
> organizational history, and every year new artists and staff members bring
> fresh perspectives.

Oregon Shakespeare Festival company members are asked to make a commitment to a classical repertory theatre and longer-than-usual contracts for regional theatre. Auditions are usually held in the Festival's home of Ashland, Oregon, as well as in Los Angeles and New York. Check the website for audition and casting information. OSF operates under a modified LORT B+ contract and hires approximately 70 Equity actors and 20 non-Equity actors annually. A special audition hotline is available at (520) 482-2111, ext. 366.

The Oregon Shakespeare Festival's mission is succinct: 'Inspired by Shakespeare's work and the cultural richness of the United States, we reveal our collective humanity through illuminating interpretations of new and classic plays, deepened by the kaleidoscope of rotating repertory.' Founded in 1935 by Angus L. Bowmer, OSF is among the oldest professional regional theatre companies in America. New Zealander Paul Nicholson is the OSF executive director and one of the United States' savviest administrators.

Casting

To apply for an audition slot, actors should send a photo and résumé to: OSF, Attn: Casting, P.O. Box 158, Ashland, OR 97520. OSF asks that résumés include current mailing (or email) addresses and phone numbers, and the names of directors with whom you have worked, as well as the theatres where you have performed. Audition information will then be sent to you. OSF does not offer internships in acting. The Oregon Shakespeare Festival operates on a special contract based on the LORT B+ tier. Contracts are either ten-month (January–October) or seven-month (April–October). Company members routinely perform in several productions, as well as understudying – auditions are for the company, not for specific roles. Check the website for additional details.

Script submissions

OSF does not accept unsolicited manuscripts, only submissions from literary agents. Playwrights who do not have an agent may send OSF a letter of introduction with a synopsis of the play, the first ten pages of the script, and a character list with specifics about age, gender, and ethnicity. If the material interests OSF, they will respond with a request for the complete script. Send submissions or synopses to: Oregon Shakespeare Festival, Attn: Literary Assistant, P.O. Box 158, Ashland, OR 97520.

General employment opportunities

Check the website for openings (including fellowships, assistantships, internships, and residencies), or write to: Director of Human Resources, Oregon Shakespeare Festival, P.O. Box 158, Ashland, OR 97520, or email: Jobs@osfashland.org.

ORLANDO-UCF SHAKESPEARE FESTIVAL

812 E. Rollins Street, Orlando, FL 32803
Administration: (407) 447-1700. Box office: (407) 447-1700, ext. 1.
Fax: (407) 447-1701
Email: info@shakespearefest.org
www.shakespearefest.org

This rapidly developing company is one of the Southeast's best-kept artistic secrets. Orlando-UCF Shakespeare Festival produces top-notch professional theatre, develops edgy new plays, and provides innovative educational and artistic experiences for Central Florida. The UCF in the title refers to the University of Central Florida, a strong Shakespeare supporter that has assisted the Festival in an innovative educational and professional theatre journey first envisioned by founder Stuart Omans in 1989.

Artistic director Jim Helsinger's vision is 'to create theatre of extraordinary quality that encourages the actor/audience relationship, embraces the passionate use of language, and ignites the imagination. Our goal is to be a nationally recognized destination theatre offering productions and education year-round for all audiences.' Today the company's season typically includes six productions, a Theatre for Young Audiences Series, a workshop series for new plays called PlayLab, the ten-day Harriett Lake Festival of New Plays, two summer Shakespeare productions performed by local high school students in their TYC and SYC programs, summer camps for children, community and professional classes, and extensive teaching in K-12 schools. The John and Rita Lowndes Shakespeare Center includes a 324-seat theatre, a 118-seat theatre, the 70-seat Studio B, and the 100-seat Studio D. Boldly situated on a lake on the edge of downtown Orlando is an amphitheatre for the summer Shakespeare plays.

Casting, general employment opportunities

Direct links from the company website provide quick access to timely audition information and job openings.

PASADENA PLAYHOUSE

39 S. El Molino Avenue, Pasadena, CA 91101

Administration: (626) 737-2869. Box office: (626) 356-7529. Fax: (626) 792-6142

www.pasadenaplayhouse.org

There's a sense of history, a sense of Hollywood, and a sense of style that permeate the air of the Pasadena Playhouse, one of America's oldest regional theatres (dating back to 1917). At press time, this note was on the website: 'Pasadena Playhouse is now in the process of successfully emerging from bankruptcy. For the next 6 to 12 months productions and services will carefully and slowly build back into full scale.'

Gilmor Brown decided to produce a season of plays in an old burlesque house in 1917 and put together the Savoy Players. By 1925, a new theatre had debuted on South El Molino Avenue and by the 1930s, the Playhouse was a Hollywood showcase. Named the State Theatre in 1937, it was eventually placed on the National Register of Historic Places. Over the years, the theatre has attracted such stars as Dustin Hoffman, Gene Hackman, Linda Hunt, Hal Holbrook, Phylicia Rashad, Harry Groener, Carol Lawrence, Stacey Keach, Bea Arthur, Shirley Knight, Diahann Carroll, Brian Stokes Mitchell, and Rebecca De Mornay. In 2004, the Balcony Theater at the Playhouse reopened to feature the Furious Theatre Company, and a reading series called 'Hothouse at the Playhouse' for the development of new work from diverse and emerging playwrights.

Casting, general employment opportunities, internships

Check the theatre's website and/or write the theatre for ongoing openings and casting information.

Script submissions

'New-play development and the creation of material for the stage from the ground up is both a responsibility and a joyous opportunity for a theatre of our stature and reputation,' notes artistic director Sheldon Epps. Check the website and write to the theatre for submission information.

PEOPLE'S LIGHT & THEATRE COMPANY

39 Conestoga Road, Malvern, PA 19355

Administration: (610) 647-1900. Box office: (610) 644-3500. Fax: (610) 640-9521

Email: pltc@peopleslight.org

www.peopleslight.org

'Simply put,' explain the folk at People's Light, their mission is:

> to bring together theatre artists of the highest caliber with large and
> diverse audiences in a welcoming environment to celebrate an increasingly
> complex world . . . We think that a diversity of age, race, cultural back-
> ground, and aesthetic goals among artists and audiences is vital to artistic
> growth and to the strength of a united community. We maintain a resident
> company of artists because we feel that continuity is essential in order to
> stay closely connected with our community, and for artists, audiences, and
> neighbors to grow together.

Celebrating over 30 years of operation, The People's Light & Theatre is located in the heart of Chester County, Pennsylvania, and averages eight to nine plays per season, mixing world premieres, contemporary plays and fresh approaches to classic texts for a Main Stage Series and Family Discovery Series. 'Project Discovery' is an arts education program serving more than 35,000 young people each year. Also, the year-round Theatre School at People's Light offers classes for adults and young people taught by the theatre's resident artists.

'People's Light was founded in 1974 by four young theatre artists who were committed to two ideals: long-term collaboration among artists with diverse aesthetics, and active participation in the life of the immediate community,' notes artistic director Abigail Adams, who joined the company in 1975. The company's ensemble includes actors, directors, designers, playwrights, dramaturgs, and teaching artists who attract an annual audience of about 100,000 patrons. The physical spaces include two black-box theatres, one with 375 seats, the other 180 seats. People's Light has produced over 300 plays and 100 world and/or regional premieres.

Casting

People's Light has a resident company of over 20 actors, but also casts some Equity and non-Equity roles from outside the company. Those interested in auditioning should send headshot and résumé to: Casting, c/o Management

Associate, 39 Conestoga Road, Malvern, PA 19355. People's Light is a member of the Theatre Alliance of Greater Philadelphia and participates in its Annual Auditions. For more information regarding these auditions, visit the website at www.theatrealliance.org/.

Script submissions, general employment opportunities, internships
To send inquiries, check the website for detailed position descriptions and openings and for a list of staff.

PHILADELPHIA THEATRE COMPANY
Plays & Players Theatre, 1714 Delancey Street, Philadelphia, PA 19103
Mailing address: 230 South 15th Street, Fourth Floor, Philadelphia, PA 19102
Administration: (215) 985-1400. Box office: (215) 985-0420. Fax: (215) 985-5800
www.philadelphiatheatrecompany.org
Philadelphia Theatre Company is 'dedicated to presenting the Philadelphia and world premieres of major works by contemporary playwrights with an emphasis on American drama. We seek to develop an audience of open-minded theatre-goers across cultural, ethnic, and social lines by producing drama that is at once challenging, entertaining, and imaginatively staged.' Founded as The Philadelphia Company in 1974, PTC has produced over 100 world and Philadelphia premieres, including Terrence McNally's *Master Class*, Alan Zweibel's *Bunny Bunny*, David Ives' *Lives of the Saint*, J.T. Rogers' *White People*, John Henry Redwood's *No Niggers, No Jews, No Dogs*, Daniel Stern's *Barbra's Wedding*, Jeffrey Hatcher's *A Picasso*, and Bruce Graham's *According to Goldman*.

Casting
PTC casts on a per-show basis and auditions are held in Philadelphia and New York. Audition notices are posted on their website as well as on the Philadelphia Actors' Equity Hotline, the Theatre Alliance of Greater Philadelphia website, and elsewhere. If you are not already on file or have updated information, send photos and résumés to: Casting Director, Philadelphia Theatre Company, 230 S. 15th Street, 4th Floor, Philadelphia, PA 19102. No phone calls or email submissions.

Script submissions

PTC does not accept unsolicited scripts or inquiries; it directly solicits playwrights of interest and accepts agent submissions. Agents may submit work to: Literary Department, Philadelphia Theatre Company, 230 S. 15th Street, 4th Floor, Philadelphia, PA 19102.

General employment opportunities, internships, fellowships

Check the website for ongoing listings. PTC Fellowships include the Career Development Initiative (CDI) in Directing and Production. Applications and details are provided on the website or email careers@phillytheatreco.com.

THE PHOENIX THEATRE

749 N. Park Avenue, Indianapolis, Indiana 46202
Administration: (317) 635-2381. Box office: (317) 635-7529. Fax: (317) 635-0010
Email: info@phoenixtheatre.org
www.phoenixtheatre.org
Founded in 1983, The Phoenix Theatre is a year-round professional company focusing on new, diverse, and challenging plays. It produces in the 150-seat proscenium Mainstage and the 70- to 80-seat Underground Stage. The artistic director is Michael Barnard.

General employment opportunities, apprenticeships, internships

Check the website or email info@phoenixtheatre.org for details.

PIONEER THEATRE COMPANY

University of Utah, Simmons Pioneer Memorial Theatre, 300 South 1400 East #325, Salt Lake City, UT 84112-0660
Administration: (801) 581-6356. Box office: (801) 581-6961. Fax: (801) 581-5472
Audition Hotline: (801) 585-3927.
www.pioneertheatre.org
Founded in 1962, Salt Lake's ambitious regional theatre is in residence at the University of Utah. The company produces a seven-play season running from September through May that includes classics, musicals, and contemporary dramas

and comedies. The theatre prides itself on being the first in Utah to produce important works by contemporary playwrights, such as August Wilson's *Fences*, Tom Stoppard's *Arcadia*, David Auburn's *Proof*, and Wendy Wasserstein's *An American Daughter*. Charles Morey is the longtime artistic director and he doesn't shy away from large-scale productions.

Casting, general employment opportunities

Check the company website for quick access to timely audition information and job openings. PTC generally holds auditions for shows in Salt Lake City and New York City. For Salt Lake auditions, check the website or call (801) 585-3927. New York audition appointments are through agent submissions only.

PITTSBURGH PUBLIC THEATER

621 Penn Avenue, Pittsburgh, PA 15222
Administration: (412) 316-8200. Box office: (412) 316-1600. Fax: (412) 316-8216
Email: info@ppt.org
www.ppt.org

This revered professional theatre has been an important part of Pittsburgh's renaissance of the arts and the downtown area. Founded by Joan Apt, Margaret Rieck, and Ben Shaktman, chartered in 1974, and opened in 1975, the Pittsburgh Public Theater's mission is to 'provide artistically diverse theatrical experiences of the highest quality.' The 650-seat O'Reilly Theater was designed by the world-renowned architect Michael Graves and is located in the heart of Pittsburgh's Cultural District. The venue was a $20 million project of The Pittsburgh Cultural Trust. The Hazlett Theater, dedicated by President Benjamin Harrison in 1889, was the Public's first home (1974-99). Ted Pappas is the artistic director.

Casting

Auditions are held on a show-by-show basis for Equity and non-Equity actors. Notices are placed in local newspapers, at local talent agencies, and on the Public Theater website. Actors may send a headshot and résumé to: Pittsburgh Public Theater, Attn: Artistic, 621 Penn Avenue, Pittsburgh, PA 15222.

Script submissions

PPT accepts full scripts only from literary agents or with a letter of recommendation from an artistic director or literary manager of an established professional theatre or playwriting organization. PPT accepts unsolicited queries only. Queries should include a cover letter with the playwright's contact information, a one-page synopsis of the play, and a dialogue sample of up to ten pages. Response time for queries is two to four months. Include a stamped, self-addressed envelope for a response. Queries should be addressed to 'Resident Dramaturg' at the PPT address. Check the website for details.

General employment opportunities, internships

Check the website for specifics. Pittsburgh Public Theater offers internships on a show-by-show, semester, and/or seasonal basis. Hours vary depending on the need and range from 20 to 40 per week. All internships are unpaid; however, academic credit is available at the discretion of the intern's enrolled institution. Internships are generally offered in production management, technical administration, costume design and construction, literary and education, sound design, lighting design, scenic art, and administration and finance. Send a letter of interest indicating internship of choice, a résumé, and three references to: Education Department Internship, Program, Pittsburgh Public Theater, 621 Penn Avenue, Pittsburgh, PA 15222.

PLAYMAKERS REPERTORY COMPANY

CB# 3235, Center for Dramatic Art, UNC Campus, Chapel Hill, NC 27599-3235
Administration: (919) 962-2489. Box office: (919) 962-PLAY(7529).
Fax: (919) 962-5791
www.playmakersrep.org

A long legacy of theatre excellence began in 1918 with the Carolina Playmakers at the University of North Carolina at Chapel Hill and developed into the PlayMakers Repertory Company, founded in 1975. In the theatre's own words,

> Our purpose is to provide a top-quality public arena for the professional implementation of the philosophy and aesthetics explored in the Department of Dramatic Art. Through the collaboration of guest artists, resident professionals, students, and audiences, we examine the theatrical event

and the methods used for its realization in contemporary performance.
We explore playmaking in our time.

The theatre's season generally runs from September through April, featuring six plays in the 500-seat Paul Green Theatre built in 1978. In 1998, the Center for Dramatic Art expanded to include the 265-seat Elizabeth Price Kenan Theatre, where each season PlayMakers also presents three plays in its second stage series. Joseph Haj is the producing artistic director.

Casting, script submissions, general employment opportunities
Check out the website (www.playmakersrep.org) for contact numbers and information.

PORTLAND CENTER STAGE

128 NW Eleventh Ave, Portland, OR 97209
Administration: (503) 445-3720. Box office, toll free: (877) 727-8587
Fax: (503) 445-3701
Email: info@pcs.org
www.pcs.org

Portland Center Stage 'dares to make theatre as ravishing, innovative and thought provoking as our wildest dreams,' explains company publications. PCS produces a blend of classical, contemporary, and premier works as well as a summer playwrights festival, Just Add Water/West. In residence at the Portland Center for the Performing Arts, PCS has nearly 8,000 subscribers and attracts an annual audience of more than 90,000 patrons. PCS began as the northern sibling of the Oregon Shakespeare Festival in Ashland and premiered in 1988 with *Heartbreak House*. In 1993, after five successful seasons, the company became an independent theatre company and Elizabeth Huddle was selected as producing artistic director in 1994. Chris Coleman became the theatre's fourth artistic director in 2000. PCS produces seven annual productions in the Winningstad and Newmark Theatres. In 2004, the company announced a $32.9 million capital campaign to build a new theatre complex in the historic Portland Armory to house a 599-seat main stage theatre, a smaller, 200-seat black-box theatre, administrative offices, a rehearsal hall and production facilities. They moved into the new complex in 2006.

Casting

Check the website for Equity and non-Equity audition information, dates, and contact numbers.

Script submissions

Portland Center Stage accepts full-length scripts from literary agents. PCS also accepts scripts directly from writers when they are recommended by the artistic director or literary manager of a professional theatre or playwrights' organization. Those without agents may query the theatre for interest in a particular script. Check the website for the six major instructions for queries. Submissions or query letters may be sent to: Literary Manager, c/o: Portland Center Stage, 1111 SW Broadway, Portland, OR 97205. Email questions to literary@pcs.org.

General employment opportunities

Detailed job descriptions are often posted on the website. For more information contact PCS at jobs@pcs.org.

PORTLAND STAGE COMPANY

25A Forest Avenue, Portland, ME 04101
Mailing address: P.O. Box 1458, Portland, ME 04104
Administration: (207) 774-1043. Box office: (207) 774-0465. Fax: (207) 774-0576
Email: info@portlandstage.com
www.portlandstage.com

This northern New England professional theatre produces a wide range of artistic works and programs that, in the theatre's own words, 'explore basic human issues and concerns relevant to the communities served by the theatre.' The company uses the theatre as a 'catalyst for discussion, debate, interpretation, and exploring the human condition, historically and currently, in our society and in the global community.' Founded in 1974 as a touring company, the Profile Theatre, Portland Stage Company has an audience of around 40,000 annual patrons and produces two festivals. The Little Festival of the Unexpected connects young American playwrights with audiences in a week-long event devoted to the development of new plays and, in a collaboration with the University of Iowa's International Writing Program, From Away brings international writers to Portland to share ideas and perspectives from other cultures.

Casting, script submissions, general employment opportunities
Check the website and write the theatre for information.

Internships
PSC internships introduce recent college graduates to professional theatre. PSC generally accepts about a dozen interns in directing/dramaturgy, stage management, marketing/development, carpentry/props, costumes, and general production. Interns generally work full-time, receive housing and a stipend, and work from late August through May. Check the company website for applications, details, descriptions, and deadlines.

PRINCE MUSIC THEATER
1412 Chestnut Street, Philadelphia, PA 19103
Business office: 100 South Broad Street, Suite 650, Philadelphia, PA 19110
Administration: (215) 972-1000. Box office: (215) 569-9700. Fax: (215) 972-1020
www.princemusictheater.org
Email: info@princemusictheater.org
In its own words, the mission of the Prince Music Theater is 'to nurture and develop the unique American art form of music theatre of the highest artistic caliber over a wide aesthetic range – including opera, music drama, musical comedy, and experimental work. Above all, we are dedicated to artists of our time seeking to break new ground, while we also celebrate the legacy of the creative mavericks and pioneers who have forged the American musical theatre.' Founded in 1984 as the American Music Theater Festival, the company worked in over two dozen venues throughout Philadelphia until 1999, when it found a permanent home in the former Midtown Theater. Marjorie Samoff is the producing artistic director. The Prince Music Theater serves a diverse local audience and 'a national community of artists and organizations dedicated to creating a body of contemporary American work as a legacy for the future.'

Casting
Audition notices are posted on the Theatre Alliance of Greater Philadelphia listserve, aka 'T@GP Listserv.' Please see the website www.theatrealliance.org for details on how to subscribe to the listserv. Actors/singers may also check the website for details or write to: Prince Music Theater, Attn: Casting Director, 100

South Broad Street, Suite 650, Philadelphia, PA 19110. Email submissions to casting@princemusictheatre.org.

Script submissions, general employment opportunities
Check the website for specific opportunities or write the theatre for information.

Internships
Internships are generally available in the administrative, marketing, or artistic departments. Applicants should send a résumé and letter of introduction to: Personnel Dept., Prince Music Theater, 100 South Broad Street, Suite 650, Philadelphia, PA 19110 or fax it to (215) 972-1020.

THE PUBLIC THEATER/NEW YORK SHAKESPEARE FESTIVAL
See the section on Shakespeare Festivals that follows.

THE REPERTORY THEATRE OF ST. LOUIS
P.O. Box 191730, St. Louis, Missouri 63119
Administration: (314) 968-7340. Box office: (314) 968-4925.
Fax: (314) 968-9638
Email: mail@repstl.org
www.repstl.org
Founded in 1966, the Repertory Theater of St. Louis has evolved into one of America's most exciting, productive, and respected regional theatres. Artistic director Steven Woolf has been at the helm since 1986; managing director Mark D. Bernstein arrived in 1987. The Rep has mixed the classics, musicals, new plays, and contemporary work in its 733-seat Mainstage theatre, 125-seat Studio theatre, and 75-seat Lab Space. 'The Rep seeks to develop audiences which become strong advocates for live performance,' notes Mr. Woolf. While the Rep operates under an Equity LORT contract, its Imaginary Theatre Company operates under a TYA (Theatre for Young Audiences) contract.

Casting
The Rep holds local, annual general auditions. Requirements vary from season to season but generally call upon actors to prepare two contrasting monologues (or

a monologue and a song for musical auditions). Both Equity and non-Equity actors are invited to audition. Actors should check the website and/or the *St. Louis Post-Dispatch* and the *Riverfront Times* for additional information and opportunities. The Rep's New York casting director is Rich Cole, who can be reached through Rich Cole Casting, 648 Broadway, Suite 912, New York, NY 10012, (212) 614-7130. New York casting is handled through agent submissions and open casting calls in New York. These calls are posted as needed or as required by the Actors' Equity Association.

Script submissions, general employment opportunities

Check the website for specific job openings and descriptions and/or email (mail@repstl.org) for information regarding employment and play submissions.

Internships

Internship opportunities are posted on the company website when available.

ROUNDABOUT THEATRE COMPANY

231 West 39th Street, Suite 1200, New York, NY 10018
Administration: (212) 719-9393. Box office: (212) 719-1300. Fax: (212) 869-8817
Email: info@roundabouttheatre.org
www.roundabouttheatre.org

Located in the heart of New York's Times Square, the Roundabout is one of America's best placed and most beloved theatres. The company achieved an amazing turnaround, moving from near bankruptcy to over two-dozen Tony Awards over the years with artistic director Todd Haimes in the driver's seat. At the very heart of the Roundabout's work is, in the company's own words, its 'commitment to teaming great theatrical works with the industry's finest artists to re-energize classic plays and musicals.' The institutional mission was expanded in 1995 to include 'the development and production of new works by today's great writers and composers. The production of these new works, alongside the production of classics, enables Roundabout to embody the crossroads of American theatre.' Playing to over 40,000 subscribers and a million patrons annually, the Roundabout operates the American Airlines Theatre, Studio 54, and the Harold and Miriam Steinberg Center for Theatre/ Laura Pels Theatre.

Founded in 1965 by Gene Feist and Elizabeth Owens, the Roundabout opened in a 150-seat theatre in the basement of a supermarket in Chelsea before moving into a converted 299-seat movie theatre on West 23rd Street in 1974. In 1984 Roundabout took up residence in Union Square's Tammany Hall, then moved again in 1991 for a brief stay at the Criterion Center on West 45th Street. The 399-seat Laura Pels Theatre opened in 1995.

Casting, script submissions, general employment opportunities

Check the website for specific opportunities in all areas or email jobs@roundabout theatre.org for information.

Internships

Roundabout internships are usually available in general management, development, marketing, ticket services, business, education, and production (including lighting, props, costume, and production management). Roundabout does not offer internships in acting or literary management. Persons interested in assistant director fellowships must apply through the Drama League's directing fellowship program. Application materials should be sent to: Education Program Associate, Roundabout Theatre Company, 231 West 39th Street, Suite 1200, New York, NY 10018, or by fax to (212) 768-0776. Roundabout's Career Development program accepts high school students, undergraduate and graduate college students, and early-career professionals. Internships typically run from September to December, January to May, or June to September and may be full-time or part-time, depending on the department. Check the website for specifics.

ROUND HOUSE THEATRE

P.O. Box 30688, Bethesda, MD 20824-0688

Bethesda Theatre: 4545 East-West Highway, Bethesda, MD 20814

Silver Spring Theatre: 8641 Colesville Road, Silver Spring, MD 20910

Administration: (240) 644-1099. Box office: (240) 644-1100. Fax: (240) 644-1090

Email: roundhouse@roundhousetheatre.org

www.roundhousetheatre.org

This large award-winning professional theatre company is led by producing artistic director Blake Robison. Based in Maryland, Round House Theatre produces around 200 annual performances in its 400-seat Bethesda theatre and 150-seat black-box theatre in Silver Spring. The company operates an education center in Silver Spring and reaches over 40,000 with strong educational programs. The theatre's critically acclaimed Literary Works Project features new adaptations of contemporary and classical novels, re-interpreted for contemporary audiences. The theatre is committed to world premiere productions, the annual Sarah Metzger Memorial Play, school residency programs ('Intersections'), the Heyday Players, and the artists' laboratory, The Kitchen.

Casting, hiring and career opportunities
Casting, hiring, apprenticeships and other career opportunities are detailed on the company website at www.roundhousetheatre.org

THE SAN FRANCISCO SHAKESPEARE FESTIVAL
P.O. Box 460937, San Francisco CA 94146-0937
Administration/Box office: (415) 558-0888, or toll free (800) 978-PLAY
Fax: (415) 865-4433
Email: sfshakes@sfshakes.org
www.sfshakes.org

The San Francisco Shakespeare Festival's debut production was a triumphant *The Tempest* in Golden Gate Park in 1983. Today, the company is a major producer and arts education provider that includes 'sister organizations' known as the Oakland–East Bay Shakespeare Festival and the Silicon Valley Shakespeare Festival. Free Shakespeare in the Park is produced every year for over 50,000 patrons in San Francisco, Oakland, Pleasanton, and Cupertino from July to October, and Shakespeare on Tour takes a 60-minute Shakespeare performance to students statewide. This includes around 300 annual performances to over 120,000 children.

The Bay Area Shakespeare Camps enable students aged seven to 18 to study Shakespeare. 'Midnight Shakespeare' offers at-risk youth the opportunity to learn communication skills, performance skills, discipline, and teamwork through Shakespeare. The Shakespeare Festival employs over 200 educators, artists, actors, directors, designers. The much-admired executive director is Toby Leavitt.

Casting, general employment opportunities

Check the company website for quick access to timely audition and job information. SFSF also offers production and administrative internships. Free Shakespeare in the Park and indoor mainstage productions operate under a LORT D, LOA contract, and employ a mix of Equity and non-Equity actors. Shakespeare on Tour is a non-Equity program. The Shakespeare Festival holds open auditions for both programs, and posts upcoming auditions in regional trade publications. For information on upcoming auditions, call (415) 865-4434, ext. 5. Those interested in employment with the Shakespeare Festival should send a cover letter and résumé to: The San Francisco Shakespeare Festival, P.O. Box 460937, San Francisco, CA 94146.

SAN JOSE REPERTORY THEATRE

101 Paseo de San Antonio, San Jose, CA 95113
Administration: (408) 367-7266. Box office: (408) 367-7255. Fax: (408) 367-7237
Email: help@sjrep.com
www.sjrep.com

Perhaps one of America's best-kept regional theatre secrets, San Jose Rep operates in a snazzy complex in the heart of downtown San Jose, a booming community that has long emerged from the shadow of San Francisco. The artistic director is Rick Lombardo. Serving the Silicon Valley and the greater Bay Area, the Rep generally produces seven mainstage shows and offers extensive community and educational outreach programs, including Red Ladder Theatre Company (for disadvantaged youth and other underserved groups) and creative dramatics classes. Founded in 1980 by James P. Reber, the company plays to over 120,000 patrons annually in its over 500-seat theatre.

Casting

San Jose Rep hires actors on a show-to-show basis, choosing Equity actors and local non-union actors (generally only for large-cast productions and as extras). Auditions are by invitation only and may include both Equity and non-Equity actors. Out-of-town actors who plan to be in the San Jose area may request an audition by contacting the casting office. San Jose Repertory Theatre holds annual auditions in late spring/early summer. Audition information is announced on the

Equity Hotline, Theatre Bay Area Hotline, *Callboard* magazine, and on the website. The Rep's artistic staff also attend the Theatre Bay Area general auditions each year. Actors may submit a headshot-résumé and cover letter to: Casting Director, San Jose Repertory Theatre, 101 Paseo de San Antonio, San Jose, CA 95113.

Script submissions, general employment opportunities, internships
Email the company (info@sjrep.com) for specific openings and opportunities.

SEATTLE CHILDREN'S THEATRE
201 Thomas Street, Seattle, WA 98109
Administration: (206) 443-0807. Box office: (206) 441-3322. Fax: (206) 443-0442
Drama School: (206) 443-0807, ext. 1186.
Email: info@sct.org. School email: dramaschool@sct.org
www.sct.org

Time magazine has hailed the Seattle Children's Theatre for its outstanding work and, in the theatre's own words, SCT 'offers the best in professional, thought-provoking performances for the entire family, from foot-stomping musicals like *Seussical* to classic adaptations like *Sleeping Beauty*.' SCT produces from September through June in its two Seattle Center theatres. SCT also runs the SCT Drama School, offering theatre arts classes for the public. Throughout its 30-year history SCT has entertained over four million children and adults. Artistic director Linda Hartzell has been at SCT since 1985 and was joined by Tim Jennings, managing director, in 2008.

Casting
SCT only accepts audition materials during general auditions in the spring. People interested in auditioning for mainstage productions should refer to SCT's auditions page on the web: www.sct.org/aboutus/workwithus/auditions.aspx.

General employment opportunities, internships
The best way to find information about jobs and internships is to visit www.sct.org/aboutus/workwithus/jobsinternships.aspx. SCT internships often include work with the Drama School and Education Outreach program, as well as assistant teaching in a variety of classes.

SEATTLE REPERTORY THEATRE

155 Mercer Street, P.O. Box 900923, Seattle, WA 98109
Administration: (206) 443-2210. Box office: (206) 443-2222, or toll free (877)
900-9285. Fax: 206) 443-2379
Email: feedback@seattlerep.org
www.seattlerep.org

One of the largest regional theatres in the country, Seattle Repertory Theatre produces a mix of classics, recent Broadway hits and cutting-edge new works in two
theatre spaces. Since SRT's founding in 1963, Lily Tomlin, Samuel L. Jackson, Meryl
Streep, Richard Gere, Richard Chamberlain, Jessica Tandy, Christopher Walken, and
many more have all 'walked the boards' at the Rep. SRT has premiered plays by
August Wilson, Neil Simon, John Patrick Shanley, Wendy Wasserstein, Sarah Ruhl
and many others with some of the world's top directors, designers and artisans.
SRT received the 1990 Tony Award for Outstanding Regional Theatre.

Casting

The Seattle Rep artistic staff, in consultation with directors, invites individual actors
to read for roles in specific productions. These auditions are held throughout the
year on an invitation-only basis in Seattle, and also possibly in New York, Chicago,
or Los Angeles as the project warrants. Seattle Repertory Theatre participates in
the annual general auditions organized by Theatre Puget Sound. These auditions
are one of the most important opportunities for Seattle Rep's artistic staff to see
and stay current with the work of local actors. The dates for general auditions and
procedures to apply are announced at least one month in advance on Theatre
Puget Sound's site. Seattle Rep also holds a yearly general audition for Equity
actors. Audition appointments are made on a first-come, first-served basis to
Equity members, and there may be remaining slots available for non-Equity
actors. The auditions (and sign-up procedures) are announced two weeks prior
through Actors' Equity Association and on Theatre Puget Sound's site.

Script submissions

SRT welcomes submissions from playwrights, literary agents, and theatre colleagues with whom we have an existing professional relationship. They do not
accept unsolicited submissions or queries. Unsolicited scripts will be returned via
a stamped, self-addresseed envelope, or recycled. The only exception to this

policy is for playwrights whose permanent address is located within the Pacific Northwest (Washington, Oregon and Idaho). Those scripts will be read by a member of the literary staff.

General employment opportunities, internships

Current job/internship listings are posted on the company website. The requested materials should be sent to: Human Resources, Seattle Repertory Theatre, 155 Mercer Street, P.O. Box 900923, Seattle, WA 98109. Email inquiries may also be sent to: humanresources@seattlerep.org. No phone calls.

SEVEN ANGELS THEATRE

Hamilton Park Pavilion/Plank Road, Waterbury, CT 06705
Mailing address: P.O. Box 3358, Waterbury, CT 06705
Administration: (203) 591-8223. Box office: (203) 757-4676. Fax: (203) 757-1807
www.sevenangelstheatre.org

Seven Angels Theatre is a professional Equity theatre founded in 1990. The company notes that it is 'the only major professional arts organization to emerge in Waterbury and the Greater Waterbury region in 60 years' and it has the region's largest subscriber base (around 2,000) with annual attendance of approximately 50,000 patrons. The company produces and presents up to 200 performances a year and has an active educational program that includes Young Angels, Bright Lights, Summer Theatre Camp, and presents various Children's Plays.

Casting, general employment opportunities, internships

SAT hires Equity, non-Equity, and community talent and provides various internships. Send résumés and headshots to: Seven Angels Theatre, P.O. Box 3358, Waterbury, CT 06705.

THE SHAKESPEARE CENTER LOS ANGELES

1238 West 1st Street, Los Angeles, CA 90026
Administrative/Box office: (213) 481-2273. Fax: (213) 975-9833
www.shakespearecenter.org

Producing artistic director Ben Donenberg founded The Shakespeare Center Los Angeles (formerly Shakespeare/LA) in 1984. He describes the company as 'driven by an underlying impulse that equates the creation of professional, award-winning theatre with the performance of tangible human services. Our evolving programs reflect this impulse as they demonstrate, in form and content, a unique, effective, and artful response to the pressing need for community development.' The Shakespeare Center Los Angeles moved into a new home in downtown Los Angeles in 2000, which allowed the organization to create new institutional partnerships (including being a part of the NEA Shakespeare project) and boost programming for teachers and inner-city youth in Los Angeles.

In addition to its summer festival and educational programs, the Center's youth employment program hires young people challenged by severe economic circumstances to 'create and perform an adaptation of a Shakespeare play' while other initiatives help teachers find unique ways to tackle Shakespeare in the classroom. Highly lauded professional performances of Shakespeare's plays are offered free of charge.

SHAKESPEARE THEATRE COMPANY

Lansburgh Theatre: 450 7th Street NW, Washington, DC 20004

Sidney Harman Hall: 610 F Street NW, Washington, DC 20004

Administrative office: The Shakespeare Theatre, 516 8th Street SE, Washington, DC 20003-2834

Administration: (202) 547-3230. Box office: (202) 547-1122, or toll free (877) 487-8849. Fax: (202) 547-0226

Email: web_admin@shakespearedc.org

www.shakespearedc.org

The Shakespeare Theatre Company's innovative approach to Shakespeare and other classic playwrights has earned it the reputation as one of the nation's premier classical theatre companies. By focusing on works with profound themes, complex characters, and poetic language written by Shakespeare, his contemporaries and the playwrights he influenced, TST's artistic mission is unique among theatre companies: to present theatre of scope and size in an imaginative, skillful and accessible American style that honors the playwrights' language and intentions while viewing their work through a twenty-first-century lens. Artistic director Michael Kahn has led the organization for over two dozen years. In its 2007–2008 season, it opened the Harman Center for the Arts, consisting of the new 775-seat Sidney Harman Hall and the 451-seat Lansburgh Theatre, both located in downtown Washington's Penn Quarter neighborhood. A dynamic hub of activity, the Harman Center showcases the company as well as outstanding local performing arts groups and nationally renowned organizations.

Academy for Classical Acting

Intended for professional actors, the Academy for Classical Acting is accredited through The George Washington University and involves 12 months of study in voice, speech, acting, text, mask, Alexander technique, movement, clown, and stage combat. Check the website for more details.

Casting

TST has a small resident acting company and casts other roles (both Equity and non-Equity) on an ongoing basis throughout the year. Most auditions are by invitation only. TST also attends the Washington, DC–Baltimore Area Wide Auditions for Equity members each winter, and the League of Washington Theatres general auditions every summer. General auditions are advertised in *Back Stage* for New York auditions and general auditions are held in DC each summer. TST also reviews photos and résumés received by mail, and contacts actors to schedule auditions based on their classical experience and training. New York casting director, Stuart Howard Associates coordinates all New York auditions. See the website for more details. Mail casting inquiries, photos and résumés to: Associate Director, The Shakespeare Theatre, 516 8th Street SE, Washington, DC 20003.

General employment opportunities

Check the website for specific openings, details and job descriptions, or email inquiries to: jobs@shakespearedc.org. No calls.

Internships

Administrative internships are generally available in artistic administration, development, education, general management, graphic design, and public relations/marketing. Production internships often surface in costumes, lighting, production management, sound, stage management, stage properties, and technical direction.

Acting Fellows

The Shakespeare Theatre provides opportunities for up to eight actors to join the Acting Fellows Company for a full season as part of established relationships with Vassar College and the Kennedy Center American College Theatre Festival. Actors who are not affiliated with a particular program may audition for remaining positions. Check the website for details.

THE SHAKESPEARE THEATRE OF NEW JERSEY

36 Madison Avenue, Madison, NJ 07940
Administration: (973) 408-3278. Box office: (973) 408-5600. Fax: (973) 408-3361
Email: information@shakespearenj.org
www.shakespearenj.org

Founded in 1962, The Shakespeare Theatre of New Jersey (formerly the New Jersey Shakespeare Festival) plays to over 100,000 audience members annually and is New Jersey's only professional theatre company dedicated to Shakespeare's canon and other classic masterworks. In its own words, the company 'strives to illuminate the universal and lasting relevance of the classics for contemporary audiences.' The vibrant artistic director, Bonnie J. Monte, has led the company since 1990. The mainstage season plays out in the F.M. Kirby Shakespeare Theatre in Madison and runs June through December. An outdoor stage production is presented each summer at The Greek Theatre, an open-air amphitheatre located on the College of Saint Elizabeth campus in nearby Morris Township. The institution's staff of 22 full-time employees works year round and is joined by more than 250 additional company members during the heart of the season.

Casting, general employment opportunities, internships

Check the website or email the theatre for details.

SIGNATURE THEATRE COMPANY

4200 Campbell Avenue, Arlington, VA 22206
Administration: (571) 527-1860. Box office: (703) 820-9771. Fax: (703) 845-0236.
Email: tickets@signature-theatre.org
www.sig-online.org

When Cameron Mackintosh, Stephen Sondheim, Fred Ebb (in memoriam), and John Kander are your honorary trustees, how far can you go? Evidently, right to the top as the Signature Theatre won the 2009 Regional Theatre Tony Award and has been producing award-winning theatre since 1990. In its own words, Signature Theatre's mission is 'to produce contemporary musicals and plays, reinvent classic musicals, develop new work, and reach its community through engaging educational and outreach opportunities.' Signature Theatre dared to produce new works in its tiny original space (a renovated auto garage) and the theatre is well known for its exciting Sondheim productions, adaptations of overlooked or forgotten works, and commitment to new projects. Signature Theatre has received over 276 Helen Hayes Award nominations and at least 70 Hayes Awards. In 2007, Signature Theatre moved into a new complex in an upbeat urban Arlington location, Shirlington Village. Eric Schaeffer is the artistic director.

THE SITI COMPANY

SITI Company Studio and Offices, 520 Eighth Avenue, Suite 310, New York, NY 10018
Administration: (212) 868-0860. Fax: (212) 868-0837
Email: inbox@siti.org
www.siti.org

Artistic director Anne Bogart founded SITI with Japanese director Tadashi Suzuki in 1992. The ensemble-based theatre company's three ongoing components are 'the creation of new work, the training of young theatre artists, and a commitment to international collaboration.' In its own words, the company was founded 'to redefine and revitalize contemporary theatre in the United States through an emphasis on international cultural exchange and collaboration.' Originally envisioned as a summer institute in Saratoga Springs, New York, SITI has expanded to encompass a year-round program based in New York City with a summer season in Saratoga. SITI believes that 'contemporary American theatre must necessarily incorporate artists from around the world and learn from the resulting cross-cultural exchange of dance, music, art, and performance experiences.' Two notable collaborations include *Reunion* (about eight aging, negative, still-angry Group Theater people who are reunited for a public symposium to discuss the story of the Group Theater in the 1930s) and *Hotel Cassiopeia*, a collage of images, events, songs, movie stars, and dances, written by Charles L. Mee.

SOUTH COAST REPERTORY

655 Town Center Drive, P.O. Box 2197, Costa Mesa, CA 92628-2197
Administration: (714) 708-5500. Box office: (714) 708-5555. Fax: (714) 545-0391
Email: theatre@scr.org
www.scr.org

David Emmes and Martin Benson made up one of the longest-running artistic teams in regional theatre history, and Marc Masterson was announced as the new artistic director in 2011. The theatre's work developing new plays is among America's most accomplished. South Coast Repertory was founded in the belief that 'theatre is an art form with a unique power to illuminate the human experience.' As testimony to its success, the company was awarded the Regional Theatre Tony Award in 1988. In the company's words, 'We commit ourselves to exploring the most urgent human and social issues of our time, and to merging literature, design, and performance in ways that test the bounds of theatre's artistic possibilities. We undertake to advance the art of theatre in the service of our community, and aim to extend that service through educational, intercultural, and outreach programs that harmonize with our artistic mission.' The esteemed managing director is Paula Tomei.

Opening with *Tartuffe* in 1964 in the Newport Beach Ebell Club, South Coast Repertory rented a former marine hardware store on Balboa Peninsula that was developed into a 75-seat proscenium stage in 1965. Don Took, Martha McFarland, Art Koustik, Richard Doyle, Hal Landon Jr., and Ron Boussom were deemed the theatre's founding artists and most still turn up 40 years later on South Coast Repertory stages. A variety store in Costa Mesa was converted into a 217-seat theatre in 1967, and in 1978–79, a new 507-seat main stage and 161-seat second stage were built in Costa Mesa on donated land. A 336-seat stage and major renovations to the complex and existing theatres were completed in 2002. Pivotal to the theatre's accomplishments over the years have been the NewSCRipts play readings, the Hispanic Playwrights Project, and the Pacific Playwrights Festival.

Casting

South Coast Repertory operates its Segerstrom and Argyros Stage theatres under LORT contracts, and produces three Theatre for Young Audience productions and a yearly educational touring production under a LORT TYA contract. The company casts its season on a show-by-show basis. Photos and résumés from Los Angeles-area actors only may be submitted for specific productions. South Coast Repertory also hires non-union talent from time to time for specific projects. Submit photos and résumés with a cover letter and contact information clearly printed on the résumé to: Casting, South Coast Repertory, P.O. Box 2197, Costa Mesa, CA 92628-2197. For more information, email the casting office or check the website for details. South Coast Repertory participates in the Actors' Equity general auditions twice each season and actors wishing to attend these auditions should contact the Equity offices for dates and times.

General employment opportunities
South Coast Repertory posts detailed position descriptions and openings on the company website (www.scr.org).

Colab and NewSCRipts
Colab is an integrated play development program employing diverse strategies to aid playwrights in creating new work. Playwright commissions support writers and help the theatre develop long-term relationships. *Rabbit Hole* by David Lindsay-Abaire, *The Violet Hour* by Richard Greenberg, *Collected Stories* by Donald Margulies, *Golden Child* by David Henry Hwang, and *The Beard of Avon* by Amy Freed were all successful South Coast Repertory commissions. Other recent commissioned playwrights include Nilo Cruz, Lynn Nottage, Howard Korder, and Tracy Letts.

NewSCRipts is a developmental staged reading series that allows playwrights to hear their work read in front of an audience, receive feedback, and work closely with the theater's literary staff for further development. The theatre does not accept direct submissions to the NewSCRipts program or the Pacific Playwrights Festival. Participation is by invitation for projects submitted according to the procedures outlined on the website. The Pacific Playwrights Festival presents six to eight new plays in readings, workshops, and productions during a three-day period.

SYRACUSE STAGE
820 East Genesee Street, Syracuse, NY 13210
Administration: (315) 443-4008. Box office: (315) 443-3275. Fax: (315) 443-9846
Email: syrstage@syr.edu
www.syracusestage.org
An exciting theatre in a great university town, Syracuse Stage generally produces eight mainstage plays, a Young Playwrights Festival, a children's touring show, and

educational programs as central New York's premier regional theatre. In its own words, the theatre's mission is 'to enrich, empower, and entertain our community through the creation of professional theatre.' Over 90,000 annual patrons attend Syracuse Stage productions and the theatre has produced a number of world premieres, including works by Tina Howe, Michele Lowe, and Cheryl West.

Syracuse Stage was founded in 1974 by Arthur Storch, a Broadway director who arrived in town as chairman of the Syracuse University Drama program. Growing audiences prompted the 1979 conversion of an old movie theatre into the flexible 499-seat John D. Archbold Theatre. The actors, directors, and designers employed by Syracuse Stage are usually professionals working in New York and Los Angeles and at resident theatres around the country. Timothy Bond is the producing artistic director.

Casting, general employment opportunities, internships
Check the website or email syrstage@syr.edu for ongoing information.

Script submissions
To submit a play for consideration, send your résumé, the plot synopsis, and ten-page dialogue sample to: Play Submissions, Syracuse Stage, 820 East Genesee Street, Syracuse, NY 13210-1508.

THEATRE FOR A NEW AUDIENCE
154 Christopher Street, #3D, New York, NY 10014
Administration: (212) 229-2819. Box office: (212) 229-2819, ext. 0
Fax: (212) 229-2911
Email: info@tfana.org
www.tfana.org
Founded by artistic director Jeffrey Horowitz in 1979, Theatre for a New Audience states that its mission is 'to help develop and vitalize the performance and study of Shakespeare and classic drama.' Theatre for a New Audience produces for audiences Off-Broadway, tours nationally and internationally, and even presented two Shakespeare productions at the Royal Shakespeare Company in England. In its own words, 'Theatre for a New Audience finds the contemporary heart of the classics' with 'a reverence for language, spirit of adventure and visual boldness.'

The company has worked with many of the world's best, including Julie Taymor, Sir Peter Hall, Robert Woodruff, Bartlett Sher, and Peter Brook. For performance venues see http://www.tfana.org. Theatre for a New Audience produces at The Duke Theater in a 199-seat flexible space.

Casting
All casting is through Deborah Brown Casting, 160 West End Avenue, Suite 15P, New York, NY 10023. No calls.

General employment opportunities
General employment opportunities are posted on Playbill.com and/or in TCG's *ARTSEARCH*. Administrative and stage management internship availability varies on a season-by-season basis. TFANA does not offer acting internships. Check the website for more information.

Script submissions
Theatre for a New Audience does not accept play submissions.

American Directors Project
The American Directors Project was established in 1997 to promote the development of American directors of Shakespeare. Through this program, TFANA invites six to eight young to mid-career directors to work with a remarkable array of professionals. Past participants have included Cicely Berry, Karin Coonrod, Scott Ellis, Bartlett Sher, Victor Garber, and Ron Rifkin. Check the website for annual information.

THEATREWORKS
P.O. Box 50458, Palo Alto, CA 94303-0458
Administration: (650) 463-1950. Box office: (650) 463-1960;
Fax: (650) 463-1963
www.theatreworks.org
Founded in 1970 by artistic director Robert Kelley, TheatreWorks 'is committed to being one of America's outstanding professional theatres . . . Our work celebrates the human spirit through innovative premieres, productions, and programs inspired by our exceptionally diverse community.' TheatreWorks employs over 300

artists annually, has a professional staff of 42, and plays to over 100,000 enthusiastic patrons each year. The company offers a year-round season of dramas, comedies, musicals, and world premieres in the 625-seat Mountain View Center for the Performing Arts and in the 425-seat Lucie Stern Theatre in Palo Alto.

Casting

TheatreWorks holds general auditions twice each year, typically in March and September. The company also attends the Theatre Bay Area regional auditions held each spring. Callbacks are by invitation for each production, throughout the year. The theatre hires Equity and non-Equity actors. Check the website for additional information. In the company's own words, 'TheatreWorks has a long history of culturally specific and non-traditional casting.' Auditions are listed in *Theatre Bay Area* magazine. Actors can also check the theatre's voicemail message at (650) 463-1950, ext. 610, email (casting@theatreworks.org), or call (650) 463-7107.

Script submissions

TheatreWorks prefers 'well-written, well-constructed plays that celebrate the human spirit through innovative productions and programs inspired by our exceptionally diverse community. There is no limit on the number of characters, and we favor plays with multi-ethnic casting possibilities.' The theatre accepts plays and musicals submitted by theatres and/or agents, including plays produced Off-Off Broadway and regionally other than in the Bay Area, plays and musicals not produced in the Bay Area within the last five years, plays and musicals that have never been produced but have had some development, and plays and musicals looking for development. The theatre does not accept unsolicited manuscripts, one-acts, or 'plays with togas.' For inquiries, send a cover letter, short synopsis, ten-page sample dialogue, the play's production history (including development), playwright's theatre résumé, and a self-addressed, stamped return envelope. See the website for more details.

General employment opportunities, internships

Open full-time and part-time positions and internships are listed in detail on the website, along with contact names and emails. Internships are often available in marketing, development, scenic construction, dramaturgical research, and costume rentals.

TRINITY REPERTORY COMPANY

201 Washington Street, Providence, RI 02903

Administration: (401) 521-1100. Box office: (401) 351-4242. Fax: (401) 521-0447

Email: info@trinityrep.com

www.trinityrep.com

Trinity Repertory Company is the largest artistic organization in Rhode Island and is a professional theatre that is 'firmly rooted in and dedicated to the life of its community. Through its principal aesthetic of great stories, well told, Trinity Rep aspires to the continuous creation of a theatre that represents all that is Rhode Island, all that is American, all that is human. With the unique performance style of a resident acting company, Trinity Rep nurtures the development of new work while keeping the classics alive and relevant to the new generation of theatre audiences.' Curt Columbus joined Trinity Rep as artistic director in January 2006.

Casting

Trinity Rep is a resident company of artists and does not audition specifically for company members. 'One is invited to join after we have worked with you on a number of projects. We cast from the resident company as frequently as possible each season.' Out-of-town auditions are for Equity only and are listed through Equity and the trade papers. Trinity Rep also uses casting directors in New York. Role-specific auditions for union and non-union actors are listed on the company website, through the *Providence Journal*, and occasionally through the Stagesource hotline in Boston. Check the website for ongoing information.

Script submissions

Trinity Rep generally produces at least one premiere production a year, as well as readings and workshops of numerous new plays. Each year Trinity Rep's Mabel T. Woolley Literary Department reads and reviews hundreds of new scripts. To submit a new play for consideration at Trinity Rep, a writer should first send a cover letter, a one-page synopsis of the play, and up to ten pages of dialogue from the play to: Mabel T. Woolley Literary Department, Trinity Repertory Company, 201 Washington Street, Providence, RI 02903.

General employment opportunities

Check the company website, where positions are listed as they become available. Send cover letter and résumé to: Human Resources, Trinity Rep, 201 Washington Street, Providence, RI 02903 or email: hr@trinityrep.com.

Internships

Trinity Rep offers college students and recent college graduates the opportunity to receive intensive professional training in theatre production and administration through its internship program. Internships are full-time positions, and interns are treated as members of the theatre staff, with all the same responsibilities and expectations. Trinity Rep provides interns with housing (furnished apartments with basic utilities) as well as a stipend. There may also be opportunities for interns to earn a small amount of overhire income at the theatre. Check the website for more details and contact names and numbers. Internships are generally available in theatre management, education, literary management, communications, marketing, development, production management, stage management, scenic carpentry, electrics, sound, costumes, and props.

TWO RIVER THEATRE COMPANY

21 Bridge Avenue, Red Bank, NJ 07701

Administration: (732) 345-1400. Box office: (732) 345-1400. Fax: (732) 345-1414

Email: info@trtc.org

www.trtc.org

Robert M. Rechnitz is the founder and executive producer and leads the theatre's production and educational programs. In the theatre's own words, 'with every production we've mounted, we've endeavored to bring something new and exciting to our audiences, to provide an intelligent complement to Broadway's flash and celebrity, and to create a body of work that bespeaks a passion for unusual and enlightening theatre.' The theatre's educational programs have 'a dynamic, integrated approach to engage the artist within every student.' For additional information, check out the company website.

UTAH SHAKESPEARE FESTIVAL

See the section on Shakespeare Festivals that follows.

VIRGINIA STAGE COMPANY AT THE WELLS THEATRE

P.O. Box 3770, Norfolk, VA 23514

Administration: (757) 627-6988. Box office: (757) 627-1234. Fax: (757) 628-5958

Email: marketing@vastage.com

www.vastage.com

The mission of Virginia Stage Company is 'to develop and sustain a fully professional theatre serving Southeastern Virginia, which enriches the region and the field through the production of theatrical art of the highest quality.' Founded in 1979, the company currently plays to an audience of more than 100,000 patrons. VSC's Education Department tours to over 50,000 Hampton Roads students annually and participates as a partner in education by providing services such as performances, drama classes, production training, and workshops to Title One schools and others at no charge. The Tony Award-winning musical *The Secret Garden* was first produced at VSC in 1989. The company operates in the 677-seat Wells Theatre, named after baseball player-turned-vaudeville entrepreneur Jake Wells. Chris Hanna is Virgina Stage Company's artistic director.

Casting, general employment opportunities, internships

Virginia Stage Company holds local auditions annually. Check the website for information and updates on employment and internships.

Script submissions

Virginia Stage Company is unable to consider unsolicited manuscripts for production. Letters of inquiry regarding potential submissions should be directed to artistic director Chris Hanna.

WALNUT STREET THEATRE

825 Walnut Street (at 9th), Philadelphia, PA 19107

Phone: (215) 574-3550. Fax: (215) 574-3598

www.walnutstreettheatre.org

Over 56,000 subscribers and 400,000 patrons flock to the historic Walnut Street Theatre, considered by many to be the oldest theatre in America. According to company officials, it stands alone as the oldest continuously operating theatre in the English-speaking world since it opened in 1809. Everyone from Edwin Booth and Helen Hayes to Houdini, George M. Cohan, and Katharine Hepburn have appeared on the Walnut Street Theatre stage. Originally opened for equestrian acts as The New Circus in 1809, Walnut Street can claim that Thomas Jefferson attended its first theatre production, *The Rivals*, in 1812. The Walnut Street Theatre has been designated both a National Historic Landmark and the State Theatre of Pennsylvania. Producing artistic director Bernard Havard returned the Walnut to a producing theatre in 1983 when it was reconceived as a nonprofit regional theatre dedicated to the preservation and development of the art of theatre. Since 1983, the company has produced over 20 world premieres and 10 American premieres.

The Walnut Street Theatre School was added in 1985. Walnut Street Theatre employs over 600 people and the annual budget is near $10 million. Walnut Street operates under a special contract with Actors' Equity and related unions.

Casting

Walnut Street Theatre is dedicated to the casting and employment of local, Philadelphia-based actors. Each mainstage and studio production begins with local auditions. The theatre also participates in general auditions as part of the Theatre Alliance of Greater Philadelphia. Send a photo and résumé for consideration to: Assistant to the Producing Artistic Director/Casting, Walnut Street Theatre, 825 Walnut Street, Philadelphia, PA 19107. See the website for further information.

General employment opportunities

General employment information is listed in detail on the website.

Apprenticeships

Positions are generally open in acting, carpentry, casting/literary management, costumes, education, fundraising, general management, house management, marketing, production management, props, public relations, running crew/stage, scenic painting, stage management (mainstage and studio series), and subscriptions. The program is a full-time commitment with a weekly scholarship, individual HMO medical coverage, gym membership, and free tuition at Theatre School classes. The terms of scholarships vary. Check the website for details and applications.

THE WILMA THEATER

265 S. Broad Street, Philadelphia, PA 19107

Administration: (215) 893-9456. Box office: (215) 546-7824. Fax: (215) 893-0895

Email: info@wilmatheater.org

www.wilmatheater.org

In the company's own words, 'The Wilma Theater exists to present theatre as an art form, engaging artists and audiences in an adventure of aesthetic philoso-phical reflection of the complexities of contemporary life. We accomplish our mission by producing thoughtful, well-crafted productions of intelligent, daring plays that represent a range of voices, viewpoints, and production styles.' Artistic director Jiri Zizka 'searches for plays, as well as new adaptations and translations, to which creative visual and musical techniques add another dimension, allowing each play to evolve beyond the confines of immediate verbal meaning into the world of metaphor and poetic vision.'

Founded in 1973 as The Wilma Project, the company engaged avant-garde theatre artists, including the Bread and Puppet Theatre, Mabou Mines, Charles Ludlam's Ridiculous Theatrical Company, The Wooster Group, Ping Chong and the Fiji Company, and Spalding Gray, until 1979, when the Zizkas 'forged a creative relationship with the Wilma as artists-in-residence.' They assumed artistic leader-ship in 1981. The Wilma soon moved to a 100-seat theatre and eventually a new 296-seat home in 1996. Over 500 students enroll in the Wilma Studio School each year for theatre training.

Casting

The Wilma encourages actors to submit a headshot and résumé for the com-pany's casting files and to 'indicate the role and production in which you are interested.' Wilma auditions are by invitation only. Send to: Casting, The Wilma Theater, 265 South Broad Street, Philadelphia, PA 19107.

Script submissions

The Wilma considers full-length plays, translations, adaptations, and musicals from an international repertoire with an emphasis on innovative, bold staging; world premieres; ensemble works; works with poetic dimension; plays with music; multi-media works; social issues. The preferred maximum cast size is 12; the stage measures 44' x 46'. Due to staffing and scheduling limitations, the

Wilma is only able to accept unsolicited manuscripts from agents. However, if accompanied by a recommendation from a literary manager, dramaturg, or other theatre professional, a query will be accepted by the theatre. Queries should include a cover letter, a synopsis, and a written résumé or description of your writing background, plus samples of the piece (optional). Check the website for other important details.

YALE REPERTORY THEATRE

Box office: 1120 Chapel Street (at York)
P.O. Box 208244, New Haven, CT 06505
Administrative office: P.O. Box 208244, New Haven, CT 06520-8244
Administration: (203) 432-1515. Box office: (203) 432-1234. Fax: (203) 432-6423
Email: yalerep@yale.edu
www.yalerep.org

The intimate and accomplished Yale Repertory Theatre was the 1991 recipient of the Regional Theatre Tony Award, having mounted over 90 world premieres, including four Pulitzer Prize-winners. Yale Rep's close relationship with the Yale School of Drama has created a grand sharing of internationally prominent artists and together they are 'committed to the rigorous, daring, and passionate exploration of our art form. We embrace a global audience.' Artistic director James Bundy notes that 'Our highest aim is to train artistic leaders – in every theatrical discipline – who create bold new works that astonish the mind, challenge the heart, and delight the senses.' Victoria Nolan is the theatre's seasoned, savvy managing director. Robert Brustein founded Yale Repertory Theatre in 1966 as the 'Master Teacher' of the Yale School of Drama.

Casting

Yale Rep casts locally (mostly non-Equity) and in New York and Los Angeles. Check out the email information line (yalerep@yale.edu) and the website (www.yale.edu/yalerep) for ongoing information.

Script submissions

Yale Rep accepts full-script submissions only from recognized literary agents. Unrepresented authors may send a letter of query, detailed synopsis, character breakdown, résumé, and ten-page dialogue sample to the literary office.

General employment opportunities, internships

Administration and production positions are generally listed in *ArtSearch* and through Human Resources at Yale University. Yale University offers internships at Yale Repertory but the theatre doesn't offer internships.

400+ TCG theatres

THEATRE COMMUNICATIONS GROUP (TCG)

520 Eighth Avenue, 24th Floor, New York, NY 10018-4156

Phone: (212) 609-5900. Fax: (212) 609-5901

Email: tcg@tcg.org

www.tcg.org

Theatre Communications Group (TCG) is the world's best link to the American theatre and is the national organization for the American not-for-profit professional theatre. Founded in 1961 (the same year as New York's La MaMa Theatre and the Utah Shakespeare Festival), TCG has provided a national forum and communications network for a field that, in its own words, is 'as aesthetically diverse as it is geographically widespread.'

According to the website's 'Theatre Profiles' – a grand collection of facts, artistic statements, contact information, and production overviews published by TCG, capturing over 250 of America's nonprofit theatres – TCG offers a 'comprehensive support system that addresses concerns of the theatre companies and individual artists that collectively represent our national theatre.'

TCG's mission is 'to strengthen, nurture, and promote the not-for-profit American theatre.' Through its artistic, management, and international programs, advocacy activities, and publications, TCG seeks to increase the organizational efficiency of its member theatres, cultivate and celebrate the artistic talent and achievements of the field, and promote a larger public understanding of and appreciation for the theatre field. Theresa Eyring has been TCG's marvelous executive director since 2007. Jim O'Quinn is longtime editor of TCG's *American Theatre*, a monthly magazine that is a terrific tool for theatre employees at every stage of their careers.

TCG's centralized services include publishing *American Theatre*, *ARTSEARCH* employment bulletin, the *TCG Theatre Directory* (a must for every theatre office), the *Dramatists Sourcebook, Stage Writers' Handbook, Stage Directors' Handbook,* and much more. *Theatre Profiles* is an online compendium of information about TCG member theatres and their productions, going back to 1995. Perhaps most important to theatre leaders and managers, TCG organizes, analyzes, and communicates pertinent, timely, factual information that is extremely useful to individuals and institutions in both their local concerns and national advocacy. TCG's artistic programs include career development programs and grants to theatres and theatre artists. Management programs offer professional development opportunities for theatre leaders.

Special advocacy alerts on lobbying efforts and legislative developments are also a key service of TCG. As mentioned in other parts of this book, every theatre person and theatre institution in America should have an ongoing collection of *American Theatre* magazines, the *ARTSEARCH* employment bulletin, and the TCG *Theatre Directory*, listing the names, addresses, phone numbers, websites, email addresses, and general information for the TCG membership. Why should everyone have these publications? Because they're the best way to keep on top of trends, key potential employers, theatre innovations, creative explorations, and the activities of your profession.

TCG offers its members networking and knowledge-building opportunities through conferences, events, research and communications; grants approximately $2 million per year to theatre companies and individual artists; advocates on the federal level, and serves as the US Center of the International Theatre Institute, connecting its constituents to the global theatre community. TCG's constituency has grown from a handful of groundbreaking theatres to nearly 700 member theatres and affiliate organizations and more than 12,000 individuals nationwide. You should consider becoming one of them.

Internships
Internships are available to qualified individuals interested in entering fields related to arts administration, management, editing, and journalism through hands-on experience. Check the website for details.

THEATRE COMMUNICATIONS GROUP/INTERNATIONAL THEATRE INSTITUTE

TCG/ITI is a network of theatre centers in 92 countries that serves as a clearing-house of information and networking source between professionals and a resource for students. Check the website for details.

The members

TCG's members are all available through direct links on the TCG website or through the web links below:

1812 Productions	Philadelphia, PA	www.1812productions.org
The 52nd Street Project	New York, NY	www.52project.org
7 Stages	Atlanta, GA	www.7stages.org
A.D. Players	Houston, TX	www.adplayers.org
About Face Theatre	Chicago, IL	www.aboutfacetheatre.com
Act II Playhouse	Ambler, PA	www.act2.org
ACT Theatre	Seattle, WA	www.acttheatre.org
The Acting Company	New York, NY	www.theactingcompany.org
Actors Co-Op Hollywood	Hollywood, CA	www.actorsco-op.org
Actor's Express	Atlanta, GA	www.actors-express.com
The Actors' Gang	Culver City, CA	www.theactorsgang.com
Actors' Shakespeare Project	Somerville, MA	www.actorsshakespeareproject.org
Actor's Theatre of Charlotte	Charlotte, NC	www.actorstheatrecharlotte.org
Actors Theatre of Louisville	Louisville, KY	www.actorstheatre.org
Actors Theatre of Phoenix	Phoenix, AZ	www.actorstheatrephx.org
Adirondack Theatre Festival	Glens Falls, NY	www.atfestival.org
Adventure Stage Chicago	Chicago, IL	www.adventurestage.org
African-American Shakespeare Company	San Francisco, CA	www.african-americanshakes.org
Alabama Shakespeare Festival	Montgomery, AL	www.asf.net
Albany Park Theater Project	Chicago, IL	www.aptpchicago.org
Alley Theatre	Houston, TX	www.alleytheatre.org
Alliance Theatre	Atlanta, GA	www.alliancetheatre.org
Amas Musical Theatre	New York, NY	www.amasmusical.org
American Blues Theater	Chicago, IL	www.americanbluestheater.com
American Conservatory Theater	San Francisco, CA	www.act-sf.org
American Folklore Theatre	Fish Creek, WI	www.folkloretheatre.com
American Players Theatre	Spring Green, WI	www.americanplayers.org
American Repertory Theater	Cambridge, MA	www.amrep.org
American Shakespeare Center	Staunton, VA	www.americanshakespearecenter.com

American Stage Theatre Company	St. Petersburg, FL	www.americanstage.org
American Theater Co	Chicago, IL	www.atcweb.org
American Theatre Co	Tulsa, OK	www.americantheatercompany.org
Amphibian Stage Productions	Fort Worth, TX	www.amphibianproductions.org
The Antaeus Company	North Hollywood, CA	www.antaeus.org
Arden Theatre Co	Philadelphia, PA	www.ardentheatre.org
Arena Stage	Washington, DC	www.arenastage.org
Arizona Theatre Company	Tucson, AZ	www.arizonatheatre.org
The Arkansas Arts Center	Little Rock, AR	www.arkarts.com
Arkansas Repertory Theatre	Little Rock, AR	www.therep.org
Artists Repertory Theatre	Portland, OR	www.artistsrep.org
Arts Center of Coastal Carolina	Hilton Head, SC	www.artshhi.com
Arvada Center for the Arts & Humanities	Arvada, CO	www.arvadacenter.org
Asolo Repertory Theatre	Sarasota, FL	www.asolo.org
Atlantic Theater Company	New York, NY	www.atlantictheater.org
Aurora Theatre Company	Berkeley, CA	www.auroratheatre.org
B Street Theatre	Sacramento, CA	www.bstreettheatre.org
Barksdale Theatre	Richmond, VA	www.barksdalerichmond.org
Barrington Stage Co	Pittsfield, MA	www.barringtonstageco.org
BATS Improv	San Francisco, CA	www.improv.org
Bedlam Theatre	Minneapolis, MN	www.bedlamtheatre.org
Berkeley Repertory Theatre	Berkeley, CA	www.berkeleyrep.org
Bickford Theatre	Morristown, NJ	www.bickfordtheatre.org
Bloomington Playwrights Project	Bloomington, IN	www.newplays.org
Bloomsburg Theatre Ensemble	Bloomsburg, PA	www.bte.org
Boise Contemporary Theater	Boise, ID	www.bctheater.org
Bond Street Theatre	New York, NY	www.bondst.org
Book-It Repertory Theatre	Seattle, WA	www.book-it.org
Borderlands Theater	Tucson, AZ	www.Borderlandstheater.org
Brat Productions	Philadelphia, PA	www.bratproductions.org
Brava Theater Center	San Francisco, CA	www.brava.org
Bristol Riverside Theatre	Bristol, PA	www.brtstage.org
Broadway By The Bay	Burlingame, CA	www.broadwaybythebay.org
The Building Stage	Chicago, IL	www.buildingstage.com
Burning Coal Theatre Co	Raleigh, NC	www.burningcoal.org
Bushfire Theatre of Performing Arts	Philadelphia, PA	www.bushfiretheatre.org
California Repertory Company	Long Beach, CA	www.calrep.org
California Shakespeare Theater	Berkeley, CA	www.calshakes.org
California Theatre Center	Sunnyvale, CA	www.ctcinc.org

Cara Mia Theatre Co	Dallas, TX	www.caramiatheatre.com
Castillo Theatre	New York, NY	www.castillo.org
The Catastrophic Theatre	Houston, TX	www.catastrophictheatre.com
Center for New Performance at Cal Arts	Valencia, CA	www.calarts.edu
Center for Puppetry Arts	Atlanta, GA	www.puppet.org
Center Repertory Company	Walnut Creek, CA	www.centerrep.org
Center Theatre Group	Los Angeles, CA	www.centertheatregroup.org
CENTERSTAGE	Baltimore, MD	www.centerstage.org
Centre Stage, Greenville's Professional Theater	Greenville, SC	www.centrestage.org
The Chance Theater	Orange, CA	www.chancetheater.com
Charleston Stage	Charleston, SC	www.charlestonstage.com
Chicago Dramatists	Chicago, IL	www.chicagodramatists.org
Chicago Shakespeare Theater	Chicago, IL	www.chicagoshakes.com
The Children's Theatre Co	Minneapolis, MN	www.childrenstheatre.org
Childsplay	Tempe, AZ	www.childplayaz.org
The Cider Mill Playhouse	Endicott, NY	www.cidermillplayhouse.org
Cincinnati Shakespeare Company	Cincinnati, OH	www.cincyshakes.com
Cinnabar Theater	Petaluma, CA	www.cinnabar.org
Citadel Theatre Company	Lake Forest, IL	www.citadeltheatre.org
City Lights Theater Company	San Jose, CA	www.cltc.org
City Theatre Co	Pittsburgh, PA	www.citytheatrecompany.org
The Civilians	Brooklyn, NY	www.thecivilians.org
Clarence Brown Theatre Co	Knoxville, TN	www.clarencebrowntheatre.org
Classic Stage Company	New York, NY	www.classicstage.org
The Cleveland Play House	Cleveland, OH	www.clevelandplayhouse.com
Cleveland Public Theatre	Cleveland, OH	www.cptonline.org
Clubbed Thumb	New York, NY	www.clubbedthumb.org
Collaboraction	Chicago, IL	www.collaboraction.org
The Colony Theatre Company	Burbank, CA	www.colonytheatre.org
Commonweal Theatre Company	Lanesboro, MN	www.commonwealtheatre.org
Company of Fools	Hailey, ID	wwwcompanyoffools.org
Company One	Boston, MA	www.companyone.org
Connecticut Repertory Theatre	Storrs, CT	www.crt.uconn.edu
Contemporary American Theater Festival	Shepherdstown, WV	www.catf.org
Cornerstone Theater Co	Los Angeles, CA	www.cornerstonetheater.org
The Coterie Theatre	Kansas City, MO	www.coterietheatre.org
CounterPULSE	San Francisco, CA	www.counterpulse.org

Court Theatre	Chicago, IL	www.courttheatre.org
Crowded Fire Theater Company	San Francisco, CA	www.crowdedfire.org
Cultural Odyssey	San Francisco, CA	www.culturalodyssey.org
Curious Theatre Branch	Chicago, IL	www.curioustheatrebranch.com
Curious Theatre Company	Denver, CO	www.curioustheatre.org
The Cutting Ball Theater	San Francisco, CA	www.cuttingball.com
Cygnet Theatre Company	San Diego, CA	www.cygnettheatre.com
Cyrano's Theatre Company	Anchorage, AK	www.cyranos.org
Dad's Garage	Atlanta, GA	www.dadsgarage.com
Dallas Children's Theater	Dallas, TX	www.dct.org
Dallas Theater Center	Dallas, TX	www.dallastheatercenter.org
Deaf West Theatre	North Hollywood, CA	www.deafwest.org
Dell'Arte International	Blue Lake, CA	www.dellarte.com
Denver Center Theatre Co	Denver, CO	www.denvercenter.org
Depot Theatre	Westport, NY	www.depottheatre.org
Detroit Repertory Theatre	Detroit, MI	www.detroitreptheatre.com
Diversionary Theatre	San Diego, CA	www.diversionary.org
Dobama Theatre	Cleveland Heights, OH	www.dobama.org
Dog & Pony Theatre Company	Chicago, IL	www.dogandponychicago.org
Double Edge Theatre	Ashfield, MA	www.doubleedgetheatre.org
East Lynne Theater Company	West Cape May, NJ	www.eastlynnetheater.org
East West Players	Los Angeles, CA	www.eastwestplayers.org
EgoPo Classic Theater	Philadelphia, PA	www.egopo.org
Elevator Repair Service Theater	Brooklyn, NY	www.elevator.org
Elm Shakespeare Company	New Haven, CT	www.elmshakespeare.org
Ensemble Studio Theatre	New York, NY	www.ensemblestudiotheatre.org
The Ensemble Theatre	Houston, TX	www.ensemblehouston.com
Ensemble Theatre Company	Santa Barbara, CA	www.ensembletheatre.com
Epic Theatre Ensemble	New York, NY	www.epictheatreensemble.org
Eugene O'Neill Theater Center	Waterford, CT	www.theoneill.org
Everyman Theatre	Baltimore, MD	www.everymantheatre.org
Fairbanks Shakespeare Theatre	Fairbanks, AK	www.fstalaska.org
First Folio Theatre	Clarendon Hills, IL	www.firstfolio.org
Florida Stage	West Palm Beach, FL	www.floridastage.org
Florida Studio Theatre	Sarasota, FL	www.floridastudiotheatre.org
Folger Theatre	Washington, DC	www.folger.edu
foolsFURY Theater	San Francisco, CA	www.foolsfury.org
Ford's Theatre	Washington, DC	www.fordstheatre.org
The Foundry Theatre	New York, NY	www.foundrytheatre.org
Fountain Theatre	Los Angeles, CA	www.fountaintheatre.com

Free Street Theater	Chicago, IL	www.freestreet.org
Freehold Theatre Lab	Seattle, WA	www.freeholdtheatre.org
Fulton Theatre	Lancaster, PA	www.thefulton.org
FUSION Theatre Company	Albuquerque, NM	www.fusionabq.org
GableStage	Coral Gables, FL	www.gablestage.org
GALA Hispanic Theatre	Washington, DC	www.galatheatre.org
Gamm Theatre	Pawtucket, RI	www.gammtheatre.org
Gamut Theatre Group	Harrisburg, PA	www.gamutplays.org
Geffen Playhouse	Los Angeles, CA	www.geffenplayhouse.com
George Street Playhouse	New Brunswick, NJ	www.georgestreetplayhouse.org
Georgia Ensemble Theatre	Roswell, GA	www.get.org
Georgia Shakespeare	Atlanta, GA	www.gashakespeare.com
Geva Theatre Center	Rochester, NY	www.gevatheatre.org
The Globe Theatre	Odessa, TX	www.globesw.org
Golden Thread Productions	San Francisco, CA	www.goldenthread.org
Goodman Theatre	Chicago, IL	www.goodmantheatre.org
Great Lakes Theater Festival	Cleveland, OH	www.greatlakestheater.org
Greenbrier Valley Theatre	Lewisburg, WV	www.gvtheatre.org
Griffin Theatre Company	Chicago, IL	www.griffintheatre.com
Guthrie Theater	Minneapolis, MN	www.guthrietheater.org
Hangar Theatre	Ithaca, NY	www.hangartheatre.org
Harlequin Productions	Olympia, WA	www.harlequinproductions.org
HartBeat Ensemble	Hartford, CT	www.hartbeatensemble.org
Hartford Stage	Hartford, CT	www.hartfordstage.org
Harwich Junior Theatre	West Harwich, MA	www.hjtcapecod.org
Hedgerow Theatre	Wallingford, PA	www.hedgerowtheatre.org
HERE Arts Center	New York, NY	www.here.org
History Theatre	St. Paul, MN	www.historytheatre.com
Honolulu Theatre For Youth	Honolulu, HI	www.htyweb.org
Horizon Theatre Co	Atlanta, GA	www.horizontheatre.com
The House Theatre of Chicago	Chicago, IL	www.thehousetheatre.com
The Human Race Theatre Co	Dayton, OH	www.humanracetheatre.org
Huntington Theatre Company	Boston, MA	www.huntingtontheatre.org
Hyde Park Theatre	Austin, TX	www.hydeparktheatre.org
The Hypocrites	Chicago, IL	www.the-hypocrites.com
Idaho Shakespeare Festival	Boise, ID	www.idahoshakespeare.org
Illinois Theatre Center	Park Forest, IL	www.ilthctr.org
Illusion Theater	Minneapolis, MN	www.illusiontheater.org
Imagination Stage	Bethesda, MD	www.imaginationstage.org
Indiana Repertory Theatre	Indianapolis, IN	www.irtlive.com

Interact Center for the Visual & Performing Arts	Minneapolis, MN	www.interactcenter.com
InterAct Theatre Company	Philadelphia, PA	www.interacttheatre.org
International City Theatre	Long Beach, CA	www.ictlongbeach.org
Intersection for the Arts	San Francisco, CA	www.theintersection.org
Intiman Theatre	Seattle, WA	www.intiman.org
Invisible Theatre Co	Tucson, AZ	www.invisibletheatre.com
Irish Classical Theatre Co	Buffalo, NY	www.irishclassicaltheatre.com
Irondale Ensemble Project	Brooklyn, NY	www.irondale.org
Japan Society	New York, NY	www.japansociety.org
The Jewish Theatre San Francisco	San Francisco, CA	www.tjt-sf.org
Jobsite Theater	Tampa, FL	jobsitetheater.org
Jubilee Theatre	Fort Worth, TX	www.jubileetheatre.org
Jump-Start Performance Co	San Antonio, TX	www.jump-start.org
Junebug Productions	New Orleans, LA	www.junebugproductions.org
The Jungle Theater	Minneapolis, MN	www.jungletheater.com
Kansas City Repertory Theatre	Kansas City, MO	www.kcrep.org
Kennedy Center Theater for Young Audiences	Arlington, VA	www.kennedy-center.org
Kentucky Shakespeare Festival	Louisville, KY	www.kyshakes.org
Kitchen Dog Theater	Dallas, TX	www.kitchendogtheater.org
Kitchen Theatre Company	Ithaca, NY	www.kitchentheatre.org
Know Theatre of Cincinnati	Cincinnati, OH	www.knowtheatre.com
L.A. Theatre Works	Venice, CA	www.latw.org
La Jolla Playhouse	La Jolla, CA	www.lajollaplayhouse.org
La MaMa E.T.C.	New York, NY	www.lamama.org
LAByrinth Theater Co	New York, NY	www.labtheater.org
Laguna Playhouse	Laguna Beach, CA	www.lagunaplayhouse.com
Lamb's Players Theatre	Coronado, CA	www.lambsplayers.org
Lamplighters Music Theatre	San Francisco, CA	www.lamplighters.org
Lantern Theater Company	Philadelphia, PA	www.lanterntheater.org
Lark Play Development Center	New York, NY	www.larktheatre.org
The Latino Theater Company	Los Angeles, CA	www.thelatc.org
Lexington Children's Theatre	Lexington, KY	www.lctonstage.org
Lifeline Theatre	Chicago, IL	www.lifelinetheatre.com
Lincoln Center Theater	New York, NY	www.lct.org
Long Wharf Theatre	New Haven, CT	www.longwharf.org
Lookingglass Theatre Co	Chicago, IL	www.lookingglasstheatre.org
Lord Leebrick Theatre Co	Eugene, OR	www.lordleebrick.com
Lorraine Hansberry Theatre	San Francisco, CA	www.lhtsf.org

Lost Nation Theater	Montpelier, VT	www.lostnationtheater.org
The Lyric Stage Company of Boston	Boston, MA	www.lyricstage.com
Mabou Mines	New York, NY	www.maboumines.org
Magic Theatre	San Francisco, CA	www.magictheatre.org
Main Street Theater	Houston, TX	www.mainstreettheater.com
Maltz Jupiter Theatre	Jupiter, FL	www.jupitertheatre.org
Manhattan Theatre Club	New York, NY	www.manhattantheatreclub.com
Marin Shakespeare Company	San Rafael, CA	www.marinshakespeare.org
Marin Theatre Company	Mill Valley, CA	www.marintheatre.org
The Marsh	San Francisco, CA	www.themarsh.org
Mary Moody Northen Theatre	Austin, TX	www.stedwards.edu/theatre
Maryland Ensemble Theater	Frederick, MD	www.marylandensemble.org
Ma-Yi Theater Company	New York, NY	www.ma-yitheatre.org
McCarter Theatre Center	Princeton, NJ	www.mccarter.org
Meadow Brook Theatre	Rochester, MI	www.mbtheatre.com
Merrimack Repertory Theatre	Lowell, MA	www.merrimackrep.org
Merry-Go-Round Playhouse	Auburn, NY	www.merry-go-round.com
Metro Theater Company	St. Louis, MO	www.metrotheatercompany.org
Milwaukee Chamber Theatre	Milwaukee, WI	www.chamber-theatre.com
Milwaukee Repertory Theater	Milwaukee, WI	www.milwaukeerep.com
Minnesota Jewish Theatre Company	St. Paul, MN	www.mnjewishtheatre.org
Miracle Theatre Group	Portland, OR	www.milagro.org
Mirror Repertory Co	New York, NY	www.mirrorrepertoryco.com
Mixed Blood Theatre Co	Minneapolis, MN	www.mixedblood.com
Mo`olelo Performing Arts Company	San Diego, CA	www.moolelo.net
Montana Repertory Theatre	Missoula, MT	www.montanarep.org
Montgomery Theater	Souderton, PA	www.montgomerytheater.org
Moving Arts	Los Angeles, CA	www.movingarts.org
MPAACT, Inc	Chicago, IL	www.mpaact.org
Mu Performing Arts	St. Paul, MN	www.muperformingarts.org
NACL Theatre	Highland Lake, NY	www.nacl.org
Naked Angels	New York, NY	www.nakedangels.com
Native Voices at the Autry	Los Angeles, CA	www.nativevoicesattheautry.org
Nautilus Music-Theater	St. Paul, MN	www.nautilusmusictheater.org
Nebraska Repertory Theatre	Lincoln, NE	www.unl.edu/rep
The Neo-Futurists	Chicago, IL	www.neofuturists.org
The New American Shakespeare Tavern	Atlanta, GA	www.shakespearetavern.com

The New Conservatory Theatre Center	San Francisco, CA	www.nctcsf.org
New Dramatists, Inc	New York, NY	www.newdramatists.org
New Georges	New York, NY	www.newgeorges.org
New Ground Theatre	Davenport. IA	www.newgroundtheatre.org
New Jersey Repertory Co	Long Branch, NJ	www.njrep.org
New Orleans Shakespeare Festival at Tulane		
	New Orleans, LA	www.neworleansshakespeare.com
New Paradise Laboratories Theatre	Philadelphia, PA	www.newparadiselaboratories.org
New Repertory Theatre	Watertown, MA	www.newrep.org
New Stage Theatre	Jackson, MS	www.newstagetheatre.com
New York Theatre Workshop	New York, NY	www.nytw.org
Next ACT Theatre	Milwaukee, WI	www.nextact.org
Next Theatre Company	Evanston, IL	www.nexttheatre.org
NightBlue Theater	Lemont, IL	www.nightbluetheater.com
A Noise Within	Glendale, CA	www.anoisewithin.org
North Carolina Stage Co	Asheville, NC	www.ncstage.org
North Coast Repertory Theatre	Solana Beach, CA	www.northcoastrep.org
Northern Stage	White River Jnct, VT	www.northernstage.org
Northlight Theatre	Skokie, IL	www.northlight.org
Odyssey Theatre Ensemble	Los Angeles, CA	www.odysseytheatre.com
The Old Globe	San Diego, CA	www.theoldglobe.org
Olney Theatre Center for the Arts	Olney, MD	www.olneytheatre.org
Ontological-Hysteric Theater	New York, NY	www.ontological.com
The Open Eye Theater	Margaretville, NY	www.theopeneye.org
Open Stage of Harrisburg	Harrisburg, PA	www.openstagehbg.com
OpenStage Theatre & Co	Fort Collins, CO	www.openstagetheatre.org
Oregon Children's Theatre	Portland, OR	www.octc.org
Oregon Shakespeare Festival	Ashland, OR	www.osfashland.org
Orlando Shakespeare Theater	Orlando, FL	www.orlandoshakes.org
Out of Hand Theater	Atlanta, GA	www.outofhandtheater.com
Palm Beach Dramaworks	West Palm Beach, FL	www.palmbeachdramaworks.org
Pan Asian Repertory Theatre	New York, NY	www.panasianrep.org
Pangea World Theater	Minneapolis, MN	www.pangeaworldtheater.org
Paper Mill Playhouse	Millburn, NJ	www.papermill.org
Parkway Playhouse	Burnsville, NC	www.parkwayplayhouse.com
Passage Theatre Company	Trenton, NJ	www.passagetheatre.org
Paul Mesner Puppets, Inc	Kansas City, MO	www.paulmesnerpuppets.org
PCPA Theaterfest	Santa Maria, CA	www.pcpa.org
The Pearl Theatre Co	New York, NY	www.pearltheatre.org

Peninsula Players Theatre	Fish Creek, WI	www.peninsulaplayers.com
The Pennsylvania Shakespeare Festival	Center Valley, PA	www.pashakespeare.org
Penobscot Theatre	Bangor, ME	www.penobscottheatre.org
Penumbra Theatre Company	St Paul, MN	www.penumbratheatre.org
The People's Light & Theatre Company	Malvern, PA	www.peopleslight.org
Perishable Theatre	Providence, RI	www.perishable.org
Perseverance Theatre	Douglas, AK	www.perseverancetheatre.org
Philadelphia Young Playwrights	Philadelphia, PA	www.phillyyoungplaywrights.org
Phoenix Theatre	Phoenix, AZ	www.phoenixtheatre.com
Pig Iron Theatre Company	Philadelphia, PA	www.pigiron.org
Pillsbury House Theatre	Minneapolis, MN	www.pillsburyhousetheatre.org
Ping Chong & Company	New York, NY	www.pingchong.org
Pistarckle Theater	St Thomas, VI	www.pistarckletheater.vi
Pittsburgh Irish & Classical Theatre	Pittsburgh, PA	www.picttheatre.org
Pittsburgh Public Theater	Pittsburgh, PA	www.ppt.org
Piven Theatre Workshop	Evanston, IL	www.piventheatre.org
Plan-B Theatre Company	Salt Lake City, UT	www.planbtheatre.org
The Play Company	New York, NY	www.playco.org
PlayGround	San Francisco, CA	www.playground-sf.org
The PlayGround Theatre	Miami Shores, FL	www.theplaygroundtheatre.com
Playhouse on the Square	Memphis, TN	www.playhouseonthesquare.org
PlayMakers Repertory Co	Chapel Hill, NC	www.playmakersrep.org
The Playwrights' Center	Minneapolis, MN	www.pwcenter.org
Playwrights Foundation	San Francisco, CA	www.playwrightsfoundation.org
Playwrights Horizons	New York, NY	www.playwrightshorizons.org
Porchlight Music Theatre Chicago	Chicago, IL	www.porchlighttheatre.com
Portland Center Stage	Portland, OR	www.pcs.org
Portland Stage Company	Portland, ME	www.portlandstage.com
Pregones Theater	Bronx, NY	www.pregones.org
Profile Theatre	Portland, OR	www.profiletheatre.org
The Public Theater	New York, NY	www.publictheater.org
The Public Theatre	Lewiston, ME	www.thepublictheatre.org
PURE Theatre	Charleston, SC	www.puretheatre.org
Red Barn Theatre	Key West, FL	www.redbarntheatre.com
Red Bull Theater	New York, NY	www.redbulltheater.com
Redmoon	Chicago, IL	www.redmoon.org
Remy Bumppo Theatre Company	Chicago, IL	www.remybumppo.org
Renaissance Theaterworks	Milwaukee, WI	www.r-t-w

Rep Stage	Columbia, MD	www.repstage.org
Repertorio Espanol	New York, NY	www.repertorio.org
The Repertory Theatre of St. Louis	St. Louis, MO	www.repstl.org
Reprise Theatre Company	Los Angeles, CA	www.reprise.org
ReVision Theatre	Asbury Park, NJ	www.revisiontheatre.org
Ripe Time	Brooklyn, NY	www.ripetime.org
Riverside Theatre	Iowa City, IA	www.riversidetheatre.org
Roadside Theater	Norton, VA	www.roadside.org
Robey Theatre Company	Los Angeles, CA	www.robeytheatrecompany.com
The Rose Theater	Omaha, NE	www.rosetheater.org
Round House Theatre	Bethesda, MD	www.roundhousetheatre.org
Roundabout Theatre Co	New York, NY	www.roundabouttheatre.org
Rude Mechanicals	Austin, TX	www.rudemechs.com
Saint Michael's Playhouse	Colchester, VT	www.saintmichaelsplayhouse.org
The Salt Lake Acting Co	Salt Lake City, UT	www.saltlakeactingcompany.org
Salvage Vanguard Theater	Austin, TX	www.salvagevanguard.org
San Diego Repertory Theatre	San Diego, CA	www.sdrep.org
San Francisco Mime Troupe	San Francisco, CA	www.sfmt.org
San Jose Stage Company	San Jose, CA	www.sanjosestage.com
Seattle Children's Theatre	Seattle, WA	www.sct.org
Seattle Public Theater	Seattle, WA	www.seattlepublictheater.org
Seattle Repertory Theatre	Seattle, WA	www.seattlerep.org
Second Stage Theatre	New York, NY	www.2st.com
SF Playhouse	San Francisco, CA	www.sfplayhouse.org
Shadowlight Productions	San Francisco, CA	www.shadowlight.org
Shakespeare & Co	Lenox, MA	www.shakespeare.org
Shakespeare Dallas	Dallas, TX	www.shakespearedallas.org
Shakespeare Festival of St. Louis	St Louis, MO	www.sfstl.com
Shakespeare On The Sound	Norwalk, CT	www.shakespeareonthesound.org
The Shakespeare Theatre Company	Washington, DC	www.shakespearetheatre.org
The Shakespeare Theatre of New Jersey	Madison, NJ	www.shakespearenj.org
Shotgun Players	Berkeley, CA	www.shotgunplayers.org
Signature Theatre	Arlington, VA	www.signature-theatre.org
Signature Theatre Co	New York, NY	www.signaturetheatre.org
Silk Road Theatre Project	Chicago, IL	www.srtp.org
Single Carrot Theatre	Baltimore, MD	www.singlecarrot.com
SITI Company	New York, NY	www.siti.org
Society Hill Playhouse	Philadelphia, PA	www.societyhillplayhouse.org

Soho Repertory Theatre	New York, NY	www.sohorep.org
Sonoma County Repertory Theater	Sebastopol, CA	www.the-rep.org
South Carolina Repertory Company	Hilton Head, SC	www.hiltonheadtheatre.com
South Coast Repertory	Costa Mesa, CA	www.scr.org
Southern Appalachian Repertory Theatre	Marshill, NC	www.sartplays.org
Southern Rep	New Orlean, LA	www.southernrep.com
Southwest Shakespeare Co	Mesa, AZ	www.swshakespeare.org
SpeakEasy Stage Company	Boston, MA	www.speakeasystage.com
St. Louis Black Repertory Co	Saint Louis, MO	www.theblackrep.org
Stage Left Theatre	Chicago, IL	www.staglefttheatre.com
Stages Repertory Theatre	Houston, TX	www.stagestheatre.com
Stages Theatre Center	Los Angeles, CA	www.stagestheatrecenter.com
Stages Theatre Company	Hopkins, MN	www.stagestheatre.org
Stageworks Theatre	Tampa, FL	www.stageworkstheatre.org
StageWorks/Hudson	Hudson, NY	www.stageworkshudson.org
Steppenwolf Theatre Co	Chicago, IL	www.steppenwolf.org
Steppingstone Theatre	St Paul, MN	www.steppingstonetheatre.org
Strawdog Theatre Company	Chicago, IL	www.strawdog.org
The Studio Theatre	Washington, DC	www.studiotheatre.org
Summer Play Festival	New York, NY	www.spfnyc.org
Sundance Institute Theatre Program	New York, NY	www.sundance.org
Swine Palace Productions	Baton Rouge, LA	www.swinepalace.org
Synchronicity Theatre	Atlanta, GA	www.synchrotheatre.com
Syracuse Stage	Syracuse, NY	www.syracusestage.org
Talking Band	New York, NY	www.talkingband.org
Taproot Theatre Company	Seattle, WA	www.taproottheatre.org
Target Margin Theater	Brooklyn, NY	www.targetmargin.org
The TEAM	Brooklyn, NY	www.theteamplays.org
Teatro Circulo	New York, NY	www.teatrocirculo.org
Teatro del Pueblo	St Paul, MN	www.teatrodelpueblo.org
Teatro IATI	New York, NY	www.teatroiati.org
Teatro Vista	Chicago, IL	www.teatrovista.org
Tectonic Theater Project	New York, NY	www.tectonictheaterproject.org
Ten Thousand Things Theater Company	Minneapolis, MN	www.tenthousandthings.org
Tennessee Repertory Theatre	Nashville, TN	tennesseerep.org

Tennessee Women's Theater Project	Nashville. TN	www.twtp.org
The Theater at Monmouth	Monmouth, ME	www.theateratmonmouth.org
Theater Breaking Through Barriers	New York, NY	www.tbtb.org
Theater for the New City	New York, NY	www.theaterforthenewcity.net
Theater Grottesco	Sante Fe, NM	www.theatergrottesco.org
Theater J	Washington, DC	www.theaterj.org
Theater Latte Da	Minneapolis, MN	www.latteda.org
Theater of the First Amendment	Fairfax, VA	www.theaterofthefirstamendment.org
Theater Wit	Chicago, IL	www.theaterwit.org
Theatre Aspen	Aspen, CO	www.theatreaspen.org
Theatre for a New Audience	New York, NY	www.tfana.org
Theatre In The Square	Marietta, GA	www.theatreinthesquare.com
Theatre of Yugen	San Francisco, CA	www.theatreofyugen.org
Theatre Project	Baltimore, MD	www.theatreproject.org
Theatre West	Los Angeles, CA	www.theatrewest.org
TheatreFIRST	Oakland, CA	www.theatrefirst.com
TheatreSquared	Fayetteville, AR	www.theatresquared.org
TheatreWorks	Palo Alto, CA	www.theatreworks.org
Theatrical Outfit	Atlanta, GA	www.theatricaloutfit.org
Third Rail Repertory Theatre	Portland, OR	www.thirdrail.org
Timeline Theatre Company	Chicago, IL	www.timelinetheatre.com
Touchstone Theatre	Bethlehem, PA	www.touchstone.org
Triad Stage	Greensboro, NC	www.triadstage.org
Tricklock Theatre Co	Albuquerque, NM	www.tricklock.com
Trinity Repertory Co	Providence, RI	www.trinityrep.com
Trustus	Columbia, SC	www.trustus.org
Two River Theater Co	Red Bank, NJ	www.trtc.org
Undermain Theatre	Dallas, TX	www.undermain.com
Unicorn Theatre	Kansas City, MO	www.unicorntheatre.org
Upstream Theater	Saint Louis, MO	www.upstreamtheater.org
Urban Stages	New York, NY	www.urbanstages.org
Valley Youth Theatre	Phoenix, AZ	www.vyt.com
Vermont Stage Company	Burlington, VT	www.vtstage.org
Victory Gardens Theater	Chicago, IL	www.victorygardens.org
The Village Playhouse and Repertory Co	Mt Pleasant, SC	www.villageplayhouse.com
Virginia Premiere Theatre	Mobjack, VA	www.vptheatre.com
Vital Theatre Company	New York, NY	www.vitaltheatre.org
Voices of the South	Memphis, TN	www.voicesofthesouth.org

Walden Theatre	Louisville, KY	www.waldentheatre.org
The Warehouse Theatre	Greenville, SC	www.warehousetheatre.com
Waterfront Playhouse	Key West, FL	www.waterfrontplayhouse.com
WaterTower Theatre	Addison, TX	www.watertowertheatre.org
Watts Village Theater Company, Inc.	Los Angeles, CA	
		www.wattsvillagetheatercompany.com
Wellfleet Harbor Actors Theater	Wellfleet, MA	www.what.org
The Western Stage	Salinas, CA	www.westernstage.com
Weston Playhouse Theatre Company		
	Weston, VT	www.westonplayhouse.org
Westport Country Playhouse	Westport, CT	www.westportplayhouse.org
WET Productions	New York, NY	www.wetproductions.org
Will Geer Theatricum Botanicum	Topanga, CA	www.theatricum.com
William Inge Center for the Arts	Independence, KS	www.ingecenter.org
Williamstown Theatre Festival	Williamstown, MA	www.wtfestival.org
The Wilma Theater	Philadelphia, PA	www.wilmatheater.org
Wing-It Productions	Seattle, WA	www.wingitpresents.com
Woolly Mammoth Theatre Co	Washington, DC	www.woollymammoth.net
The Wooster Group	New York, NY	www.thewoostergroup.org
The Working Theater	New York, NY	www.workingtheater.org
Writers' Theatre	Glencoe, IL	www.writerstheatre.org
Yale Repertory Theatre	New Haven, CT	www.yalerep.org
Young Playwrights' Theater	Washington, DC	www.yptdc.org
Youth Ensemble of Atlanta	Atlanta, GA	www.youthensemble.org
Youth Performance Co	Minneapolis, MN	www.youthperformanceco.com
The Z Space Studio	San Francisco, CA	www.zspace.org
ZACH Theatre	Austin, TX	www.zachtheatre.org

200+ Shakespeare festivals

Will power rules as Shakespeare thrives in American theatres

Four centuries have passed since the birth of William Shakespeare but the world's bookstores are still brimming with new editions of his plays and a dozen new volumes about who he was, who he might have been, or who we'd like him to be! Year after year, his plays are always the most produced of all of the world's playwrights and movie rental firms have dozens of copies of his plays as copycat film directors and producers continue to turn the originals into cute romantic comedies or dark dramas filled with teenage angst. Attendance is up. People are traveling hundreds, even thousands of miles to see the latest, greatest production. Indeed, the Bard is back!

Who would believe that as the twenty-first century began, John Updike's latest novel would feature *Hamlet*'s Gertrude and Claudius, Nintendo would put Shakespeare next to Mario Brothers on its hand-held game devices, and Julie Taymor's version of *Titus Andronicus* would be on the 'must see' new movie list (along with *The Tempest* in 2010)? Did *Shakespeare in Love* really win seven Academy Awards and gross $100 million in North America, or are pop culture fanatics simply caught up in the same dream that captured Michelle Pfeiffer and Kevin Kline in one of the two *A Midsummer Night's Dream* movies still renting on DVD shelves throughout America? Over 50,000 Royal Shakespeare Company *Hamlet* DVDs (with David Tennant in the title role) have been sold worldwide and nearly two million people watched it on BBC and PBS. It's Bard-mania on a grand scale!

Big bucks for the Bard?

Even the world's Shakespeare Festival leaders are scratching their heads and chuckling over the resurgence of all things linked to the great William. So far in the twenty-first century, England's Sir Peter Hall moved to America to join the boom in all Bard-related business, the Royal Shakespeare Company farmed out Shakespeare to the hinterlands of Great Britain, and the Stratford Festival of Canada sold over 600,000 tickets in one year with an estimated economic impact of over $170 million.

In a world where audiences for serious plays and non-musical work are often waning, tickets to Shakespeare plays are hot, hot, hot. There are over 200 Shakespeare companies in North America, and over 150 international Shakespeare festivals and companies around the world, including companies in Japan, Spain, South Africa, New Zealand, China, France, and Germany. Indeed, new Shakespeare festivals and timely, sometimes outrageous productions are popping up throughout America from Maine to California, and internationally from Tasmania to Tanzania. I recently returned from seeing a brilliant Taiko-drum/Asian-inspired *Pericles* at the Sydney Opera House and consulted with the new Australia Shakespeare Festival that opened recently on the island of Tasmania – with an artistic director from Shakespeare South Africa!

Over a million people braved America's great outdoors for Shakespeare's sake at the beginning of the new century, while millions of others attended Shakespeare productions in indoor theatres throughout the world. England's Royal Shakespeare Company typically hosts over a million patrons each year and the Oregon Shakespeare Festival welcomed nearly 400,000 audience members in a recent season. Add 600,000 attending the Stratford Festival of Canada and that's two million tickets to three theatres alone!

Shakespeare up the creek?

Certainly, producers have almost always enjoyed producing Shakespeare. Aside from the diversity of comedies, romances, histories, and tragedies, there's a great bonus to budgeting Shakespeare: no royalties. There is also good news for actors, directors, stage managers, and production personnel: you don't have to travel to Stratford-Upon-Avon or even Stratford, Canada, to belly up to the Bard! The United States leads the way in Shakespeare productions. It might be Shakespeare-on-the-Rocks or Shakespeare under the Stars (both in Texas), Shakespeare in the Park (New York), Shakespeare in the Parking Lot (Tacoma, Washington), the Shakespeare Free-For-All (in Washington, DC), or the Fairbanks Shakespeare Theater (in chilly Alaska). From coast to coast, the Bard is alive and well in the United States.

Without question, Shakespeare is the most-produced playwright in world theatre. Fortunately, given the large size of his casts, the Shakespeare phenomenon translates into myriad annual opportunities for artists, craftspersons, and producers.

The Shakespeare Theatre Association (STA) provides direct links to many of the major festivals. Four other related websites offer insights into Shakespeare festival work and career opportunities. One website (http://ise.uvic.ca) is hosted by Internet Shakespeare Editions (ISE) and the Shakespeare in American Communities program (www.shakespeareinamericancommunities.org), is sponsored by the National Endowment for the Arts (NEA). Other useful Shakespeare Festival related websites include:

www.curtainrising.co

www.unc.edu/depts/outdoor

shakespeare.palomar.edu/festivals.htm

www.shakespearefellowship.org/linksfestivals.htm

www.jrol.org/Arts/Performing_Arts/Theater/Shakespeare/Festivals/United_States

dir.yahoo.com/arts/humanities/literature/authors/playwrights/shakespearewilliam_15
     64_1616_/shakespeare_festivals

www.google.com/Top/Arts/Performing_Arts/Theatre/Shakespeare/Festivals/United_
     States

www.dmoz.org/Arts/Performing_Arts/Theatre/Shakespeare/Festivals/United_States/

www.amazon.com/Shakespeare-Festivals-Around-Marcus-Gregio/dp/1413459064

partyguideonline.com/cultures/arts/Shakespeare.html

www.shakespeare.cz/en/about-festivals/1/

The Shakespeare Theatre Association (STA)

www.staaonline.org

The Shakespeare Theatre Association was established to provide a forum for artistic and managerial leadership of theatres whose central activity is the production of Shakespeare's plays; to discuss issues and share methods of work, resources, and information; and to act as an advocate for Shakespearean productions and training in North America. Membership is open to any producing theatre organization worldwide that is primarily involved with the production of Shakespeare's plays. Limited associate membership is also possible. STA membership now includes approximately 75 theatres, representing diverse types (indoor, outdoor, year-round, seasonal, university-affiliated, free) with wide-ranging budgets ($25,000 to $27,250,000), and Equity as well as non-Equity companies.

History

The Shakespeare Theatre Association was founded in 1991 by Sidney L. Berger, producing director of the Houston Shakespeare Festival, and Douglas N. Cook, longtime producing artistic director of the Utah Shakespeare Festival. The first meeting was held on January 12, 1991, in the Library Board Room of the Folger Library in Washington, DC. Over the years, STA has met at the Royal Shakespeare Company in Stratford, England; Shakespeare's Globe in London; the Stratford Festival of Canada; and at festivals large and small throughout the United States. The STA's *Quarto* is published twice a year and details plans, productions, statistics, and strategies related to Shakespeare in production. STA also holds an annual conference hosted by a member theatre and hosts an online directory for access to member theatres.

The STA website offers lists of officers, an institutional history, an updated directory, links to member theatres, and recent copies of *Quarto*. The STA secretary handles membership information. Check out the website for ongoing information and direct links to many of America's producing festivals. *Quarto* is edited by Jim Volz. Editorial information or *Quarto* questions may be sent to jvolz@fullerton.edu. Information about the association is available from STA co-founder Sidney Berger at sberger@uh.edu.

A few high-profile companies

While the diversity of Shakespeare production in America is vast, here is a sampling of some high-profile companies whose work focuses on the Bard:

STRATFORD SHAKESPEARE FESTIVAL

P.O. Box 520, Stratford, Ontario, Canada N5A 6V2

Administration: (519) 271-4040. Box office: (800) 567-1600. Fax: (519) 271-2734

www.stratfordfestival.ca

Starting with two Shakespeare productions in a tent in 1953, the festival prospered in the early years thanks to the founding vision of Sir Tyrone Guthrie and Tom Patterson. Now with more than $57 million budgeted for production and salaries for actors, musicians, artisans, and craftspeople, the Stratford Shakespeare Festival employs roughly 1,000 people who generally work on 12 to 14 productions in more than 600 performances annually. Over 60,000 students from Canada and the United States attend student performances and related enrichment programs each year. Stratford's mission is 'to produce the best works of theatre in the classical and contemporary repertoire, with special emphasis on the works of William Shakespeare, to the highest standards possible.'

According to the casting office of the Festival, actor résumés are collected in July and August – check the website for details on casting and other positions. Email resumes@stratfordfestival.ca to submit a résumé.

OREGON SHAKESPEARE FESTIVAL

15 South Pioneer Street, Ashland, OR 97520

Administration: (541) 482-2111. Box office: (541) 482-4331. Fax: (541) 482-0446

Email: administration@osfashland.org

www.osfashland.org

The Tony Award-winning Oregon Shakespeare Festival (OSF) is the USA's largest nonprofit theatre and employs approximately 600 theatre professionals (around 375 full-time). OSF produces 11 plays in three theatres (four by Shakespeare and seven by classic and contemporary playwrights). Recent audiences have exceeded 400,000 patrons, with a budget exceeding $26 million. The artistic director is Bill Rauch, a 20-year veteran of the Cornerstone Theater Company. In his own words:

When I first directed Handler *at OSF in 2002, I sensed that I had found a new artistic home. Each successive artistic adventure in Ashland has continued to deepen that conviction. I've taken risks in every project that I've undertaken at the Festival, and those risks have been rewarded by the response of a literate and passionate audience. I am moved by the sheer eclecticism of the programming – Shakespeare and other classics, contemporary work, and brand new plays commissioned for our company. I am energized by the scale of the operation: the largest audience and acting company in the country, 11 plays, 3 stunningly different theatre spaces, a wide range of educational programs. There is invaluable legacy and history, including individuals with 20, 30, even 50 years of organizational history, and every year new artists and staff members bring fresh perspectives.*

Oregon Shakespeare Festival company members are asked to make a commitment to a classical repertory theatre and longer-than-usual contracts for regional theatre. Auditions are usually held in the Festival's home of Ashland, Oregon, as well as in Los Angeles and New York. Check the website for audition and casting information. OSF operates under a modified LORT B+ contract and hires approximately 70 Equity actors and 20 non-Equity actors annually. A special audition hotline is available at (520) 482-2111, ext. 366.

The Oregon Shakespeare Festival's mission is succinct: 'Inspired by Shakespeare's work and the cultural richness of the United States, we reveal our collective humanity through illuminating interpretations of new and classic plays, deepened by the kaleidoscope of rotating repertory.' Founded in 1935 by Angus L. Bowmer, OSF is among the oldest professional regional theatre companies in America. New Zealander Paul Nicholson is the OSF executive director and one of the country's savviest administrators.

THE PUBLIC THEATER/NEW YORK SHAKESPEARE FESTIVAL

425 Lafayette Street, New York, NY 10003
Administration: (212) 539-8500. Box Office (Tele-Charge): (212) 967-7555.
Fax: (212) 784-3856
www.publictheater.org
New York Shakespeare Festival productions have captured the imaginations of audiences worldwide. Joseph Papp founded The Public Theater/NYSF in 1954 and the NYSF held its first free production of Shakespeare at the Emmanuel

Presbyterian Church on East 6th Street. Three years later, Papp staged his first Shakespeare in Central Park. The Delacorte Theater was completed in 1962. Of course, the rest is history. Upon Papp's death, JoAnne Akalaitis, his hand-picked successor, became artistic director for 20 months. George C. Wolfe took over in 1993; Oskar Eustis was appointed in 2005.

In its own words, here is the mission of the Public Theater:

> As the nation's foremost theatrical producer of Shakespeare and new work, The Public Theater is dedicated to achieving artistic excellence while developing an American theatre that is accessible and relevant to all people through productions of challenging new plays, musicals and innovative stagings of the classics.

Now, the Public stages two classics as part of Shakespeare in the Park at the Delacorte every summer free of charge and 80,000 to 100,000 patrons flock to the productions. The Shakespeare Lab is a nine-week summer program providing intensive classical training to young and culturally diverse actors, and the company continues Joseph Papp's emphasis on innovative stagings of classic drama and the development of new American plays and musicals. Over the years, the Public's productions have won 42 Tony Awards, 151 Obie Awards, and four Pulitzer Prizes.

Auditions for the Public are held on a show-by-show basis. Equity principal auditions are held with other Off-Broadway theatres annually and the NYSF casting office keeps headshots and résumés on file for ongoing consideration. The company operates under a LORT B contract. Check the website for current casting director, audition, and job employment information. Internships are available in various areas, including Joe's Pub cabaret.

SHAKESPEARE THEATRE COMPANY
Lansburgh Theatre: 450 7th Street NW, Washington, DC 20004
Sidney Harman Hall: 610 F Street NW, Washington, DC 20004
Administrative Office: The Shakespeare Theatre, 516 8th Street SE, Washington, DC 20003-2834
Administration: (202) 547-3230. Box office: (202) 547-1122 or toll free (877) 487-8849. Fax: (202) 547-0226
Email: web_admin@shakespearedc.org

www.shakespearedc.org

The Shakespeare Theatre Company's innovative approach to Shakespeare and other classic playwrights has earned it a reputation as one of the nation's premier classical theatre companies. By focusing on works with profound themes, complex characters and poetic language written by Shakespeare, his contemporaries and the playwrights he influenced, the Company's artistic mission is unique among theatre companies: to present theatre of scope and size in an imaginative, skillful and accessible American style that honors the playwrights' language and intentions while viewing their work through a twenty-first-century lens. Artistic director Michael Kahn has led the organization for 24 years. In its 2007–08 season, the Company opened the Harman Center for the Arts consisting of the new 775-seat Sidney Harman Hall and the 451-seat Lansburgh Theatre, both located in downtown Washington's Penn Quarter neighborhood. A dynamic hub of activity, the Harman Center showcases the Company as well as outstanding local performing arts groups and nationally renowned organizations.

Academy for Classical Acting

Intended for professional actors, the Academy for Classical Acting is accredited through The George Washington University and involves 12 months of study in voice, speech, acting, text, mask, Alexander technique, movement, clown, and stage combat. Check the website for more details.

Casting

STC has a small resident acting company and casts other roles (both Equity and non-Equity) on an ongoing basis throughout the year. Most auditions are by invitation only. STC also attends the Washington, DC–Baltimore Area Wide Auditions for Equity members each winter, and the League of Washington Theatres' general auditions every summer. General auditions are advertised in Back Stage for New York auditions and general auditions are held in DC each summer. STC also reviews photos and résumés received by mail, and contacts actors to schedule auditions based on their classical experience and training. New York casting director Stuart Howard Associates coordinates all New York auditions. See the website for more details. Mail casting inquiries, photos and résumés to: Associate Director, Shakespeare Theatre Company, 516 8th Street SE, Washington, DC 20003.

General employment opportunities

Check the website for specific openings, details and job descriptions, or email inquiries to: jobs@shakespearedc.org. No calls.

Internships

Administrative internships are generally available in artistic administration, development, education, general management, graphic design, and public relations/marketing. Production internships often surface in costumes, lighting, production management, sound, stage management, stage properties, and technical direction.

Acting Fellows

The Shakespeare Theatre provides opportunities for up to eight actors to join the Acting Fellows Company for a full season as part of established relationships with Vassar College and the Kennedy Center American College Theatre Festival. Actors who are not affiliated with a particular program may audition for remaining positions. Check the website for details.

ALABAMA SHAKESPEARE FESTIVAL

One Festival Drive, Montgomery, AL 36117

Administration: (334) 271-5300. Box Office: (334) 271-5353 or toll free: (800) 841-4273. Fax: (334) 271-5348

Email: asfmail@asf.net

www.asf.net

Located in the heart of Dixie, the Alabama Shakespeare Festival is the sixth-largest Shakespeare festival in the world and attracts more than 300,000 annual visitors from more than 60 foreign countries. Martin L. Platt founded ASF in 1972. ASF typically produces 14 plays year-round in the 750-seat Festival Stage and the 225-seat Octagon. It contracts around 57 Equity actors and 16 non-Equity actors for the repertory season based in Montgomery, the state capital. In 1985, ASF moved into a 100,000-square-foot, $21.5 million complex christened the Carolyn Blount Theatre. Designed by Thomas Blount and Perry Pittman, the architecture of the complex reflects the style of one of Shakespeare's contemporaries, Italian architect Andrea Palladio, and houses two theatres – the 750-seat Festival Stage and the 225-seat Octagon. Landscape architect Russell Page planned the estate-like grounds and lake that make up the 250-acre park, which is also home to the Montgomery Museum of Fine Arts. The Southern Writers' Project festival of new plays was founded by former artistic director Kent Thompson in 1991 as an exploration of the South's rich cultural heritage. It is dedicated to creating a theatrical voice for Southern writers and topics. Artistic director Geoffrey Sherman joined the company in 2005.

Check the website's Career Opportunities area for job opportunities, casting plans and internship openings.

CHICAGO SHAKESPEARE THEATER

800 East Grand Avenue on Navy Pier, Chicago, IL 60611
Administration: (312) 595-5656; Box office: (312) 595-5600
Fax: (312) 595-5607
www.chicagoshakes.com
Email: customerservice@chicagoshakes.com

The fastest growing Bard on the block is the Chicago Shakespeare Theater on Navy Pier, winner of the 2008 Regional Theatre Tony Award. The gorgeous seven-storey theatre complex features a 500-seat courtyard-style theatre and 200-seat flexible black-box theatre, serving 225,000 audience members annually. It is dazzling critics and attracting visitors from all over the world. 'There is no better view of Chicago than standing on Navy Pier. And there is no better view into the heart of mankind than through the eyes of William Shakespeare,' proclaims the sassy and jubilant founder and artistic director, Barbara Gaines.

Since moving to its state-of-the-art facility on Navy Pier in 1999, CST has garnered great acclaim under the leadership of Gaines and executive director Criss Henderson, including three Laurence Olivier Awards and more than 30 Joseph Jefferson Awards (Chicago's own version of the Tony Awards). The 2011–12 season marks Chicago Shakespeare's 25th anniversary.

The 38-play canon of William Shakespeare forms the core of CST's work and Subscription Series, complemented by other dramatic works, from traditional classical theatre to new classics that resonate with Shakespeare's timeless insights into the human condition. Through a 48-week season encompassing more than 600 performances, Chicago Shakespeare leads the community as the largest employer of Chicago actors. CST also contributes to an international community of creative exchange through its World's Stage Series, which affords Chicago audiences prime opportunities to experience the cultural and artistic traditions of some of the world's iconic theatre troupes as well as sending some of CST's best works abroad. Chicago Shakespeare is committed to making theatre an expansive, ever-changing and lifelong relationship. For family audiences, CST Family presents abridged Shakespeare productions, timeless fables and fairy tales, interactive music concerts and world-premiere musical theatre created with families in mind. CST's education outreach program, Team Shakespeare, has served over a million students and teachers throughout the Midwest, introducing the Bard's legacy to a new generation of theatregoers.

Visit www.chicagoshakes.com for casting and career opportunities.

UTAH SHAKESPEARE FESTIVAL

351 W. Center Street, Cedar City, UT 84720
Administration: (435) 586-7880. Box office: 800-PLAYTIX
Email: usfinfo@bard.org
www.bard.org

The Tony Award-winning Utah Shakespeare Festival, located in scenic southern Utah, hires over 250 actors, administrators, musicians, technicians, and educational tour positions for the summer and fall seasons, as well as actors, technicians, and managers for its touring production. Applications are accepted beginning October 1 for the following year. Seasonal hiring is completed by March of each year. For detailed information and application instructions for current positions, check out the company website.

Fred C. Adams founded the Festival in 1961 and continues to serve as executive producer emeritus. 'I believe in dreams, and in the need we all have to be children again,' he says. Committed to entertaining, enriching, and educating audiences 'through professional rotating repertory productions of Shakespeare and other master dramatists,' the company is happily situated within a day's drive of seven national parks, in the tiny, Bard-booming town of Cedar City.

'We are seeking classically trained actors eager to work in a repertory environment in scenic southern Utah,' explains Executive Director R. Scott Phillips. A headshot and résumé are required for auditions, which are held in Los Angeles, San Francisco, New York, Chicago, and other spots around the nation.

The Festival's budget is over $6 million and nearly 150,000 audience members attend annually. Founder Adams notes, 'We are looking forward to the future with nothing short of an adrenaline rush.' In 2010, two long-time USF actors and directors were named as artistic co-directors: David Ivers and Brian Vaughn.

Shakespeare Theatre Association members and select other Shakespeare producing theatres

A Company of Fools Theatre, Inc	Ottawa, Ontario, Canada	www.fools.ca
A Noise Within	Glendale, CA	www.anoisewithin.org
Abilene Shakespeare Festival	Abilene, TX	www.acu.edu/sponsored/asf
Actors Shakespeare Company at New Jersey Center University	Jersey City, NJ	www.ascnj.org
Actors' Shakespeare Project	Somerville, MA	www.actorsshakespeareproject.org
Actors' Theatre of Columbus	Columbus, OH	www.theactorstheatre.org
Advice to the Players	North Sandwich, NH	www.advicetotheplayers.org
African-American Shakespeare Company	San Francisco, CA	www.african-americanshakes.org
Alabama Shakespeare Festival	Montgomery, AL	www.asf.net
American Bard Theater Company	New York, NY	americanbard.org
American Globe Theatre Ltd	New York, NY	www.americanglobe.org
American Players Theatre	Spring Green, WI	www.americanplayers.org
American Shakespeare Center	Staunton, VA	www.americanshakespearecenter.com
American Shakespeare Repertory	St. Paul, MN	american-shakespeare.com
American Stage Theatre Company	St. Petersburg, FL	www.americanstage.org
The Aquila Theatre Company	New York, NY	www.aquilatheatre.com
Arcadia Shakespeare Festival	Glenside, PA	www.arcadia.edu
Arkansas Shakespeare Theatre	Conway, AR	www.arkshakes.com
Arizona Classical Theatre	Prescott, AZ	www.azshakes.com
Austin Shakespeare	Austin, TX	www.austinshakespeare.org
Baja Shakespeare c/o Marin Shakespeare Company	Los Barriles, Mexico	www.marinshakespeare.org
Baltimore Shakespeare Festival	Baltimore, MD	www.baltimoreshakespeare.org

Band of Brothers Shakespeare Company	Johnstown, PA	www.bandofbrothersshakespeare.org
Bard on the Beach Shakespeare Festival	Vancouver, BC, Canada	ww.bardonthebeach.com
Bell Shakespeare	Millers Point, NSW, Australia	www.bellshakespeare.com.au
Boston University Shakespeare Society	Boston, MA	http://people.bu.edu/bard
California Shakespeare Theater	Berkeley, CA	www.calshakes.org
Capistrano Shakespeare Festival	San Juan Capistrano, CA	www.capistranocenter.com/capistranoshakespeare.htm
Capital Classics Theatre Company	Hartford, CT	www.capitalclassics.org
Carolinian Shakespeare Festival	New Bern, NC	www.muse-of-fire.org
Central Coast Shakespeare Festival	San Luis Obispo, CA	centralcoastshakespeare.org
Chesapeake Shakespeare Company	Ellicott City, MD	www.chesapeakeshakespeare.com
Chicago Shakespeare Theater	Chicago, IL	www.chicagoshakes.com
Chicspeare Production Company	Chicago, IL	www.chicspeare.org
Cincinnati Shakespeare Company	Cincinnati, OH	www.cincyshakes.com
The Classical Theatre Project	Toronto, Ontario, Canada	www.classicaltheatreproject.ca
The Cleveland Shakespeare Festival	Cleveland, OH	www.cleveshakes.org
The Colonial Theater	Westerly, RI	thecolonialtheatre.org
The Colorado Shakespeare Festival	Boulder, CO	www.coloradoshakes.org
Commonwealth Shakespeare Company	Boston, MA	www.freeshakespeare.org
Communicable Arts	Brooklyn, NY	www.communicablearts.org
Connecticut Free Shakespeare	Bethany, CT	www.ctfreeshakespeare.org
The Coronado Playhouse	Coronado, CA	www.coronadoplayhouse.com
Cromulent Shakespeare Company	Minneapolis, MN	www.cromulentshakespeare.org
Delaware Shakespeare Festival	Claymont, DE	www.delshakes.org
Door Shakespeare	Baileys Harbor, WI	www.doorshakespeare.com
The Elm Shakespeare Company	New Haven, CT	www.elmshakespeare.org
Fairbanks Shakespeare Theatre	Fairbanks, AK	www.fstalaska.org
Festival Theatre Ensemble	Los Gatos, CA	www.festivaltheatreensemble.org
First Folio Theatre	Clarendon Hills, IL	www.firstfolio.org
Flatwater Shakespeare	Lincoln, NE	www.flatwatershakespeare.org
Folger Theatre	Washington, DC	www.folger.edu
The Foothill Theatre Company	Santa Fe, NM	www.foothilltheatre.org
The Four County Players	Barboursville, VA	www.fourcp.org

Freewill Shakespeare Festival	Edmonton, Alberta, Canada	
		www.rivercityshakespeare.com
Freeport Shakespeare Festival	Freeport, ME	www.freeportshakespearefestival.org
Georgia Shakespeare	Atlanta, GA	www.gashakespeare.org
Grand Marais Playhouse	Grand Marais, MN	
		www.grandmaraisplayhouse.com
Grand Valley Shakespeare Festival	Allendale, MI	www.gvsu.edu/shakes
Great Lakes Theater Festival	Cleveland, OH	www.greatlakestheatre.org
Great River Shakespeare Festival	Winona, MN	www.grsf.org
GreenStage: Seattle's Shakespeare in the Park Company	Seattle, WA	www.greenstage.org
Hamilton Urban Theatre	Hamilton, Ontario, Canada	www.hwcn.org/link/huta
Hampshire Shakespeare Company	Amherst, MA	www.hampshireshakespeare.org
Hamptons Shakespeare Festival	Amagansett, NY	www.hamptons-shakespeare.org
Harrisburg Shakespeare Festival	Harrisburg, PA	www.gamutplays.org/hsf
Hawaii Shakespeare Festival	Honolulu, HI	www.hawaiishakes.org
Heart of America Shakespeare Festival	Kansas City, MO	www.kcshakes.org
The Hofstra Shakespeare Festival	Hempstead, NY	
	www.hofstra.edu/academics/Colleges/HCLAS/DD/dd_shakespearefestival.html	
Houston Shakespeare Festival	Houston, TX	www.houstonfestivalscompany.com
Hudson Shakespeare Company	Weehawken, NJ	www.hudsonshakespeare.org
Hudson Valley Shakespeare Festival	Cold Springs, NY	www.hvshakespeare.org
Idaho Shakespeare Festival	Boise, ID	www.idahoshakespeare.org
Illinois Shakespeare Festival	Normal, IL	thefestival.org
Independent Shakespeare Co	Chatsworth, CA	www.independentshakespeare.com
Inwood Shakespeare Festival/ Moose Hall Theatre Company	New York, NY	www.moosehallisf.org
Island Players	Anna Maria, FL	www.theislandplayers.org
Ithaca Shakespeare Company	Ithaca, NY	www.ithacashakespeare.org
Judith Shakespeare Company	New York, NY	www.judithshakespeare.org
Kentucky Shakespeare Festival	Louisville, KY	www.kyshakes.org
Kings County Shakespeare Company	Brooklyn, NY	www.kingscountyshakespeare.org
The Kingsmen Shakespeare Company	Thousand Oaks, CA	www.kingsmenshakespeare.org
Lake Tahoe Shakespeare Festival	Incline Village, NV	www.laketahoeshakespeare.com
Lark Play Development Center	New York, NY	www.larktheatre.org
Las Vegas Shakespeare Company	Las Vegas, NV	lvshakes.com
Lexington Shakespeare Festival	Lexington, KY	www.tw3w.com/LSF
Livermore Shakespeare Festival	Livermore, CA	www.livermoreshakes.org

Long Beach Shakespeare Company	Long Beach, CA	www.lbshakespeare.org
Los Angeles Women's Shakespeare Company	Santa Monica, CA	www.lawsc.net
Marin Shakespeare Company	San Rafael, CA	www.marinshakespeare.org
Maryland Shakespeare Festival	Frederick, MD	www.mdshakes.org
Merced Shakespearefest	Merced, CA	www.mercedshakespearefest.org
Michigan Shakespeare Festival	Jackson, MI	www.jtvpodcast.com/msf
The MIT Shakespeare Ensemble	Cambridge, MA	www.mit.edu/~ensemble
Mixed Magic Theatre	Pawtucket, RI	mixedmagicri.com
The Montana Shakespeare Company	Helena, MT	www.montanashakespeare.org
Montana Shakespeare in the Parks	Bozeman, MT	www2.montana.edu/shakespeare
The Montford Park Players	Asheville, NC	www.montfordparkplayers.org
Murphys Creek Theatre	Murphys, CA	www.murphyscreektheatre.org
Murray Shakespeare Festival	Murray, KY	www.murraystate.edu/chfa/english/shakespeare.htm
The Nashville Shakespeare Festival	Nashville, TN	www.nashvilleshakes.org
Nebraska Shakespeare Festival	Omaha, NE	www.nebraskashakespeare.com
Nevada Shakespeare Company	Dayton, NV	www.nevada-shakespeare.org
The New American Shakespeare Tavern	Atlanta, GA	www.shakespearetavern.com
The New England Shakespeare Festival	Deerfield, NH	www.newenglandshakespeare.org
New Theatre	Coral Gables, FL	www.new-theatre.org
New Orleans Shakespeare Festival at Tulane	New Orleans, LA	www.neworleansshakespeare.com
New York Classical Theatre	New York, NY	newyorkclassical.org
North Carolina Shakespeare Festival	High Point, NC	www.ncshakes.org
Northeast Shakespeare Ensemble	New London, NH	www.nesetheatre.org
Notre Dame Shakespeare Festival	Notre Dame, IN	shakespeare.nd.edu
Oak Park Festival Theatre	Oak Park, IL	www.oakparkfestival.com
Ohio Shakespeare Festival	Akron, OH	www.ohioshakespeare.com
Ojai Shakespeare Festival	Ojai, CA	www.ojaishakespeare.org (on hiatus)
Oklahoma Shakespeare in the Park	Oklahoma City, OK	www.oklahomashakespeare.com
The Old Globe	San Diego, CA	www.oldglobe.org
Olympic Shakespeare Productions	Port Townsend, WA	www.olympus.net/community/olyshakespeare
Oregon Shakespeare Festival	Ashland, OR	www.orshakes.org
Orlando Shakespeare Theater in Partnership with UCF	Orlando, FL	orlandoshakes.org

Oxford Shakespeare Company	New York, NY	www.osctheatre.org
Oxford Shakespeare Festival	University, MS	shakespeare.olemiss.edu
Pacific Repertory Theatre	Carmel, CA	www.pacrep.org
Park Players	Warrior, AL	www.bhamparkplayers.com
Pax Amicus Castle Theatre	Budd Lake, NJ	www.paxamicus.com
The Pella Shakespeare Festival	Pella, IA www.pmscasting.com/festival (on hiatus)	
Pennsylvania Renaissance Faire	Manheim, PA	www.parenaissancefaire.com
Pennsylvania Shakespeare Festival at De Salles University	Center Valley, PA	www.pashakespeare.org
Penobscot Theatre Company	Bangor, ME	www.penobscottheatre.org
The Philadelphia Shakespeare Theatre	Philadelphia, PA	www.phillyshakespeare.org
Poor Players Theatre Company	San Marcos, CA	www.poorplayers.com
The Public Theater/ New York Shakespeare Festival	New York, NY	www.publictheatre.org
Quintessence: Language & Imagination Theatre	Portland, OR	www.qlit.org
Rebel Shakespeare Company	Salem, MA	www.rebelshakespeare.org
Reduced Shakespeare Company	Sonoma, CA	www.reducedshakespeare.com
Revolving Shakespeare Company	New York, NY www.milesphillips.com/page16.html	
The Richmond Shakespeare Festival	Richmond, VA	www.richmondshakespeare.com
Riverside Theatre	Iowa City, IA	www.riversidetheatre.org
Rochester Community Players/ Shakespeare Players	Rochester, NY www.rochestercommunityplayers.org	
Rosebriar Shakespeare Theatre	Groveport, OH	www.rosebriarshakespeare.org
Sacramento Shakespeare Festival	Sacramento, CA www.sacramentoshakespeare.net	
Salt Lake Shakespeare	Salt Lake City, UT	saltlakeshakespeare.org
The San Francisco Shakespeare Festival	San Francisco, CA	www.sfshakes.org
San Jacinto Valley Shakespeare Festival	Hemet, CA	www.ramonabowl.com
Sandstone Productions	Farmington, NM www.fmtn.org/city_government/parks_recreation_ and_cultural_affairs/sandstone_productions.html	
Saratoga Shakespeare Company	Saratoga Springs, NY www.saratogashakespeare.com	
Seattle Shakespeare Company	Seattle, WA	www.seattleshakespeare.org
Sebastopol Shakespeare Festival	Sebastopol, CA the-rep.com/index.php/sebastopol_shakespeare	

Shady Shakespeare Theatre Company	Saratoga, CA	www.shadyshakes.org
Shakespeare '70, Inc	Lawrenceville, NJ	www.shakespeare70.org
Shakespeare & Company	Lenox, MA	www.shakespeare.org
Shakespeare & Company	White Bear Lake, MN	shakespeareandcompany.org
Shakespeare at Chaffin's Barn	Nashville, TN	www.dinnertheatre.com
Shakespeare at Clemson	Clemson, SC	www.clemson.edu/caah/shakespeare
Shakespeare at Winedale	Austin, TX	www.utexas.edu/cola/progs/winedale
Shakespeare by the Sea	Halifax, NS, Canada	www.shakespearebythesea.ca
Shakespeare by the Sea	San Pedro, CA	www.shakespearebythesea.org
The Shakespeare Center	Los Angeles, CA	www.shakespearecenter.org
The Shakespeare Company of Greater Rochester	Rochester, NY	www.shakeco.com
Shakespeare Dallas	Dallas, TX	www.shakespearedallas.org
Shakespeare Festival of St. Louis	St. Louis, MO	www.shakespearefestivalstlouis.org
Shakespeare in Action	Toronto, Ontario, Canada	www.shakespeareinaction.org
Shakespeare in Delaware Park	Buffalo, NY	www.shakespeareindelawarepark.org
Shakespeare in the Park	Arlington, MA	www.acarts.org/shakespeare.php
Shakespeare in the Park	Calgary, Alberta, Canada	www.mtroyal.ca/AboutMountRoyal/MediaRoom/FeaturedEvents/sitp
Shakespeare in the Park	Henderson, NV	www.hendersonlive.com/special-events/shakespeare
Shakespeare in the Parking Lot	New York, NY	shakespeareintheparkinglot.com
Shakespeare in the Ruins	Winnipeg, MB, Canada	www.shakespeareintheruins.com
Shakespeare-in-the-Schools	Pittsburgh, PA	www.play.pitt.edu/sits
Shakespeare in the Valley	Campton, NH	www.shakespeareinthevalley.com
Shakespeare in the Vines	Riverside, CA	www.shakespeareinthevines.org/SITV/Home.html
Shakespeare Kelowna	Kelowna, BC, Canada	www.shakespearekelowna.org
Shakespeare Now! Theatre Company	Brookline, MA	www.shakespearenow.org
Shakespeare NYC	New York, NY	www.shakespearenyc.net
Shakespeare on the Green	Wilmington, NC	www.whatsonwilmington.com
Shakespeare on the Saskatchewan Festival	Saskatoon, SK, Canada	www.shakespeareonthesaskatchewan.com
Shakespeare on the Sound	Norwalk, CT	www.shakespeareonthesound.org
Shakespeare Orange County	Orange, CA	www.shakespeareoc.org

The Shakespeare Project of Chicago	Chicago, IL	www.shakespeareprojectchicago.org
Shakespeare Santa Cruz	Santa Cruz, CA	www.shakespearesantacruz.org
Shakespeare Sedona	Phoenix, AZ	
		www.shakespearesedona.com (on hiatus)
The Shakespeare Society	New York, NY	www.shakespearesociety.org
Shakespeare Theatre Company	Washington, DC	www.shakespearetheatre.org
The Shakespeare Theatre of New Jersey	Madison, NJ	www.shakespearenj.org
Shakespeare Under the Stars	Wimberley, TX	www.emilyann.org/sus.cfm
Shakespeare's Globe	London, UK	www.shakespeares-globe.org
Shenandoah Shakespeare's American Shakespeare Center	Staunton, VA	www.americanshakespearecenter.com
The South Carolina Shakespeare Company	Columbia, SC	georgedinsmore.com/shakespeare
Southwest Shakespeare Company	Mesa, AZ	www.swshakespeare.org
Southwest Shakespeare Festival	Odessa, TX	www.globesw.org
St. Lawrence Shakespeare Festival	Prescott, Ontario, Canada	www.stlawrenceshakespeare.ca
St. Louis Shakespeare	St. Louis, MO	www.stlshakespeare.org
Stage West	Fort Worth, TX	stagewest.org
Sterling Renaissance Festival	Sterling, NY	www.sterlingfestival.com
Stratford Shakespeare Festival	Stratford, Ontario, Canada	www.stratfordfestival.ca
Summer Shakes, Inc	Virginia Beach, VA	www.summershakes.com
Sun Valley Shakespeare Festival	Sun Valley, ID	www.nexstagetheatre.org/productions/shakespeare.html
Tennessee Shakespeare Festival	Bell Buckle, TN	www.tennesseeshakespearefestival.com
Tennessee Stage Company	Knoxville, TN	www.tennesseestage.com
Texas Shakespeare Festival	Kilgore, TX	www.texasshakespeare.com
The Artists Formerly Known as Milwaukee Shakespeare	Milwaukee, WI	http://milwaukeeshakespeare.wordpress.com/
The Summer Theatre at New Canaan	New Canaan, CT	www.stonc.org/home/
The Theater at Monmouth	Monmouth, ME	www.theatreatmonmouth.org
Theater Arts, Oregon State University	Corvallis, OR	www.oregonstate.edu/dept/theatre
Theatre for a New Audience	New York, NY	www.tfana.org
Theatreworks	Colorado Springs, CO	www.theatreworkscs.org
Theatricum Botanicum	Topanga, CA	www.theatricum.com

Trinity Shakespeare Festival	Fort Worth, TX	www.trinityshakes.org
Two Pence Shakespeare	Chicago, IL	www.twopenceshakespeare.org
Unseam'd Shakespeare Company	Pittsburgh, PA	www.unseamd.com
Upstate Shakespeare Festival	Greenville, SC	www.upstateshakespearefestival.org
Utah Shakespeare Festival	Cedar City, UT	www.bard.org
Vermont Shakespeare Company	North Hero, VT	www.vermontshakespeare.org
Virginia Shakespeare Festival	Williamsburg, VA	www.wm.edu/as/vsf
Vpstart Crow Productions Inc.	Manassas, VA	www.vpstartcrow.com
Washington Shakespeare Company	Crystal City, VA	www.washingtonshakespeare.org
Water Works Theatre Company Inc.	Royal Oak, MI	www.waterworkstheatre.com
Westerly Shakespeare in the Park/ The Colonial Theater	Westerly, RI	www.thecolonialtheatre.org
Woman's Will	San Francisco, CA	www.womanswill.org
Woodward Shakespeare Festival	Fresno, CA	www.woodwardshakespeare.org
Yonkers Shakespeare Project	Yonkers, NY	www.alltheworldsastage.org
The York Shakespeare Company	New York, NY	www.yorkshakespeare.org
York Shakespeare Festival	Newmarket, Ontario, Canada	www.resurgence.on.ca
Young Shakespeare Players	Madison, WI	www.ysp.org

130+ children's theatre and youth theatre programs

Children's theatre, educational theatre, participatory youth theatre, or theatre for young audiences (known as 'TYA' in contract terminology at Actors' Equity and throughout the business) is a growing enterprise in America.

'Leading artists in every discipline are finding that working in this field not only expands their aesthetic possibilities but connects them to an audience which challenges, inspires, and reconnects them to the profound power of theatre,' notes Peter Brosius, artistic director of The Children's Theatre Company in Minneapolis. 'We need artists of skill, passion, and dedication,' adds Mr. Brosius.

Many theatres and theatre leaders are firmly committed to the goals of theatre for young audiences, believing in the artistic, cultural, social, audience-building, family-values virtues of theatre for children and teens. Some companies perform for children using adult actors, others perform with children in their casts, and many produce plays for family audiences including children and adults. Anyone who thinks that children's theatre is for beginners obviously hasn't directed, acted, or produced children's theatre or visited any of the major children's theatres in America. Long a staple in community theatres, schools, and parks and recreation programs, children's theatre is now in remarkably creative hands. Check out the work of the Tony Award-winning Minneapolis wonder The Children's Theatre Company, and the Seattle Repertory Theatre's commissioning work from Pulitzer Prize-winning playwright Robert Schenkkan. St. Louis's Metro Theater Company, Tempe, Arizona's Childsplay, Dallas's Children's Theater, Bethesda, Maryland's Imagination Stage, and many others have elevated the art form and continue to entertain children and their families.

However, it should be noted that many theatre outreach and educational programs have surfaced to a prominent place in theatre schedules for financial, fundraising, marketing, and audience-development purposes. For example, at various times in our nation's recent history when art and theatre were being threatened by censorship issues and minimized by business, corporate and government granting institutions, many theatres broadened their horizons to include significant educational programs as a way of attracting individual, business, corporate, foundation, and government support. Some theatre leaders have turned into 'true believers' and others simply enjoy the subsidies. In either case, it's always good to research the theatre's philosophy, mission, and real commitment to youth theatre before plunging in.

Theatre for Young Audiences/USA

Theatre for Young Audiences/USA is the national service organization promoting the power of professional theatre for young audiences through excellence, collaboration and innovation across cultural and intenational boundaries. The address is: Theatre for Young Audiences/USA, Attention: Chris Garcia Peak, c/o Emerald City Theatre Administrative Offices, 2936 N. Southport Avenue, 3rd Floor, Chicago, Illinois 60657. For questions about membership, call (703) 403-5820. Fax: (773) 529-2693. Email: info@tyausa.org. Website: www.assitej-usa.org.

The website includes listings for over 100 producers with contact numbers. A few are listed below to give you an idea of the range of producers in this genre.

ARIZONA

Childsplay, Inc
Tempe, AZ
www.childsplayaz.org

CALIFORNIA

Active Arts: Theatre for Young Audiences
Oakland, CA
www.activeartstheatre.org

Palo Alto Children's Theatre
Palo Alto, CA
www.city.palo-alto.ca.us/theatre

South Coast Repertory
Costa Mesa, CA
www.scr.com

COLORADO

Denver Center Theatre Academy
Denver, CO
www.dcpa.org

DISTRICT OF COLUMBIA

The Children's Theatre Workshop, Inc
Washington, DC
www.thechildrenstheatreworkshop.com

The Smithsonian Associates' Discovery
    Theater
Washington, DC
www.discoverytheatre.org

FLORIDA

Eckerd Theater Company
Clearwater, FL
www.rutheckerdhall.com

Fort Lauderdale Children's Theatre
www.flct.org

Orlando Repertory Theatre
Orlando, FL
www.orlandorep.com

The PlayGround Theatre
Miami Shores, FL
www.theplaygroundtheatre.com

Riverside Children's Theatre
Vero Beach, FL
www.riversidetheatre.com

GEORGIA

Alliance Theatre Education Department/TYA
Atlanta, GA
www.alliancetheatre.org

HAWAII

Honolulu Theatre for Youth
Honolulu, HI
www.htyweb.org

IDAHO

Velma V. Morrison Center for Performing Arts
Boise, ID
www.mc.boisestate.edu

ILLINOIS

Adventure Stage Chicago
Chicago, IL
www.adventurestage.org

Emerald City Theatre
Chicago, IL
www.emeraldcitytheatre.com

INDIANA

Children's Museum of Indianapolis
Indianapolis, IN
www.childrensmuseum.org

Indiana Repertory Theatre
Indianapolis, IN
www.irtlive.com

KENTUCKY

Lexington Children's Theatre
Lexington, KY
www.lctonstage.org

Stage One
Louisville, KY
www.stageone.org

LOUISIANA

Playmakers of Baton Rouge
Baton Rouge, LA
www.playmakers.net

MARYLAND

AATE
Bethesda, MD
www.aate.com

Adventure Theatre
GlenEcho, MD
www.adventuretheatre.org

Children's Theater Association
Towson, MD
www.ctabaltimore.org

Imagination Stage
Bethesda, MD
www.imaginationstage.org

MICHIGAN

Flint Youth Theatre
Flint, MI
www.flintyouththeatre.org

MINNESOTA

The Children's Theatre Company
Minneapolis, MN
www.childrenstheatre.org

CLIMB Theatre
Inver Grove Heights, MN
www.climb.org

Great River Educational Arts Theatre
(G.R.E.A.T)
St. Cloud, MN
www.greattheatre.org

Ordway Center for the Performing Arts
St. Paul, MN
www.ordway.org

Prairie Fire Children's Theatre
Barrett, MN
www.prairiefirechildrenstheatre.com

Stages Theatre
Hopkins, MN
www.stagestheatre.org

Stepping Stone Theatre for Youth
    Development
St. Paul, MN
www.steppingstonetheatre.org

Youth Performance Company
Minneapolis, MN
www.youthperformanceco.com

MISSOURI

Coterie Theatre
Kansas City, MO
www.coterietheatre.org

TRYPS Children's Theatre
Columbia, MO
www.tryps.missouri.org

NEBRASKA

Omaha Theater Company
Omaha, NE
www.otcyp.org

NEW JERSEY

George Street Playhouse
New Brunswick, NJ
www.gsponline.org

The Growing Stage – The Children's
    Theatre of New Jersey
Netcong, NJ
www.growingstage.com

Youth Stages
Princeton, NJ
www.youthstages.com

NEW YORK

Bardavon Opera House
Poughkeepsie, NY
www.bardavon.org

Family Opera Initiative
New York, NY
www.familyoperainitiative.org

iTheatrics
New York, NY
www.itheatrics.com

Making Books Sing, Inc
New York, NY
www.makingbookssing.org

Music Theatre International
New York, NY
www.mtishows.com

The New Victory Theater
New York, NY
www.newvictory.org

NYS Theatre Institute
Troy, NY
www.nysti.org

The Open Eye Theater
Margaretville, NY
www.theopeneye.org

Paper Bag Players
New York, NY
www.thepaperbagplayers.org

TADA! Theatre
New York, NY
www.tadatheatre.com

NORTH CAROLINA

Children's Theatre of Charlotte
Charlotte, NC
www.ctcharlotte.org

OHIO

The Children's Theatre of Cincinnati
Cincinnati, OH
www.thechildrenstheatre.com

Cincinnati Playhouse in the Park
Cincinnati, OH
www.cincyplay.com

Madcap Productions Puppet Theater
Cincinnati, OH
www.madcappuppets.com

Playhouse Square Theatre
Cleveland, OH
www.playhousesquare.org

OREGON

Oregon Children's Theatre
Portland, OR
www.octc.org

PENNSYLVANIA

Arden Theatre Company
Philadelphia, PA
www.ardentheatre.org

Fulton Theatre/Fulton Opera House
Lancaster, PA
www.fultontheatre.org

Pennsylvania Youth Theatre
Bethlehem, PA
www.123pyt.org

People's Light and Theatre Co
Malvern, PA
www.peopleslight.org

Philadelphia Theatre Company
Philadelphia, PA
www.philadelphiatheatrecompany.org

Walnut Street Theatre
Philadelphia, PA
www.walnutstreettheatre.org

SOUTH CAROLINA

South Carolina Children's Theatre
Greenville, SC
www.scchildrenstheatre.org

TENNESSEE

Artistree, Inc/Wood & Strings Theatre
Centerville, TN
www.woodandstrings.net/Dolly
wood.htm

Nashville Children's Theatre
Nashville, TN
www.nashvillechildrenstheatre.org

TEXAS

AC Lamplight Youth Theatre
Amarillo, TX
www.aclamplight.com

Alley Theatre
Houston, TX
www.alleytheatre.org

Angelo Civic Theatre
San Angelo, TX
www.angelocivictheatre.com

Austin Theater Alliance
Austin, TX
www.austintheatre.org

Dallas Children's Theater
Dallas, TX
www.dct.org

Magik Theatre
San Antonio, TX
www.magiktheatre.org

Main Street Theater
Houston, TX
www.mainstreettheater.com

UTAH

Noorda Regional Theatre Center for
Children and Youth
Orem, UT
www.uvu.edu/theatre/noorda/index.html

VIRGINIA

The Children's Theatre of Hampton Roads
Norfolk, VA
www.40thstreetstage.com

JMU Children's Playshop
Harrisonburg, VA
www.jmu.edu/theatre/child.htm

Kennedy Center Theater for Young
Audiences
Arlington, VA
www.kennedy-center.org

WASHINGTON

Olympia Family Theater
Olympia, WA
www.olyft.org

Seattle Children's Theatre
Seattle, WA
www.sct.org

WISCONSIN

First Stage Children's Theater
Milwaukee, WI
www.firststage.org

In addition to Theatre for Young Audiences/USA, there are many other TYA companies who use the Equity contract. Some are LORT theatres, others are TCG theatres, and all of these are recent Equity Theatre Contract companies (contact the Actors' Equity Association for the full list and contact numbers):

ALABAMA SHAKESPEARE FESTIVAL, Montgomery, AL	www.asf.net
AMERICAN STAGE, St. Petersburg, FL	www.americanstage.org
BILINGUAL FOUNDATION OF THE ARTS, Los Angeles, CA	www.bfatheatre.org
CASA MANANA PLAYHOUSE, Fort Worth, TX	www.casamanana.org
CLASSICS ON STAGE, Chicago, IL	www.classicsonstage.com
CLEVELAND PLAYHOUSE, Cleveland, OH	www.clevelandplayhouse.com
DRURY LANE CHILDREN'S THEATRE, Oakbrook Terrace, IL	www.drurylaneoakbrook.com
FANFARE THEATRE ENSEMBLE, New York, NY	(212) 674-8181
FIRST STAGE PRODUCTIONS, Milwaukee, WI	www.firststage.org
FLAT ROCK PLAYHOUSE, Flat Rock, NC	www.flatrockplayhouse.org
FREEDOM THEATRE, Philadelphia, PA	www.freedomtheatre.org
LARK THEATRE COMPANY, New York, NY	www.larktheatre.org
LINCOLN CENTER INSTITUTE, New York, NY	www.lcinstitute.org
NORTH SHORE MUSIC THEATRE, Beverly, MA	www.nsmt.org
OLD LOG CHILDREN'S THEATRE, Greenwood, MN	www.oldlog.com
PITTSBURGH CIVIC LIGHT OPERA, Pittsburgh, PA	www.pittsburghclo.org
PUSHCART PLAYERS, Verona, NJ	www.pushcartplayers.org
SEEM-TO-BE PLAYERS, Lawrence, KS	www.lawrenceartscenter.com/STB
SESAME STREET LIVE, Minneapolis, MN	www.sesamestreetlive.com
SHAKESPEARE & COMPANY, Lenox, MA	www.shakespeare.org
SHAKESPEARE LIVE!, Madison, NJ	www.njshakespeare.org/tour/live.html
STORYBOOK MUSICAL THEATRE, Philadelphia, PA	www.storybookmusical.org
THEATREWORKS/USA, New York, NY	www.theatreworksusa.org
WHEELOCK FAMILY THEATRE, Boston, MA	www.wheelock.edu/wft

140+ musical theatres
including an introduction to NAMT and ASCAP

NATIONAL ALLIANCE FOR MUSICAL THEATRE (NAMT)

520 Eighth Avenue, Suite 301, 3rd Floor, New York, NY 10018

Phone: (212) 714-6668. Fax: (212) 714-0469

Email: info@namt.org

www.namt.org

Musical theatre is all the rage in theatres, arts centers, and civic light operas throughout America, and the National Alliance for Musical Theatre (NAMT) is a national service organization dedicated exclusively to musical theatre. Founded in 1985, the NAMT membership includes theatres, presenting organizations, higher education programs and individual producers. NAMT recently reported that its members 'cumulatively staged over 16,000 performances attended by over 11 million people and reached revenues of over $500 million, employing over 15,500 people.'

In the organization's own words, the mission of NAMT is 'nurturing the creation, development, production, and presentation of new and classic musicals; providing a forum for the sharing of resources and information relating to professional musical theatre through communications, networking, and programming; and advocating for the imagination, diversity, and joy unique to musical theatre.'

Programs and services

Member benefits include a Festival of New Musicals, two annual conferences, new works summits and writers' roundtables, a set and costume rental registry, and a new granting program: the National Fund for New Musicals.

Members

This geographical index of NAMT members is listed in alphabetical order by state, and reveals theatres nationally and abroad. The main website provides direct links to each theatre.

Red Mountain Theatre Company	Birmingham, AL	www.redmountaintheatre.org
Arizona Theatre Company	Tucson, AZ	www.arizonatheatre.org
Cabrillo Music Theatre	Thousand Oaks, CA	www.cabrillomusictheatre.com
FCLO Music Theatre	Fullerton, CA	www.fclo.com
Broadway/LA	Los Angeles, CA	www.broadwayla.org
McCoy Rigby Entertainment	Yorba Linda, CA	www.mccoyrigby.com
Musical Theatre West	Long Beach, CA	www.musical.org
California Musical Theatre (Music Circus, Broadway Sacramento & Cosmopolit)		
	Sacramento, CA	www.californiamusicaltheatre.com
TheatreWorks	Palo Alto, CA	www.theatreworks.org
Western Stage	Salinas, CA	www.westernstage.com
Relevant Theatricals, LLC	Culver City, CA	
42nd Street Moon	San Francisco, CA	www.42ndstmoon.org
Academy for New Musical Theatre	North Hollywood, CA	www.anmt.org
Las Positas College	Livermore, CA	
		www.laspositascollege.edu/performingarts
Old Globe, The	San Diego, CA	www.theoldglobe.org
Slater, Stewart	San Jose, CA	
California State University, Fullerton	Fullerton, CA	www.fullerton.edu/arts/
1113 Productions, Inc	Marina Del Rey, CA	www.fallingforevemusical.com
Center Theatre Group	Los Angeles, CA	www.CenterTheatreGroup.org
R and R Productions, Inc/ Standing O, Inc	Penngrove, CA	
SenovvA, Inc	Los Angeles, CA	www.SenovvA.com
M2 Consulting	San Jose, CA	
La Jolla Playhouse	La Jolla, CA	www.lajollaplayhouse.org/
Woodminster Summer Musicals	Oakland, CA	www.woodminster.com
California Conservatory of the Arts/ Musical Theatre University	Newport Beach, CA	www.musicaltheatreuniversity.com
University of Northern Colorado – School of Theatre Arts and Dance	Greeley, CO	www.unco.edu
Goodspeed Musicals	East Haddam, CT	www.goodspeed.org
Spirit of Broadway Theater, The	Norwich, CT	www.spiritofbroadway.org

Hartt School – Theatre Division, University of Hartford	West Hartford, CT	www.hartford.edu/hartt
Van Hill Entertainment	Stamford, CT	www.vanhillentertainment.com
Ford's Theatre	Washington, DC	www.fords.org
V.J. Colonna Productions, Inc	Miami Beach, FL	
Stage Aurora Theatrical Company, Inc	Jacksonville, FL	www.stageaurora.org
International Broadway Productions	Boca Raton, FL	
Florida State University College of Music – Music Theatre Program	Tallahassee, FL	www.music.fsu.edu
Maltz Jupiter Theatre, Inc	Jupiter, FL	www.jupitertheatre.org
University of Miami, Department of Theatre Arts/Jerry Herman Ring Theatre	Coral Gables, FL	www.miami.edu/tha
Theater of the Stars	Atlanta, GA	www.theatreofthestars.com
Coeur d'Alene Summer Theatre, The	Coeur d'Alene, ID	www.cdasummertheatre.com
Light Opera Works	Evanston, IL	www.light-opera-works.org
Marriott Theatre	Lincolnshire, IL	www.MarriottTheatre.com
Chicago Muse	Chicago, IL	www.chicagomuse.org
Little Theatre On The Square, The	Sullivan, IL	www.thelittletheatre.org
Porchlight Music Theatre Chicago	Chicago, IL	www.porchlighttheatre.com
Millikin University, Department of Theatre and Dance	Decatur, IL	www.millikin.edu/theatre/
Northwestern University, American Music Theatre Project and Music Theatre	Evanston, IL	www.amtp.northwestern.edu
Chicago Shakespeare Theater	Chicago, IL	www.chicagoshakes.com
Derby Dinner Playhouse	Clarksville, IN	www.derbydinner.com
Ball State University – Department of Theatre and Dance	Muncie, IN	www.bsu.edu/theatre/
Music Theatre of Wichita	Wichita, KS	www.MTWichita.org
Reagle Music Theatre of Greater Boston	Waltham, MA	reaglemusictheatre.com
Boston Music Theatre Project at Suffolk University	Boston, MA	www.suffolk.edu/college/3199.html
Fiddlehead Theatre Company	Dedham, MA	www.fiddleheadtheatre.com
Boston Conservatory, The	Boston, MA	www.bostonconservatory.edu
Lyric Stage Company of Boston, The	Boston, MA	www.Lyricstage.com
Barrington Stage Company	Pittsfield, MA	barringtonstageco.org
NETworks Presentations	Columbia, MD	www.networkstours.com
Phoenix Entertainment	Frederick, MD	www.phoenix-ent.com

Pack The House Productions	Germantown, MD	www.packthehouseproductions.com
Maine State Music Theatre	Brunswick, ME	www.msmt.org
Ogunquit Playhouse	Ogunquit, ME	www.ogunquitplayhouse.org
Ordway Center for the Performing Arts	St. Paul, MN	www.ordway.org
Theatre Latté Da	Minneapolis, MN	latteda.org
Municipal Theatre Association of St. Louis (The MUNY)	St. Louis, MO	www.muny.org
University of Montana – College of Visual and Performing Arts	Missoula, MT	http://www.umt.edu/umarts
North Carolina Blumenthal Performing Arts Center	Charlotte, NC	www.blumenthalcenter.org
North Carolina Theatre	Raleigh, NC	www.nctheatre.com
Flat Rock Playhouse- the State Theatre of North Carolina	Flat Rock, NC	www.flatrockplayhouse.org
Seacoast Repertory Theatre	Portsmouth, NH	www.seacoastrep.org
Paper Mill Playhouse	Millburn, NJ	www.PaperMill.org
ReVision Theatre (The Genesius Guild, Inc.)	Asbury Park, NJ	www.ReVisionTheatre.org
NYU, Tisch School of the Arts Graduate Musical Theatre Writing Program	New York, NY	www.nyu.edu/tisch/musical/
Brooks & Distler, Attorneys at Law	New York, NY	
Gorgeous Entertainment Inc.	New York, NY	www.gorgeousentertainment.com
Berlind, Roger	New York, NY	
Prince, Harold	New York, NY	
Artpark and Company	Lewiston, NY	www.artpark.net
BMI Lehman Engel Musical Theatre Workshop	New York, NY	www.bmi.com
ASCAP Musical Theatre Workshop	New York, NY	www.ascap.com
Town Square Productions	New York, NY	www.townsquareproductions.com
321 Theatrical Management	New York, NY	
Lark Play Development Center	New York, NY	www.larktheatre.org
Musical Mondays Theatre Lab, Inc.	New York, NY	www.musicalmondays.org
Ball, Leland	New York, NY	
East of Doheny	New York, NY	www.eastofdoheny.com
CAP21 - Collaborative Arts Project 21	New York, NY	www.cap21.org
Collaborations Limited	Centerport, NY	collaborationsltd.com
Junkyard Dog Productions	New York, NY	www.jydprod.com
P2 Creations LLC	New York, NY	

Demos Bizar Entertainment	New York, NY	www.demosbizar.com
Stacey Mindich Productions, LLC.	New York, NY	
Adirondack Theatre Festival	Glens Falls, NY	www.ATFestival.org
Playing Pretend	New York, NY	www.playingpretend.com
Sharon Carr Associates, Ltd.	New York, NY	
Pace New Musicals	New York, NY	

www.pace.edu/pace/dyson/academic-departments-
and-programs/performing-arts/musical-theatre-bfa-program/

AWA Touring	New York, NY	www.awatouring.com

NYU, Steinhardt School of Culture, Education and Human Development

	New York, NY	steinhardt.nyu.edu/music/theatre

NYU, Steinhardt School of Culture, Education and Human Development

	New York, NY	steinhardt.nyu.edu/music/theatre
Van Hill Entertainment	New York, NY	www.vanhillentertainment.com
Margot Astrachan Production	New York, NY	
Amas Musical Theatre	New York, NY	www.amasmusical.org
New York Theatre Barn	New York, NY	www.NYTheatreBarn.org
Public Theatre, The /		
New York Shakespeare Festival	New York, NY	www.publictheatre.org
Vineyard Theatre	New York, NY	www.vineyardtheatre.org
Playwrights Horizons, Inc.	New York, NY	www.playwrightshorizons.org
Human Race Theatre Company, The	Dayton, OH	www.humanracetheatre.org
University of Cincinnati,		
Department of Musical Theatre	Cincinnati, OH	www.ccm.uc.edu/musical_theatre
Baldwin Wallace College		
Conservatory of Music	Berea, OH	www.bw.edu

Wright State University Department of Theatre, Dance & Motion Pictures

	Dayton, OH	www.wright.edu/tdmp
Lyric Theatre of Oklahoma	Oklahoma City, OK	www.lyrictheatreokc.com

Weitzenhoffer Department of Musical Theatre, University of Oklahoma

	Norman, OK	www.ou.edu/finearts/musicaltheatre
Dancap Productions Inc.	Toronto, Ontario,	www.dancaptickets.com
April 30th Entertainment Inc.	Toronto, Ontario, Canada	
		april30thentertainment.com
Broadway Rose Theatre, The	Tigard, OR	www.broadwayrose.com
Actors Cabaret of Eugene	Eugene, OR	www.actorscabaret.org
Pittsburgh Musical Theatre	Pittsburgh, PA	www.pittsburghmusicals.com
Pittsburgh CLO	Pittsburgh, PA	www.pittsburghCLO.org
Walnut Street Theatre	Philadelphia, PA	www.walnutstreettheatre.org
Pennsylvania Centre Stage	University Park, PA	www.pacentrestage.psu.edu/

Gray, Charles	Pittsburgh, PA	
Fulton Theatre	Lancaster, PA	www.thefulton.org
Temple Theatres	Philadelphia, PA	www.temple.edu/sct/theatre/
Act II Playhouse	Ambler, PA	www.act2.org
Bristol Riverside Theatre	Bristol, PA	www.BRTstage.org
Allen, Judith	Charleston, SC	
Cumberland County Playhouse	Crossville, TN	www.ccplayhouse.com
Dallas Summer Musicals	Dallas, TX	www.dallassummermusicals.org
Theatre Under The Stars	Houston, TX	www.tuts.com
Ostrow, Stuart	Houston, TX	
ZACH Theatre	Austin, TX	www.zachtheatre.org
Franks, Bud	Houston, TX	
Uptown Players	Dallas, TX	www.uptownplayers.org
Dallas Theater Center	Dallas, TX	www.dallastheatrecenter.org
Alley Theatre	Houston, TX	www.alleytheatre.org
Royal Scottish Academy of Music and Drama	Glasgow, Scotland	www.rsamd.ac.uk
Utah Festival Opera Company	Logan, UT	www.ufoc.org
Brigham Young University	Provo, UT	tma.byu.edu
Charlie Fink	Vienna, VA	www.newmusicalfoundation.org
Weston Playhouse Theatre Company	Weston, VT	www.westonplayhouse.org
5th Avenue Theatre, The	Seattle, WA	www.5thavenuetheatre.org
Village Theatre	Issaquah, WA	www.villagetheatre.org
Tacoma Musical Playhouse	Tacoma, WA	www.tmp.org
West Virginia Public Theatre	Morgantown, WV	www.wvpublictheatre.com
Rainbow Stage	Winnipeg, Manitoba, Canada http://www.rainbowstage.net/	
Mercury Musical Developments	East Sussex, UK	www.mercurymusicals.com
HoriPro	Tokyo, Japan	www.horipro.co.jp
2Entertain	31123 Falkenberg, Sweden	www.2entertain.com
Danish Academy of Musical Theatre	Fredericia,Denmark	www.musicalakademiet.dk
Royal & Derngate	Northampton, UK	www.royalandderngate.co.uk
Perfect Pitch Musicals Ltd	London, UK	www.perfectpitchmusicals.com

AMERICAN SOCIETY OF COMPOSERS, AUTHORS AND PUBLISHERS

ASCAP/New York, One Lincoln Plaza, New York, NY 10023

Phone: (212) 621-6000. Fax: (212) 724-9064

Email: info@ascap.com

www.ascap.com

ASCAP/Los Angeles, 7920 West Sunset Blvd., Third Floor, Los Angeles, CA 90046

Phone: (323) 883-1000. Fax: (323) 883-1049

If you plan to focus on musical theatre, you should also be aware of ASCAP, the association of over 200,000 US composers, songwriters, lyricists, and music publishers. In its own words, 'through agreements with affiliated international societies, ASCAP also represents hundreds of thousands of music creators worldwide. ASCAP is the only US performing rights organization created and controlled by composers, songwriters, and music publishers, with a board of directors elected by and from the membership.'

112+ outdoor theatres

INSTITUTE OF OUTDOOR DRAMA (IOD)

East Carolina University, College of Fine Arts and Communication,
310 Erwin Building, Greenville, NC 27858-4353
Phone: (252) 328-5363. Fax: (252) 328-0968
Email: outdoor@ecu.edu
http://outdoordrama.unc.edu

The Institute of Outdoor Drama, a public service agency, has recently found a new home base at East Carolina University in Greenville, North Carolina. Based at the University of North Carolina in Chapel Hill for the 47 years prior to the move to Greenville, the IOD is the only organization in the United States providing national leadership in fostering artistic and managerial excellence and expansion of the outdoor drama movement through training, research, and advisory programs. The Institute serves as a national clearinghouse for more than 101 constituent theatre companies across the nation. The IOD represents outdoor theatres in the following categories:

- ➤ Historical dramas (original plays, often with music and dance, based on significant events and performed in amphitheatres located where the events actually occurred)
- ➤ Religious plays (faith-based plays that dramatize significant events in the major world religions)
- ➤ Shakespeare festivals (producing full-length Shakespearean plays, often in repertory with the works of modern and other classical playwrights)
- ➤ Musical theatre
- ➤ Non-musical productions
- ➤ Children's Shows

Institute of Outdoor Drama member theatres

Each company has a direct link on the IOD website:
http://outdoordrama.unc.edu/directory/bycompany

Actors' Theatre Company of Columbus
Actors' Theatre Company, 1000 City Park Ave., Columbus, OH 43206, (614) 444-6888

Airmid Theatre Company
Airmid Theatre Company c/o 844 Bay Shore Ave., West Islip, NY 11795, (631) 704-2888

American Players Theatre
American Players Theatre, P.O. Box 819, Spring Green, WI 53588, (608) 588-2361 (box office), (608) 588-7401 (administration)

The Amistad Saga: Reflections
African American Cultural Complex, 119 Sunnybrook Road, Raleigh, NC 27610-1827, (919) 231-0625 (box office and administration)

The Aracoma Story, Inc
P.O. Box 2016, Logan, WV 25601, (304) 752-8222 (box office), (304) 752-0253 (administration)

Austin Shakespeare
701 Tillery St. # 9, Austin, TX 78702, (512) 474-8497 (box office), (512) 470-4505 (administration)

Baltimore Shakespeare Festival
3900 Roland Ave., Baltimore, MD 21211, (410) 366-8596 (box office), (410) 366-8594 (administration)

California Shakespeare Theater
701 Heinz Ave, Berkeley, CA 94710, (510) 548-9666 (box office), (510) 548-3422 (administration)

The Charlotte Shakespeare Festival
P.O. Box 32875, Charlotte, NC 28232, (704) 625-1288 (box office and administration)

Chesapeake Shakespeare Company
8510 High Ridge Road, Ellicott City, MD 21043, (866) 841-4111, (ticket agency), (410) 313-8874 (administration)

The Cleveland Shakespeare Festival
The Cleveland Shakespeare Festival, P.O. Box 93494, Cleveland, OH 44101-5494.

Colorado Shakespeare Festival
Campus Box 277 UCB, Boulder, CO 80309-0277, (303) 492-0554 (box office),
(303) 492-1527 (administration)

Commonwealth Shakespeare Company
539 Tremont St. # 308 Boston, MA 02116, (617) 426-0863 (box office and administration)

Door Shakespeare, Inc
P.O. Box 351, Baileys Harbor, WI 54202-0351., (920) 839-1500 (box office and
administration)

The EmilyAnn Theatre & Gardens
P.O. Box 801, Wimberley, TX 78676, (512) 847-6969 (box office and administration)

Fairbanks Shakespeare Theatre
P.O. Box 73447, Fairbanks, AK 99707, (907) 457-7638 (box office and administration)

First Folio Theatre
146 Juliet Court, Clarendon Hills, IL 60514, (630) 986-8067 (box office and administration)

First For Freedom
Eastern Stage, Inc. 145111 NC Hwy. 903, Halifax, NC, 27839, (252) 883-7119 (box office
and administration)

From This Day Forward
Old Colony Players, P.O. Box 112, Valdese, NC 28690, 879-2129 (box office),
(828) 879-2126 (administration)

The Great Passion Play
The Elna M. Smith Foundation, P.O. Box 471, Eureka Springs, AR 72632, (866) 566-3565
(box office and administration)

Greenstage
P.O. Box 9594, Seattle, WA 98109, (206)748-1551 (administration)

Happy Canyon Co., Inc
The Happy Canyon Night Show P.O. Box 609 Pendleton, OR 97801, (800) 457-6336 (box
office), (541) 276-2553 (administration)

Harrisburg Shakespeare Festival
605 Strawberry Sq, Harrisburg, PA 17101, (717) 238-4111 (box office and administration)

Heart of America Shakespeare Festival
3619 Broadway, Suite 2, Kansas City, MO 64111, (816) 531-7728 (administration)

Hill Country Arts Foundation/Point Theatre
Hill Country Arts Foundation, P.O. Box 1169, Ingram, TX 78025, (830) 367-5121 (box office and administration)

The Hill Cumorah Pageant
The Church of Jesus Christ of Latter-Day Saints, 44 Woodstone Lane, Rochester, NY 14626-1754, (315) 597-6808 (box office), (585) 314-1681 (administration)

Honey in the Rock
Theatre West Virginia, Inc. P.O. Box 1205, Beckley, WV 25802, (304) 256-6800 (box office and administration)

Horn in the West
Southern Appalachian Historical Association, Inc. P.O. Box 295, Boone, NC 28607, (828) 264-2120 (box office and administration)

Hudson Valley Shakespeare Festival
155 Main St, Cold Spring, NY 10516, (845) 265-9575 (box office), (845) 265-7858 (administration)

Houston Shakespeare Festival
University of Houston School of Theatre, 113 Wortham, Houston, TX 77204-4016, (713) 743-2929 (box office), (713) 743-3003 (administration)

Idaho Shakespeare Festival
P.O. Box 9365, Boise, ID 83707, (208) 336-9221 (box office), (208) 429-9908 (administration)

Illinois Shakespeare Festival
Illinois State University, 212 Centennial West, Campus Box 5700, Normal, IL 61790-5700, (309) 438-2535 (box office), (309) 438-8974 (administration)

Jenny Wiley Theatre
P.O. Box 22, Prestonsburg, KY 41653, (877) 225-5598 (box office), (606) 886-9274 (administration)

Kentucky Shakespeare Festival
1387 S Fourth Street, Louisville, KY 40208, (502) 637-4933 (box office and administration)

Lake Tahoe Shakespeare Festival
948 Incline Way, Incline Village, NV 89451, (800) 747-4697 (box office), (775) 832-1616 (administration)

Laura's Memories
Ozark Mountain Players P.O. Box 113, Mansfield, MO, 65704, (417) 924-3415 (box office), (417) 924-3383 (administration)

Liberty: The Saga of Sycamore Shoals
Sycamore Productions, 1651 W Elk Ave, Elizabethton, TN 37643, (423) 543-5808
(box office and administration)

Lincoln
Lincoln Amphitheatre, 15043 N CR 300 W, P.O. Box 7-21 Lincoln City, IN 47552,
(800) 264-4223 (box office) and 812-937-9730 (administration)

Little Shepherd of Kingdom Come
Cumberland Mountain Arts & Crafts Council, Inc. 255 Amphitheatre Road, P.O. Box 1482
Jenkins, KY, 41537, (606) 832-1453 (box office and administration)

The Living Word Outdoor Drama
P.O. Box 1481, Cambridge, OH 43725, (740) 439-2761 (box office and administration)

The Lost Colony
Roanoke Island Historical Association 1409 National Park Drive, Manteo, NC 27954,
(252) 473-3414 (box office), (252) 473-2127 (administration)

Marin Shakespeare Company
P.O. Box 4053, San Rafael, CA 94913, (415) 456-4488 (box office), (415) 499-4485
(administration)

Medora Musical
Stagewest Entertainment, P.O. Box 198, Medora, North Dakota, 58645, (701) 623-4444
(box office and administration)

Miracle on the Mountain
The Crossnore School, P.O. Box 249, Crossnore, NC 28616, (828) 733-4305 (box office),
(828) 733-5241 (administration)

The Miracle Worker
Helen Keller Birthplace Foundation Board, 300 West North Commons, Tuscumbia,
AL 35674, (888) 329-2124 or, (256) 383-4066 (box office and administration)

Montana Shakespeare in the Parks
P.O. Box 174120, Bozeman, MT 59717-4120, (406) 994-9301 (box office), (406) 994-1220
(administration)

The Montford Park Players
P.O. Box 2663, Asheville, NC 28802, (828) 254-5146 (box office and administration)

The Mormon Miracle Pageant
Church of Jesus Christ of Latter-Day Saints, P.O. Box 40, Manti, UT 84642, (866) 961-9040
(box office), (435) 340-1075 (administration)

Mountain Play Association
Mountain Play Association P.O. Box 2025 Mill Valley, CA 94942, (415) 383-1100 (box office and administration)

Murphys Creek Theatre
580 S. Algiers Rd., Murphys, CA 95247, (209) 728-8422 (box office and administration)

Nashville Shakespeare Festival
161 Rains Ave., Nashville, TN 37203, (615) 255-2273 (administration)

Nauvoo Pageant
Nauvoo Pageant Box 267, Nauvoo, IL 62354, (217)453-2429 (administration)

Nebraska Shakespeare Festival
c/o Department of Fine Arts, Creighton University, 2500 California Plaza, Omaha, NE 68178, (402) 280-2391 (administration)

New York Shakespeare Festival
New York Shakespeare Festival/The Public Theater, 425 Lafayette St, New York, NY 10003, (212) 539-8671 (box office), (212) 539-8500 (administration)

Oklahoma!
Discoveryland! U.S.A., 5529 S Lewis, Tulsa, OK 74105, (918) 245-6552 (box office), (918) 742-5255 (administration)

Oklahoma Shakespeare in the Park
P.O. Box 1437, Oklahoma City, OK 73101-1437, (405) 235-3700 (box office and administration)

Old Homestead Association
P.O. Box 10414, Swanzey, NH 03446, (603) 352-4184 (box office and administration)

Opera in the Ozarks at Inspiration Point
P.O. Box 127 Eureka Springs, AR 72632, (479) 253-8595 (box office and administration)

Oregon Shakespeare Festival
15 S. Pioneer St., Ashland, OR 97520, (541) 482-4331 (box office), (541) 482-2111 (administration)

Pacific Repertory Theatre
P.O. Box 222035, Carmel, CA 93922, (831) 622-0100 (box office), (831) 622-0700 (administration)

The Passion Play in the Smokies
The Passion Play in the Smokies, (865) 640-8903 (administration)

Pine Knob Theatre, Inc

2250 Pine Knob Rd, Caneyville, KY 42721, (270) 879-8190 (box office and administration)

Pioneer Playhouse

840 Stanford Rd., Danville, KY 40422, (866) 597-5297 (box office), (859) 236-2747 (administration)

The Promised Land

Walk in the Light Productions, Inc. P.O. Box 260 Bath, NC 27808, (252) 923-9909 (box office), (919) 612-2136 (administration)

The Promise in Glen Rose, Inc

The Promise in Glen Rose, Inc. 122 E. Church St., Weatherford, TX, 76086, (254) 897-3926 (box office);, (817) 599-3022 (administration)

Ramona

Ramona Bowl Amphitheatre 27400 Ramona Bowl Rd, Hemet, CA 92544-8108, (951) 658-3111 (box office and administration)

Richmond Shakespeare

Richmond Shakespeare, P.O. Box 27543, Richmond, VA 23261, (804) 232-4000 (box office and administration)

Riverside Theatre

Riverside Theatre Shakespeare Festival, 213 N Gilbert St, Iowa City, IA 52245, (319) 338-7672 (box office), (319) 887-1360 (administration)

Salado Legends

Tablerock Festival of Salado P.O. Box 312, Salado, TX 76571, (254) 947-9205 (box office and administration)

Sandstone Productions

901 Fairgrounds Rd., Farmington, NM 87401, (505) 325-2570 (box office), (505) 599-1140 (administration)

San Francisco Shakespeare Festival

Box 460937, San Francisco, CA 94146, (415) 865-4434 (box office), (415) 558-0888 (administration)

Shakespeare & Company/MN

Century College-West Campus, 3300 Century Ave N, White Bear Lake, MN 55110, (651) 779-5818 (box office and administration)

Shakespeare by the Sea
777 Centre St., San Pedro, CA 90731, (310) 217-7596 (box office), (310) 619-0599 (administration)

Shakespeare Dallas
3630 Harry Hines Blvd, 4th Floor, Dallas, TX 75219, (214) 559-2778 (administration)

Shakespeare Festival of St. Louis
462 N. Taylor Ave., Suite 202, St Louis, MO 63108, (314) 531-9800 (administration).

Shakespeare in Delaware Park
P.O. Box 716, Buffalo, NY 14205-0716, (716) 856-4533 (box office and administration)

Shakespeare in the Ozarks
P.O. Box 780, Eureka Springs, AR 72632, (479) 270-1278 (box office and administration)

Shakespeare on the Green
208 N 17th Street, Wilmington, NC, 28401, (910) 399-2878 (box office and administration)

Shakespeare on the Sound
Shakespeare on the Sound, Inc., P.O. Box 15, Norwalk, CT 06853, (203) 299-1300 (box office and administration)

Shakespeare Orange County
P.O. Box 923, Orange, CA 92856, (714) 590-1575 (box office), (714) 744-7016 (administration)

Shakespeare Santa Cruz/Theater Arts UCSC
University of California, 1156 High St, Santa Cruz, CA 95064, (831) 459-2159 (box office), (831) 459-5810 (administration)

The Shakespeare Theatre of New Jersey
36 Madison Avenue, Madison, NJ 07940, (973) 408-5600 (box office), (973) 408-3278 (administration)

Shakespeare's Associates
P.O. Box 2616, Livermore, CA 94551-2616, (800) 838-3006 (box office), (925) 443-2273 (administration)

Shepherd of the Hills Outdoor Theatre
5586 West Highway 76, Branson, MO 65616, (800) 653-6288 (box office), (417) 334-4191 (administration)

Sleepy Hollow Summer Theatre
P.O. Box 675 Bismarck, ND 58502, (866) 811-4111 (box office), (701) 319-0894 (administration)

The Stephen Foster Story
Stephen Foster Productions, 411 East Stephen Foster Ave., Bardstown, KY 40004, (800) 626-1563 (box office), (502) 348-5971 (administration)

The Story of Jesus
Power & Light Productions P.O. Box 97, Wauchula, FL, 33873, (863) 375-4031, (box office and administration)

The Sword of Peace
Snow Camp Historical Drama Society, Inc. P.O. Box 535, Snow Camp, NC 27349, (336) 376-6948 (box office and administration)

Tecumseh!
The Scioto Society, Inc. P.O. Box 73, Chillicothe, OH 45601-0073, (740) 775-0700 (box office), (740) 775-4100 (administration)

Texas Musical Drama
Texas Panhandle Heritage Foundation, Inc. 1514 5th Ave, Canyon, TX 79015, (806) 655-2181 (box office and administration)

Theatre in the Park, Inc
225 East Cook St., Springfield, IL 62704, (217) 632-5440 (box office), (217) 241-3241 (administration)

Tom Dooley: A Wilkes County Legend
Wilkes Playmakers, Inc. P.O. Box 397, North Wilkesboro, NC, 28659, (336) 838-7529 (box office and administration)

Trail of the Lonesome Pine
Lonesome Pine Arts and Crafts, Inc. P.O. Box 1976, Big Stone Gap, VA 24219, (276) 523-1235 (box office and administration)

Trumpet in the Land
Ohio Historical Drama Association, Inc. P.O. Box 450, New Philadelphia, OH 44663, (330) 339-1132 (box office), (330) 364-5111 (administration)

Under the Cherokee Moon
Cherokee National Historical Society P.O. Box 515, Tahlequah, OK 74465. (918) 456-6007 (box office and administration)

Unto These Hills
Cherokee Historical Association P.O. Box 398, Cherokee, NC 28719, (828) 497-2111 (box office and administration)

Upstate Shakespeare Festival

37 Augusta St, Greenville, SC 29601, (864) 787-4016 (box office and administration).

Utah Shakespearean Festival

351 West Center St, Cedar City, UT 84720, (435) 586-7878 (box office), (435) 586-7880 (administration)

Viva! el Paso

El Paso Association for the Performing Arts P.O. Box 512351, El Paso, TX, 79951, (915) 231-1165 (administration), (915) 544-8444 (box office/ticketmaster)

Will Geer Theatricum Botanicum

1419 N. Topanga Cyn. Blvd., Topanga, CA 90290, (310) 455-3723 (box office), (310) 455-2322 (administration)

300+ theatre opportunities you seldom hear about in major trade magazines

Murder mystery cafés, glitzy cruise ship theatres, and a wild assortment of related dinner theatre, touring theatre, and theme park entertainments offer employment opportunities in virtually every area of the theatre, including producing, direction, design, production, construction, costuming, acting, dance, and musical performance. If your interests and tastes include popular entertainment, musical entertainment, and contracts that might include a food plan with your paycheck, the possibilities are extensive!

25+ cruise line producers

Even the sublime Cirque du Soleil has joined the 'at-sea' business of sailing entertainment. Since cruise ships navigate the world 365 days a year featuring actors, singers, dancers, magicians, musicians, comedians, and storytellers, providing welcome breaks from the buffet lines, this might be your best chance for exotic travel. With the most popular cruises visiting Alaska's glaciers, Europe's historic capitals, Russia's palaces, Greece's magical islands, and the glorious waterfalls and fjords of Scandinavia, there are perks that might be even better than the salary and stateroom. Having sailed to all of these spots myself, I've enjoyed the combination of 'Vegas-style shows,' 'Broadway musical revues,' and 'MTV-wannabe' productions that dominate the entertainment and I am always surprised by the quirky specialty shows that spotlight unique individual performances and group exhibitions reminiscent of vaudeville and burlesque

Although some cruise lines book their own entertainment for their travels, many use entertainment agencies, booking agencies, independent contractors, and casting agents to help in their search for talent and productions. If you are interested, it's best to keep an eye on *Back Stage East* and *West* and the '10 Pertinent Publications' mentioned earlier in this book. It may also be useful to check directly with the cruise lines.

Websites devoted to cruise ship jobs offer a very positive view of working at sea. However, before signing a contract, most theatre professionals would suggest talking to past cruise-ship entertainers and employees to make sure that cruising is right for you.

SELECTED MAJOR CRUISE LINES

CARNIVAL CRUISE LINES, www.carnival.com

CELEBRITY CRUISES, www.celebrity.com

COSTA CRUISE LINES, www.costacruise.com

CRYSTAL CRUISES, www.crystalcruises.com

CUNARD LINE, www.cunard.com

DISNEY CRUISE LINES, www.disneycruise.com

HOLLAND AMERICA LINE, www.hollandamerica.com

NORWEGIAN CRUISE LINE, www.ncl.com

ORIENT LINES, www.orientlines.com

PRINCESS CRUISES, www.princess.com

REGENT SEVEN SEAS CRUISES, www.rssc.com

ROYAL CARIBBEAN CRUISE LINE, www.royalcaribbean.com

SEABOURN CRUISE LINE, www.seabourn.com

SILVERSEA CRUISES, www.silversea.com

Selected cruise line agents and producers

ANITA MANN PRODUCTIONS, www.anitamannproductions.com (Santa Monica, CA)

BIG BEAT PRODUCTIONS, INC., www.bigbeatproductions.com (Coral Springs, FL)

BLUE MOON TALENT, INC., www.bluemoontalent.com (Evergreen, CO)

BRAMSON ENTERTAINMENT BUREAU, www.bramson.com (New York, NY)

BROADWAY BOUND, www.broadwayboundinc.com (New York, NY)

CIRQUE DU SOLEIL, www.cirquedusoleil.com (Montreal, Canada)

FIRST CLASS ENTERTAINMENT, www.gotofirstclass.com (Maplewood, NJ)

GREG THOMPSON PRODUCTIONS, www.gregthompsonproductions.com (Seattle, WA)

JEAN ANN RYAN PRODUCTIONS, www.jeanannryanproductions.com
   (Fort Lauderdale, FL)

MIKE MALONEY ENTERTAINMENT, www.mmec.com (Las Vegas, NV)

PETER GREY TERHUNE PRESENTS, www.pgtpi.com (Cape Canaveral, FL)

SPOTLIGHT ENTERTAINMENT, www.barryball.com (Miami, FL)

STILETTO ENTERTAINMENT, www.stilettoentertainment.com (Inglewood, CA)

30+ dinner theatres

Historically, dinner theatres represent the only home-based professional theatre operation in many American cities and have nurtured loyal and dedicated follow-ings. Opportunities for directors, designers, dancers, singers, musicians, actors, and production personnel abound. The National Dinner Theatre Association (NDTA) had lost their website at press time. Founded in 1978, the NDTA historically holds auditions and conferences annually and, in its own words, 'includes some of the top theatrical producers in the country (both union and non-union).' Readers might try a website search for the National Dinner Theatre Association as they were seeking a new site at press time. In the meantime, here are other NDTA contact numbers, and the theatres listed below may be accessed through the direct links to their websites.

NATIONAL DINNER THEATRE ASSOCIATION (NDTA)

Charles Carnes, Executive Secretary,
3925 Sherman Boulevard, Des Moines, IA 50310
Phone: (515) 252-1942. Fax: (515) 334-5021
Email: ndta@mac.com
www.ndta.us

Alhambra Dinner Theatre

12000 Beach Blvd., Jacksonville, FL 32246
www.alhambrajax.com

Arizona Broadway Theatre
7701 West Paradise Lane, Peoria, AZ 85382
www.azbroadwaytheatre.com

The Armory Inc.
10 South High Street, P.O. Box 8038, Janesville, WI 53548
www.janesvillearmory.com

The Barn Dinner Theatre
120 Stage Coach Trail, Greensboro, NC 27409
www.barndinner.com

The Bartolotta Restaurants
6005 West Martin Drive, Wauwatosa, WI 53213
www.bartolottas.com

Black Bear Jamboree Dinner and Show
119 Music Road, Pigeon Forge, TN 37863
www.blackbearjamboree.com

Bravo! Dinner Playhouse
1476 West Route 6, Ottawa, IL 61350
Box Office: (815) 433-4331

Broadway Palm Dinner Theatre
1380 Colonial Blvd., Fort Myers, FL 33907
www.broadwaypalm.com

Broadway Palm West Dinner Theatre
5247 East Brown Road, Mesa, AZ 85205
www.broadwaypalmwest.com

Candlelight Pavilion Dinner Theater
455 Foothill Blvd., Claremont, CA 91711
www.candlelightpavilion.com

Chaffin's Barn Dinner Theatre
8204 Highway 100, Nashville, TN 37221
www.dinnertheatre.com

Circa '21 Dinner Playhouse
1828 Third Avenue, Rock Island, IL 61201
www.circa21.com

Conklin's Barn II Dinner Theatre
P.O. Box 310, Goodfield, IL 61742
www.barn2.com

Crown Uptown Professional Dinner Theatre
3207 East Douglas Avenue, Wichita, KS 67218
www.crownuptown.com

Derby Dinner Playhouse
525 Marriott Drive, Clarksville, IN 47129
www.derbydinner.com

Dutch Apple Dinner Theatre
510 Centerville Road, Lancaster, PA 17601
www.dutchapple.com

Empire Theatre Company
2825 North Avenue, Grand Junction, CO 81501
Phone: (970) 248-9091

The Fireside, Inc. Dinner Theatre
1131 Janesville Avenue, P.O. Box 7, Fort Atkinson, WI 53538
www.firesidetheatre.com

The Gaslight Dinner Theatre
The Renaissance Center, 855 Highway 46 South, Dickson, TN 37055
www.rcenter.org

Hunterdon Hills Playhouse
88 Route 173 West, Hampton, NJ 08827
www.hhplayhouse.com

Jackson Hole Playhouse
135 Deloney Street, P.O. Box 2788, Jackson, WY 83001
www.jhplayhouse.com

Marriott Theatre
Ten Marriott Drive, Lincolnshire, IL 60069
www.marriotttheatre.com

Murder Mystery Inc.
18 Hollywood Place, Huntington, NY 11743
www.murdermysteryinc.com

Murry's Dinner Playhouse
6323 Colonel Glenn Road, Little Rock, AR 72204
www.murrysdinnerplayhouse.com

Mystery Dinner Playhouse
2025 East Main Street, Suite 206, Richmond, VA 23223
www.mysterydinner.com

Rainbow Dinner Theatre
Route 30 East, Box 56, Paradise, PA 17562
www.rainbowdinnertheatre.com

The Riverside Inn
One Fountain Avenue, Cambridge Springs, PA 16403
www.theriversideinn.com

Sleuths Mystery Dinner Shows
8267 International Drive, Orlando, FL 32819
www.sleuths.com

The Station Dinner Theatre
4940 Peach Street, Erie, PA 16509
www.canterburyfeast.com

Three Little Bakers Dinner Theatre
3540 Three Little Bakers Blvd., Wilmington, DE 19808
www.tlbinc.com

Tommy Gun's Garage
2114 South Wabash, Chicago, IL 60616
www.tommygunsgarage.com

Welk Resort San Diego Theatre
8860 Lawrence Welk Drive, Escondido, CA 92026
www.welkresort.com

Westchester Broadway Theatre
75 Clearbrook Road, Elmsford, NY 10523
www.broadwaytheatre.com

Wohlfahrt Haus Dinner Theatre
170 Malin Drive, Wytheville, VA 24382
www.wohlfahrthaus.com

60+ touring theatre companies

Whether it's Baltimore's Funkopolis Central (www.funkopolis.org), an experimental touring theatre that creates original plays by melding urban and tribal experiences, or Blue Lake, California's Dell'Arte, Inc. (www.dellarte.com), a touring theatre company committed to physical theatre traditions, touring theatre opportunities still exist for theatre professionals who like to stay on the move.

Just a few of the other American theatres committed to touring include Aesop's Touring Theatre Company, The Act!vated Storytellers (www.activated-story tellers.com), American Magic-Lantern Theatre (www.magiclanternshows.com), Atlantic Coast Theatre (www.atlantic-coast-theatre.com), Elevator Repair Service (www.elevator.org), Guerrilla Girls On Tour (www.guerrillagirlsontour.com), Hampstead Players (www.hamplay.com), Mad River Theatre Works (www.madriver theatre.org), National Players (www.nationalplayers.org), Paper Bag Players (www.paperbagplayers.org), Traveling Jewish Theatre (www.atjt.com), and The Black Rep (theblackrep.org).

The National Endowment for the Arts' Shakespeare in American Communities project and funding has inspired a number of companies temporarily to hit the road, but others tour on an ongoing basis to tell their stories and find new audiences. Direct links to the theatres mentioned below may be found in the 400+ TCG Theatres section or on the National Endowment for the Arts website (www.shakespeareinamericancommunities.org). Many are TCG or LORT members. The largest Shakespeare tour in American history comprised: Alaska Theatre of Youth, Eccentric Theatre Company, Edgware, American Players Theatre, Asolo Theatre Company, Cincinnati Playhouse in the Park, Hartford Stage Company, Idaho Shakespeare Festival, Indiana Repertory Theatre, Montana Shakespeare in the Parks, People's Light and Theatre Company, Perseverance Theatre, San Diego Repertory Theatre, Shakespeare and Company, The Shakespeare Festival at Tulane, Shakespeare Santa Cruz, The Shakespeare Theatre, The Shakespeare Theatre of New Jersey, The Theater at Monmouth, Utah Shakespeare Festival, Will Geer Theatricum Botanicum, Yale Repertory Theatre, A Noise Within, The Acting Company, Actors Theatre of Louisville, American Shakespeare Center, The Aquila Theatre Company, Arkansas Repertory Theatre, The Atlanta Shakespeare Company, Fairbanks Shakespeare Theatre, Georgia Shakespeare Festival, Idaho Shakespeare Festival, Long Wharf Theatre, Nevada Shakespeare Company, The Old Globe, Oregon Shakespeare Festival, The Pennsylvania Shakespeare Festival,

San Francisco Shakespeare Festival, Seattle Shakespeare Company, Shakespeare Dallas, Shakespeare Festival of St. Louis, Shakespeare Festival/LA, Teatro Avante, Trinity Repertory Company, The Warehouse Theatre, Artists Repertory Theatre, Alabama Shakespeare Festival, and Chicago Shakespeare Theater.

100+ murder mystery theatres and innovative new live theatre opportunities

There's *Here's Killing You, Kid; Frankly Scarlett, You're Dead!*; and *Marriage Can Be Murder* at the Great Smoky Mountain Murder Mystery Theatre in Pigeon Forge, Tennessee – and that's just the beginning! Murder mystery theatres are among the hottest, fastest-growing theatre industries in America and you might want to check out the 17 million hits in the Google search for 'Murder Mystery Theatre.'

Comedy Theater Productions, TeambondingTM; Experience the Power of Play!, Scaventures; Team Building Scavenger and Treasure Hunts; and Mystery Café are just some examples of the innovative industries (check out www.mysterycafe. com) that have been developed by one company (Comedy Theater Productions). A whole new world is out there for theatre folk, and this book doesn't even touch on video game and other digital-media employment opportunities! For example, Comedy Theater Productions, founded in 1986, 'combines interactive events, athletic challenges, and theatre-based games to increase social interactivity.' From America's first murder mystery dinner theatre, the Mystery Café in Cambridge, Massachusetts, to the licensing of the business-to-theatre producers in 21 cities in the United States, the genre has taken off and opened doors to a whole new generation of actors, directors, designers, and craftspersons.

You can find state-by-state listings of over 100 murder mystery dinner theatres at www.partypop.com/Categories/Murder_Mystery_Dinner_Theatre.html. And more than 100 mystery dinner theatres can be found in the Yahoo! Directory: http://search.yahoo.com/search/dir?p=Mystery+Dinner+Theatres&srch=. You'll also find over 30 listings at www.mysteryplayers.com.

110+ theme and amusement parks

Over 75 million people attend America's top ten theme parks on an annual basis, so if you dream of dressing up as a cuddly mammal, drool at the thought of singing and dancing in a Wild West saloon, or just enjoy surrounding yourself with sunshine, roller coasters, and silly families, theme parks are for you. There are hundreds of theme parks and amusement parks in America. Florida and California have at least 20 playful parks each, including Orlando's The Holy Land Experience and Tampa's Weeki Wachee Springs (where you could be the live Mermaid), and SeaWorld San Diego (where you can hang out with the real animals).

Theme parks are generally looking to hire street entertainers, tour guides, jugglers, directors, designers, choreographers, stage managers, impersonators, choreographers, musicians, dancers, emcees, voice-over specialists, prop masters, costumers, carpenters, sound engineers, lighting technicians, and administrators to mention a few of the usual positions.

America's largest parks, according to Arthur Levine's theme park research, include Florida's The Magic Kingdom at Walt Disney World, California's Disneyland, Florida's Epcot at Walt Disney World, Disney–MGM Studios at Walt Disney World, Disney's Animal Kingdom at Walt Disney World, Universal Studios at Universal Orlando, Islands of Adventure at Universal Orlando, Disney's California Adventures in California, SeaWorld Florida, and Universal Studios Hollywood. The 110 theme and amusement parks are listed alphabetically and by state with direct links at http://themeparks.about.com.

40+ universities affiliated with professional theatres

UNIVERSITY/RESIDENT THEATRE ASSOCIATION
1560 Broadway, Suite 1103, New York, NY 10036
Phone: (212) 221-1130. Fax: (212) 869-2752
Email: info@urta.com
www.urta.com

A key resource for emerging theatre professionals is also the country's oldest and largest consortium of professional theatre-training graduate programs and partnered professional theatre companies. The professional companies these universities with graduate programs are 'consorting with' may be LORT and/or TCG, and some produce on the Equity-URTA Contract. They offer the opportunity for graduate students to develop a network, meet directors, designers, Equity actors, Equity stage managers, and others in the field, and to take classes at the schools from some of the best theatre-training faculty in the United States.

Here's a thought for you. If you are a 20-year-old woman just graduating from college and heading into professional theatre, you are competing with the thousands of other recent college graduates, as well as with all the Equity professionals who can still play roles in the 18–25 age range. Your key 'competitive edge and venue' at 20 is your audition (plus perhaps your enthusiastic recommendations and support from your college faculty members). Of course, you are generally competing for the one ingenue or one young character woman available in the typical classical play or new play – where there are, all too often, 15 male roles and three women's (two of which will most likely be cast from former employees).

On the other hand, if you are successful in your graduate school auditions and are offered a scholarship in a reputable graduate school, you have two to three years to make friends with other professionals and prove yourself on stage (competing against younger undergraduate students). At the same time, you are presumably receiving advanced training, maturing in the eyes of casting directors, and developing your résumé and skills. Finally, instead of being judged on a three-minute audition, you have been networking with actors, directors, and artistic directors who will hopefully remember you from your larger body of work. Graduate school is well worth considering. Make sure you read the debate on education and training in other sections of this book.

U/RTA helps make these connections and nurtures relationships between students, graduate schools, and professional theatre. Scott L. Steele is U/RTA's longtime savvy, personable executive director.

History and services

U/RTA encourages the professional training of artists, and of future teachers in the performing arts for all levels of education. Founded in 1969, it provides a variety of service, management, and informational programs to its members, and to theatre professionals, non-member students, and producing companies, while serving as the primary liaison between the professional and educational theatres.

Services include the National Unified Auditions and Interviews held each winter in New York, Chicago, and San Francisco, with candidates coming from around the world. Students interested in acting, design (scenic, lighting, costume, sound, media), directing, theatre technology, stage management, and theatre management are given the opportunity to vie for numerous positions with graduate schools, and for seasonal employment with summer theatre companies, Shakespeare festivals, and other professional producing organizations. Membership in U/RTA is not required for students to participate.

U/RTA also has the Contract Management Program that offers a complete contracting and employment system to organizations that, for many different reasons, are unable to directly engage professional, union artists. Finally, U/RTA negotiates and maintains important agreements with Actors' Equity Association (AEA), the Stage Directors and Choreographers Society (SDC), and United Scenic Artists (USA) geared toward the needs of resident and university theatres. These agreements make it possible to successfully integrate professional actors, stage managers, directors, choreographers, and designers with theatre students both on stage and in the classroom.

U/RTA members include
in alphabetical order

University of Alabama, www.as.ua.edu/theatre

University of Arizona–Arizona Repertory Theatre,
   http://arts.music.arizona.edu/theatre

Brandeis University, www.brandeis.edu/theatre

University of California, Irvine, http://drama.arts.uci.edu

University of California, Los Angeles, www.tft.ucla.edu

California Institute of the Arts, www.calarts.edu

California State University, Fullerton, www.fullerton.edu

California State University, Long Beach/Cal Rep, www.calrep.org, www.csulb.edu

University of Cincinnati College/Conservatory of Music, www.ccm.uc.edu

University of Connecticut/Connecticut Repertory Theatre, www.drama.uconn.edu

Florida State University, www.theatre.fsu.edu

Florida State University/Asolo Conservatory for Actor Training,
   www.asolo.org/fsuconsv/fsu-intro.htm

University of Florida, www.arts.ufl.edu/theatreanddance

Illinois State University/Illinois Shakespeare Festival, www.cfa.ilstu.edu/theatre

University of Illinois, Urbana/Champaign, www.theatre.illinois.edu

Indiana University, www.theatre.indiana.edu

University of Iowa/Iowa Summer Rep., www.uiowa.edu/~theatre

University of Maryland, www.tdps.umd.edu

University of Minnesota, http://theatre.umn.edu

University of Missouri, Kansas City/Missouri Repertory Theatre, ww.umkc.edu/theatre

University of Nebraska, Lincoln/Nebraska Repertory Theatre, www.unl.edu/TheatreArts/

University of Nevada, Las Vegas/Nevada Conservatory Theater, www.theatre.unlv.edu

University of North Carolina, Chapel Hill/Playmakers Repertory Company,
   www.drama.unc.edu

Northern Illinois University/Summer NITE, www.vpa.niu.edu/theatre

Northwestern University, www.communication.northwestern.edu/theatre

Ohio University/Cincinnati Playhouse in the Park, www.ohio.edu/theatre

The Ohio State University, www.theatre.osu.edu

Pennsylvania State University/Pennsylvania Centre Stage, www.theatre.psu.edu

Purdue University, www.purdue.edu/theatre

University of South Carolina, www.cas.sc.edu/THEA

Southern Methodist University/Dallas Theatre Center, www.smu.edu

Temple University, www.temple.edu/theatre

University of Tennessee, Knoxville/Clarence Brown Theatre, www.clarencebrowntheatre.com

University of Texas – Austin, www.finearts.utexas.edu.tad

University of Virginia/Heritage Theatre Festival, www.virginia.edu/drama/

University of Washington, http://depts.washington.edu/uwdrama

University of Wisconsin – Madison, www.theatre.wisc.edu

U/RTA partnered theatre companies include

Arizona Repertory Theatre, www.tftv.arizona.edu

Asolo Repertory Theatre, www.asolorep.org

California Repertory Theatre, www.calrep.org

Clarence Brown Theatre, www.clarencebrowntheatre.com

Connecticut Repertory Theatre, http://www.crt.uconn.edu

Dallas Theatre Center, www.dallastheatrecenter.org

Heritage Theatre Festival, www.virginia.edu/heritagetheatre/

Illinois Shakespeare Festival, www.arts.ilstu.edu

Iowa Summer Rep, www.uiowa.edu/~theatre

Kansas City Repertory Theatre, www.umkc.edu/theatre

Nebraska Repertory Theatre, www.unl.edu/rep

Nevada Conservatory Theatre, www.nct.unlv.edu/

Pennsylvania Centre Stage, www.pacentrestage.psu.edu

Playmakers Repertory Company, www.playmakersrep.org/

SummerNITE Festival, www.niu.edu

Part 6

Survival
strategies and
directories for
lifelong planning

12 tips for stress reduction: staying fit for life

" *Live as long as you can. Die when you can't help it*
James Brown

Every opening night is a serious, strenuous, soul-searching series of deadlines if you work in the arts. In regional theatre, artistic directors strive to achieve their vision and satisfy, sway, or soothe guest directors, actors, designers, board members, and critics with each new production. Actors, designers, and craftspeople work mightily to make directors and audiences happy while remaining true to the playwright and committed to their own sense of artistic integrity. Marketing directors have sky-high sales goals, development directors are on the line to meet wildly optimistic fundraising goals, and production managers coordinate the complex creation of hopefully dazzling scenery, costumes, lights, and sound with a generally unrealistic budget that would make most Broadway or movie producers gasp (or laugh – or cry)! Add the realities and frailties of a personal life to a highly charged, competitive workplace, throw in high rates of unemployment, overwork, and low pay, and the arts are often a prime breeding ground for stress. On the commercial side, Broadway producers have to keep audiences, critics and investors happy.

Unfortunately, few nonprofit arts organizations employ a human resources staff or even a specific individual who handles personnel matters. Most professional theatres have a company manager who is burdened with housing, transportation, scheduling, and contract assistance, with little time to tend to the morale of the company. Artistic directors, managing directors, and business managers often 'handle' or 'deal' with tense contract concerns or unhappy employees. Stage managers usually do their best to keep actors on track, and individual supervisors tend to bear the brunt of the personnel load. Actors are usually left to handle their own personnel problems, and if you are the Equity deputy – look out! This is not an ideal situation and there's a reason that most businesses and corporations have a personnel office or a human resources division. It's important that employees work within their realm of training and experience, and few arts employees are hired first and foremost for their personal counseling skills, medical diagnostic training, or first-aid expertise.

With this in mind, it's crucial for artists, production personnel, and arts managers to know and communicate their expectations and personal boundaries. It's also a good idea for everyone to be familiar with referral sources (local counselors, doctors, psychiatrists, psychologists, etc.) and options when it comes to 'handling personnel matters' vs. 'personal counseling' or 'offering advice.'

1. Understand your limitations

As an individual, work to clarify the source of your stress and determine if the problem is within your control. Agonizing over concerns that are impossible for you to influence is most likely an exercise in futility. Are the sources of your stress related to fear, anger, anxiety, depression, low self-esteem, passivity, conflicts with friends, or control issues at work? Or are they related to world events, ethical concerns, family frustrations, or current or recent crises?

It is certainly appropriate to be helpful, provide a listening ear, and assist your friends, colleagues, or employees within your level of experience, training, and comfort. However, whether you are a supervisor, employee, friend, or colleague, make sure you understand your limits as a counselor and as an individual. If you are an employer, devise a company referral list of professional services for your staff to use when an employee's stress levels stray 'beyond the norm.'

> *'Anger is a momentary madness, so control your passion or it will control you.'*
>
> Horace

2. Pay attention to number one

If you are in poor mental or physical health, it's difficult for you to be of help to anyone else. See your doctor for a complete physical and make sure you are healthy, eating appropriately, and meeting your sleep needs.

> *'Adversity is the first path to truth.'*
>
> Lord Byron

3. Work out

Physical activity and exercise help break up the day and may help you sort out myriad problems, achieve perspective, and relieve a host of psychological and physical challenges. If you've dedicated your life to the arts, you've certainly been taught that the mind and body work together in wonderful and mysterious ways. A consistent workout regimen may also assist with weight control, lowering cholesterol, and sound eating and sleeping habits. A brisk walk, yoga class, 50-minute racquetball game, or biking to work could make all the difference in the world.

4. A little research goes a long way

Every Borders, Barnes & Noble, and downtown bookstore has a plethora of self-help, stress-reducing techniques. Many of them may work for you. In addition, many community centers and nearby universities offer stress-reduction seminars, and the more progressive healthcare providers are scheduling ongoing stress reduction programs as part of their proactive health-screening services

5. Accept reality . . . or change your realities

Don't waste time fighting institutional policies, horrid employers, or events that you can't control. Sometimes it's best simply to cut your losses and move on. Working with unethical, rude, or wildly obnoxious colleagues or employers can impact your day-to-day attitude, self-image, and long-term health. If you can make a difference and create change and a positive work environment, more power to you! If your work environment is getting the best of you and influencing your health and psyche, it's time to step back and evaluate your values, goals, and strategic plans

6. Hunt for a mentor and develop a support group

Sometimes, just having someone or a group of people you respect with whom you can discuss issues, try out ideas, explore the corporate culture, share concerns, or help with priorities will make all the difference. Ask for help.

'Never go to a doctor whose office plants are dead.'
Erma Bombeck

7. Use those acting exercises

Many arts professionals started as actors, dancers, or theatre students. Remember those deep-breathing exercises, muscle-tension release improvisations, and sensory awareness seminars that seemed so silly in Acting 101 or Beginning Dance? Now is the time to revisit these great stress-reducing techniques that can lighten up your day and add a sense of balance to a tense moment.

8. Look out for burnout! Consider a time-out

Often, just hiding away, finding quiet time, vacationing, and regaining perspective can work wonders for the battered soul. Monitor sudden weight loss, rise in blood pressure, emotional swings, withdrawal, self-destructive thoughts or actions, feelings of desperation, or physical symptoms (ulcers, teeth-grinding, nail-biting, back pain, colds, flu, rashes, neck pains, headaches, lowered sexual interest, fatigue, reliance on alcohol or drugs, shaking, unusual sweating, or facial tension).

> *'Never trouble trouble till trouble troubles you.'*
>
> Anonymous

9. Choose your battles

I once had a colleague who would consistently pick fights with subordinates in the morning, drive to McDonald's at lunch, and argue with the serving staff about cold French fries and long lines, return to work to irritate his direct supervisor, and leave at five every evening to complain to his wife about her housework. His extreme competitiveness, charged, accusatory speech patterns, relentless impatience, and body tension reflected his hyper-stress-filled existence. When he finally mellowed and decided to select his battles more carefully, he was a much happier individual (and do I need to mention the relief of everyone around him)?

10. Know the big triggers

Stress lists typically include these 'events' – death or illness of a family member, marriage, separation, divorce, personal illness or injury, being fired at work, going back to school, pregnancy, supervisor troubles, quitting smoking, change in residence, sexual concerns, financial difficulties, arguments with spouse, work changes, burnout/overwork, sleeping-habit changes, eating habit hanges, major holidays, large purchases, family concerns, and legal problems.

11. Don't play doctor

Avoid self-medication and self-prescribed, over-the-counter drugs to temporarily avoid the main problem (which is whatever is causing the stress in the first place). See a doctor. Don't procrastinate!

12. A mini-list of stress relievers

Play soothing music, get a massage, learn to prioritize, limit the hours you work, take a walk in the woods, read adventurous fiction, take a coffee break, go to an upbeat movie, read a little Norman Vincent Peale, think optimistically, question negative thoughts that haunt you, write down everything that's going right in a journal (and review it often) – and finally believe that your personal best is just around the corner.

> *'If I knew I was going to live this long, I'd have taken better care of myself.'*
>
> Mickey Mantle

15 notes for for actors from New York professionals

Over the years, I've had the opportunity to meet with many of New York's most prominent agents and casting directors. Recently, in a small National Theatre Conference session at the Players Club in Gramercy Park (Edwin Booth's former home), I was able to visit with talent agent Philip Adelman, casting director Harriet Bass, casting director Rich Cole, and casting director Mark Simon as they shared their advice with producers, professors, directors and actors. Their key points included:

1 Remember that auditioning/casting/hiring is not a science – it is an art.

2 Not every actor can do every role – know what you can and can't do and what you want to do!

3 Most university actors coming to New York could benefit from more screen time (especially to assist with auditions for film, television, and commercials, but also for times when theatre audition tapes are necessary).

4 Jobs are won or lost in the audition! Audition classes must be taught by working professionals as the rules change every year!

5 For actors, unless you are an international star, you will be auditioning for the rest of your life!

6 Audition fears must be conquered and considered a 'nice positive way to spend time.' Auditions should be the best part of your day – someone sits and watches you act!

7 Directors want to see you 'live in the role' and we no longer read 'sides,' you have to come in memorized and work/play with the readers and show as much of a final result as possible.

8 If, in a call-sheet breakdown or casting notice, it says 'scripts available' and you don't ask for one (especially of a new play), you are dead.

9 The reality is that electronic auditions and web casts are here – but no one likes it. Still, 'I have cast many actors from tapes,' notes one casting director.

10 You owe it to yourself to enter the business with the best haircut, body size and 'physical best' of your life – unless you want to limit yourself. Actors need to be physically fit.

11 We don't tell people 'you are not going to make it.' It's not my job to take away someone's dream. There's a lot of talent and good training out there and it depends on what each person brings to the table in terms of talent, experience, curiosity, and imagination.

12 Bring discoveries into the audition room!

13 One casting director noted that 'University or professional school show-cases have made life easier for agents but the hook is usually that I know someone in the cast – and the rest of the cast benefits.' One casting director noted that they were invited to more than 100 showcases annually – but only went to 15. 'I'm not a snob,' he explained, 'but I have other work to do.'

14 The concept of a well-rounded actor has more to do with actors who knows themselves and what they want out of their careers.

15 The best actors are those who do their homework, let you know that they want to be a part of your project, research the director, the play, other productions, and know the play well. Winging it does not work.

A brief directory of theatre-related labor unions, guilds, and associations

Actors' Equity Association (AEA)
New York, (212) 869-8530
www.actorsequity.org

Alliance for Inclusion in the Arts
(formerly Non-traditional Casting Project)
New York, (212) 730-4750
www.inclusioninthearts.org

American Alliance for Theatre and Education
Maryland, (301) 951-7977
www.aate.com

American Arts Alliance (AAA)
Washington, DC, (202) 207-3850
www.americanartsalliance.org

American Federation of Television and Radio Artists (AFTRA)
New York, (212) 532-0800
www.aftra.org

Americans for the Arts
Washington, DC, (202) 371-2830
www.artsusa.org

American Guild of Musical Artists (AGMA)
New York, (212) 265-3687
www.musicalartists.org

American Guild of Variety Artists (AGVA)
New York, (212) 675-1003
www.agvausa.com

American Theatre Critics Association (ATCA)
New Mexico, (505) 856-2101
www.americantheatrecritics.org

Association of Fundraising Professionals (AFP)
Virginia, (703) 684-0410
www.afpnet.org

Association of Theatre in Higher Education (ATHE)
Colorado, (888) 284-3737; (800) ATHE-737
www.athe.org

Association of Performing Arts Presenters (APAP)
Washington, DC, (202) 833-2787
www.artspresenters.org

Association of Theatrical Press Agents and Managers (ATPAM)
New York, (212) 719-3666
www.atpam.com

Business Committee for the Arts (BCA)
Business Volunteers for the Arts (BVA)
www.americansforthearts.org

The Dramatists Guild of America (DGA)
New York, (212) 398-9366
www.dramatistsguild.com

The Foundation Center
New York, (212) 620-4230
www.foundationcenter.org

Institute of Outdoor Drama (IOD)
North Carolina, (919) 962-1328
www.outdoordrama.unc.edu

International Alliance of Theatrical Stage Employees (IATSE)
New York, (212) 730-1770
www.iatse-intl.org

International Theatre Institute of the United States (ITI/US)
New York, (212) 697-5230
www.tcg.org

League of Historic American Theatres (LHAT)
Baltimore, (410) 659-9533
www.lhat.org

League of Resident Theatres (LORT)
New York, (212) 944-1501
www.lort.org

National Alliance for Musical Theatre (NAMT)
New York, (212) 714-6668
www.namt.org

National Assembly of State Arts Agencies (NASAA)
Washington, DC, (202) 347-6352
www.nasaa-arts.org

National Association of Performing Arts Managers and Agents (NAPAMA)
New York
www.napama.org

National Center for Nonprofit Boards
Washington, DC (202) 452-6262
www.boardsource.org

National Endowment for the Arts (NEA)
Washington, DC (202) 682-5400
www.arts.endow.gov

National Endowment for the Humanities (NEH)
Washington, DC (800) 634-1121
www.neh.gov

National Theatre Conference (NTC)
c/o The Players Club, New York
www.nationaltheatreconference.org

Screen Actors' Guild (SAG)
Los Angeles, (323) 954-1600
www.sag.org

Shakespeare Theatre Association (STA)
www.staaonline.org

Stage Directors and Choreographers Society (SDC)
New York, (212) 391-1070, toll free (800) 541-5204
www.sdcweb.org

Theatre Communications Group (TCG)
New York, (212) 609-5900
www.tcg.org

Theatre Development Fund (TDF)
New York, (212) 912-9770
www.tdf.org

United States Institute for Theatre Technology (USITT)
New York, (315) 463-6463, toll free (800) 938-7488
www.usitt.org

University/Resident Theatre Association (U/RTA)
New York, (212) 221-1130
www.urta.com

United Scenic Artists (USA)
New York, (212) 581-0300
www.usa829.org

Volunteer Lawyers for the Arts (VLA)
New York, (212) 319-2787
www.vlany.org

Part 7
Leaving a legacy

Lively stories of mentoring glories

It's time to write your own book! So many pioneers in regional theatre are still around to tell their stories. A few will sit down and commit their thoughts and histories to paper, but many more need the next generation of theatre professionals and writers to be their spokesmen. As I've discovered over the 35 and more years that I've been attending and researching regional theatres, these stories are adventurous, poignant, humorous, and heartbreaking. In my truncated 'A Brief History of Theatre in America,' I couldn't begin to mention all the self-made pioneers and dedicated teachers who influenced our generation of theatre professionals. But many names surfaced in my discussions and correspondence with so many of the nation's working theatre professionals, and I wanted to share our inheritance from a few of the mentors, role models, and pioneering theatre professionals in my interviewees' own words.

The question I posed is: 'Are there key figures in American theatre who have been crucial to your career or informed your work?'

John Houseman sat behind his enormous desk at the Juilliard, looked me in the eye, and said, 'You're good enough. Take the job.' It was my first LORT artistic directorship and I didn't know if I could handle it. John put some small part of his power into me, for which I shall always be thankful. Alan Schneider sat across from me in a Chicago bar and said, 'Screw 'em, do the shows you want.' I was uncertain about putting Brecht and Beckett in my next season. Alan put some of his courage into me, for which I shall always be thankful. Jean-Louis Barrault told me, 'It's our responsibility to pass along what we've learned to the next generation.' I thanked him – I've tried. I sat in the Guthrie Theater for the first season of that legendary director's productions in Minneapolis and I said out loud to myself, 'I have to do this. At least I have to try.' The list of figures and events that have shaped all our lives and careers stretches out to the crack o' doom. To paraphrase Sartre, 'We are the sum total of our mentors.'

Tom Markus, Author/Director/Longtime Artistic Director

I, of course, worked in a number of theatres in the 1980s – God, that's a long time ago . . . I was blessed by being mentored by a number of people, of whom two rose to the top: the late Tom Haas, who was perhaps the most important figure for me, steering me towards graduate school, nurturing me as a director, teaching me how to read text in an uncluttered but heartfelt way; and the late Peter Zeisler, who during my NEA days taught me to see a field, not a string of separate theatres, while teaching me to value concepts of service and leadership.

Ben Cameron, former Executive Director, Theatre Communications Group

Joe Papp. He dared to do what he thought important. His reward was an audience of interested, earnest, and informed people.

Gilbert Cates, Producing Director, Geffen Playhouse

Richard Wilbur, Tennessee Williams, Charles Ludlam, Julie Taymor, and David Ives.

Dana Gioia, Chairman, National Endowment for the Arts

A young and vital Zelda Fichandler with her dream of an Arena Stage, a school teacher named Angus Bowmer with his passion for Shakespeare, an immigrant Brit called Tyrone Guthrie who founded not one but two regional theatres, stand out amongst the hundreds that have played a major role in my love of theatre and love for my region of this land. The list could go on and on with Margo Jones, Craig Noel, and Keith Engar adding confirmation to my every decision.

Fred C. Adams, Founder, Utah Shakespeare Festival

Let's look at The Kentucky Cycle. *One play (of the nine) was read at New Dramatists and then produced at EST, both in New York City. The rest of the plays were first produced at EST West (in LA) or at two separate*

workshops at the Mark Taper Forum (thanks to artistic director Gordon Davidson). The play also received readings in Colorado Springs and New Haven. I owe special thanks to Liz Huddle, then artistic director of Seattle's Intiman Theatre, who read The Kentucky Cycle on a Friday and called Saturday to say she was going to produce the play – 'even if I have to play the rest of my season on a unit stage.' Which, in fact, she did. The play was later produced at the Mark Taper and then the Kennedy Center before finally arriving on Broadway.

Other places/people in the regional theatre who have been crucial to me include Lloyd Richards and the O'Neill Theatre Conference, David Kranes and the Sundance Theatre Conference, Jon Jory and the Humana Festival, and Vinny Murphy at Theatre Emory. Most recently, Libby Appel, artistic director at Oregon Shakespeare Festival, has championed my work.

Robert Schenkkan, Playwright

When we were starting Bay Street and we hit a bumpy period about five years into our development, the great Jack O'Brien said something I'll never forget, and which had been said to him when he started out at the Old Globe: 'For the first five years they'll love you, for the next five years they'll try to get rid of you, and if you can make it to fifteen you can do whatever you want.' So far, truer words were never spoken! He also wrote an extraordinary article once called 'Here Be Dragons' about the nature of risk-taking in theatre that resonated for us way beyond its original intentions.

Emma Walton, Co-founder, Bay Street Theatre

All of those pioneers who participated in the diaspora of proven theatre people from New York in the 1960s, 70s, and 80s: Zelda Fichandler, Jules Irving, Herbert Blau, Gordon Davidson, Des McAnuff, et al. The successful creation of a regional network (crystallized by TCG and collective bargaining agreements such as LORT) has made it possible for generations of theatre students to believe they can have careers without migrating to New York.

Andrew Barnicle, Laguna Playhouse

Almost all of the founders of the regional theatre movement have impacted on my thinking and expectations of theatre and myself. Their vision and fortitude are amazing. I think of the courage of Gordon Davidson, the intellectual *brilliance of Zelda Fichandler, the genius of Bill Ball, the dogged determination of Adrian Hall, the vision of Mac Lowry, the commitment of Peter Zeisler, the consummate skill of Arvin Brown, the abstract imagination of JoAnne Akalaitis, and the work of so many others. All have supplied inspiration and an experience that I often wish that I had the courage to emulate.*

Arthur Bartow, Artistic Director,
Department of Drama, Tisch School of the Arts, New York University

God, yes! I've been very lucky. Joseph Anthony, Harold Clurman, Lloyd Richards, and Lillian Hellman changed my life. We all need teachers, mentors, people to turn to for all our lives.

Craig Belknap, Director, Theatre, Film and Television,
Senior Faculty, California Institute of the Arts

Artistic leaders who have informed my work include Gerald Freedman (former artistic director of Great Lakes Theater), Libby Appel, and Daniel Sullivan. Crucial to my work have been the pioneers of the American Shakespearean theatres, such as Fred Adams and Michael Addison.

Kathleen Conlin, Director, Utah Shakespeare Festival

Philip Meister, National Shakespeare Conservatory; Josephine Farsberg, Second City; Michael Langham; Des McAnuff; Jack O'Brien; Michael Kahn; and my therapists.

Ben Donenberg, Artistic Director, The Shakespeare Center Los Angeles

As a theatre critic/journalist, it would be another theatre critic/journalist. The one I most admire is Frank Rich of the New York Times *. . . thanks to his searing insight, uncommon eloquence, and tremendous love for the art form of theatre.*

Iris Dorbian, Former Editor-in-Chief, *Stage Directions* Magazine

The writers and composers of the American 'Broadway' musical. The Cohans, Kerns, Berlins, Rodgers and Hammerstein, Lerner and Loewe, Andrew Lloyd Webber, etc. They have defined this art form and made it dynamic. Also, the Shuberts, Nederlanders, etc., who have produced these shows

and created facilities to do this work, and Agnes de Mille, Jerome Robbins, Harold Prince, etc., who have made this art form so distinct and exciting.

Jan and Griff Duncan, Artistic and Executive Director, Fullerton Civic Light Opera

Of course we would have to consider Mr. William Ball a pivotal figure in terms of our approach to the work, and to our passion for live theatre in general, and classical work in particular . . . His passion for dynamic productions of the great authors of world literature, and his unabashed love for actors are powerful elements of his legacy that we hope we carry on. Another person who looms large in our consciousness is Mr. Sydney Walker, a longtime member of ACT's acting company. He was such a generous, passionate teacher, whose extraordinary exuberance on stage taught everyone who watched that truth has no size.

Julia and Geoff Elliot, Artistic Directors, A Noise Within

Yes, Milton Smith, Milton Goldman, Harold Clurman, Robert Anderson, Audrey Woodward, and Robert Edmond Jones.

Richard G. Fallon, Dean Emeritus, Florida State University,
Co-founder, Asolo Theatre Company

Producers and directors I was influenced by include Robert Porterfield at the Barter Theatre, Douglas Seale at Center Stage, John Reich and Douglas Campbell at the Goodman Theatre . . . The biggest influences, however, were the actors I met in regional theatre . . . I knew that was the kind of life-in-the-theatre that I wanted.

Joel Fink, Associate Dean, Chicago College of the Performing Arts

Peter Donnelly in Seattle and Peter Culman in Baltimore were great leaders in the regional theatre movement.

Bernard Havard, Producing Artistic Director, Walnut Street Theater

Later influences included Sir Tyrone Guthrie and his work as a director and administrator, and Douglas Campbell, an actor whose strong, fearless, invigorating risks on stage (and off) have always reminded me that life need never be dull.

Theodore Herstand, Professor Emeritus, University of Oklahoma

Joseph Papp, Gregory Mosher, Bernard Gersten, Tim Sanford, Adam
Guettel, Jon Robin Baitz, Dan Sullivan, Hugh Masekela, Josh Rosenbaum,
John Guare, Jose Rivera, Chris Durang, Spalding Gray, Scott Elliot.

Lynn Landis, Managing Director, The Wilma Theatre

I've been fortunate to have worked with leaders in a generation of theatre
that saw the birth of the regional theatre movement and the Off-Broadway
movement. I was close to Joe Papp from the mid-1980s until his death.
I was very close to Jose Quintero for that same period. I was and still am
associated with many leaders who crossed over from educational theatre to
professional theatre, especially in the LORT system at the Asolo and other
venues, and was president of ATHE at a very fruitful time of exchanges in
both directions between academic and professional theatre. People such as
Lloyd Richards, Gerald Freedman, Zelda Fichandler, Edward Albee, Ming
Cho Lee, John Ezell, and many others still work in both arenas.

Gil Lazier, Dean, Florida State University/Asolo Theatre Conservatory

The key figures in my life in the American theatre, those whose philosophy I
have followed or have guided me personally, are Zelda Fichandler, Don
Schoenbaum, and Richard Fallon. Zelda because she believed in a company
of actors, Don because he was the most innovative managing director in
the early days, and Dick Fallon because he was my mentor for so many
years.

Howard J. Millman, Producing Artistic Director, Asolo Theatre

One individual in particular. Sally Stearns Brown was managing director of
the Peterborough Players, a small New Hampshire summer theatre, from
1963 to 1983. She was the managing director by title, producer in fact,
and truly the heart and soul of the place . . . she ran a summer theatre
not out of any desire to make a career for herself, but to give others
opportunity and because she simply couldn't imagine a summer without
ahouse full of actors.

Charles Morey, Artistic Director, Pioneer Theatre Company

Sharon Ott, Joseph Papp, Tina Landau, Ingmar Bergman, Robert LePage.

Jonathan Moscone, Artistic Director, California Shakespeare Theater

Zelda Fichandler, Ellis Rabb, Garland Wright, Andre Bishop. Lots more . . .

Robert Moss, Artistic Director, Syracuse Stage

Absolutely! I would have no career at all were it not for the influence, kindness, and great generosity of many people – Eva Le Gallienne, William Ball, Ellis Rabb, and Adrian Hall, in particular. As a young man living in Los Angeles I saw Le Gallienne's touring National Repertory company play Ibsen and Molière. I went backstage and timidly asked Ms. Le Gallienne for advice. She met with me daily for the two weeks her company was in Los Angeles and much of my thinking about the theatre – particularly regarding the importance of the classics, resident companies, and rotating repertory – was forged by those conversations. It was the annual visits of APA, the Guthrie, and ACT to Los Angeles (as well as many subsequent trips to see them in New York, Minneapolis, San Francisco, and my travels to Providence to see Trinity Rep) that forged my taste and taught me by example most of what I know about acting and directing. I saw Ellis's School for Scandal, The Wild Duck, *and* Right You Are if You Think You Are *18 times each and Guthrie's* The House of Atreus *and* The Resistable Rise of Arturo Ui *(directed by Edward Payson Call) 20 times each. I would hide in the men's room after the matinee on two-show days so I could sneak back into the theatre for the evening performance. And I saw every production at ACT for almost ten years, most of them multiple times. It was the work of Bill Ball, Ellis Rabb, Tyrone Guthrie, and Adrian Hall that inspired me to train for the theatre (I went to Carnegie because that is where Bill and Ellis had studied) and to pursue a career working in, and preparing others to work in, the regional theatre with an emphasis on classic plays . . .*

Sandy Robbins, Director, Professional Theatre Training Program,
University of Delaware

Many. Some positive. Some negative. I won't say which are which. For me, Adrian Hall (Trinity Rep), Hal Prince, Zefferelli, Jon Dillon (Milwaukee Rep), Michael Maso (Huntington), Martin Charnin, Victoria Crandell (Brunswick Music Theatre), Chuck Abbott (director), Arthur Laurents, Jo Loesser, Dan

Schay, and a pile of others. I have been an avid collector of information from which to learn. I am in regional theatre today because I consciously decided that I did not like the commercial world of theatre despite a possible direct career path to Broadway. I just did not like the way that art was created on Broadway or the way decisions were made: not always for the benefit of the play, but frequently for politics. I learned a lot from all of those whom I was able to watch and with whom I was able to work.

Richard Rose, Producing Artistic Director, Barter Theatre

Robert Whitehead, Julie Harris, and a great many American playwrights.

Alan Rust, Director, The Hartt School Theatre

Joe Papp embodied that entrepreneurial spirit, melding a fierce advocacy that theatre deserved government support like libraries and schools with an equally indefatigable commercial producer's instinct for working the market-place. Under his leadership, The Public Theatre/New York Shakespeare Festival championed a highly eclectic program, something we emulate at the Laguna Playhouse. He certainly fired my passion for this career when I met him and heard him speak while I was a graduate student.

Richard Stein, Former Executive Director, Laguna Playhouse

Richmond Crinkley was an influence and mentor. He is not well remembered, in part because unlike many artistic directors, producers, or founding fathers, he kept moving on to the next organization, which was often the next company he started. Richmond came to Washington from a tiny Virginia town, and started the Folger Theatre Group, now the Shakespeare Theatre. He produced the bicentennial season at the then relatively new John F. Kennedy Center for the Performing Arts, and then moved to New York City and helped develop Off-Broadway by establishing a producing arm of a long dormant organization called ANTA (where he produced, among other works, the original The Elephant Man and Tintypes). Richmond then moved to the Beaumont Theater and built the organization, or board structure, for the Lincoln Center Theater Company, which eventually achieved lasting success under Greg Mosher and Bernie Gersten. Richmond possessed an extraordinary intellect . . .

Scott L. Steele, Executive Director, University/Resident Theatre Association

As a director, I learned enormously from assisting both Michael Langham (at the Stratford Festival in Canada) and Mark Lamos (at Hartford Stage) . . . Michael is the single best director with text, language, and verse that I have ever observed. Further, he's brilliant, charismatic, insightful, and articulate – sometimes to a fault, he can be lacerating as well as illuminating. But his ability to bring clarity to a Shakespeare text is astonishing. Mark had been a protégé of Michael's at the Guthrie, but turned into a wholly different kind of Shakespeare director – he is an imaginative, daring reconceiver of classical plays for a contemporary audience. He always pushes the boundaries of design and storytelling, with a restless, impulsive creative energy. Mark is a visionary. Two people gave me much-needed perspective in running a major institution: Peter Zeisler and then Ben Cameron, both executive directors of TCG. Peter was irascible, outspoken, and courageous – he always pushed me towards better work and into rethinking my ideas about how to build a theatre company. And Ben is simply astonishing in his cogency of thought, his deep and heartfelt belief in the power of live theatre, and his passionate, articulate, and inspiring preaching – both to the field and about the field.

Kent Thompson, Artistic Director, Denver Center Theatre Company

Howard Millman, who saved and re-established both the Geva Theatre in Rochester, New York, and the Asolo Theatre in Sarasota, Florida . . . From Howard, I truly learned what it takes to make a LORT theatre stay alive both artistically and financially. He is a master of understanding an audience while still pushing the artistic envelope. Ed Stern, who co-founded Indiana Rep and reestablished Cincinnati Playhouse in the Park, showed me a way of dealing with artists that was loose, exciting, and filled with care and devotion. Gordon Davidson of the Mark Taper Forum, who served as a living example . . .

Stephen Rothman, Chair, Department of Theatre Arts and Dance,
California State University, Los Angeles

Key figures: hard question. Gerald Freedman and John Houseman.

Steven Woolf, Artistic Director, Repertory Theatre of St. Louis.

Having gone to undergraduate school at the University of Virginia, I became aware in the 60s of the remarkable work Zelda Fichandler was doing at Arena Stage. I grew up in New York City but, ironically, did not see in New

York the range of work that was being done in Washington by Zelda. These productions solidified in my mind how regional theatre is the American national theatre in this country. I would, in the same vein, include Bill Ball and the remarkable work he did at ACT San Francisco for being a pioneer in demonstrating the remarkable vitality and strength that is the regional theatre movement.

Ed Stern, Producing Artistic Director, Cincinnati Playhouse in the Park

A final note: discover a life worth living

Pursue a career you enjoy and treat those you love with warmth and sincerity, and chances are pretty good that you'll discover a life that's worth living. This book was written and assembled out of love for America's artists, respect for America's producers and craftspeople, and true admiration for the pioneers and ongoing leaders of America's professional theatres.

Thanks again to everyone who offered his or her advice, guidance, and encouragement for this book. There are a lot of 'would-be/could-be' mentors out there – go out and find individuals who may be able to help you establish a network, discover the joys of the arts, and take advantage of the ever-changing career opportunities in today's American theatre.

If you have suggestions or advice regarding additions or changes to this book, please don't hesitate to contact me at jvolz@fullerton.edu.

Bibliography

Branson, Clark and Mary Mann. *The Los Angeles Theatre Book*. North Hollywood: LA Theatre Book Publishers, 1984.

Brown, Lenora Inez. 'West is West.' *American Theatre*. New York: Theatre Communications Group, 2001.

Brubaker, Edward and Mary. *Golden Fire, The Anniversary Book of the Oregon Shakespearean Festival*. Ashland: Oregon Shakespearean Festival, 1985.

Case, Evelyn Carol, and Jim Volz. *Words for Lovers: Snippets, Sonnets and Sensual Sayings from William Shakespeare*. Columbiana: WaterMark Inc., 1990.

Celentano, Suzanne Carmack, and Kevin Marshall. *Theatre Management*. Studio City: Players Press, 1998.

Churnin, Nancy. *The Old Globe at 60*. San Diego: Performing Arts, 1995.

Cincinnati Playhouse 30th Anniversary. Cincinnati Playhouse Press, 1990.

Cory, Joyce Burke. *The Dallas Theater Center: An Idea that was Big Enough*. Dallas Theater Center Press, 1980.

Eustis, Morton. *B'way, Inc! The Theatre as a Business*. New York: Dodd, Mead, 1934.

Farren, Mick. *Words of Wisdom*. London: Chrysalis Book Group, 2004.

Flanagan, Hallie. *A Brief Delivered by Hallie Flanagan, Director, Federal Theatre Project, Works Progress Administration, before the Committee on Patents, House of Representatives, Washington DC, February 8, 1938*.

Flanagan, Hallie. *Dynamo*. New York: Duell, Sloan and Pearce, 1943.

Hewitt, Barnard. *Theater USA, 1665 to 1957*. New York: McGraw-Hill, 1959.

Holmes, Ann Hitchcock. *The Alley Theatre: Four Decades in Three Acts*. Alley Theatre Press, 1986.

Hoyt, Harlowe R. *Town Hall Tonight: Intimate Memories of the Grassroots Days of the American Theatre*. New York: Bramhall House, 1955.

Humana Festival of New American Plays. Louisville: Actors Theatre of Louisville Press, 1986.

Klotkin, Joel. *The City: A Global History.* New York: Modern Library, 2005.

Kragen, Ken and Jefferson Graham. *Life is a Contact Sport.* New York: William Morrow and Company, 1994.

Krows, Arthur Edwin. *Play Production in America.* New York: Henry Holt, 1916.

Langley, Stephen. *Theatre Management and Production in America.* New York: Drama Book Publishers, 1990.

Langley, Stephen, and James Abruzzo. *Jobs in Arts and Media Management: What They Are and How to Get One!* New York: American Council for the Arts, 1989.

Livingston, Sheila. *The Guthrie Theater: 25th Year Anniversary.* Minneapolis: Guthrie Press, 1988.

London, Todd. *The Artistic Home, Discussions with America's Institutional Theatres.* New York: Theatre Communications Group, 1988.

Lynch, Margaret. *The Making of a Theater, The Story of the Great Lakes Theater Festival.* Cleveland: Great Lakes Lithograph Company, 1986.

Macgowan, Kenneth. *Footlights across America, Towards a National Theater.* New York: Harcourt, Brace, 1929.

Malloy, Merritt, and Shauna Sorensen. *The Quotable Quote Book.* New York: Citadel Press, 1990.

McDaniel, Nello and George Thorn. *The Workpapers: A Special Report – The Quiet Crisis in the Arts.* New York: FEDAPT, 1991.

Meserve, Walter J. *An Outline History of American Drama.* New Jersey: Littlefield, Adams, 1965.

Moe, Christian, Scott J. Parker, and George McCalmon. *Creating Historical Drama: A Guide for Communities, Theatre Groups, and Playwrights.* Carbondale: Southern Illinois University Press, 2005.

Mordecai, Benjamin. *Indiana Repertory Theatre* . New York: FEDAPT, 1977.

Morison, Bradley G., and Julie Gordon Dalgleish. *Waiting in the Wings: A Larger Audience for the Arts and How to Develop It.* New York: American Council for the Arts, 1987.

Newman, Danny. *Subscribe Now! Building Arts Audiences Through Dynamic Subscription Promotion.* New York: Theatre Communications Group, 1977.

Peale, Norman Vincent, and Kenneth Blanchard. *The Power of Ethical Management.* New York: Blanchard, Morrow,, 1992.

Peter, Dr. Laurence. *Peter's Quotations.* New York: Bantam Books, 1987.

Poggi, Jack. *Theater in America, The Impact of Economic Forces, 1870–1967.* Ithaca: Cornell University Press, 1968.

Price, Steven D., Editor. *1001 Smartest Things Ever Said.* Connecticut: Lyons Press, 2004.

Ratcliffe, Susan (editor). *Little Oxford Dictionary of Quotations.* Oxford: Oxford University Press, 2005.

Samuels, Steven (editor). *Theatre Profiles 12.* New York: Theatre Communications Group, 1996.

Shakespeare Theatre Association Member Directory. Cedar City: STAA Publishers, 2011.

Sheehy, Helen. *Margo: The Life and Theatre of Margo Jones.* Dallas: Southern Methodist University Press, 1989.

South Coast Repertory 40. South Coast Repertory Press, 2004.

Steinberg, Mollie B. *The History of the Fourteenth Street Theaterr.* New York: Dial Press, 1931.

Steppenwolf @ Twenty-Five. Chicago: Steppenwolf Press, 2001.

TCG Theatre Directory. New York: Theatre Communications Group, Inc., 2010.

Volz, Jim. *Shakespeare Never Slept Here: The Making of a Regional Theatre.* Atlanta: Cherokee, 1986.

White, Rolf B. (editor). *The Great Business Quotations.* New York: Dell, 1986.

Wilson, Garff B. *Three Hundred Years of American Drama and Theatre, From Ye Bare and Ye Cubb to Hair.* New Jersey: Prentice-Hall, 1973

Special note: The basic facts for each theatre and institution overview generally derive from each institution's website, theatre directories, brochures, programs, historical information, email correspondence, and/or from the author's own experience with the theatre.

About the Author

Jim Volz is an international arts consultant, author, producer and professor at California State University, Fullerton. He has produced over 100 professional productions, consulted with over 100 companies, and published more than 100 articles and books on management, arts criticism, Shakespeare, and theatre. He served as a longtime critic/columnist for both New York's *Back Stage* and Hollywood's *Drama-Logue*, and has published in *American Theatre*, *Horizon* magazine, *Equity News*, *SSD&C Journal*, *Theatre Management Journal*, *Theatre Research International*, for Methuen Drama and BackStage Books, and in a myriad other international publications. He has been the editor of the Shakespeare Theatre Association of America's international publication, *Quarto*, since 1991. He is the author/editor of eight books including *A Back Stage Guide to Working in Regional Theatre*, *How to Run a Theater* and *Shakespeare Never Slept Here*. *Buffett and the Bard*, edited with Cindy Melby, and *Phaneuf* and *Shakespeare Around the World*, with Evelyn Carol Case are books in progress.

Jim is Past President of the National Theatre Conference, an associate member of the American Theatre Critics Association and a longtime voting member for the prestigious Tony Award's Regional Theatre Award. He serves on the National Advisory Council for the Institute of Outdoor Drama, the National Artistic Board of Directors for Florida's Orlando Shakespeare Festival, and the Editorial Board of distinguished scholars for the ISE Shakespeare Project, based at the University of Victoria in Canada. He has served as a Strategic Planning/Time Management Program presenter for the National Association of Schools of Music, the National Association of Schools of Dance, and the National Association of Schools of Theatre. His loyalties to the Rocky Mountain region include longtime service as associate editor for the University of Colorado's *On-Stage Studies*, consulting services for the Colorado Shakespeare Festival, and continued work as national adjudicator for the University of Wyoming's National Theatre Essay Competition.

Jim is President of Consultants for the Arts, an international arts consulting service that works with a revolving team of highly qualified theatre professionals contracted to bring their specific area of expertise to each project. His service over three decades includes work with professional theatres, Shakespeare festivals, and arts centers in Tasmania, San Francisco, Atlanta, Boulder, Hilton Head Island, Telluride, Sedona, Orlando, and dozens of other cities throughout America in areas of Strategic planning, executive search, board of trustee advisement, producing, marketing, fundraising and institutional development. In California, arts projects include work with the cities of Irvine, Cypress, Brea, La Quinta, San Jose, and Fullerton, and with arts organizations ranging from South Coast Repertory, the Laguna Playhouse, Marin Theatre Company, the San Francisco Mime Company, and San Jose Repertory Theatre to the Irvine Barclay Theatre, Hunger Artists Theatre Company, Irvine Museum, and Arts Orange County.

The Alabama Shakespeare Festival's Board of Trustees recruited Jim to spearhead the ASF's historic expansion from a small summer operation in Anniston, Alabama, to the world's fifth largest Shakespeare Festival in Montgomery, Alabama. From 1982 to 1991, Jim orchestrated the tremendous growth of the Alabama Shakespeare Festival as Managing Director in partnership with Artistic Directors Martin L. Platt and Kent Thompson.

Devoted to arts education, Dr. Volz has taught at over a dozen universities, administered MFA programs in acting, stage management, and arts administration, and served as Head of the BFA in Arts Administration program and acting Chairman of the Department of Theatre and Dance at Wright State University. He is a Ph.D. graduate from the University of Colorado, Boulder. At California State University, Fullerton, Dr. Volz served for many years on the Board of Trustees for the Philanthropic Foundation and has received honors, grants and recognition for Teaching, Mentoring in the Arts, Publishing, Service to the Campus as a Community, Enhancing Learning in the Classroom, External Community Service, Contributions to Student Leadership, Shakespearean Research, Student Career Planning Service, Professional Theatre Research, and Service to the University.

Over the years, he has served as a presenter at Stratford, England's Royal Shakespeare Company, as chair of New York's Stavis Playwright Award for emerging playwrights, and as grant reviewer for the National Endowment for the

Humanities and National Endowment for the Arts. As a concerned community member, Jim has served on the Board of Directors of Humana Hospital, the World Affairs Council, the Southeastern Theatre Conference, and the National Theatre Conference. As a civic leader, he has worked on Chamber of Commerce and State Tourism Committees and volunteered services for struggling artists, theatres, arts centers, arts councils museums and dance companies.

On a national level, Jim has served as a steering committee member for the American Council for the Arts and a longtime member of the League of Resident Theatres, the University/Resident Theatre Association, the American Arts Alliance, the Theatre Communications Group, the Authors Guild, the Dramatists Guild, and the Association for Theatre in Higher Education.

His speaking engagements have covered every area from the Kiwanis, Rotary, Lions, and Optimists clubs to the Volunteer Lawyers for the Arts, Alabama Youth Foundation, Montgomery Business Committee for the Arts, National Conference of State Legislatures, American Council for the Arts, National Society of Fund Raising Executives, National Business Committee for the Arts, Association of Independent Colleges and Universities, and the Association of Government Accountants.

In the past few years, he has devoted his spare time to community service, travel, basketball, and writing. Jim is married to professional actress and award-winning educator Evelyn Carol Case. As a writing team, they edited *Words for Lovers: Snippets from William Shakespeare*. They have two adventurous children, Nicholas and Caitlin.